Socialist Price Theory and Price Policy

Socialist Price Theory and Price Policy

by

Béla Csikós-Nagy

Akadémiai Kiadó, Budapest 1975

Translated by

Elek Helvey (Parts I—II)

and

István Véges (Parts III—VI)

Translation revised by

Tamás Bácskai

ISBN 963 05 0357 3

Printed in Hungary

Contents

Preface

In this study attempt has been made to give a scientific presentation of socialist price theory and price policy. I am fully aware of the difficulties that necessarily arise in preparing a book with such an objective. These difficulties can be traced back to two sources.

First, the planned economies of socialist societies have *general* and *specific* features alike. The characteristics shared by all socialist societies are: (1) public ownership of the means of production; (2) state planning and management of the national economy. Specific is, however, the way the concrete tasks of socialist construction emerge, since socialist societies also differ in respect of their levels of development of production forces, their social-economic structure and the conditions of their economic growth. Therefore, the socialist countries cannot have a certain type of economic control system that should be uniformly applied with all of its elements. Each country has to identify for itself requirements arising from its specific social-economic realities. The utilization of the possibilities inherent in socialist production relations depends in no small measure on how these requirements are met. Price under socialism performs its function not in isolation but as an organic part of the system of economic control. Price mechanism is affected by all factors that determine the circumstances and the development of the economy as a whole. *Differences that can be found in the economic mechanism are also reflected, for objective reasons, in the national price systems.*

Secondly, the socialist system of economic control is being improved amidst heated debates. National price debates and, to an even greater extent, discussions on the mechanism of the national economy, throw up different views voiced and accepted in various countries. Thus, differences in economic thinking also make themselves felt in the critical analysis of the economic situation and in the proposals preparing decisions of economic policy. Consequently, quite apart from objective reasons, the national price systems of the individual socialist countries also differ from one another because they *interpret the concept of planned regulation differently*. As a result of the Complex Programme of the economic integration of the CMEA countries, a convergence of the economic views can be observed. In this process a prominent role is being played by the economic debates organized at CMEA level. Yet, at present, these tendencies are still in their initial stage.

In this book I have summarized the common as well as the divergent features of the national price systems of the CMEA countries. In this respect I have relied on the findings of the comparative analysis of the various price systems. But these findings do not constitute the main body of my work. I have approached the questions of price theory not from the angle of a critique of the principles and methods of economic control prevailing in the various CMEA countries. Such an exposition of socialist price theory would be all the less scientifically justified as planned economy is being carried on in these countries under different conditions. Consequently, this book will only exercise criticism in this sense – at least intentionally – in such instances when a country has modified its system of economic management, having also specified, by way of self-criticism, the causes that had induced it to make the changes.

While expounding socialist price theory, however, I deemed it practicable to drawn on the extremely rich body of knowledge derived from the debates on questions of prices and economic mechanism referred to above. If in a country different views are voiced on the problems of economic control, then it may also be justified to assume that a given mechanism, merely because it exists, cannot be regarded as objectively determined in all its elements for the country concerned. If we regarded it as such, it would be simply impossible to explain the changes that are carried out with a view to improving these systems of economic control.

The history and development of Marxian economics presuppose that the representatives of this science openly express their views. It may, therefore, appear only natural that in discussing the various problems of price theory, I will always defend the statements of which I have a definite opinion. For this reason, I would like to stress emphatically: intention and reality may deviate from one another. Thus the possibility exists that I have not always been able to get divorced from the circumstances under which the tasks of socialist construction have to be solved in Hungary. And besides, I cannot even claim that the view I adopt is always the best alternative. It is almost twenty years that I have been engaged in exploring the problems of socialist price theory. During that time, I have revised and changed my views on several questions. Nevertheless, I do hope that, despite all its deficiencies, my book will prove a useful contribution to the further development of socialist price theory.

Budapest, March 1, 1974.

The Author

Introduction

The classics of economics built up their science as a study of the economics of *production,* and regarded labour necessary for producing commodities as the substance of value. *Smith* and *Ricardo* revealed the laws of the exchange of equal quantities of labour as laws regulating social production, through which human needs exert an influence on production, and needs, in turn, adjust themselves to production.[1] In further developing the labour theory of value, *Marx* worked out the theory of surplus value. He emphasized: equilibrium, as a rule, governs market prices either below or above value level, yet the exchange of commodities at their labour value is the rational, natural law of their equilibrium.[2]

The theory of surplus value brought capitalist exploitation into the limelight. Therefore, it was in the interest of the apology of capitalism to invent a new basis for the theory of the capitalist mode of production. This historical change was brought about by the school of marginal utility. Its followers turned the economics of production into the economics of *consumption.* The basis for this theory was provided by the laws of the satisfaction of needs set out by *Gossen.*[3] Labour value measured in the field of production was replaced by marginal utility measured in that of consumption. A large-scale experiment was undertaken to provide an explanation, based on consumers' sovereignty, of the economic phenomena. Praxeology, the theory of rational economic behaviour was created.[4] *Pareto* laid the foundations of the economics of praxeology.[5] *Mises*

1 SMITH, A.: *Inquiry into the Nature and Causes of the Wealth of Nations.* Edinburgh, 1776. RICARDO, D.: *Principles of Political Economy and Taxation.* London, 1817.

2 MARX, K.: *Das Kapital.* Vol. I. Hamburg, 1867, Vol.II. 1885, Vol.III. 1913.

3 GOSSEN, H.M.: *Entwicklung des Gesetzes des menschlichen Verkehrs.* Braunschweig, 1854.

4 The notion of praxeology originates from *Espinas.* On the theory of praxeology see: SLUTSKY, B.: Ein Beitrag zur formal-praxeologischen Grundlegung der Ökonomik. *Wirtschaftswissenschaftliche Informationen,* H.46, 1966, Berlin.

5 PARETO, V.: *Cours d'économie politique.* Lausanne, 1897.

changed price theory into a theory of decision-making alternatives.[6]

In this way, two main trends of economic thought can be clearly identified. They can also be called Marxist and non-Marxist economic schools. This is at the root of the basic differences between socialist and capitalist price theories, too. Socialist price theory regards *labour value* in the context of the economics of production, as a category providing the starting point from which the concept of the price phenomenon can be explained. Capitalist price theory derives price, in the context of the economics of consumption, from the category of *marginal utility*. This is also the dividing line if we interpret socialist price theory in the sense as used by the economists of the socialist countries. But *the first theory of socialist pricing* was created before the socialist societies came into existence and was, strangely enough, *formulated on the basis of the marginal utility theory*.[7]

Immediately following the overthrow of capitalism by the revolution in Russia, *Mises* challenged, with a claim to scientific truth, the socialization of the means of production. He tried to prove that capitalist private property and a free market were indispensable conditions of rational behaviour. In his view, where there was no free market, there was no pricing mechanism either, and without a pricing mechanism there was no economic calculation. Further, he pointed out that exchange relations between production goods could only be established on the basis of private ownership of the means of production, consequently, every step taken in the direction away from private ownership of the means of production, would also remove us from rational thinking.[8]

The theory of marginal utility and, in general, the explanation of economic phenomena based on the principle of consumers' sovereignty, dominated economic thinking throughout the world, except in the Soviet Union, between the two World Wars. This makes it easier to understand that even Marxist economists tried to prove that the social ownership of the factors of production and state planning did not impede rational calculation interpreted in the sense of the approach of the school of marginal utility, in other words, that the *Pareto*-op-

[6] MISES, L.: *Nationalökonomie.* Theorie des Handels und Wirtschaftens. Geneva, 1940.

[7] BARONE, E.: Il ministerio della produzione nello stato colletivista (The Ministry of Production in the Collectivist State). *Giornale degli Economisti e Rivista di Statistica,* Nos. 8–10, 1908.

[8] MISES, L.: Die Wirtschaftsrechnung im sozialistischen Gemeinwesen. *Archiv für Sozialwissenschaften,* April 1920.

timum could be created under socialism too. This answer given to *Mises*'s challenge is known in the history of economic thought as the *Lange-Lerner* solution.[9] The term "solution" is meant to imply the logical correctness of the model.

One might think that with this the "western" debate on socialist pricing has come to an end. But some economists argued that the contention was not that rational calculation was logically inconceivable under socialism, but that there was no practicable way of applying it.[10] Thus attention was focussed on the ability of a socialist economy to operate sucessfully. *Schumpeter* argued if there were no "practicable" basis for rational calculation under socialism, socialist economy ought to break down.[11] *Hayek* answered as follows: It was not the possibility of planning as such which has been questioned, but the possibility of *successful* planning. What we should anticipate is that output would be lower than if the price mechanism of a market operated freely under otherwise similar circumstances.[12] Thus a justified doubt was raised as to the scientific foundation of the debate. It can hardly be ignored that the Soviet Union was the only country that was left unaffected by the world crises between the two wars, and that its superiority based on economic growth was particularly conspicuous during the time of the debate.

Socialist price theory formulated on the basis of the marginal utility school is represented in our days primarily by economists operating in capitalist countries and displaying a special interest in the questions of socialist economy. Dealing with socialist calculation, *Bergson* interprets the insistence on the labour theory of value as one of the principal causes of wasting economic resources.[13] In characterizing the labour theory of value, *Bergson* and others use the attribute "obsolete". This can only be interpreted as a statement that the labour theory of value might have been valid in the 18th and 19th centuries, but has lost its validity in the 20th century. But such a statement would be obviously absurd. First, producing value and making calculations are two different things. If it is accepted that value can only be created by human labour – and this was convincingly proved by

9 Lange, O.: On the Economic Theory of Socialism. *Review of Economic Studies*, October 1936, February 1937. Lerner, A.P.: Economic Theory and Socialist Economy. *Review of Economic Studies,* October 1936.

10 Robbins, H.: *The Great Depression.* London, 1934.

11 Schumpeter, J.A.: *Capitalism, Socialism, and Democracy.* 2nd ed., New York, 1947.

12 Hayek, F.A.: Socialist Calculation: The Competitive Solution. *Economica,* May 1940.

13 Bergson, A.: *Essays in Normative Economics.* Cambridge, Massachussetts, 1966.

Marx–, then its validity cannot realistically be challenged on the basis that marginal analysis does have a role to play in economic calculation, or that relative prices reflect in a definite way the relative scarcity of economic resources or products. Secondly, rational calculation is not the discovery of the theory of marginal utility. The laws of commodity production (the laws of return, of the satisfaction of needs of equilibrium) asserted themselves in the same way in the past as in our days. Rational human activity has always been governed, one way or another, by the "*lex minimi*". From this point of view, the theory of marginal utility has incorporated – by means of a number of very questionable axioms – the "*lex minimi*" into the context of general economic equilibrium.

The criticism of the marginal utility theory began to unfold after the Second World War. Several economists have critically analysed the system of assumptions under which the *Pareto*-optimum can assert itself. *Little* writes: Probably the great majority of socialist economists are already convinced that the marginal cost scheme is absurd.[14] And really, economists working in socialist countries would have to face a serious dilemma if we set to them the requirement to consider the *Lange-Lerner* solution in socialist pricing. The *Lange-Lerner* model cannot be applied in pratice, just as the system of assumptions under which price mechanism can optimize economic efficiency is virtually void of any reality.

Socialist price theory has, of course, its affinities to marginal utility theory, and praticularly to *welfare economics.* At first, the market model of general equilibrium neglected the sociological interdependences and thus the elements of essential importance to socio-economic development. The incorporation of sociological factors into the equilibrium model, or the endeavour to achieve it, has given rise to welfare economics.[15] The social welfare function introduced by *Bergson* wished to indicate that a state of optimum could only be determined as a function of *social utility.*[16] But it is obvious that the concept of social utility as formulated in welfare economics is given a basically different interpretation under socialism.

The structural lay-out of the book deviates from that of the works on price theory which expound the general equilibrium theory in terms of a market model. Is socialist price theory suitable to be formulated in this way? The answer is partly affirmative, partly negative. It is affirmative if we identify socialist price

[14] LITTLE, I.M.D.: *A Critique of Welfare Economics.* Oxford, 1957.
[15] PIGOU, A.C.: *Economics of Welfare.* 1st ed., London, 1920.
[16] BERGSON, A.: *op. cit.*

theory with the *shadow price theory.* But even in this sense, socialist price theory is an integral part of state planning and not an abstract representation of a spontaneous price mechanism. The answer is negative if we think of the possible alternatives of the role of price as incorporated in the system of a centrally controlled economy. The shadow price theory presupposes that state planning is based on mathematical programming. This is easier to formulate in an abstract model than to apply in practice. Such method of planning could not have been introduced so far even though there had been otherwise a general consensus on the progressive character of its application. On the other hand, traditional socialist planning has been formulated exactly in terms of restriction of the price function. Thus, this is an equilibrium theory, from the point of which price theory cannot, at least directly, be justified. It is for this reason, among other things, that socialist price theory cannot be identified with the shadow price theory displaying features similar to those of the *Lange-Lerner* approach. But this does not mean that there is no relevant theory for socialist pricing. Socialist pricing cannot be interpreted as a merely pragmatic price policy. Of this, the present work will probably provide conclusive evidence for the reader.

This fact also accounts for the method of expounding socialist price formation different from the price theories interpreted in the free-market system. Works dealing with price theory on the basis of the free-market hypothesis, present the ideal model of the operation of the market mechanism, or critically analyse their assumption system. In addition, those are models that ignore the intricate relationships of the international division of labour and even the specific sectoral characteristics. If, however, the task is assigned to theory to support practice, then it is justly expected to provide answers to all current questions. This theory can only be a complex one, price theory can only be interpreted in an organic interrelationship with price policy. Hence the title of this work: Socialist Price Theory and Price Policy.

This book is aimed at giving an account of the problems of socialist pricing in the context of its practical application as evolved in the European socialist countries, and of the scientific debates forming this practice. Since 1969, the price institutes operating in association with the Price Offices of the CMEA have been incorporating into a joint document studies on socialist pricing and such official publications which may be of international interest. How great an attention has been paid to questions of pricing is evidenced by the fact that the body of knowledge is being enlarged, year to year, by 1,000 publications of about 700 socialist economists. These studies partly provide information on the pricing measures already introduced, partly comment critically on the established systems of socialist price formation. In assessing socialist price theory it should not be ignored that, as a result of the economic reforms already implemented or being in the state of preparation, the role of commodity and money relations has greatly increased and, as a consequence, the price debates have become extremely lively. It is to be assumed as natural that the author of the present study professes a definite view of the price phenomenon under socialism, yet the expectation is justified that this book should also give a survey of the more important relevant theories.

Part I

Value and Price

1. Labour Value and Value Price

Value: the Key-Question of Price

Value is the key question of price. *Accordingly, input has become the central problem of the socialist price theory.* Naturally, this cannot characterize by itself the trends developed in the socialist price theory. The existing trends differ, among other things, from one another in some of them reducing the price theory to the theory of input price. In expounding the socialist price theory it is expedient to set out from these trends.

The identification of the socialist price theory with the input price theory relies on the hypothesis, according to which the socialist state *can solve satisfactorily the regulation of production based on needs within the system of planned economy.* If the problem of equilibrium can be considered settled *a priori* by the planned regulation of the production and distribution process, then the correct expression of labour input in monetary terms is indeed the most important problem of the price theory. Under such circumstances the entire problem becomes simplified to the following formula: the value orientates the price while the price orientates the planning of the national economy. In this case the main function of the price is to enable state planning to establish balanced conditions at value prices. If the price corresponds to the value and the plan meets the requirements of equilibrium, efficiency has been provided for and socialist economy can function at optimum conditions.[17] This conveys in the main the postulate of *economic perspicacity* expressed by the large camp of Marxist economists as the main requirement with respect to the socialist price system.[18]

It is a matter of course that socialist societies are greatly interested in the *efficient utilization of available resources* and in perpetuating a rate of economic growth, as a result of which socialist societies can catch up, may overtake, advanced capitalist societies. Antagonism and struggle between various socio-economic systems called forth economic challenge and

[17] Csikós-Nagy, B.: *Árpolitika az átmeneti gazdaságban* (Price Policy in a Transitional Economy). Budapest, 1958.

[18] Péter, Gy.: *A gazdaságosság és a jövedelmezőség jelentősége a tervgazdálkodásban* (The Significance of Efficiency and Profitability in a Planned Economy). Budapest, 1956.

competition. However, not only this is at stake. The improvement of the Socialist social order is inseparable from the improvement of the intellectual and material conditions of society. This is why economics focussed attention on the price problem under socialism as early as the fifties. The mainspring of the investigations conducted in this field were deficiencies which came to light in the course of economic calculations.

Decisions underlying the plan of the national economy are *economic efficiency calculations.* In this domain, calculations regarding the efficiency of investments and that of foreign trade are of particular importance. Mathematical formulae have been worked out to determine the order of rank of efficiency of the productive branches (products) so that state planning should approximate the development concept by an efficient transformation of the actual economic structure. Economic calculations are equally called for in the case of long-term, medium- or short-term decisions. In the case of such decisions it is important to know the changes that will ensue in medium- and long-term value (price) relations. Thus, efficiency investigations have required price forecasts (price planning) from the very outset.

On the basis of critical analysis the conclusion has been drawn that the administrative price system – in its actual pattern – does not provide sufficient information even in case of short-term decisions. It appeared that the price level of productive branches (products) deviates to a different degree, upward or downward, from the value level. At first, it was thought that this problem can be solved by price corrections, that is, by an evaluation system worked out for state planning purposes. However, the question instantly arose: can the optimum functioning of the socialist economy be satisfactorily ensured if state planning makes use of an evaluation system detached from the price system and microeconomy relies on a price system considered unsatisfactory by the state from the point of view of obtaining information for economic decision-making.

An evaluation system detached from the price system, the only function of which is to serve the purpose of state planning, has been considered by many a *temporary* solution from the outset, though opinions were also voiced, according to which *duality is inherent* in socialist planned economy.[19] In judging this question, two aspects of the matter must be taken into account. (1) The differentiation of domestic prices from foreign trade prices and within domestic prices the separation of con-

[19] Csikós-Nagy, B.: *Általános és szocialista árelmélet* (General and Socialist Price Theory). Budapest, 1968.

sumer prices from producer prices have developed into a characteristic feature of the socialist price system. The former is offset by subsidizing or levelling off foreign trade prices when accounts are settled between foreign trade enterprises and the budget while the latter is adjusted by the turnover tax and/or price subsidies in the relationship between productive (commercial) enterprises and the budget. Since the socialist state cannot regulate world market prices, on the other hand, however, prices have to function as equilibrating prices in the commodity supply of the population, many economists interpreted the input price principle a priori as a price category limited to producer prices. (2) The dual evaluation considered effective in respect to the producer price category emerged in a system of economic control in which the state regulates the management of enterprises by compulsory plan targets. It was therefore thought possible that the evaluation system ensuring perspicacity in economic matters will become a specific requirement of national planning.

Nevertheless, the discussion on the methodology of economic efficiency calculations has become a price debate for objective reasons. Investigations on the national economy which started from the point of view of the consumer and the producer revealed the organic relationship between macro-and micro-economic decisions and the comprehensive character of economic efficiency which can only become effective in a uniform evaluation system. The demand of the population is regulated by the price too, even in an economy based on central directives. Now, if the state aims at expanding the economy, taking into account the efficient transformation of the structure, it is of primary importance that the consumer price should conform to the value. If the two deviate, the state controlled regulation of production can maintain equilibrium only in case of an accordingly determined demand structure. It also appeared that even if control of the economy is firmly centralized, enterprises have a fairly wide freedom in decision making. This was also taken into account by the mechanism relying on plan directives as shown by bonuses granted in case of fulfilment or overfulfilment of plan targets. Thus, the control of the economy based on a system of compulsory plan indicators to be observed by enterprises reckoned with the possibility of enterprises being in a position to organize production according to a product pattern which differs from the prescribed one or being able to change the material input of products and so forth.

The logic of preferences and alternatives in decision making are immanent elements of economy on all levels of activity. Owing to this recognition, the discussion which started as a polemic on state planning aiming at economic efficiency turned into a general price discussion which – in the fifties – in fact was "purely" a price debate searching for a solution of the price problem within the given system of socialist economic control. At that time very few people only connected prices with the actual system on the basis of which socialist economy was functioning.[20] The discussion identified planned price formation with the administrative fixing of prices; accordingly, the main subject of the debate was the kind of guidelines administrative price formation has to adopt so that prices should provide correct orientation when it comes to decision making. Finally, the working out of value calculation produced the conditions which made it possible to turn the discussion to practical account.

Value Calculation

The formula value is

$$c + v + m,$$

where:

c represents value of the consumed means of production;

v stands for that part of the new value produced by work which embodies the value of labour; and

m is that part of the new value produced by work which appears as surplus value (social net income).

Social labour input can be expressed by both *worktime and costs.* Investigations aiming at the expression of value relations based on the direct amount of worktime-input are, for the time being, in an initial, experimental stage. Socialist countries have no operative accountancy system which allows to directly measure expenditures in terms of worktime. Although the manufacturing technologies, among others the operative time norms per unit of product are known, this is insufficient for accounting the worktime spent on a product. The degree of elaborateness of the operations needed for the production of commodities is different. Thus, operative time norms could only be added up if they were first reduced to time norms reckoned in terms of simple work. Operative time norms only refer to the last production phase and do not contain the worktime requirement of products produced in a previous production phase and used thereafter as means of production.

[20] Brus, W.: *Role of the Law of Value in Socialist Economy.* (Manuscript) Report introducing the debate of Polish Economists' Second Conference, July 7–10.1956. Péter, Gy.: *op.cit.*

Value, however, can also be expressed by costs.[21] In recent years this method of value calculation has been generally accepted on an international scale and is also used in organizing the economic co-operation of CMEA countries. As a result of scientific research work

– the value levels of economic branches and their deviation from the price level are established by the input-output balance system, and

– the values of products worked out in the price model system representing the price system of the national economy and/or the price and value deviations from product to product are already known today.

The social costs of production are not to be confounded with the prime costs of products. The social cost of a commodity ($c + v + m$) is the value of a commodity. The prime costs of a product ($c + v$) is that part of the value of a commodity which includes the costs of the remuneration of labour and of the consumed means of production. In spite of differences between social costs and the prime costs of commodities, it stands to reason that if the prime costs of products are known, the social costs can easily be determined. How is it to be explained that the numerical expression of the value of commodities is disputable when that of prime costs brings no problems in its train? How can one acquaint oneself with one part of the value expressed in monetary terms when the value as such is unknown in the same terms?

This inconsistency becomes unravelled if it is taken into account that *in the light of political economics the interpretation of prime costs differs from that of prime costs in reality.* The prime cost means $c + v$ only qualitatively. Quantitatively the prime cost may deviate – and in fact generally does deviate – from the $c + v$ part of the value of the product. *By the cost accounting method as applied by enterprises social costs cannot be established. In practice the prime cost is, as a matter of fact, the prime cost of a certain phase of production accounted at current prices.* If the relationship between price and cost is analysed in a given price system in order to establish how costs develop in the last production phase, it is indifferent whether the prime cost of a product contains through the prices of the means of production – that is to say indirectly – social net income and to what this amounts to.

Economists are at home in prime cost investigations because the question to be answered is not what the cost of a product is

[21] Csikós-Nagy, B., Ganczer, S. and Rácz, L.: Az első termékrendszerű ármodell (The First Product Type Price Model). *Közgazdasági Szemle,* No. 1, 1964, Budapest.

from the point of view of society but only how much the product costs the enterprise under review. From the point of view of an enterprise the identification of the input price and value of means of production is self-evident. However, the value calculation cannot be limited to the last production-phase only. The investigation of the social costs of production must cover all previous phases, too. If economists well-versed in prime cost calculation were asked to calculate the value of products whose prime costs are known they would find themselves in an impasse. Therefore it has become necessary to introduce a new category, that of prime costs in real terms. *Prime costs in real terms are equal to unit prime costs cleared from social net incomes, that is, they are tantamount to prime costs at wage levels.*

Society's productive organization is an integral entity. Except for consumer goods, one and the same product is the product of a certain working process while it is an instrument of production in the case of another working process. In every working process means of production are applied which have been produced earlier. The product put into use in a new working process continues to function as the material factor of live work (dead labour). Live work purposefully puts to use the objects of work transferring their value into the value of the commodity. The value of the commodity ($c+v+m$) expresses that the working process separated in time and space is the aggregate of *subsequent* phases of one and the same working process. c included in the value of one or another product – i.e. in the product of previous working processes – is also divided into $c+v+m$. The latter c also consists of the components $c+v+m$ and so on. Thus, c itself (dead labour) which constitutes a component part of the value of the product, is traceable – in the form of a convergent infinite series – to $v+m$, to live work in the past. The formula of the commodity value can also be written down in the following way:

$$c+v+m = (V+M)+v+m$$

This formula directly points to live work input (quantity of worktime). As a rough approximation it can be assumed that the ratio of v and m is identical in the case of every product. If this is so, the relative value of products also becomes known through wage income ratios ($V+v$) expressed in them accumulatively. This means, as a matter of fact, that relative *prime costs in real terms correspond to the relative values.*

In this context that idea of economics is expressed according to which both modes of the implementation of social net incomes bring about completely consistent results whether m is proportionated either to wage incomes (v) in the case of prime costs ($c+v$) in a politico-economical sense, or to prime costs in the case of prime costs in real terms ($V+v$). Thus, one can arrive at value in two ways: either by determining values a priori or by establishing prime costs in real terms and raising them to value level. It should be added *that the accounting of the magnitude of value causes a lesser problem, the main point is the approximation of the relative value.*

The essence of the real prime cost category was first expounded by *A. Smith*. Since the value of every commodity is produced by work – says *Smith* – and every kind of commodity producing work is reduced to necessary work (v) and surplus work (m), the commodity value ($c+v+m$) must also become reduced to these two elements; when all is said and done, the commodity value can only consist of $v+m$.[22]

When the socialist price theory was worked out it caused confusion that while *Marx* adopted the labour value theory, he disapproved of and condemned *Smith*'s thesis a dogma, according to which the commodity value is "made up" of incomes and "becomes resolved" in incomes.[23] These confusions came to light when modern mathematical apparatuses and computers opened the road to value calculations based on reducing the c value element to $v+m$. It seemed therefore important to throw light upon the real aim of *Marx*'s criticism.

It is obvious that from a practical point of view the commodity value does *not* "resolve" in incomes for besides changing capital (v) and surplus value (m), the reproduction of the permanent capital value (c) must also take place. *Marx* reproached *Smith* for having prevented the comprehension of the social reproduction process. *Smith* dealt with commodities which were the outcome of the capitalist production process. Consequently he ought to have analysed both the value forming process and the sales process.

However, *A. Smith*'s analyses are important for getting acquainted with the laws of the movement of social capital. Summing up *A. Smith*'s economic views on this subject, *Marx* acknowledged that in the flow of *social capital* – under which the aggregate of individual capitals is to be understood – *the matter appears in another light than in the case of isolated single capitals*. For the single capitalist the commodity value becomes reduced to a permanent element as well as to the aggregate of wages and surplus value. From a social point of view, however, the constant capital value disappears. This means that the views of *Marx* and *A. Smith* have reached a common platform in connection with the prime cost formula in real terms.

22 Smith, A.: *op.cit.*
23 Marx, K.: *op.cit.*

The category of prime costs in real terms can indirectly be met with also in the case of *Marx*, namely, when the conceptually different components of the commodity value are expressed by parts commensurate with the product. *Marx*'s example about the input components of twenty pounds of cotton yarn is known:

Input components of twenty pounds of cotton yarn

Input		Value elements expressed in cotton yarn	Value components of yarn	Quantity of work in material form
		pound	shilling	Working hours
used cotton		13⅓	20	40
consumed auxiliary materials, means of production, spindles etc.		2⅔	4	8
needed work of spinners		2	3	6
surplus work of spinners		2	3	6
	total:	20	30	60

Regarding its character the prime cost formula in real terms completely corresponds to this formula. The prime cost in real terms of 20 pounds of yarn amounts to 15 shillings of which 10 shillings are wages of cotton workers, 3 shillings wages of spinners and 2 shillings wages paid for the production of the consumed auxiliary materials, means of production, spindles etc. Thus, if the ratio of v and m is known, one can arrive at prime costs in real terms starting from the commodity value and vice versa.

Why has *Marx*'s formula had to be redrafted? Because the calculations just dealt with were applied by Marx to elucidate the value components only based on the assumption that prices equal values. However, for a method which aims at obtaining information on the value, a formula must be found which removes distortions caused by the price system. This has been the purpose of the redrafting of the formula.

Even an economist well-versed in price calculations does not know what to do with the value formula. *On a micro-economic level price calculations are enterprise centred.* From this follow the following characteristics:

1. Enterprises calculate on the basis of the actual cost structure applying approximating methods for the price calculation:

– production costs generally arise as a result of the wearing out of machinery, buildings and vehicles, materials purchased and wages paid,

– the costs are – dependent upon the character of the working process – technical development, production, storage, marketing, transport etc. costs,

– costs can be *directly charged* to single products, on the one hand, while there are *overhead costs* on the other. Products can be directly charged with those costs only of which it can be established with the production of which product they are connected. A basis of projection has to be found for the distribution of overhead costs between products. This is determined by means of the complementary postcalculation method which can rely, for example, on direct material costs, direct wage costs, direct costs and so on. This has to be done for it is known that the choice of the basis of projection influences the *relative costs* of productions.

2. The calculation of enterprises aims at a profit. To *recover the capital* is the criterion of the calculation. However, enterprises producing various products simultaneously by different technologies would have to face an insoluble task if they had to determine the prices of products starting from the principle of proportional profit projected on the capital tied up in production. It is, therefore, preferable to convert average capital refundment into another (available) projection basis for purposes of price calculations. This projection basis can be prime costs, value added etc. This is done knowing that the choice of the projection basis influences the *relative prices* of manufactured products (performed services).

3. Social production functions in the framework of a determined *organizational structure:*

– The activities of enterprises cover various *stages of production.* Accordingly, differences are made between material prices and prices of semi-finished and finished goods.

– Enterprises fulfil different *functions* in the production process. The terms producer price, wholesale and retail prices, transport costs, and so on are used accordingly.

It is in fact not easy to find one's way in the intricate interconnections of prices. Yet a common denominator can be found for the price structure and the value structure on a macrolevel. This is solved by the cost calculation on a national economic level. Here *the question to be answered is not the quality and quantity of materials used for the manufacture per unit of a certain product of one or another enterprise but what kinds and quantities of products have to be produced in all branches of the social production as a whole.* There is a difference between the two:

(a) In the case mentioned first only those sorts of material which are directly used for the manufacture of a product are taken into account while in the latter case every kind of material is taken into account whose production was needed directly or indirectly. The former is direct accounting on the level of enterprises, the latter is total accounting on a national economic level. In the comprehensive cost accounting all existing means of production are taken into account because all of them are in some way, indirectly, connected with all others.

(b) In comprehensive cost calculation aggregate technical coefficients are applied, whereas in the cost calculation of enterprises only direct material consumption is taken into account.

(c) In the case of comprehensive accounting the aggregate technical coefficients of every product of own consumption is generally larger than one. Since the product had first to be produced, it is a matter of course that it amounts to one at least. However, it generally surpasses one because it had partly been consumed either when the product itself was manufactured or had partly been used for the production of other means of production.

When comprehensive cost calculations are prepared, overhead costs are eliminated; these costs are then reduced to material and wage costs by estimation, while material costs are converted into physical terms, that is to say, into technical coefficients. Technical coefficients denote the quantity of materials directly consumed for the production per one unit of a certain product. The difference between technical coefficients and material norms applied for calculations is that the former express the total direct material consumption directly chargeable in price calculations.

According to the rules of algebraical matrices, if matrices of technical coefficients are substracted from the matrix unit and a quadratic matrix inverse is calculated, the matrix obtained includes coefficients which contain the aggregate material input of the product. If the price calculation relies on the aggregate (national economic) technical coefficient *there is no reason for dividing costs into material costs and wage costs, for in this case costs of every kind assume the form of wage costs.* Accordingly, in the price structure of the national economy, wage costs are only supplemented by elements of social net income. This is due to the fact that in price calculations at the level of enterprises, material costs express those wage costs and incomes which have arisen in the course of previous working processes. Thus, when price calculations do not rely on the last phase of production but on accounting as a whole, material costs disappear. In the structure of the national economy the price is made up of those items of wage costs and net incomes which are related to aggregate technical coefficients.

If the price structure of products is known on a national economic level, the prime costs in real terms of products can also be calculated by eliminating net incomes. Knowing the prime cost in real terms, the working time spent on the product can also be determined: if wage costs expended on products are divided by the average wages of those industrial branches which did the bulk of the work in manufacturing the products, the working time spent is obtained.

Thus, the price of every product can be worked out in two structures: according to the structure of enterprises and to that of the national economy. In the former case the quantity of materials used by an enterprise for the production of products per unit (that is, in the last phase of production) is multiplied with the price of these materials. To the thus calculated material costs the wage costs arisen and the net income realized by the enterprise are added. In the latter case products are taken into account according to systematization and quantities as needed by the aggregate production of the national economy (for the manufacturing of a given product) and the thus obtained quantities are multiplied with price amounts (with value added) of the last production phase.

The Single and Dual Level Price System

Meisenberg published a book in 1953, in which the socialist price system was scientifically expounded for the first time.[24] Those European countries which took to socialism after the Second World War established a planned economy by turning to experiences of the Soviet Union. In this way an identical type

[24] MEISENBERG, L.I.: Die Preisbildung in der Volkswirtschaft der UdSSR. Berlin, 1954.

of price systems evolved in these countries. This so-called traditional socialist price system is *based on the differentiation of the price formation of products within and outside state ownership.* It is, in the main, a dual-centred price system. The prices of products within state ownership centre around *prime costs* whereas in the case of products outside state ownership prices centre round *values.*

In respect of products within state ownership planned price formation starts from the requirement of *self-accounting ("khozraschet") of enterprises.* The main condition of the smooth functioning of self-accounting is that price receipts should cover the costs of simple reproduction when enterprises function according to plan. This cannot be a self-financing price for it is applied in a system of economic control in which the budget allocates the financial means of development at the disposal of enterprises – and free of charge at that – through the centralization and redistribution of social savings. Prices also must contain a moderate profit, for the conditions of production of enterprises functioning along the same line, differ. Prices are determined, as a rule, according to the prime costs of enterprises functioning at average conditions plus a moderate profit. In the case of products outside state ownership, prices must be adjusted to the value level; otherwise the tasks of income distribution and redistribution could not be solved. As a general rule the budget draws off in the sphere of products outside state ownership that part of incomes that came into being in the value producing process which is necessary to statisfy overall social needs.

The basic idea underlying the two-centred price system is that price changes within the sphere of state ownership do not influence the financial relationship between budget and enterprise, further, that from the point of view of alignment with related values it is indifferent whether this is effectuated on value level or on prime cost level. The former is justified by the "zero balance solution", the latter by the "prime cost solution in real terms".

The following is an appropriate example which will keep the readers straight in respect of the *zero balance solution.* Let us suppose that the branches of the state extracting industry work at a deficit while branches of the processing industry yield high profits. In the case of such price conditions the budget supplements price incomes of the former with the latter's profits skimmed off. If prices of the processing industry continue to remain unchanged while the prices of extracting industries are raised, subsidy granted by the budget can be discontinued but because in line with this the profit which has been drawn off from the processing branches decreases, the position of the budget remains unchanged. Nor can a general rise of the industrial price level within the sphere of state ownership bring about a budget surplus because in this case expenditure of the state as consumer or investor increases in conformity with the increased income. The specific features of socialist economy's price system are primarily due to problems of the zero balance. It should, however, be added that every price rearrangement within the sphere of state ownership practically always *charges the budget.* Since enterprises taking part in the price rearrangement are interested in the situation arisen as a result of new price conditions, "reserves" are built in the cost accounting which, centrally, can hardly or not at all be checked; the impact of changes of input prices on prime costs is overrated while the impact of changes of output prices on profits is underrated. This possibility cannot be eliminated if "average" prices are applied in cost calculations because of the great variety of inflowing and outflowing commodities. The thus ensued readjustment of incomes between the budget and state enterprises can subsequently be corrected in a mechanism based on plan directives because in this case every enterprise settles accounts with the budget in a system of the three months' financial plan.

The zero balance also plays a role in the price regulation of products outside state ownership. If the non-state productive sector or the population as a whole is surveyed it is fairly easy to work out measures which bring about a zero balance. For example, the agricultural price level can be raised without raising the consumer prices of foodstuffs, while the surplus income of agriculture can be drawn off by taxes. Such measures can be expedient under given circumstances with the zero balance manifesting itself in every respect. These measures do not touch upon the population because consumer prices of foodstuffs have not changed. They are indifferent from the point of view of the budget because the decrease of taxes included in foodstuff prices or subsidies granted is evened up by the increased tax burdens of agriculture. Agriculture, however, passes on the sums obtained as a result of higher prices in the form of taxes.

Similar measures can be worked out in connection with consumer prices. The state can raise prices of single products and refund the thus withdrawn incomes either by reducing prices of other products or by raising wages. This too is an absolutely neutral measure. The price reduction of products decreases net incomes which are included in prices and can be drained off. Wage raises decrease profits included in prices and incomes reducible on this account. All this is evened up by surplus incomes realized by higher prices. Society, however, has recovered what it has been deprived of by price rises of certain articles, in the form of price reduction and wage raises.

In both cases, however, the zero balance is correct on a national economic average only. Looking at the matter from the point of the quoted agricultural example: producers do not share in the advantages of the price rise in proportion to the higher taxes to be paid. This measure which is indifferent as regards the average of agriculture exerts different effects on single agrarian producers. Some get in a more advantageous position and others in a more disadvantageous one. Hence, such a measure should only be applied if it aims at differentiation. The same can be said about consumer price measures as mentioned by way of example.

The background of the *"solution of prime costs in real terms"* has been discussed in connection with the quantification of value. If it is true that "$c+v+m$" can be reduced to "$v+m$" and "m" is constant, then it also follows that the "v" ratios correspond to the "$c+v+m$" ratios. Thus, the specific feature of the two-centred price system is that it develops relative prices on "v" level in the sphere of products within state ownership and on the "$c+v+m$" level in the sphere of products outside state ownership. It is even more justified to emphasize here what has already been stressed in connection with the "zero balance solution" regarding deviations of theory and practice. This is not only so because in the interest of the smooth functioning of the self-accounting system, prime costs have to be supplemented with profits to a differentiated measure from sector to sector but also because in an administrative price system prices can only fix the cost relations of a given period.

The conditions of production perpetually change. However, the socialist price system – in the form as discussed above – does not follow these changes except when it actualizes them at times by a *readjustment of prices* (every 6–8 years). It is characteristic of this price system that the new prices approximate actual costs when being introduced, subsequently the "frozen" prices lose touch more and more with actual costs, one might say they get age-worn, until relationship between prime costs and prices later becomes restored once again. The temporary separation between self-costs and prices is solved by operative financial planning in the form of drawing off profits in the relationship between budget and enterprise. Thus, while the budget theoretically solves the centralization of a part of net incomes which come into being in the value producing process through prices of products outside state ownership, the periodically effected drawing off of incomes in the sphere within state ownership is also considerable. This is in fact the drawing off of effective savings because this kind of income derives from decreased prime costs and improved productivity.

Criticism of the traditional socialist price system started at about the mid-fifties. In his introductory report *J.A. Konrad* criticized the low price level of the means of production in a discussion which started on the law of value and price formation at the Institute of Economics of the Academy of Sciences of the Soviet Union in December 1956. He advocated, together with others, the creation of a uniform (one-level) price system.[25] In these and other discussions held in a number of socialist countries real problems got mixed up with erroneous hypotheses. A number of economists thought that the dual-centred price system is in fact the expression of *Stalin*'s thesis according to which means of production are not "real" commodities in the socialist economy.[26] On this basis it was criticized that socialist price formation applies *different criteria for the determination of prices of consumer goods and of means of production.*

It would, however, be a misinterpretation if the dual-centred price system would be characterized in this way. In this price system, as a rule also consumer goods are realized at prime cost prices within the sphere of state ownership, while means of production are sold at value level when being removed from the sphere of state ownership. Although the great majority of the produced means of production remains within the sphere of state ownership (let us disregard export for the time being) and the commodities leaving state ownership are mainly consumer goods, it is not right to speak about two-levelled prices in the case of means of production and consumer articles. It is more characteristic of the dual centred price system that prices are lower within the sphere of state ownership and higher outside it. Therefore, the dual centred price system can also be referred to as a "sectoral" price system. One and the same product can have two or even more prices, for example, the price of a product is the lowest when it is purchased in the state sector, higher when it is bought in the co-operative sector, and the highest when it is bought in the private sector.

The erroneous hypothesis of low prices of the means of production vs. high prices of consumer goods gave rise to the opinion that *price rises of the means of production could be coupled with the price reduction of consumer prices.* According to this view: the total amount of prices corresponds to the total amount of values also in a socialist economy with the difference

[25] See: *Voprosy Ekonomiki,* Nos. 2 and 3, 1957, Moscow.
[26] STALIN, J.: Economic Problems of Socialism in the USSR. *Supplement to New Times,* No. 44, 1952, Moscow.

though that prices of the means of production are set below their value whereas those of consumer goods are above their value. On this basis certain economists arrived at the conclusion that by creating the single-centred (one level) price system the living standard could be raised "with one stroke".

The dual centred price system can be interpreted in one way only: the price level of products outside state ownership corresponds to the value level, while prices of products within state ownership are lower than the value level; the total amount of prices is *lower* than the total value sum. This price system can only be converted into a one-level price system by raising the prices of products within the sphere of state ownership to the value level. A price reform carrying this into effect can – without touching upon the price level of products outside the sphere of state ownership – only change those channels through which the budget centralizes a part of the incomes realized in the value production. In a dual-centred price system the indirect (turnover) tax is the main income source of the budget whereas in the one-level price system it is the direct (income) tax.

It is easily understandable that the living standard cannot be influenced advantageously merely through a price reform. The living standard develops as a function of economic real processes. Wages and prices, being nominal magnitudes, are only reflections, forms of expression, of real processes. Price reforms can also focus on improving conditions of life. This, however, is prepared by changing economic real processes. It must be assumed that those who took part in the price discussions were fully aware of these elementary interdependences and wanted to influence state planning by referring to the living standard. These price discussions took place at a time when socialist countries allocated an inordinately large part of the produced national income to accumulation.

Criticisms of the dual-centred price system also included the *problem of the relative evaluation of live work* (wages) and *dead work* (material costs and depreciation). Some of the economists were of the opinion that if wages are determined as a function of consumer prices, the price determination of the means of production must centre round the same principle. Low prices of the means of production may bring about irrational mismanagement of enterprises. It was pointed out that enterprises are financially interested in the decrease of prime costs and that technical-organizational measures decreasing costs change, among other things, the proportions between live and dead work. Thus, if live work is related to cost calculations of enterprises at a higher evaluation level, and dead work at a lower one, it may happen that savings in live work will be associated with a lavish spending of means of production socially surpassing savings; prime costs will decrease at the level of enterprises while economic efficiency will deteriorate on a social level. In the price discussions some attached importance to the one-level price system just in view of these considerations.

This opinion is unwarrantable because of the specific features of the category of "prime costs in real terms". If it can be proved that relative prime costs in real terms are relative values then it also follows that *this kind of price system is consistent from the point of view of the logical choice.* In this price system, theoretically speaking, the price of the means of production is prime cost on wage level, that is, the evaluation of wages, material costs and depreciation is homogeneous. In other words: if the consistent price system of prime costs is converted into a consistent price system of values, only the price level increases but the relative prices of products as well as the relative costs of wages, depreciation and materials remain unchanged.

Greater importance must be attached to criticisms of the traditional socialist price system in connection with technical development, social benefits above wages and the gratuitous use of capital engaged in production and of land.

Value Price – Production Price

The "pure" price discussion developed into a debate on the so-called *price centre.* Of course the value debate also was carried on starting from a statement by *Marx* which related value not simply to input but to socially necessary expenditure. In socialist countries administrative price formation relies on actual conditions of production, that is, on the hypothesis according to which the effective production costs equal the amount of socially necessary expenditure. The price discussion focussed just on this element of administrative price formation intensifying the debate by revealing relationships between national and international values. In this discussion on the price centre problems of both the autarchical and nonautarchical price system and those of the national and/or world market (foreign trade) centric price system came to the fore.

The term price centre also indicates that the discussion did not primarily touch upon concrete prices but on the main criteria of administrative price formation. It is common knowledge that prices to be applied in practical life cannot be worked out according to a stereotyped pattern. The disputing partners, however, thought that if the question of the price centre got cleared up it will become the main characteristic of the price system worked out on the basis of administrative price whereas prices deviating from it will present unique cases. The "price centre" created in this way the concept of "price deviation". The "pure" price discussion considered the former as belonging to the sphere of science, while the latter was considered a matter of practice.

The "pure" price discussion employed the following categories: value price, production price, self-financing price, as well as one and multi-channel price systems. In the case of the *value price,* prime costs become refunded in the price of all products while social net income is realized in proportion to wages. In the case of the *production price* prime costs become refunded in the price of all products while social net income is divided among product prices in proportion to the embodied capital. In the case of *self-financing prices,* prime costs become refunded in each product price while a part of the social net incomes is realized according to the financing of investments in conformity with the planned development of the single branches.

The value price and the production price are *one-channel* price systems while the self-financing price is a *multi-channel* price system. The term "channel" refers to the case of a supplement to net incomes and/or to the system of drawing-off state incomes. The self-financing price is, necessarily, a multi-channel system because the financial demands needed for the development of branches are less than social savings. In this price system it must be determined in each case separately through which channels state incomes are to be drawn off. In the price discussion there also emerged different value price-production price variants, that is, alternatives in the case of which prices are formed on the basis of net incomes partly in proportion to wage costs and partly in proportion to the capital embodied in production. These are two-channel systems. Since the majority of the participants in the discussion considered it inevitable to separate consumer prices from producer's prices within a determined sphere and in a determined measure, the turnover (consumer) tax also had to be taken into account as a separate channel.

The substitution of the concept of value by that of the price centre was not considered by Marxist economists deflection from the labour value theory. *Marx* regarded the "production price", the realization of the average profit, a modified form of value whereas he integrated the "monopolistic price", the realization of monopolistic profit, with the law of value.

Different types of price centres were not only discussed theoretically but were also quantified by *price modelling.* Price modelling did not come up against difficulties because when the value calculation is solved, a solution for every other type of price centre can also be found. Thus, it could be investigated what kind of deviations of related prices appear in the case of different types of price centres and the branches (products) would be pointed out in the case of which the influence of the price centre type on the magnitude of the price is particularly striking.[27]

Strumilin and others advocated the cause of a *uniform value price system of the national economy.*[28] The standpoint of the adherents to the value price is clear: they adopted the socialist policy of distribution according to work. It is easy to demonstrate that wages according to work and the value price comply with this principle of distribution. This is so because

– when every member of society obtains personal income in proportion to the work performed for society, the relative incomes are in harmony with the principle of distribution according to work,

– when relative prices reflect relative values, nominal incomes become transformed into real incomes without changed relative incomes.

In such a case wages are income regulators whereas prices are factors ensuring the equivalents of the exchange of commodities. All this gives the impression of matters being quite in order. He who holds an opposite view encroaches on the fundamental interests of socialist society by attacking distribution according to work.

Malishev and others took sides with a *production price system of the national economy.*[29] In the sense of this system price centres have duly to express the different needs for capital of various branches (products). The economic justification of this concept is based on two important characteristics of the modern forces of production:

– as regards the production of different kinds of products (branches) equal labour input is accompanied by a very different degree of capital input,

[27] In Hungary, e.g. – according to data obtained by price modelling first of all the production of electric energy, transport, metallurgy required capital above the average, whereas construction, the production of textile garments, etc. required capital below the average in the second half of the 1960s.

[28] Strumilin, S.: K voprosu ob uchote stoimosti produktsii (On the Question of the Value of Products). *Voprosy Ekonomiki,* No.12, 1956, Moscow.

[29] Malishev, I.S.: Nekotoriye voprosy tsenoobrazovaniya v sotsialisticheskom khozyaistve (Some Questions of Pricing in Socialist Economy). *Voprosy Ekonomiki,* No.3, 1957, Moscow.

– the magnitude of labour input needed for the production per unit of one or another kind of product (that is, the efficiency of labour) depends to a considerable extent upon the degree of capital input, i.e. upon the application of a more equipment intensive or more labour-intensive technology.

The "production price" was dealt with in detail in price discussions held within the CMEA. It appeared that the extent of expressing different needs for capital by relative prices is determined by the magnitude of the *charge on capital,* which should render it possible to select from the different investment alternatives the ones the aggregate of which ensures maximum rate of growth of the national income.

Maximum increment of the national income can generally be reached in such a way that, in addition to making use to the full of that part of the national income which is devoted to increasing the assets engaged by the national economy, the full employment of the labour force is also ensured at the same time. Therefore correctly chosen charges on capital should theoretically enable the development of a combination of labour and capital input when decisions are made in respect to investment alternatives so that

– the aggregate of all requirements aiming at the increase of capital input should equal that part of the national income which is allotted to productive accumulation and

– that there should be no possibility to change (regroup) the investment pattern which would bring about a greater national income than the established variant.

The discussion on value price vs. production price was very sharp particularly at the beginning. The zealous backers of the production price were reproached for wanting to introduce stealthily the law of average profits into the mechanism of the socialist economy. They were accused of paving the way to spontaneity under the guise of the production price and of fomenting elements of anarchy in production. These kinds of discussions did much damage to economics. It would have been easy to make a boomerang of the stick they wanted to strike down with. For he who identifies the production price with capitalist production relations, with the specific capitalist economic mechanism, must refuse to admit the adoptability of the value price under socialism. If the first thesis holds good, then the value price is identical with simple commodity production relations. This too would substitute the planned control of the economy by spontaneity. A discussion on this basis leads into a blind alley and only those can see the point of the price centre discussion who understand that the type of prices and the principle on which the functioning of the economy relies are two different things.

The adherents of the value price subsequently referred to the fact that value expresses, among other things, the different capital intensity of various branches (products) through *amortization.* However, it could be proved that the character of depreciation differs from that of charge on capital. What do economists overlook when criticizing the production price with reference to depreciation? In the first place the fact that in the case of price formation which takes into account capital intensity the point is not only that the charge on capital should surpass the depreciation of assets, but that this additional cost should be of an "adequate" order of magnitude. Secondly, that the "adequate" magnitude can only be determined in accordance with capital efficiency.

Through the exploration of the different character of depreciation and charge on capital the advocates of the production price formula finally succeeded to point out elements which influenced price formation. In economic calculations *two time factors* have to be taken into account simultaneously.

1. During the time of wear the *value of assets engaged in production must be recovered.* This must be provided for by amortization. Through the latter the asset value manifests itself in the value of the commodity in accordance with the principle of materialization and is determined by socially necessary labour input. It derives from the particular features of social production i.e. that socially necessary input assumes the form of live work ($v+m$) and dead work (c); that dead work (c) is embodied partly in means of work (such as real estate, machines etc.) and partly in objects of work, such as raw materials, fuel, auxiliary materials etc; and that the means of work maintain their original form in the production process gradually transmitting their value into the value of the commodity in porportion to wear.

2. The new capital input should be more efficient than the previous one. Backers of the production price are justified in differentiating between present and future products as well as between the present and future evaluation of products taking into account regular technical development and increase of labour productivity. The socialist economy is a dynamic one with production regularly increasing at a considerable and fast rate. Hence, the time factor must be taken into account by all means when products are evaluated. If this is so one has to take the same pattern in the case of price formation; accordingly, the prices of products of identical value but produced by capital inputs of different order of magnitude cannot be identical either; thus, the relative price of various products can only be adjusted to their relative value if they had been turned out in case of equal capital input.

The production price formula solves, as a matter of fact, two countervailing economic processes. One of the processes aims at drawing off means of the available funds of the national income in order to develop the national economy. The other process shows that labour productivity increases as a result of expanded production and in conformity with this, the value relations also change. The formula of the production price takes into account deviations due to different capital input starting from the fact that capital input has an active role in the upswing of production.

National and International Value

Value expresses socially necessary labour input. But how can a society be characterized which regards labour input a socially necessary matter? Does the international or the national value provide an explanation of the price phenomenon? Should the concept of value be deduced from supra-national society or from national societies?

In the "pure" price discussion the world market price was defined as the centre of the domestic price supplemented with value price vs. production price variants and considered, in general, a *standpoint against autarchical price systems.*[30] According to this if a price only exists as an accounting price it cannot be determined in economic terms. In other words: *the price as it exists under socialism is not suitable to play the role of a signalling system.* Since, however, such a price is indispensable as a means of economic decisions, the *capitalist world market price* (that is, prices applied in foreign trade between socialist and capitalist countries) must and can be applied for this purpose. In socialist price discussions the world market price – the centre of the national price – manifests itself as a price which determines, besides the formation of profits and losses realized in the prices of single products, also the relationship between price and prime cost. According to certain opinions this price system is best suited for the socialist society.

What arguments are usually adduced *for the application of the world market price* as domestic price centre? First of all, that this kind of price serves best the economic competition between the two socio-economic systems. Every other concept – all variants of price systems reflecting national value relations – keeps autarchical requirements to the fore and does not provide suffi-

[30] Liska, T.: Kritika és koncepció (Criticism and Concept). *Közgazdasági Szemle,* No.9, 1963, Budapest.

cient orientation in the rational development of the international division of labour.

This view bears a relation to two aspects of the organizational work of the socialist economy.

(a) In inter-trade between CMEA countries such contractual prices are applied which take into account – in a specific manner – capitalist world market prices.

(b) In a number of socialist countries, in addition to the order of profitability of branches based on actual prices, also the order of efficiency is established where domestic prices are substituted by capitalist world market prices.

It is easy to understand that a suitable relation between domestic and foreign trade prices is of vital importance particularly from the point of view of the economy of foreign trade sensitive socialist countries. When a considerable quotient of the national income is redistributed through foreign trade

– the *prime costs of products* only reflect adequately the socially necessary costs in case the *import price regulates* the domestic price of import products used in production;

– the socially acknowledged extent of expenditure of export products is regulated by export prices.

It must, however, clearly be seen that the discussion on the type of price centres and the observance of foreign trade prices are matters of very different character. The discussion on the price centre is a problem of the calculation system, whereas the relationship between domestic and foreign trade prices is an important condition of putting economic efficiency into effect. In a foreign trade sensitive economy, economic efficiency can only be interpreted on an international scale – from the point of view of developing the macrostructure – and its true yardstick is international competitiveness.

However, the national price system *cannot be absorbed* in the world market price system. Even the possibility of getting to know world market prices is only limited. The single socialist countries can only follow world market prices in connection with their foreign trade commodity structure. At the same time it is known that prices applied in trade between capitalist and socialist countries deviate from the price quotations applied by capitalist countries when trading among themselves. There is no country in the world whose national price system could become identified with any of the world market price systems worked out artificially.

For the clearer comprehension of the value problem one has to take into account the *historical process of the regional expansion of the market.* Economic development created national markets by integrating local markets, and international markets came into being by the economic co-operation between countries. In world trade – to borrow a term from *Marx* – commodities unfold their value on a world scale. From this, however, it does not follow that *national value categories are withering away. This is the characteristic way of thinking of those who firmly believe that commodities can only have one magnitude of value.* From Marx's comments on the theory of value one cannot arrive at such conclusions.

Marx expounded the functioning of the law of value on a national basis in connection with the natural conditions of single countries, separately analysing those factors which modify the law of value on an international scale. In every country there exists a certain medium intensity of work and if for the production of certain commodities the time consumed exceeds the socially needed average, this kind of work as a whole cannot be considered value producing work. Only the degree of intensity above the national average changes a country's magnitude of value.

Since single countries are integral parts of the world market a different situation prevails on the latter. The medium intensity of work changes from country to country. These national averages form a flight of steps whose unit of measure is the average unit of universal work. National work of higher intensity produces more values during the same time than less intensive work.

However, the international effectiveness of the law of value becomes modified to an even greater degree due to the fact that on the world market more productive national work is rated as more intensive work except for the case when keen competition compels the more productive nation to reduce the prices of its commodities to their value.

The local, national, international and world markets can be considered co-existing markets having established contacts with each other. Accordingly, commodities can have simultaneously *different* magnitude of value between which there exists a reciprocal state of dependence. The development of national values does not necessarily mean the vanishing of local values. Similarly, the coming into being of the world market does not do away with national values. The simultaneous existence of different (local, national, international) magnitudes of value is the result of (local, national, international) markets co-existing separately in a determined manner.

For the easier comprehension of the national and international value of commodities it is particularly important to keep the following in mind:

(a) The international value is the weighted average of national values of products introduced by foreign trade. Thus, the international value is a category derived from national values.

(b) The socially necessary work input is determined on the national market in accordance with national conditions. This national magnitude of value changes in foreign trade into international value. Interaction between these two orders of value asserts itself without differences between these two magnitudes of value becoming resolved.

(c) The tendency of integrating national markets on an international scale differs from product to product. Gold is, for example, a typically world trade commodity. There are, however, products whose existence is limited to national (or local) markets. The latter have therefore no international value. Labour force, a highly important commodity in capitalist world economy, is limited in the main to national markets and only the tendency of its becoming international manifests itself.

(d) In case of products which are traded in international business, only that part which is turned over in foreign trade represents international value.

All these factors make it clear: *one cannot speak about national values "becoming absorbed" in international values; the independent existence of national values cannot be denied; national values cannot be set against international values.* All this would furnish a wrong theoretical value basis of the price phenomenon. From what has been said hitherto it follows: socially necessary labour input concerns one or another "field" which has become an economic unit as a result of the social division of labour. In the interrelationship between *different* economic units only the investigation of relative values is of importance.

Labour Value and the Price of the Three Factors of Production

In everyday parlance the notion of price becomes identical with the price of a commodity and with the tariff of services. This is in fact the *narrower* notion of price. In a *wider* sense price is an economic category related to every element of the production process which becomes cost in one place and income in the other. Not only products and services but also land, labour and capital have a price. The categories of these are land rent, wages and interest. This goes to say that even *things which have no value, can have a price.* This, however, only indicates that part of the new value produced by work which appears as surplus value can assume different income forms. These forms of income are determined in socialist countries by taxes connected with the production process.

In capitalism the production process shapes in a system of market relations which developed between the entrepreneur, the capitalist, the landowner and the labourer. Thus, not only that seems natural that the labourer works for wages but also that the landowner (capitalist) wants to participate in the surplus value in return of the land (capital) let for use. In capitalism this participation (land rent and interest) as well as wages are determined by the market relations of the factors of production. A market mechanism functioning on a broad basis substantiates opinions according to which the value of a commodity is made up of the three factors of production plus the value of the work of the entrepreneur. In this sense the price theory cannot be expounded on the basis of the labour value theory but only relying on the theory of the three factors of production.

The counterposing of the three production factors and the labour value theory may play a role insofar that when the socialist price theory is discussed many leave out of consideration the problems of the association of the factors of production. In conformity with this, socialist political economics basically represents *socialist production as simple commodity production characteristic of the degree of development preceding capitalism.* This prevailing opinion is based on the hypothesis that every change of form taking place in simple commodity production under capitalist relations is characteristic only of capitalist production and is not valid under socialist relations. Now let us deal with the relevant theses of socialist political economics.[31]

First thesis. Three factors are needed for commodity production in any society: work, the subject of work and working tools. The commodity production has a twofold character. On the one hand, it is a *working process* aiming at the manufacture of products of use value. On the other hand, it is a *value producing process* insofar that work materializes through the product into value. This duality is characteristic of every production process in which commodities are turned out.

Second thesis. In capitalist commodity production the labourer creates value using tools and working on objects alienated from him. The labour force appears as a commodity.

[31] *Politicheskaya Ekonomiya* (Political Economy). Moscow, 1958. 3rd ed. Members of the Collective of Editors: Ostrovityanov, K.V., Leontev, L.A., Laptev, I.D., Gatovsky, L.M. and Kuzminoy, I.Y.

Capitalist private property is a title and a possibility for the capitalist dispossession of products produced by workers. Under capitalist relations the value producing process must turn into a *realization process.* Surplus value comes into being whose source is the new value produced by the worker.

Third thesis. Profit, interest and land rent *express capitalist exploitation* and are categories reflecting specific production relations. The characteristic feature of these production relations is that the means of production are owned by a part of society while another part of society is not in command of means of production.

According to these theses the rational organization of production in a socialist economy is not a correct combination of land, work and capital, but *of live and dead work.* In this connection reference is frequently made to *Marx* although he did not dispute the existence of the factors of production. *Marx* has proved that in spite of the existence of profit, interest and land rent, work is the only value producing factor. The hypothesis of the three factors of production is not the negation of the labour value theory – as it is frequently assumed. *Marx* could only be referred to on the ground that he considered surplus value, profit etc. specific categories of capitalism. However, *Marx* was of the opinion that commodity production in general does not suit the socialist society. He thought that socialist society would introduce the direct exchange of goods (barter economy). The delimitation of capitalist production form commodity production only took place later, taking into account practical experience gained in the course of the building of socialism. This was expressed in the following way. In socialist production

– money, price etc. *continue* to exist for these are categories of commodity production independent of capitalists, but

– capital, interest, etc. cease to exist, for these are connected to capitalist exploitation.

If land and capital are socialized they can of course be put to the disposal of enterprises free of charge. In this case the price calculation is a so-called calculation of wage character. In the production costs the wage costs of the last phase of production are aggregated with the wage costs (material costs) of the previous phases of production; this, supplemented by the gain, constitutes the price. Earlier, however, socialist societies found it quite natural to exclude capital and land from price calculations but recently a contrary tendency has come to the fore. The role of credit is on the increase, tax is imposed on capital engaged in production, use charge has to be paid for land and so on.

How is it to be explained that the above are expressed in terms of costs in the production process? The reasons of this are to be found in the criteria of rational calculation. Socialist society makes the available forces of production work not as an unorganized body but in the form of enterprises which are self-accounting units. Commodity and money relations are the form of the division of labour between enterprises. Rational behaviour is expected from every unit. In the interest of rational behaviour *everything that is available to a limited extent only, must be drawn into the orbit of economy.*

Of course, economy can be managed in different ways. The state as the owner of mines can regulate the rhythm and method of exploitation of mineral resources according to a preconceived plan. Empty plots available free of charge can be turned to account according to central allocation etc. These methods of central economic management devoid of prices are known and are necessary. However, central economic management of capital and natural resources *without prices* cannot substitute for regulation based on the application of the price category. The factors of production can be replaced in the production process within narrower or wider bounds. One of the criteria of the rational behaviour of enterprises is the optimum association of the factors of production. If natural resources were made available for an enterprise free of charge, ruthless exploitation of these resources would bring about the best result for this particular enterprise. The state can of course set limits to this. However, no kind of state prescription can bring about the optimum association of the factors of production which are in a substitutive relationship with each other although this is the condition of an efficient functioning of the forces of production. This can only be solved by means of the price category.

2. Market Value and Relative Prices

Use Value

The explanation of price based on the value of labour looks upon production in its state as adjusted to needs. This is a *natural* state as the aim of production is the satisfaction of human wants. In this situation input (sacrifice) coincides with the utility (enjoyment) of products when consumed. Input and utility, these mark the relationship between production and consumption. This also finds expression in the *dual nature of products* which are

- partly values of human labour,
- partly use values suited to satisfy human wants.

In the first Volume of his Capital, *Marx* regards value as a magnitude, and use value as a characteristic of commodities. Use value is the carrier of the exchange value of commodities. The use values of various commodities are *qualitatively different,* therefore, they are not commensurable in this respect. Different commodities have one characteristic in common making them comparable in the exchange, namely that they are products of labour. What provides the basis of equality between two commodities to be exchanged is the socially necessary labour to produce them.

It is this point that some economists critically comment upon when they object to the deviation from the input principle in the practice of pricing of the socialist countries, or to the adoption in the price system of these countries *of the principle of price proportionality based on the comparison of use values.* They are of the opinion that this deflection of price from value weakens the role price plays in the planning of the national economy, a basis for the value indicators of the plan.[32] But what *Marx* characterized was merely the dual nature of commodity which follows from the dual character of labour embodied in a commodity.

[32] Kotov, V.: Tseny – instrument narodnokhozyaistvennogo planirovaniya i osnova stoimostnykh pokazateley plana (Price as a Means of Economic Planning and the Basis of Plan Indices). *Planovoye Khozyaistvo,* No.9, 1972, Moscow.

At the same time, *Marx* interpreted the *labour theory of value together with rent theory.* Rent incomes are earned by certain productive branches (products) which have a high social utility and whose production cannot, or can only be expanded within narrow limits. Rent income is directly or indirectly the consequence of *natural factors*, of the fact that the satisfaction of wants cannot be confined to the extraction of mineral resources made possible by favourable natural endowments, or to products of high-quality lands, or those situated close to the market. Let us take coal as an example. The costs of coal extraction must be realized in the price of coal. But the relative prices of different qualities and varieties of coal must be adjusted to relative use values. This is the reason why coal deposits with favourable natural endowments can earn rent incomes. The price (price level) of qualitatively "undefined coal" corresponds to the value of "undefined coal", but the income produced by labour is redistributed, and this is governed by use value. This is how value and use value are connected in the price system. Similarly, oil mining enjoys a rent income compared with coal mining. Fuel oil and coal are commensurable on the basis of their use values, and thus the specific input of oil extraction so interpreted is less. Hence, rent income itself points to such specific features of the price phenomenon which can only be investigated from the angle of consumption.

If we approach the price phenomenon from the point of view of the consumer, then what appears to be of particular interest is *the differentiation between the products of labour and the so-called free goods*. Goods provided free by nature (the heat of the sun, the force of winds, etc.) are also use values, but not values since they are free gifts of the nature. The consumer does not appreciate free goods as they are available to him free of charge. By contrast, products of labour are always available in limited quantities, which *forces man to economize on them*. Therefore, the consumer develops his scale of preferences. Consumers' preference asserts itself as a function of prices. To put it in a simplified way: in the case of a given price proportion, the consumer accords preference to one product over the other.

The hypothesis continues to be valid: goods are produced when there is a demand for them. Now the following question arises: if production adjusts itself to demand, how can consumers' preference give rise to such elements of the price phenomenon which cannot be explained by labour value? This is conceivable only if the producer acts, in certain cases, under the pressure of coercion; he produces even if he cannot sell at value price. But what can compel a producer, who is able to assess demand and to decide freely the assortment and quantity of commodities, to act in this way? This coercion can only be explained by *characteristics of the product structure.* Thus, *regularities* must be attached to the *product structure* and therefore the law of value can only function in harmony with these regularities. *If the regularities of the product structure are based on the quantification and comparability of use values, the latter's role as price regulator has also to be acknowledged.*

Products Interlinked in Production

Experts in economic calculations cannot consider the use value an "empty" category for the use value often is indispensable when prices and cost accountings are worked out. This is particularly striking in the case of *products interlinked in the production process*. It is characteristic of the production process that a number of products can be produced side by side. The economics of industrial management classifies these products into main products, by-products and waste products just for the sake of solving accounting problems; main products produced simultaneously are considered twin products.

The terms by-product and waste-product show that their use value is insignificant as compared to the main product which originates at the same time. In plant cultivation grains are the main product and straw is the by-product. In vine growing grapes are the main products whereas vine and marc are by-products. In animal husbandry increase in weight is the main product and dung the by-product. Waste (iron, textile, wood etc.) originates in almost every production process. Although the aim of production is to turn out the main product, by-products and even waste can have use value. But just because of differences of the use value, the relative prices of main products, by-products and waste products cannot be approached from the side of input which cannot be divided between these products proportionately.

Economic calculations can apply different methods in order to co-ordinate value and use value if by-products (waste) develop; the latter can be considered expenditure if its market price is known. This is called the *substraction method*: the expenditure of the main product is obtained by subtracting price incomes deriving from the sale of by-products (waste) from the production costs. The *separating method* is applied if the market price is dubious and economic calculations must decide the minimum price at which it is still worth while to sell the by-product (waste product). In this case the costs of manipulation, storage, transport etc. of by-products (waste) are separated from the costs of production.

The value of by-products and waste is unknown in the production process they originate from; only their market price is known. However, the market price can express the value because by-products (waste) of one branch of production can be the main product of another one. The relationship between the market price of waste of the wood processing industry and the value of firewood, the main product lumbered in forests, is obvious. Manure is the by-product of animal breeding whereas artificial fertilizer is a main product of the chemical industry; the two use values are in substitutive relationship with each other. If, however, such a relationship does not exist as, for example, in the case of scrap-iron, the user's evaluation is the only determinant. This kind of product turns into a commodity only if on the ground of the user's evaluation its conversion into money is more advantageous for the producer than its destruction.

Economic calculation based on use value is not restricted to by-products and waste products. The *relative prices of twin products* connected with each other by an identical manufacturing technology *cannot be explained by proportional input in every case*. For example, in sheep-breeding four twin products (lamb, meat, milk and wool) originate. From the point of view of use value these twin products are related to different groups of products. Consequently the price of lamb, mutton, ewe-milk and wool can only be interpreted in the light of the value relations of those branches of production they are connected with on the ground of use value. Accordingly, in the economic calculation of sheep-farming the *value proportional method* is applied; expenditures are divided between twin products on the basis of relative prices.

Twin products also are characteristic of certain branches of the chemical industry. In the course of the fractional destillation of coal a number of products originate produced with the same distilling apparatus. The raw material (coal) is not perceptible in either of the products separately, that is, the proportion of the basic material per product cannot be established. The single products are related to different groups of products. *Mass produced articles belonging to different groups of products* are connected with each other through the rational functioning of the *productive unit* (plant) without being related by the *manufacturing technology*.

Seen from the side of expenditure, all possible methods of economic calculation based on use value are expressed by the *deviating cost-bearing capacity* of articles produced side by side. Differences in the cost-bearing capacity of products (twin products) related to each other by the manufacturing technology are determined by the comparison of prices established on the basis of proportional expenditure with actual prices. In the case of products linked together by the productive unit (enterprises with a mixed special line of production) differences in the cost-bearing capacity are indicated by the mode of dividing overhead expenses between products.

Complementary and Substitutive Products

Use value can become a price factor because there are relationships between products which rely on their physical properties. This is the case when *products are complementary to each other or substitute each other in consumption*. Complementary products are, for example, motorcar and petrol because a petrol-driven car cannot be used without gasoline. Substitutive products are, for example, fat and edible oil for they are equally suited to satisfy the same demand. Products in substitutive relationship can complete each other; the degree and conditions of substitution may differ. *Demands of complementary products change in an unidirectional way whereas demands of substitutive products change* – under unchanged conditions – *in opposite directions*.

The independent demand of various products establishes different kinds of relationship between demand and price in the sphere of complementary and substitutive products. *Complementary products can be considered "one product" from the point of view of demand whereas substitutive products can be considered "one product" from the point of view of prices*. The fact that complementary products are "one product" from the point of view of demand means that demand is uniform. In the demand of a motorcar the demand of petrol is implicitly included. Now what does it mean that substitutive products are "one product" from the point of view of prices? It means that the consumer reduces the prices to a common denominator. If society consumes about equal quantities of both fat and edible oil and the price of fat rises against that of oil it is certain that the consumption structure will change to the advantage of edible oil while a contrary change will take place when edible oil becomes more expensive. The effect of changes of relative prices on the consumption structure is decided in the main in addition to the degree of relative prices by the degree and mode of substitutionability.

Value is the regulator of relative prices in the sphere of complementary products while use value is the regulator of relative prices in the sphere of substitutive products. The production costs of lignite may be higher than those of brown-coal and the production costs of the latter may be higher than the production costs of hard coal, the fact remains that lignite is cheaper than brown coal and brown coal is cheaper than hard coal. This is so because the different kinds of coal of different quality are comparable and measurable according to their physical properties and utility in consumption. The degree of steaming power of a certain quality of coal, an energy bearer used as steam generator, can be determined and expressed by thermal energy coefficients. If the consumer has a choice, demand will always centre on the cheaper energy bearer and that energy bearer is cheaper whose price is lower in case of identical thermal energy efficiency. In this way are substitutive products reduced to a common denominator in the sphere of consumption from the point of view of prices. This tendency is based on the consumer's natural aim to satisfy needs by the smallest sacrifices. For this reason *relative prices of products in substitutive relationship with each other adapt themselves to relative use values*.

The complete or partial substitution of products asserts itself *on a wide range*. In the case of coal this does not only refer to the substitution of certain qualities of coal for other ones but also to that for all energy bearers. Coal can be replaced by other kinds of solid fuels, crude oil products, natural gas and electricity. Thus, quantification based on use value is not only possible as regards different varieties and qualities of one product, but also in respect to different kinds of products.

To take an example let us look into the question of *transport rates*. Seen from a historic outlook the prevalent role of railroads and the complementary character of other branches of transport characterizes the development of transport. It is understandable that when new transport services developed, investigations centred on the question whether the new means of transport will be taken advantage of and/or under which conditions will the new services be chosen instead of railroads. The most important point of view of the policy of new transport services was to bring it into accord with railway rates. Parameters related to use value play an important role in the fixing of transport rates. Criteria are of importance as, for example, slowness of water transport, relative speed of railroads, mobility of cars and the very high speed of airplanes; shipping is dependent upon waterways, weather and so on.

Technical sciences have investigated for long the qualitative factors of industrial materials, among other things, the effect different varieties of raw materials and the different assortments of certain kinds of material have on the prime cost of products processed of these materials. The aim is to determine in this way the *industrial value* of the single varieties of products. The approach to this is made by quantitative comparisons for the main point is that per quantitative unit of a product obtained by the processing of a certain raw material different quantities of various varieties of the raw material are needed. The greater this quantity the smaller is the industrial value of the given assortment.

As regards the industrial evaluation of coal: three qualitative parameters determine the industrial value of coal, calorific value (kcal/kg), specific ash content and the degree of classification. The calorific value shows the combustible proportion of one kilogramme of coal, the specific ash content the proportion of ash and wetness in the non-combustible part of coal whereas the degree of classification indicates the homogeneity of the mass of coal. From all this it does not follow that by means of the industrial value (i.e. use value) the price system of coal can be determined. The industrial value can be approached both by fewer and more parameters; the weight of the parameters as a function of the price can be worked out in different ways. It is obvious that in this case the properties changing from country to country play an important role.

Coal is only a case in order to show that in subsequent manufacturing processes the *substitutive products of the previous phase of production are always evaluated as a relationship between price and use value*. In a like manner the price system of iron ore, coke, timber, cotton and so on can only be understood as described in the case of coal. In other words: from the side of value coal, iron ore, coke etc. are only "one product" whereas from the side of use value they are a "system of products".

The relative use value of subsitutive products as a regulator or relative prices *determines downwards starting from the end product*. The final aim of production is the present consumption and that of the future. On this basis a difference is made between consumer articles and investment goods. In society's productive organization industrial evaluation adjusts itself to those criteria with which articles of consumption and investment goods are qualified.

In connection with the industrial value it has been emphasized that an objective yardstick by means of which the use value of substitutive products can be reduced to a common denominator can always be established. This is done by economic calculation (prime cost calculation). In this case, however, it is assumed that the quality of the product will not change by different variants of material input. This holds good in the case of absolute substitutability and can mainly be met with in the lower stages of production, but is not always characteristic even there. The more a semi-finished product comes close to becoming a consumer article (investment good), the more characteristic *non-substitutability* of this kind of product is.

Theoretically speaking energy bearers can be conceived as products being in absolutely by substitutional relationship with each other. Practically, however, difference is made between variable and invariable quantities of energy bearers. This differentiation relies on the fact that the consumer has not always the alternative of choice. Technology may prescribe the use of a certain energy bearer. Apart from this the same energy bearer can be put to use with different net efficiencies in different furnaces. The order of energy bearers according to their use value is different from consumer group to consumer group. Thus, absolute substitution is mostly characteristic of new consumers.

Up to now mainly the *technical* limits of substitution have been discussed. However, there also are *qualitative* limits which are quite independent from the technical ones. Theoretically speaking fat can be substituted for edible oil but it is known that in some countries fat is the main basis of fat for household consumption whereas in other ones it is edible oil. It would therefore be a mistake to explain fundamental differences of the consumer pattern on the basis of deviating relative prices. Nor can it be explained on the basis of prices why more beer is consumed in some countries and more wine in others. Climatic conditions, consumer habits, conditions of production etc. also play a role in this. The aforesaid already touch upon criteria playing a role in the qualification of consumer articles, criteria not at all or scarcely quantifiable.

In respect to the evaluation of characteristics of the quality of agricultural produce, in addition to the nutritive value (calories) and biological value the *"relish" value* also plays a role. Nutritive and biological values are measurable properties of foodstuffs for they can be determined by the effective material content per unit of product. But in the case of a number of foodstuffs, the "relish" value is the main property from the point of view of the consumer. It is often a condition of delectable consumption, moreover, it is to a certain degree a condition of the beneficial utilization by the organism of the nutritive and biological value of foodstuffs.

The qualitative factors of industrial articles are in conformity with usances (standards). However, substandard products marketed at reduced prices can also be used in accordance with their original function. Use value measured in consumption does not make a distinction between standard and substandard commodities. Price relations rely on a more complicated systematization of products than that. Consumer preferences created categories such as branded goods, fashion articles and modern products. *Branded goods* are products which, owing to excellent properties, deserve to be given prominence to (as compared to similar commodities), *articles of fashion* are products manufactured according to the prevalent fashion whereas *modern products* are the ones whose parameters comply with world standards. Although the above do not cover the entire range of criteria characteristic of the consumer's judgement they suffice to give an idea that these are scarcely or not at all quantifiable properties of products.

Factors such as "relish" value, fashion and modernity a priori cannot be determined as price factors but become quantified through relative prices, and it is not known that these relative prices are formed with a view to *consumer preferences.* It is perhaps most of all in the modernity factor that the relative use value becomes quantified through the input ratio. However, consumer preferences keep even this under control. More precisely: the modernization process of products must make itself felt by such parameters to which the consumer gives preference too. In the case of investment goods this is determined by economic considerations (e.g. the effect more modern machines exert on productivity) whereas it is determined in the case of consumer articles by the general trend of expanded and refined needs.

We have arrived at the conclusion that consumer preferences regulate the relative prices of consumer articles (investment goods) in the sphere of products in substitutional relationship and that the consumer influences through this the industrial value of raw materials (semi-finished goods), that is, the relative prices of raw materials (semi-finished goods) which are also in substitutional relationship with each other. Consumer preferences have no direct influence provided that the substitution of materials does not alter the quality of the product turned out with a substitute. If the quality changes the industrial value must be deduced from the qualification of the end product.

Labour Value and Use Value

It should be noted that the price regulating role of the use value is curtailed by *two limiting factors:* (1) It is a price regulator in the sphere of substitutional products only, hence, it is not a general price regulator and (2) it is not a price level regulating factor, but a factor regulating relative prices. It is necessary to make this point repeatedly, for arbitrarily expanding the principle of substitution and confusing price level and relative prices when the regulating role of consumer preferences is dealt with leads to the negation of labour value, in consequence of which either the value category is thrown overboard or the objective concept of labour value is confounded with the concept of subjective value.

In analysing the world of commodities one can get relatively easily acquainted with the relationships between different products based on use value and with the limit beyond which such relationships do not exist. Many economists have worked out price sequences based on the use value of different types (assortments) of coal, shoes, motorcycles, machine tools and so on but it would be a futile attempt to work out price sequences based on use values of the relationship between coal – shoes – motorcycles and machine tools.

In agriculture though, large-scale experiments were made to express different kinds of products in "grain units". This endeavour is in connection with the opinion of many who challenge the possibility of separating agricultural expenditures on one produce from those on another. In fact, from that time on when *Howard* worked out the agricultural accounting system[33] – following in the wake of double entry book-keeping – a school of economists queried the existence of prime costs in agriculture. The followers of this school declare that a farm (agricultural plant) is a uniform organization made up of productive sections completing one another organically and because of the close connections between them the single production lines have no reason for a separate existence. They refer among other things to the fact that plant cultivation produces fodder and litter for animal keeping; on the other hand, animal keeping provides plant cultivation with manure, draught-animals also contribute to plant cultivation and so on. On the ground of these and similar reasons they counter the principle that agricultural accounting can be performed in the close system of double-entry book-keeping, they are against breaking down agricultural plants to branches in accounting and against handling the single production lines independently from each other.

Aeroboe restricted accounting in terms of money in agricultural book-keeping to external turnover. In his opinion the

[33] HOWARD, H.: *Landwirtschaftliche Buchführung mit vollständigem ganzjährigem Ausführungsbeispiel.* Unterlagen und Abschluss aus der Praxis. Zum Selbststudium, 1–3 Bd. 2. Aufl., Hannover, 1913.

domestic produce and animal economy should be accounted in physical terms, for only these show the expenditure required by and yields of the single production lines. *Aeroboe* disregards the evaluation of non-marketable produce such as manure, straw, pastures etc.[34] *R. Manteuffel* worked round to this old-standing discussion when he pointed out that the distributing methods – which he compared to ruthlesly used pruning knives – applied by rigid accounting, cut to pieces the internal relationships within agriculture, artificially isolating the single production areas from each other.[35]

Manteuffel suggests to apply the *organic method* of prime cost calculation. According to *Manteuffel* the simplified organic method can be applied in the following way: production as a whole is to be expressed in one kind of produce (for example in grain units) whereas the total costs of production of a farm are distributed among the single kinds of produce by the proportioning method; finally the thus accounted costs per produce are to be divided with the quantity produced. The *equivalent of grain unit* taken as a basis of the prime cost calculation of agricultural produce (products) means that an approach to the prime costs starts from the aggregate production costs of a farm on the basis of the useful content of the produce (products).[36]

A number of countries have worked out the grain unit system and the aggregate grain unit index of agricultural production. This is also applied for international comparative analyses as a yardstick for measuring the development of intensive farming.

[34] AEROBOE, FR.: *Allgemeine landwirtschaftliche Betriebslehre.* Berlin, 1917. HORRING, J.: Die Kostenkalkulation in der Landwirtschaft. *Agrarwirtschaft,* No.1, 1954. ZÖRNER, H.: Nochmals Kalkulation oder Produktionskostenrechnung. *Berichte über Landwirtschaft,* VIII, 1928, Berlin.

[35] MANTEUFFEL, R.: Mwtoda organitszna badania oplacalnoshtsi productiy rolnitszey (Organic Research Method of Efficiency in Agricultural Production). *Ekonomista,* No.1, 1958.

[36] For long it has been an endeavour of experts of agriculture to bring to a common denominator the quantitative data of different kinds of agricultural produce by using equivalences. In the beginning of our century, THAER introduced the notion of hay unit in foddering. At the same time FJORD used the unit of fodder in dairy farming. At the Copenhagen Congress on Foddering held in 1915, the barley unit, recommended by HANSSON, was accepted as the unit of foddering in the Scandinavian countries. In Germany, on the basis of RUBNER's examinations, Kellner established by exact scientific methods the notion of starch value. Even today this calculation provides the basis for highly developed calculations of fodder. WOERMANN was the first to use the unit he termed grain unit in measuring quantitative output. Today the grain unit is generally used to express in a quantitative unit the production yield and the gross produce of agriculture work. – In greater detail see: LONKAI, J.: Gabonaegységgel való teljesítménymérés a mezőgazdaságban (Measuring Output in Agriculture by means of the Grain Unit). *Gazdálkodás,* No.3, 1958, Budapest.

However, experts well-versed in various accounting methods know that, outside the sphere of substitution, equivalent coefficients cannot be determined satisfactorily in a strict sense of the word. Therefore, they have recourse to prices or put up with very dubious methods.

In order completely to eliminate labour value from the analysis of the price phenomen it has to be assumed that the *entire price formation process can be explained by the consumers' behaviour.* This was the starting hypothesis of the demand theories which came to the fore after *Marx.* Recently *indifference surfaces* have become the main theorem of demand theories. This theory considers the *various products as elements of general and uniform needs.* This general and uniform global need is satisfied by different kinds of products. As a result, the consumer can precisely appreciate the total utility of the sets of goods (consumption baskets) of different compositions. He can establish which combinations of sets of goods he considers of equal utility (which are thus indifferent) and which ones provide smaller or greater advantages as compared to another combination.[37] This theory is, as a matter of fact, a variant of the marginal utility theory further developed; it came into being in the course of discussions about the measurability of utility. Thus, some are of the opinion that although utility is non-measurable, a judgement can be formed on the degree of utility of different combinations of sets of goods. In fact, however, the negation of one opinion includes the negation of the other one. The mistake is ascribable in both cases to the error that the substitution of products can be adopted universally.[38]

According to this concept the individual consumer can directly regulate only the price relations of consumer goods. If, however, the consumer price relations are given, the latter "adjust", retrogressively, the price relations of the factors of production too. In the case of given consumer prices the conditions are also determined from which the price of compensation due to the various factors of production for their contribution to the production process can be deduced.[39] The theory relies on the hypothesis of the complete substitutionability of the factors of production. According to this hypothesis, work, capital and land mutually substitute each other. This theory demonstrates

[37] Edgeworth, Fr. J.: *Papers relating to Political Economy.* Vols. I–III, London, 1925. Pareto, V.: *Cours d'économie politique.* Paris, 1896.

[38] Neubauer, Gy.: Közgazdaság és metodika (Economy and Methodology). *Közgazdasági Szemle,* Vol. 73, 1930.

[39] Thünen, J.H.: *Der isolierte Staat.* 3. Aufl. Sammlung Sozialwissenschaftlicher Meister. Bd. 13, 1930, Jena. Clark, J.B.: *The Distribution of Wealth.* New York, 1912.

through the laws of return that each factor of production participates – on the basis of marginal productivity – in the value produced.

Even experts well versed in economic calculation frequently confound the role of use value in regulating relative prices with the price level regulating role of value. If the price of a certain product is given then the prices of the materials used for the manufacture of this product can of course also be determined in conformity with it. If the price of electric current is given, the price of coal can be calculated from the former. This is the natural outcome of price and cost interdependences within society's productive organization. This is why the price of a product of a higher grade of finish seemingly regulates prices retrospectively. If this were true the price phenomenon could not be explained on the basis of the conditions of production but on the ground of factors outside society's productive organization. In this case it ought to be supposed that prices develop in the sphere of distribution which of course is an absurdity.

The demand for synthetics is a case in point showing the *consumer's actual possibilities and limits in shaping the price level of commodities.* The gradual spreading of synthetics is well known. In line with the mass production of synthetics and with the return of considerable initial costs the prices of synthetics decreased by and by. The lower prices improved the efficiency of substitution for the technology of applicability of synthetics was worked out on a wide range at a time when demand was still far less because of too high prices. Changes have taken place between prices of traditional raw materials and those of synthetics and the resulting decline of prices of synthetics gradually improved the efficiency of substitution and increased the demand for synthetics.

Fully aware of this process it would be hardly well founded to contend that the price level of synthetics is regulated by consumption. The price level of synthetics can primarily be explained on the basis of the conditions of production. For lack of excellent properties or failing the possibility to substitute synthetics for traditional material at high economic efficiency, the production of synthetics could, of course, never have become mass production. Demand which keeps up and develops the production of synthetics under such conditions, reacts on both price relations of synthetics and on those of traditional materials which are in substitutional relationship with the former.

Public Goods and Individual Products

In a commodity producing economy work expended on the production of commodities is expressed in terms of money and input is expressed by the price. Therefore social products can be added up in terms of money. From this, however, it does not follow that the distribution of every product is regulated by the price. A part of the products provides for social supply and is available for consumption free of charge. For example, national defence, the road network, public lighting are organized in the form of social supply, hence, arms, roads, streetlamps are objects of social consumption i.e. public goods the financing of which is provided for by the state. A part of the incomes originating in production is centralized in the budget for these purposes. Another part of the products is allocated to personal consumption and can be purchased at market prices. Products which are subject to personal consumption such as foodstuffs, wearing apparel etc. are sold as commodities. Consumers have to provide themselves for the supply of these *individual products* and finance their purchases out of original and secondary incomes deriving from production after taxes.

Supply with public goods is provided for by the political mechanism whereas that with individual products by the market mechanism. *The mixed system of distribution is characteristic of both the socialist and the capitalist economy.* The prevalent tendency in *capitalism* is that as many goods as possible should become commodities and that public goods should be reduced to a narrow sphere where the market is incapable of functioning. On the other hand, in *socialism* such products are also included in the sphere of social supply which could be distributed by the market too. The mixed system of distribution is based on the technical criteria of products in capitalism and on the criteria of needs in socialism.[40]

A product can be converted into a commodity (a) if it has use value from the point of view of the individual consumer, (b) if it is available in a manner suited to satisfy individual needs and (c)

[40] The mixed distribution system in capitalism can be studied in: Wicksell, K.: *Vorlesungen über Nationalökonomie.* Jena. I. Bd. 1913, II. Bd. 1922. Johansen, L.: *Public Economics.* Amsterdam, 1965. Buchanau, J.: *The Demand and Supply of Public Goods.* Chicago, 1968. The 1970 Leningrad Congress of the Institute of International Public Finance dealt with a comparative analysis of capitalism and socialism. See: Musgrave, R.A.: Provision for Social Goods in the Market System. Csikós-Nagy, B.: Uses and Limits of Markets in Government – Co-ordinated Economics. Problems of Public Finance in the field of Research and Technical Development and New Approaches in Public Finance. Institut International de Finances Publiques. Lyon, (Paris), Saarbrücken, 1971.

if consumption has a competitive character i.e. if there is a possibility of excluding a commodity from consumption. In short: *a commodity is a divisible product.* The market mechanism has developed accordingly: a television set is a commodity because it is produced in a manner suited to satisfy individual needs; costs and benefits are internal for those who take part in the goods exchange; thus, the market can regulate distribution and the price can fulfil its selective function.

Public goods are (a) either a priori unsuited to satisfy individual needs (e.g. products of labour serving the purposes of national defence) or (b) are not divisible products of labour (e.g. public lighting), (c) or are theoretically divisible but (d) nobody can be excluded from their consumption for technical reasons and/or (e) there is no reason for excluding anybody – say – from the use of roads. The consumption of public goods by certain individuals does not influence consumption by others. Therefore, this kind of consumption is not competitive. Should, however, competition arise in case of overcrowding this cannot be solved by exclusion through prices.

The individual consumer does not *appreciate public goods which from his point of view are unrestrictedly available.* What appears to be unrestricted from the point of view of the individual consumer is limited on a social scale because free use only extends as far as it is available for society.

The divisibility and non-divisibility of products of labour, internal and external effects, competitive and non-competitive consumption as well as the principle of exclusion and non-exclusion from consumption are technical criteria of differentiating between commodity and non-commodity. These criteria do not always render an unambiguous classification of products possible. Those who consider goods exchange the most efficient way of product distribution, obviously regard also such products divisible the supply of which is socially organized. (In some countries toll is taken for the use of motorways, bridges etc.) In certain cases society has a choice between technical alternatives which also decide whether certain products of labour are suited to satisfy individual needs or supply is to be organized on a social basis.[41] (For example, one can combat drought by irrigation equipments or by artificially producing precipitation of rain-clouds.) In this way the sphere of public goods can be narrowed down. This, however, does not touch upon the essentials. The structure of social production can be deduced not only from the process through which a product of labour becomes a commodity. Society also needs public goods.

41 HEAD, J.G. and SHOUP, C.S.: Public Goods, Private Goods, and Ambiguous Goods. *The Economic Journal,* LXXIV, September, 1969.

For the better understanding of the mechanism of mixed distribution under socialism *one has to make a difference between socially organized consumption and public goods.* Supply is organized on a social basis whenever the preconditions of the functioning of the market are failing. In this sense the concept of public goods is also valid in the socialist economy. However, social consumption also extends to spheres where – from a purely technical point of view – distribution also could be performed by the market because costs and benefits are internal, consumption is competitive and the principle of exclusion from the market is enforceable. Although costs and benefits of educational and health institutions are internal, they yet appear as public goods. Educational, health and social institutions cannot be taken advantage of unrestrictedly. For example, the number of those who want to matriculate at the university always exceeds by far the number of those who can be admitted and besides there is always a possibility to put in a claim for social benefits when supply cannot be yet ensured. Since in the system of social consumption products have no price at all or the price only covers a part of the actual costs, prices do not perform a selective function and exclusion from consumption must be determined by mechanisms outside the sphere of prices. (The criteria for claims for admittance to the university or for taking advantage of social institutions etc. must be determined.)

If social supply is not determined by the technical criteria of products, the difference between commodity vs. non-commodity can only be traced back to *ideological aspects of the economy.* Established social norms are compulsory for the socialist organization of the economy. As a general rule *social supply* includes social care for the aged and for children, culture and education as well as health services. In a socialist society this is put into practice by two co-existing systems of distribution: *distribution according to work and distribution according to needs.* Distribution according to needs refers to needs which from the point of view of the members of society are basic requirements but are ethical requirements from the point of view of society as a whole.

Social benefits are granted partly in monetary form (family allowance, pensions, social subsidies etc.) or in physical terms (education, medical attendance etc.) Benefits in monetary terms provide sound demand for individual products. Benefits in physical terms provide a possibility for socially organized consumption. Thus, there is a mixed system of distribution in the socialist economy, a complementary functioning of the market mechanism and the non-market one.

Labour Value and Market Value

In the case of individual products, the relationship between labour value and price *is tansmitted by market value.* Public goods – as they are not distributed by the market – have no market value, only price. The inputs expended on the production of public goods must be covered by state (social) organizations. In the sphere of individual products it is only concrete varieties that command a market price. It is true, we often refer to the prices of coal, oil, cotton, etc., but then we think either of their average prices or of the prices of their definite varieties. It is not coal in general but a given quality of coal that has a market price. It is this which expresses the input on the one hand and the use value of a given quality of coal in its relationship with energy carriers that can substitute it, on the other.

The market can only evaluate a commodity as a relation between the participants involved (producers and consumers). In this context it is frequently mentioned that the market only takes internal effects into account while external effects are left out of consideration. From the point of view of market value, input is expenditures concentrating on the producer while benefit is the utility of the consumer. In the case of fully divisible commodities producer costs coincide with social costs while consumer utility corresponds to the social benefits of the commodity. This means that in the case of *fully divisible commodities there are no external effects.* However, in addition to fully divisible individual products and indivisible public goods there also are products which become commodities although they are only partly divisible. The market cannot evaluate in accordance with social judgement commodities which are only partly divisible.

Experts frequently refer to difficulties in working out economic calculations because of the *unequal position of commodities.* To take one example: when the competitiveness of railroads as against road traffic is the question at issue it is often mentioned that railway construction and track maintenance are internal factors in the case of railroads, whereas they are external ones in the case of road traffic. It is well known too that the same industrial capacity is less capital intensive in an industrial centre than in an agrarian region because among other things the infrastructural background is available at the former while it has to be set up at least partly by industrial co-operation in an agrarian area. Town planners have often mentioned that in overcrowded industrial areas accessory infrastructural investments – necessary for the foundation of new productive works – surpass many times the operative investments.

The concept of socially necessary labour input includes the fulfilment of the condition according to which costs covered by society in the interest of the production of a commodity are truly disclosed by the productive unit. This materializes when the gratuitous use of public goods does not lead to the exclusion of others in the course of the production of a product and/or if all elements which are the condition of production are included in the costs. It has been shown that these conditions are not always fulfilled. Seen from the side of costs, external effects are on the increase in line with the development of the forces of production, particularly as a result of the scientific-technical revolution. A number of analyses have pointed out that there is a close organic relationship between the rate of economic growth and research-development activities. The rate of technical progress increases due to the government's research development policy. The state supports this activity, directly and indirectly. The more this is so, the higher is the probability that the market value of *basic research intensive commodities* is lower than social sacrifices made in the interest of the latter for the simple reason that a part of the social costs is refunded by the state budget and does not become converted into production costs.

The partial divisibility of commodities also *manifests itself in the external effect of utility.* The dangerous nature of commodity production increases in line with the development of the forces of production manifesting itself in water, air and soil polution and intolerance in noise. This is why *environment protection* has come to the fore. When the production and consumption of commodities is associated with such effects a commodity

– is undervalued from the aspect of the producer (because expenditures devoted to the protection of the environment have been neglected) while

– utility is overestimated from the viewpoint of the consumer (because social injuriousness in left out of account).

The concept of socially necessary input includes the fulfilment of the condition according to which products do not decrease the use value of free goods. If they yet decrease the use value of free goods (either because investments in connection with nature conservation have been neglected or technologies protecting the environment are still unknown) the social product does not reflect correctly the social utility of production. If the expansion of production brings about the increase of environmental injuriousness, social utility falls behind the rate of development of the GNP.

The interest of the socialist society requires that production and goods exchange should be organized in accordance with social utility and the price should become in this way signalling system of economic decisions. The approximation of work performed on a social scale to market value calls for the correctly interpreted system of cost-interdependences between productive units, that is, for the assertion of the principle that nothing is gratuitously available in production that has demanded sacrifices from society. However, the protection of the environment is not a price problem only. It must also include the ban of technologies which are particularly injurious to health further prohibit or limit in industrial areas the production of certain types of commodities injurious to health.

However, it is impossible completely to eliminate external effects. These external effects manifest themselves to a different degree from type to type of commodities. Therefore the order of values developed by socially *necessary* input differs from the order adapted to effective labour input while the latter differs from the order according to the market value.

Market Value and Equilibrium Price

The market value of commodities governs the market price, however, price and value do not coincide necessarily. The relationship between the two, that is, the degree and trend in case of their congruence or differences depends upon the *quantitative relationship between demand and supply.* The price fulfils the role of a stabilizer in the market mechanism. Goods exchange partly encumbers and partly facilitates the balancing of production and consumption. It makes the situation more difficult insofar that needs become embodied on the market in the form of demand and in some cases there is no demand at all or demand is slighter than expected for products aimed at the satisfaction of society's needs. The goods exchange, however, also facilitates to keep up equilibrium because demand takes a definite shape through the price and, theoretically speaking, there always exists a low or high price in the case of which equilibrium can be ensured. This also indicates that the price can only establish a relationship with the value *in conformity with the laws of the market.*

The organic connection between price and market relations has induced many economists to reject the value category for they think that the knowledge providing the criteria of the equilibrium price in the framework of the law of demand and supply is a satisfactory explanation of the price. In this context *B. Croce's* statement according to which economics without value is just like logic without concept, ethics without moral obligation and aesthetics without expression, is particularly appropriate.[42] But is it true that the value of every product is expressed in its actual price, namely, that the value of a product is known by its price and/or becomes manifest as soon as the misdetermined price is changed and transformed into an equilibrium price. This cannot be true. The opinion conceiving value as an equilibrium price only explains short term price phenomena but does not give an answer to the question what kind of regularities prevail on a *longer term* on the average.

Differences made between *long-term* price tendencies and *short-term* price movements run right through the history of economics of the past two centuries. *A. Smith* differentiates between "natural price" and market price. The "natural price" develops according to the law of costs, whereas the market price evolves according to the law of demand and supply. The "natural price" asserts long-term price tendencies, while the market price brings about an equilibrium which changes time and again at short periods. According to *Marx* the rational thing is to exchange or sell commodities at their value for this is the natural law of their equilibrium, hence, deviations must be explained starting on this basis and not the other way round, namely, by explaining the law itself by the deviations. In the modern non-Marxist price theory *Marshall* has substituted the concept of "long period normal supply price" by the term "natural price".[43]

The total price necessarily coincides with the total market value. Hence, deviations of value from price can only be interpreted as *deviations of relative prices from relative values.* The price of a certain product can only exceed its value because the price of another product is lower than its value. That is, incomes are redistributed through the functioning of market laws. The price of a certain product is higher on the average as compared to the work expended on it, whereas another product realizes less than the average income. This is so because supply in one product is less while it is higher in another product than the demand determined as a function of the value price.

Price relations also express in this way the degree of scarcity of commodities. From the point of view of the consumer the utility of a commodity does not only depend upon its physical properties (use value) but also upon whether this particular

42 Croce, B.: Historical Materialism and the Economics of Karl Marx. See also: Dobb, M.: *Political Economy and Capitalism.* London, 1953. Göncöl, Gy.: Az értéktörvény a kapitalizmusban és a szocializmusban (The Law of Value in Capitalism and Socialism). *Közgazdasági Szemle,* No. 5, 1958, Budapest.

43 Marshall, A.: *The Principles of Economics.* 8th ed., London, 1890.

commodity is available and the purchasable quantities satisfy the demand as determined by the market value. The consumer attaches greater or lesser utility to a commodity dependent upon whether the purchasable quantity is more or less than demand. The relationship between demand and price is expressed by the *demand curve* which follows the laws of the satisfaction of needs. The demand curve develops differently from commodity to commodity. The term elasticity of prices is generally used in this sense. The relationship between supply and price is expressed by the *supply curve* which is governed by the laws of returns; prices lower than the market value have a supply restrictive effect while higher prices than the market value have a supply expanding effect. The supply structure adjusts itself in this way to the demand structure determined by the market value.

Part II

Law of Value and Price Function

1. Plan and Market

The System of Economic Control

The control system of the socialist economy is a structure consisting of
- the planning system,
- the regulating system and
- the system of organization.

In building socialism, socialist countries continually strive for a more perfect economic control system. At the same time the control system is adjusted to changing conditions associated with the development of the forces of production; on the other hand, certain elements of the system are improved in order to overcome negative features. Accordingly, the control system changes its form time to time. An economic reform is a peculiar form of changes, but the term itself is an inexact one. The "economic reform" is, essentially, a set of measures whose aim it is to fundamentally change the regulating system (the mechanism of plan-implementation). Changes of the planning system are generally considered the consolidation of the scientific foundations of planning while changes of the organizational system are called reorganization.

The three interconnected systems of economic control conceived in a comprehensive sense form an organic unity but within it *state planning has primacy.* In other words: although planned development is implemented by economic control interpreted in a comprehensive sense, within this system planning is of fundamental importance. Requirements deriving from the economic laws of socialism must be expressed and the objective course of planned development must be determined in a given phase of development by up-to-date state planning of the national economy. The socialist state carries the plan of the national economy into effect by regulating the economy. The organizational system must be instituted in a way that makes the efficient organization of the economy possible. These are the characteristic features of state planning which differentiate it from "indicative" planning, which presents a specific feature of the state economic policy of certain capitalist countries.

Self-regulation of the market based on price automatism is incompatible with socialist planned economy. Further, the man-

agement of socialist economy fundamentally differs from the anticyclic economic policy of capitalist states, whose vital element is capitalist private property relying on conformity with the free market. The socialist state *derives the criteria of social utility from the equality of the members of society* and develops the planning, regulating and organizational system with this end in view.

This, of course, does not exclude discussions about the actual system of economic control. The possibility of such discussions has already been foreshadowed by price discussions. However, if one logically thinks over the matter it appears that *price discussions abstracted from the function of the price are absolutely useless.* Price is the central category of commodity production. Every economic manifestation, for example, every process regulation induced by the state, directly or indirectly affects the price and/or its efficiency mechanism. Hence it was inevitable that pure price discussions concerned with the relationship between value and price had to grow into a discussion covering general economic mechanism. *The price theory investigates the system of economic control in connection with the functioning of the law of value in socialism.* Research work in the field of socialist price theory covers all three systems of control, that is, relationship between the price mechanisms of the planning, the regulating and the organizing system.

1. *In the state planning of the national economy the "law of input-output balances" plays a decisive role.*[44] State planning quantifies both the demand and the sources satisfying demands for the means of production and consumer articles as it is to be expected in line with the expansion of production and rise of the living standard. State planning can, theoretically, be considered complete if the balances of the means of production and of consumer articles are in equilibrium accompanied by a general external and internal equilibrium. This is primarily indicated by the balance of the national income, the balance of international payments and by the global financial balance of the national economy. However, the state can decide to tolerate disequilibria in certain spheres.

From the point of view of price theory particular attention is paid to the *criteria of planning.* More precisely: does the price have a role in the planning of the production structure and in that of the distribution (redistribution) of the national income and if it does, what role is it? This is related to the discussion about whether planning should be volume – or value – oriented. Further, standpoints of price theory stimulate mathematical

[44] Lange, O.: *Politikai gazdaságtan* (Political Economy). Budapest, 1965.

programming connecting the theory of the optimum functioning of the socialist economy with the shadow price theory.

2. The implementation of the plan is decisive *in the state regulation of the national economy*. The regulating system must be plan-conform. The system of means applied by the state in the interest of plan implementation is adequate if it leads to the objective process of development as laid down by the plan.

From the point of view of price theory the *interpretation of the unity* of planning and regulation is the main point. The question is whether the economic units are simply technical executive agencies of plan indicators or whether they are allowed to act in an environment where the economically determined price gives orientation. The discussion of regulation based on compulsory plan indicators and economic regulators is related to the aforesaid. The substitution of a rigid administrative price system by a flexible price mechanism is also furthered by considerations of price theory.

3. *The organizational system of the socialist economy* relies on the broad basis of a monopolistic organization. Certain economic activities are granted state monopoly. In agriculture the co-operative form of property prevails. The non-socialist sector is restricted to the small-scale production of commodities and plays a complementary role.

From the point of view of price theory the *parameters of action* (the criteria of success) of socialist economic units and the *interpretation of the state monopoly* are the main points of interest. These are in connection with discussions going on about productivity and profit motivation. Positions taken up in matters of price theory also prompt to establish an organizational system which renders competition possible.

Discussions about volume-oriented or value-oriented planning, regulation based on plan indicators or economic instruments, interest in productivity or profit, the elimination or freedom of competion are problems closely connected with the functioning of the law of value in socialism. In the following we are going to concentrate on these questions. First, however, one has to get to the bottom of the problem. In the background of the price discussions there are different opinions formed on the *nature of socialist commodity production*. The discussions have become more difficult because certain economists beat about the bush and while discussing prices think it most desirable to discontinue commodity production altogether or approach the price question from the aspect of administratively managed economy, which, by the way, is justifiable, if considered in a historical context.

Socialist Commodity Production

Socialist society can organize economy, theoretically, in two ways: on the basis of barter economy and on that of commodity economy.

If *barter economy* is carried on, society's needs are precisely taken stock of and production is organized in conformity with needs. The products manufactured are distributed among the members of society according to needs. In the barter economy, categories of the commodity economy such as money, price and trade, are not applied. The *direct exchange* of goods makes the application of these categories unnecessary. Productive units organize production under directives passed by society. The working people obtain products from society directly, according to their needs. The distribution of production is regulated in this way. In brief: consumers obtain use values in the direct system of the barter of goods. Production and needs are in this case economic processes organically determining each other.

In a *commodity economy* products are distributed by way of the market. Production appears in the form of supply whereas needs in the form of demand. Exchange is transacted in the market. The flow of commodities is followed by the flow of money. Productive units obtain price receipts for the products sold, whereas workers obtain money incomes. For the money they buy commodities chosen to preference. In this economic system money, price and trade are objective necessities, for

– there must be a universal equivalent (money) which mediates the exchange of goods,

– there must be a product price expressing value in terms of money and

– there must be a market where the exchange is transacted.

Human society carried on barter economy at the time people lived in primitive communities. Money and price appeared at a later phase of the development of human society. Commodity economy with its complicated mechanism was further developed by the capitalist mode of production and became the general system of economic organization. This transformation was the objective outcome of the development of the forces of production and of production relations changing in conformity with the former. Subsequently, *socialist revolutions radically changed the production relations on a part of our globe.* The worker-peasant state power expropriated the concentrated functioning means of production and carried on a policy as a result of which small-scale commodity producers have by and by united in co-operatives. Where the socialist revolution has been victorious the socialist basis of the people's economy, the state ownership and co-operative forms of property have come into being after a transitional period.

However, commodity economy has continued to exist also under socialist production relations. The question *whether the application of the categories of commodity economy is compatible with the aims of* socialist society is raised time and again. The communist way of thinking considers the direct exchange of goods, that is, barter economy, the natural regulator of relations between people because the communist principle of distribution according to needs is conditional on the direct exchange of goods. *Marx* envisaged the economic pattern of the socialist society in which the state directly organizes production according to needs. In this case both market commodity exchange and monetary economy are eliminated. Instead of this direct exchange of goods, barter economy is introduced provided that *Marx's* assumption becomes true who supposed that the forces of production would reach such a degree of development which would enable the unrestricted satisfaction of human needs if production were not limited by the profit motivation of capitalists. In his opinion this shows, among other things, the superiority of economy organized on a socialist basis as compared to economy organized on a capitalist basis.[45] *Engels* had the same in mind when he declared: When society takes possession of the means of production, commodity production will cease and together with it the rule of products over those who had produced them.[46]

It should, however, be added that both *Marx* and *Engels* thought that socialist revolutions would be triumphant simultaneously first of all in industrially advanced capitalist countries and that developed socialist societies would overthrow market economy together with capitalist ownership. *Marx's* thesis was first reexamined by *Lenin* on the basis of the historic process of socialist transformation and subsequently *Marx's* ideas on the economic pattern of the socialist society too. Before the First World War *Lenin* had already arrived at the conclusion that socialism would be victorious at first in a number of capitalist countries or only in one and prospects for the success of a socialist revolution were more favourable in countries where the links of the worldwide chain of capitalism were the weakest. *Lenin* was proved right by the October Revolution of 1917 and

[45] MARX, K.: *op.cit. – A gothai program kritikája* (Criticism of the Gotha Programme). Budapest, 1949.

[46] ENGELS, F.: *Herr Eugen Dühring's Revolution in Science* (Anti-Dühring). International Publ., Marxist Library, Vol. 18, New York, 1966.

by the foundation of the Soviet Union. However, at that time the Communist Party of the Soviet Union under the leadership of *Lenin* still followed Marx's direction in respect to society's socialist build-up especially because of the compelling circumstances of civil war and foreign intervention, disrupting the economy. Barter economy was introduced for a period and was called *war communism.* It soon appeared that the liquidation of trade and of money was associated with many drawbacks and that a way out of the chaotic economic conditions caused by the First World War and the boosting of social activities to achieve economic development could scarcely be reached in this way. Therefore categories of the market economy such as money, price and commerce were re-introduced and set into action in the Soviet Union once again. Lenin rendered the reason for this very succinctly: Life has shown that we erred.[47] He proclaimed and introduced the new economic policy (called NEP) in the Soviet Union in accordance with the guiding principles he had worked out. Since then a number of books, amounting to an entire library, have revealed the causes due to which commodity and money relations provide a better opportunity for pursuing a more efficient economy at a certain phase of development of the forces of production than the switch over of socialist societies to the system of barter economy.

In forming an opinion on the economic organization of the socialist society political economics starts from the assumption that *commodity production and capitalist production are two different matters.* Capitalist production is unimaginable without the dominant character of commodity production, but commodity production is possible in the absence of capitalist production. According to Stalin: One cannot identify commodity production with capitalist production. Capitalist production begins with the concentration of the means of production in private ownership, while the workers deprived of their instruments of production have no other choice than to sell their working capacity as a commodity. Failing this there is no capitalist production.[48]

Socialist society regulates the methods of production and distribution dependent upon the development of the forces of production and upon the prevailing conditions of economic growth. In the first phase of building communism the principle of distribution according to work is applied because of the scar-

[47] Lenin, V.I.: *The Tax in Kind. The Significance of the New Policy and its Conditions.* Moscow, 1965.

[48] Stalin, J.: Economic Problems of Socialism in the USSR. *Supplement to New Times,* No.44, 1952, Moscow.

city of commodities. It is only expedient to change over to the communist principle of distribution according to needs if abundance of goods prevails. Under such conditions the extreme development of the forces of production and the abundance of commodities make it unnecessary to apply exclusion from distribution. Hence, the objective conditions of the elimination of commodity and monetary economy come about. From the point of view of the socialist society the *price is a transitional economic category* which, considered in a historic context, continues to exist for a relatively long time.

Thus, the socialist and the capitalist economy fundamentally differ from each other with respect to production relations and also as regards the property relation of the means of production. However, the mechanism of economic control of the two social economic systems shows some similar traits. In capitalism, categories of commodity economy are connected with capitalist exploitation. In socialism the fact that the means of production are in social ownership makes exploitation impossible. Thus, the social content of the categories of a commodity economy is different, for it is determined by the socio-economic systems. In spite of this the process regulating content of the categories of a commodity economy can be identical. For this reason the foundation of the investigations on price phenomena under socialism must be laid on the comprehensive and general knowledge of commodity economy.

Plan and Market

Oddly enough, elements of the direct exchange of goods can become integrated with commodity production. This is due to certain peculiar features of the market mechanism. The market can function as a comprehensive and as a partial regulator. In the commodity economy there is no "vacuum". The market regulates everything, provided the state does not put obstacles in the way of its functioning. Thus, the alternatives of market restrictions depend upon whether the state wants to have recourse to the market mechanism in regulating economic processes and, besides, upon where and to what extent it carries on a market eliminating policy.

The self regulation of the market is comprehensive, for in case of self-propelled prices the market simultaneously regulates supply, demand and incomes. When the state eliminates a part of the market, the latter yet continues to function in fields where it is allowed to operate. On this relies the market eliminating policy of the state. A market regulated by *price re-*

striction excludes (in case of administrative prices) or curtails (in case of maximum prices) the functioning of self-propelled prices. In spite of this the price can fulfil its function in regulating supply, demand and incomes. A market regulated by *production restriction* exerts its influence through incomes, on the one hand, and through the relationship between demand and price, on the other. A market regulated by *consumption restriction* becomes effective through incomes and through the relationship between price and supply. When the state eliminates the market by the *direct regulation of incomes*, automatism brings about harmony between prices as well as the supply and consumption structure. The elimination of the market is not necessarily restricted to a single function of the market mechanism. The market price is kept within the narrowest bounds when state regulation allows the market to make itself effective in one direction only. This, however, is the minimum condition under which one still can speak about the functioning of the market. In the case of complex central regulation the *price can have only an accounting function.* This also indicates that the price has become *completely* separated from the market mechanism.

Stalin explained the integration of the direct barter of goods with socialist commodity production in the following way: "In our country, the sphere of operation of the law of value extends, first of all, to commodity circulation, to the exchange of commodities through purchase and sale, the exchange, chiefly of articles of personal consumption . . . under our system means of production can certainly not be classed in the category of commodities . . . in the sphere of foreign trade, but only in this sphere, our means of production really are commodities, and really are sold . . . but in the sphere of domestic circulation, means of production lose the properties of commodities . . . retaining only the outward integument of commodities (calculation, etc.). Furthermore: Wherever commodities and commodity production exist, there the law of value must also exist . . . But the operation of the law of value is not confined to the sphere of commodity circulation. It also extends to production. True, the law of values has no regulating function in our socialist production, and this fact cannot be ignored when directing production . . . In brief, there can be no doubt that under our present socialist conditions of production, the law of value cannot be a regulator of the proportions of labour distributed among the various branches of production."[49]

[49] Stalin, J.: *op.cit. Stalin's explanations did not stop the doubts about the contradictory features of commodity production and planned development.* See: Hessin, H.: *V.I. Lenin sushchnosti i osnovnikh prizkanakh tovarnogo*

Stalin generalized the practice of planned economy of a given historic period and expounded *one of the possible variants of the restricted price functions.* This can be described as follows: (1) In the sphere of products (means of production) circulating *within the state sector of the national economy,* prices are only employed for accounting; distribution is centrally regulated by the state in the system of technical-material supply. (2) The state applies commodity relations *between state and non-state production sectors* (supply of agriculture with industrial means of production, purchase of agrarian produce and so on). (3) The state applies the same method-relying on state (co-operative) trade – in the interest of influencing the *demand of the population.* (4) Only in the *relationship between non-state sectors* (in the case of unorganized markets) is state regulation generally limited to market supervision.

It is not due to chance that discussions about the recognition or negation of the market have become particularly strained as a result of endeavours to carry out economic reforms. In recent years a number of Marxist economists have wanted to give the impression that the discussions about the economic reform were an alternative between *socialist planned economy* or *socialist market economy.*[50] These economists start from the as-

←

proizvodstva (Lenin, V.I. on the Essence and Basic Features of Commodity Production). Moscow, 1968. MALISHEV, I.: *Obshchestvenniy uchet truda i tsena pri sotsializme* (Social Registration of Work and the Price in Socialism). Moscow, 1960. SOBOL, V.: *Ocherki po voprosam balansa narodnogo khozyaystva* (Studies on Questions of National Economic Balances). Moscow, 1960. *Some economists believe that actual economic relations in socialist countries have nothing to do with commodity production. It is on this ground that they consider money only as a mere substitute for product vouchers.* KULIKOV, V.: *Tovarno-denezhnie otnosheniya v systeme planomerno-organizovannogo sotsialisticheskogo proizvodstva* (Commodity and Money Relations in the System of Socialist Planned Production). Moscow, 1960. SHEKHET, N.: Planovaya tsena v systeme ekonomicheskikh kategoriy sotsialisma (Planned Prices in the System of Economic Categories of Socialism). Moscow, 1972. *A good survey of the whole debate can be found in*: VOLOVAY, D.: O planomernom ispolyzovanii tovarnodenezhny otnosheniy (On a Planned Utilization of Commodity and Money Relations). *Planovoe Khozyaystvo*, No. 2, 1974, Moscow.

50 BERGER, W. and KEINBOLD, O.: Megjegyzések a "terv és piac" problémájához (Remarks on the problem of "Plan and Market"). *Béke és Szocializmus,* No.7, 1968, Budapest. LISITCHKIN, G.Sz.: *Terv és piac* (Plan and Market). Budapest, 1967. PETRAKOV, N.J.: *A szocialista gazdálkodási módszerek vitatott problémái* (Debated Questions of Controlling Socialist Economy). Budapest, 1970. REICHENBERG, R. and TITTEL, G.: Gegen fehlerhafte Darstellung des Verhältnisses von Plan und Markt im Sozialismus. *Wissenschaftliche Zeitschrift der Hochschule für Ökonomie,* No.3, 1970, Berlin. TUREK, O.: Csehszlovák közgazdászok a terv és a piac szerepéről a szocializmusban (Czechoslovak Economists on the Role of Plan and Market in Socialism). *Béke és Szocializmus,* No. 4, 1968, Budapest.

sumption that the discussion centres on the question whether socialist societies should continue to develop in the system based on planned economy or should become transformed into market economies. They so to speak set the plan against the market as well as social consciousness against economic spontaneity. On this basis, however, a fruitful discussion can scarcely be carried on. A true alternative only exists between commodity production and direct exchange of products (barter economy). If economists subscribe to the view that commodity production is to be maintained, the economic mechanism can only rely on the assumption according to which

– there is no purposeful economic development without *state planning* and planned regulation;

– that economy cannot be organized rationally without the functioning of the *market mechanism.*

Practically, the main point always is the *synthetizing of plan and market* for market economy without plan or planned economy without market are out of the question. If the means of production are in public ownership the necessity of state planning simply cannot be denied. Commodity and money relations are market relations. This is why the anti-market standpoint seems so pointless, particularly if somebody denies the role of the market and considers at the same time activation of the commodity and money relations an important requirement for the improvement of the socialist economic mechanism. Some socialist countries embarked upon an economic reform not because they found a market wanting but because they became aware of the *objective existence of market relations in socialist commodity production and if the state yet carries on an anti-market policy the disadvantages thereof outweigh the advantages.*

The formula according to which the socialist society consciously employs the law of value has become, one migth say, an *axiom.* However, the law of value is the law of the commodity producing society which asserts itself through the market law of demand and supply. Thus the question must emerge how the law of value can be applied if economic policy *aims at narrowing the effectiveness of the market instead of making use of it according to plan.* What can the role of the law of value be in a control system which separates domestic prices from foreign trade prices and, in the sphere of domestic prices, producers' prices from consumer prices? In this case economic policy does not lean on the economic law of value any more but introduces pricing which is cut off from the assertion of the law of value. This would be justifiable if this price policy would also set aside the market laws. However, in a commodity producing society economic rationality cannot make itself effective

– in the *consumption structure* if relative consumer prices are separated from relative values, further

– in the *foreign trade commodity pattern,* if domestic prices are separated from foreign trade prices.

Thus it is understandable that the barter economy is attacked particularly sharply in those countries where the *consumer price considerably deviates from value, on the one hand, and the participation of foreign trade in the national income is significant, on the other.* In these countries the requirement came necessarily to the fore that the relationship between plan and market should be synthetized more appropriately than before and that the *market mechanism should have a more efficient controlling role in economic decisions.* This is the essence of the reform of the socialist economic mechanism.[51]

Non-Marxist economists are pleased about discussions concerning plan and market because this diverts attention from the main questions of socio-economic systems i. e. from property and class relations. Those who advocate the cause of capitalism prefer discussions on the economic mechanism to the ones on class and property relations. In the former case the main point is only how the state should control economy, while in the latter case the question is whose interests motivate economic control.

[51] Boychev, J.: *Zakon't za stoynostta pri socializma* (The Law of Value in Socialism). Sofia, 1970. Cipek, K.: Diskuse o ekonomickych reformách v socialistickych zemich (Debate on Economic Reforms in Socialist Countries). *Politicka ekonomie,* Prague, 1969. Friss, I.: Terv és gazdasági reform Magyarországon (Plan and Economic Reform in Hungary). *Társadalmi Szemle,* No.6, 1970, Budapest. Kaczmarek, Z. and Chweduk, R.: *Produkcija, towarowa, prawo wartosci i ceny wo gospodarce socjalistycznej* (Commodity Production, the Law of Value and Price in Socialist Economy). Warsaw, 1969. Marinescu, J.: *Preturile, legea valorii și relatiile diutre plan si piata* (Prices, the Law of Value and the Connection between Plan and Market). Bucharest, 1969. Nyers, R.: *Gazdaságpolitikánk és a gazdasági mechanizmus reformja* (Our Social Policy and the Reform of the Economic Mechanism). Budapest, 1968. Pajestka, J.: Proces doskonalenia systema funkcionowanie gospodarki socjalistycznej v Polsee (The Perfectioning Process of the Operating System of Socialist Economy in Poland). *Zycie Gospodarcze,* Nos. 5–6, 1970, Warsaw. Rachmuth, I.: Legea valorii. Cu priviro la determinarae mecenismului de actiune si utilizaro in Socialism (The Law of Value. On the Mechanism of the Determination of its Operation and Implementation in Socialism). *Viate Economica,* No.2, 1969, Bucharest. Sliwa, J.: Warunki wykorzystania cen jako instrumentu wiazania produkcji z rynkiem (Conditions of the Utilization of Prices as Means of Connecting Production and Market). *Gospodarka Planowa,* No.4, 1969, Warsaw. *The Soviet Economic Reform.* Main features and aims. (Liberman, Baybakov, Vorobyev, Kulagin, etc.) Novosti Press Agency Publishing House, Moscow, 1966. Timár, M.: *Gazdasági fejlődés és irányítási rendszerek Magyarországon* (Economic Development and Control System in Hungary). Budapest, 1968.

The replacement of discussions on production relations by discussions on the economic mechanism provides matter for *theories on the convergence of different socio-economic* systems.[52] If the opinion is plausible that the mode of control is the essence of the socio-economic system then the convergence of socio-economic systems is justifiable because, in line with the development of the forces of production,

– elements of state planning become more marked in capitalist societies and

– elements of the market mechanism grow firmer in socialist societies.

It must be clear to all that the socio-economic system of a country depends upon the characteristics of the state power and upon the prevailing property and class relations. The system of economic control develops on the basis of these relations, one might say it is formed to serve these relations. Competition between socialism and capitalism increasingly brings to the fore economic growth based on economic efficiency. Although the social conditions of the two systems fundamentally differ, *the means applied are probably not very dissimilar.* This is what the convergency theory welcomes and erroneously interpretes as the decrease of differences of the socio-economic systems. However, seen from this point of view the most important elements, the prime-movers of social and economic development, are left out of consideration.

[52] GALBRAITH, J.K.: *The Affluent Society.* Boston, 1958.

2. State Planning

Volume-Oriented Planning

Although socialist countries regulate the process of economic development by *five-year* plans, the annual plan underlies the operative control of the economy. CMEA member countries have agreed to work out the economic community's *long-term* plans up to 1990 and to synchronize the perspective plans on an international scale. Long-term planning with a view to the harmonized transformation of the internationally co-ordinated structure is considered important for it lays national development concepts on firmer foundations.

From the point of view of price theory it interests us greatly whether and how changes ensuing in value relations are taken into account when economic processes broken down to different time spans are projected. In socialist planned economy currently mostly *volume-oriented planning* is carried on. Planning is based on processes in real terms and not on price (value) relations. According to the starting hypothesis the condition of society's economy and the welfare of the people is determined as a function of processes in real terms. The decisive issue is the physical capacity of the productive organization, that is, what the available mass of capital goods and consumer articles amounts to in terms of use value, as well as what the favourable changes to be expected in processes in real terms due to the expansion of the economy are.

Thus, this is the essence of planning in *physical terms at constant prices.* The plan does not determine value processes but processes in real terms. The transformation process of the structure combined with economic growth is determined with a view to the commodity and monetary (market) relations characteristic of the period when the plan is being prepared, and not of those which will become effective during the time-span when the plan under preparation will operate. The price category is only employed in programming the transformation of the structure because the aggregate economic processes, lacking homogeneity, cannot be expressed in physical terms, only in homogeneous productive branches (such as coal mining or the building material industry). Value indicators must be applied where production relies on many-sided structures, that is, where the set of use values can only be added up by means of prices. In this case the price can be conceived as an instrument for the aggregation of use values.

If plans are drafted in the relationship of processes in real terms, the price does not provide information – or at least not sufficient information – when the structure transformation process is determined, and it comes to the distribution – between branches – of limited resources. However, *volume-oriented* planning does not want to depend in the first place on prices but on *technical-material information.* In this planning system prices can only provide information for the solution of matters of detail. A case in point is when planners of investment projects are bound to work out economic efficiency calculations.

Let us have a closer look at the role of technical-material information in planning. This kind of information is related to the *quantitative* and *qualitative* aspects of processes in real terms and planning establishes connections with the latter in the system of technical interdependences. *The two methods planning operates with are (a) establishing equilibrium of the material balances in respect to quantitative aspects and (b) raising the technological standard in respect to qualitative aspects.* Of course, planning cannot control the flow of commodities and movements in technologies in all their elements. Hence, planning focusses attention a priori on *processes which determine the economic structure.* In this way it, in fact, determines planned development under the impact of the spread-effect of technical interdependences. Relying on technical-material information planning can theoretically ensure development *maintaining equilibrium* at the same time, but it is hardly predictable on which level of economic efficiency this will become effective.

First let us examine the *quantitative aspects of processes in real terms.* If, from the point of view of planning, all material balances are in equilibrium, matters are seemingly quite all right. However, the question arises: why does that particular structure of consumption, as stipulated by the plan, determine production. The material balances are in close correlation with each other through technical interdependences and are, in the last analysis, determined by the distribution of scarce economic resources between branches. Even within the closed system of the national economy resources can be distributed in different proportions between branches. In the case of an open economy, the transformation of structure becomes determined by various combinations of import substitution and of the export pattern. In this case an answer is also to be given to the question whether the commodity structure of foreign trade – which has been determined with a view to planned development – coincides with the possible variant still practicable and most efficient from the point of view of foreign trade, too. It is obvious that these problems cannot be solved merely within the system of quantitative interdependences.

Some economists are of the opinion that this problem could be solved by having recourse to the *qualitative side of processes in real terms.* Starting from the assumption that the inadequacy of a country's economy derives from a lag in the field of science and technology they tend to think that the unambiguous solution of the problems is to catch up with the world standard in manufacturing technologies. In other words: every advance which diminishes the technical gap is also a step towards improving economic efficiency. According to this view it suffices therefore to rely in planning on technical information.

It is a matter of course that small countries cannot come abreast of the world standard along the whole line. However, *a selection can be made on a purely technical basis.* By a survey of world's technical standards and their expectable development, those lines of technical trends can be eliminated which surpass the country's intellectual and economic capacities and which therefore cannot play a significant role in the country's economic development. This selection, however, which is carried out on the ground of scientific-technical considerations, still allows a too wide margin with respect to *adapting the world standard,* thus it confronts the national economy with unreal problems. Managers are aware of the standard of development in advanced countries and regularly compare this with the state of development at home. Although their ambition to catch up with the world standard is understandable, this often brings about an irrational mentality. The remark: "it is only a matter of money" can often be heard. Their financial problem is, so to speak, separated from the capacity of the national economy and that particular branch whose interests they represent is detached from the social organization in which it exists and is bound to develop.

Under such conditions state planning *comes nolens-volens under the influence of technocratic trends.* Discussions and compromises in planning are in many respect conflicts between technocratic trends in order to decide which branches are to be considered *progressive* ones and what the *prospective system of technical development should be.* Technocratic trends also avail themselves of the price category. All details of the modernizing process cannot be regulated by directives even in a centrally managed economy. Hence, technocrats make the demand that the price should establish financial motivation for the adopted technocratic trends.

This way of thinking can also be characterized in the following way: although the price cannot govern the allocation of resources, it must have a prompting effect on the development trends as laid down by the plan; the process of developing the economic structure according to plan must be combined with *planned* price formation; therefore, price regulation must be considered a priori the concern of the state. The state is in a position to stimulate technical development by *price constructions*. This seems to be necessary in many cases because if a new technology is more expensive it must be promoted by a higher price in production and by a lower price in utilization.

The aforesaid enables us to describe the *erroneous interpretation of the relationship between economy and technology* in more actual terms. The technocratic mentality rejects the role of the price function where it is closely connected with economic efficiency, whereas it attributes exceptional faculty to the price where it fails to work. This is a topsy-turvy way of thinking. Technology takes the place of economy and economy is expected to solve problems which belong to the province of technology. In other words: technical trends determine a priori what can be determined by economics only. Criteria which came into being outside the economy are built-in the economy and are expected to make themselves felt with a force equalling economic laws.

The question how economic efficiency can be taken into account to a higher degree within the framework of volume-oriented planning (at constant prices) has also emerged. This started the discussion on one plan variant vs. several. For the time being *planning on the basis of "one" plan variant is prevalent and seems to be natural to planners of the traditional school of planning*. They think along the following line: starting from the original idea the plan concept comes into being in the spirit of discussions and compromises. Timely discussions cannot be converted into discussions of plan variants at the various phases of planning. If the plan concept – adapted to the inner logic of planning – is not acceptable a new concept has to be worked out. This approach to the plan concept is first of all disapproved of by those who are not members of the machinery of state-planning but bear the political responsibility for the national plan; they think that this system of planning restricts their freedom in decision making.

Planning with particular attention devoted to economic efficiency also gives preference to "several" plan variants, but for other reasons. From the point of view of economic efficiency such a system of planning is considered desirable which submits various plan variants representing different degrees of efficiency and thus can be compared and become a matter of alternatives presenting a choice. At this point the discussion of "one" plan variant vs. "several" becomes connected with the interpretation of the relationship between economy and technology. Which criteria should planning keep to the fore? To what degree and how should requirements deriving from economic efficiency be taken into consideration?

The *concept of returns* aims at a solution of the above questions.[53] According to it, the increment of the GNP measured at constant prices (increment of volume) is to be considered the increment of the use value. The aim of planning is to *maximize the mass of the use value.* Accordingly, the task is to optimize the amounts of the increment of the use value as a function of inputs by ensuring the most advantageous returns. This concept rejects the principle of market simulation in programming the structure, and shows the way to economic development and to the ranking of branches to be developed in the norm system of processes in real terms with a view to economic efficiency. In this case returns are returns in real terms and also efficiency is to be understood as *efficiency in real terms.* When planning is based on frozen prices the development of processes in real terms is confronted with the development of inputs. However, in the case of unchanged prices and wages, input, too, can only change as a function of processes in real terms (worktime, material input per unit of product, etc.).

The administrative price system derives from volume-oriented planning (at constant prices). It is a matter of course that – if planning in physical terms has been adopted by the state – producer prices must be separated from foreign trade, and consumer prices and that producer prices can only function as a means of self-accounting of enterprises. The concept of returns introduces a new qualifying element into this price system: it establishes the category "supply equilibrium" and the "producer price of return" as the *condition* of market equilibrium. This relies on the following hypothesis: from the point of view of the satisfaction of needs there exists not only one equilibrium variant but a number of them. Supply, however, picks out one of them. That price system and the structure pertaining to it have an outstanding significance which also comply with the requirements of the "supply equilibrium". The transformation of the structure of supply on the basis of the order of rank of returns must be ensured by state planning, whereas the adjustment of demand in accordance with it must be brought about by means of consumer price policy.

[53] Hoch, R.: *Fogyasztás és ár* (Consumption and Price). Budapest, 1973.

Value-Oriented Planning

Objections against planning in physical terms were raised as early as the beginning of the sixties. In the case of planning at constant prices, *the price plan is replaced by the planning of production costs*. The problem to be solved is to forecast changes in the productivity in line with the development of the forces of production. This must be planned because the increment in incomes deriving from the development of the national economy must be determined. This is done by prime cost planning and the particular kind of prime cost underlying this planning is called *"phase prime cost."* For example, in the case of the electric energy industry all prices are constant and prime costs can only change if the material input per unit of product changes per unit of the end product and/or the costs of live work change. This is known as "phase prime cost calculation" because every enterprise projects changes of the conditions of production subject to its proper phase of production. Since changing costs cannot spread in the form of prices, the *connection of the enterprise with the state budget* provides the only possibility for the settling of accounts arisen due to changed conditions. This problem is solved separately between the budget and each phase of production. Now what conclusions can be drawn from this system of planning?

1. *The budget has to shoulder the risk of price changes* the state has no influence on (this refers first of all to foreign trade prices). Countries whose total demand is small cannot considerably influence import prices. Their only alternative is to abstain from importing certain products. If, nevertheless, they import them, they have to adjust themselves to the prices quoted. If the latter deviate from fixed domestic prices, the difference must be borne by the budget. The same applies to export. The only thing a small country can do which scarcely influences supply is to abstain from the export of certain products. If it yet exports it must adjust itself to world market prices. In this planning system price deviations remain outside the self-accounting mechanism of enterprises. Things are the same if an enterprise produces unsaleable products. Losses suffered because of unmarketable products or such as can be sold at reduced prices only manifest themselves in the balance of the enterprise but the budget has to run the risk in the last analysis.

2. In case of fixed prices the *conditions of economic calculations become detached from value relations.* This is so because the law of value functions in a system of products interrelated with each other in price and cost interdependences. The essence of the law of value is that in the conditions of production of all

productive branches changes ensuing in value relations manifest themselves jointly. The profitability of the garment industry can improve or deteriorate in two ways: either the conditions of production improve or worsen in the different phases of the garment production, or the conditions of production change for the better or become worse in the phases of production preceding the garment production proper. In the case of fixed prices the latter are not reflected in the calculation of the garment trade.

The main point of the functioning of the law of value is that it takes into consideration the organic unity of the social production as it de facto exists in the relationship between the productive branches. This interdependence can only make itself felt if the price system does not put obstacles in the way of the impact of spreading changes, that is, if legal dispositions do not hinder the spreading of these kinds of changes. Just this is paralysed by the administrative price system, which does not lay stress on the planning of value processes but on planning in physical terms.

3. Fixed and frozen prices raise special problems in *the sphere of consumption.* The application of frozen consumer prices means that a frozen consumer structure has been applied. In this case planning only examines changes ensuing in the structure of comsumption as a result of increased money incomes. The matter at issue is not whether the consumer structure has changed or not but that changes have taken place in the system of constant prices.

The demand to switch-over to value-oriented planning (at changing prices) was increasingly raised in the sixties.[54] Let there be no mistake: objections were not raised against indicators in physical terms. It is a matter of course that when objective processes of planned development are determined on short, medium and long terms these are fixed by processes in real terms. Thus, differences between volume and value-oriented planning do not appear in the outward form of the state plan but in *the criteria underlying state planning.* The question is, as a matter of fact, whether the price should play a role at all – and if so, what kind of role – in determining planned de-

[54] BAUM, H.: Aufgaben und Erfahrungen der Preisplanung bei der Entwicklung des sozialistischen Planungssystems in der DDR. *Wirtschaftswissenschaft,* No. 1, 1970, Berlin. PIETRAS, Cz. and STYBER, W.: *Planowanie cen w krajach socjalistycznych, Pra ce Zakladu Badania cen* (Price Planning in Socialist Countries). Warsaw, 1969. SICA, G.: *Preturile pot deveni obiect de planificare* (Plan Can be Subject to Planning). Bucharest, 1969. SITNIN, V.K.: Problemy planovogo tsenoobrazovaniya v SSSR. – In: *V.I. Lenin i problemy planovogo tsenoobrazovaniya* (Problems of Planned Pricing in the Soviet Union. Book entitled: V.I. Lenin and Price Planning). Moscow, 1970.

velopment and whether or not a product should be regarded a commodity. Those who take sides with value-oriented planning believe that in a commodity producing economy the price of products determined by the economy and changing as a function of time is a real phenomenon. In other words: as soon as the use value enters the system of the exchange of commodities, it only can exist as a commodity and cannot be endowed with properties independent of it.

Discussions on the planning system increasingly influence state planning. In the seventies a number of socialist countries have decided to work out plans also at current (changing) prices. Accordingly, they have made preparations to draw up *price plans*. A change-over from planning at constant prices to planning at changing prices brings about a qualitative change from the point of view of employing the price category. In this case the price already plays a role in the formation of the economico-political concept.

The introduction of price planning calls for the solution of a number of new kinds of tasks. In the first place the *expectable movements of world market prices* have to be surveyed. Without forming a judgement of the expectable movements on the world market no efficient structural policy can be carried on. From the point of view of taking into consideration expectable changes of world market prices, it is more important to approximately know changes of the relative prices of similar or substitutional articles than price changes of one or another article. The planning of economic structures means the planning of variants. Identical tasks of production can be fulfilled on the basis of different variants of material input. Which variants should be given preference to? Changes observable in international value relations are fairly reliable bases of this kind of price planning. However, in world market price movements boom effects and elements of power politics are also expressed. If a country decided to determine its structural policy on the basis of the "efficiency" order of the productive branches measured at capitalist world market prices, it would have no other choice but to change its structural policy every year. This, however, does not alter the essentials. The analysis of world market prices reminds us how important it is to draw up structural policy while maintaining *flexibility*.

The other element of the price plan is the *projection of the production costs*. Planners are confronted with the same task in the case of volume-oriented planning; there is, however, a difference between the two modes of planning in this respect: in the case of price planning it is not phase prime costs that must be projected but changes of price and prime costs. In such cases, as a general rule, plans have to be drawn up not one-sidedly in the system of the relationship between enterprise and the budget, but within the context of price and costs.

The planning of the price-forming and price-modifying role of demand and supply emerges as a new task in price planning. It may seem strange that in the case of long – and medium – term plans, when there apparently exists a possibility of planning equilibrium, the problem of tension can come up at all. To make this clearer it should be pointed out that in the course of planned development disequilibria may arise, which sometimes cannot be overcome even for a longer period. Reactions to disequilibria are different: the function of the price as an allocation-factor can be restricted; or else one has to put up with the fact that equilibrium can only be ensured by price changes. This is closely connected with the planning of the rise of the price level. This problem has not yet been cleared up sufficiently. If the plan prescribes a rise in the price level and income relations are planned accordingly, the rise in prices – which has so far been considered a possibility only – may in fact have been induced in this way. On the other hand, if changing prices are planned at an unchanged price level, the principle of the zero balance opens up an avenue of speculation to planning, diverting it from reality.

Efficiency-Oriented Planning

Volume-oriented planning and planning with "one" variant considers the national plan a *summing up of political preferences*. Seen in this light the plan as a whole and all of its elements represent planned development as laid down by party policy. For this reason it was thought for a long time that the law of value cannot be built-in in the planning system. However, sooner or later the question had to be raised as to which criteria give rise to political preferences in order to assume in time the form of concrete plan objectives. The fact that the state plan is considered a system of aims, carried in itself the dilemma of a confusion of aims and means. Let us take for a starting point the consistence of the plan. *A plan is consistent if it can be implemented in keeping with the actual economic conditions and if the programming targets are in harmony with each other.* In other words: a plan is consistent if it is in conformity with the law of input-output balances of production. This makes clear the *differences of characteristics between the various objectives*, some of which

– are the constraints of planning and have to be considered theoretically determined fundamentals while

– others are not predetermined but become concrete objectives through planning, that is, a political decision in respect of these objectives can only be reached by accepting a certain plan variant.

The law of input-output balances can be conceived as a system of aims by imagining a *hierarchical structure of objectives*. Now let us substitute the concept of equilibrium for consistency. The idea of a number of equally consistent plan variants can also be expressed in the following way: there can be different systems of objectives each of which ensures economic equilibrium in case the hierarchical structure of objectives corresponds to the law of input-output balances. *The hierarchical structure of objectives expresses the relationship between objectives and means*, that is, the programming system of objectives is, from the viewpoint of a separate and superimposed objective, a particular system of means. Yet it is a system of means in which the relationship objective vs. means manifests itself. For example, the objective of iron ore mining is the production of rolled articles, which in turn supplies the machine industry. In the same way, the objective of the manufacture of yarns is the production of textile piece goods, whereas the latter is a means of the manufacture of clothing and so on.

In the national economy equilibrium can be established by different structures – under conditions otherwise unchanged – merely by a changed pattern of foreign trade. Sticking to this example, it might be said that every structure variant can be carried out – provided it is consistent with a realistic foreign trade structure variant. The basic requirement of any variant is adjustment to the organic interconnections of the unified social production process. Precisely this is what the law of input-output balances expresses and this shows that in the case of programming the system of objectives has the nature of means. The aims at the peak of the hierarchy (e.g. the rate of development of industry and agriculture) are objectives from the point of view of all subordinate aims of programming but are means from the viewpoint of a separate, superimposed aim. Of course, the aims at the peak of the hierarchy differ in the various plan variants and the hierarchical structure of the objectives changes accordingly. The fact that to each of the plan variants there belongs a specific system of objectives should also be interpreted in the above sense. The systems of objectives are – taken separately – consistent as such, but each is a system of a definite concept of economic policy.

Mathematical programming leads us to a better understanding of the relationship of ends and means.[55] Mathematical programming is the framework of an extremely complicated, multiple working series employing various methods of economic and technical calculations that are performed in different branches of production and systematized in the development plans. The importance of mathematical programming lies in its making a comparison of development plans of different branches from the point of view of efficiency possible and thus providing a suitable standard for rational decisions. Optimization of the plan means that the factors of production are regrouped in the course of programming into branches where they can be turned to good account at a higher degree of efficiency until they reach a phase where the marginal efficiency is approximately the same in all branches of production. This is that plan variant which programming considers the optimum plan of the national economy and which does not require further changes. Every kind of deviation from the optimum plan deteriorates the maximum efficiency of the national economy.

The term optimum plan refers to that plan variant which reflects social interests to the highest degree and is thus distinguished from other plan variants: it provides for optimum economic growth by boosting the results of the national economy to the maximum. The possibility of working out optimum plans relies on the assumption that the different plan variants *are comparable and can be judged in the light of their relationship to each other.* But how is this possible in view of the fact that there is no equivalence on the basis of which the different objectives can be compared, measured and determined according to their quantitative relationship? This possibility is due to the *comparability of the different hierarchical structures of the autonomous objectives of economic policy.*[56] Therefore, if the exogenous objectives of the different plan variants are given and the latter only differ in the hierachical structure of the endogenous objectives, the plan variants will differ from one another in that each of them *approaches the maximum returns*

←

55 Fedorenko, N.P.: Cena i optimalynoye planirovaniye (Price and Optimal Planning). *Communist,* No.8, 1966, Moscow. Gaston-Marin, G.: Preturile optime – instrument de optimizare a pranurilor (Optimal Prices – Means of Plan). *Optimisatio Viata Economica*, No. 42, 1970, Bucharest. Kornai, J.: *A gazdasági szerkezet matematikai tervezése* (Mathematical Planning of the Economic Structure). Budapest, 1965. Novozhilov, V.V.: *Problemy izmereniva zatrat i rezultatov pri optimalynom planirovanii* (Problems of Measuring Costs and Returns in Optimal Planning). Moscow, 1967. Nemchinov, V.S.: *A népgazdasági tervezés és az irányítás problémái* (Problems of Planning and Control of the Economy). Budapest, 1966. Simon, Gy. and Kondor, Gy.: *Gazdasági hatékonyság, árnyékárak* (Economic Efficiency, Shadow Prices). Budapest, 1965. Urseanu, V.: *Ansupra unor proprietati ale preturilor umbra* (optime) I. [On Some Qualities of the Shadow (Optimum) Price]. Bucharest, 1969.

56 Lange, O.: *op.cit.*

of the national economy on a different standard, so that each variant will eventually produce another rate of economic growth. All this is due to the fact that the various plan variants represent different degrees of economic efficiency, that is, they meet the macro-economic requirements of rationality to a different extent.

Since the different plan variants are compared as a function of the maximization of the returns of the national economy, the *preparation of the plan is identical with the optimization of the plan.* This is carried out by means of mathematical programming. In mathematical programming, in each of the plan variants the *system of objectives of economic policy is adjusted to the given amounts of means.* Although the amount of means is determined by the available factors of production in all plan variants, their quantity in the single plan variants differs. This is because although the starting quantity is the same at the outset (as compared to the basic period) it becomes differentiated in respect to the projected (planning) period because of the different hierarchical structure of the objectives.

To the best of our present knowledge, large-scale models can only be solved by linear programming, on account of reasons of mathematical and computing techniques. In case of linear programming it has to be assumed that the marginal increments of the objective function are constant values. However, the fact is that the relative efficiency of the single branches of production is not constant. An additional input of capital allocated to a certain branch can improve the efficiency of that productive branch to a considerable extent, as a result of which it can take precedence over a number of other branches which were previously ahead of it in efficiency. At the same time, branches of production can take the lead in the order of efficiency where additional input scarcely improves efficiency or even diminishes it. Therefore, the tendency prevails in mathematical programming to retain linear programming as a framework and, at the same time, to make use of the results obtained by marginal calculations as far as possible.

Mathematical programming produces (1) a volume plan and (2) shadow prices. The volume plan is the primary solution, the shadow-price system the secondary one. This means that to *every plan variant obtained by mathematical programming there pertains an inseparable shadow-price system.* The programme variants drafted in this way give information on the marginal efficiency of the factors of production of the single branches. This information is expressed in shadow prices. In a given programme variant the marginal returns of the factors of production of the separate branches are compared in terms of money. In this way the quantitative aspects of a plan variant can be compared with the optimum plan variant. The greater the deviation between the marginal returns of the factors of production of the separate branches, the less does the plan variant meet the requirements of a rational development of the economy. Mathematical programming expressed these deviations and produces plan variants taking into account the differences in marginal returns; as a result the *shadow prices of the factors of production of the separate branches become gradually equalized and the uniform optimum prices – these inseparable characteristics of the optimum plan – develop.*

In these price systems consistency prevails between the price relations of products and of the factors of production, and further, between the general price relations and the economico-political concept expressed by the actual plan variants. These price relations meet the requirements of *long-term (medium-term) equilibrium prices* in harmony with the single plan variants. The different programme variants can in the main be prepared by the following methods: programmes which take into account economic properties of the past to a lesser degree and bring about a more dynamic rate of the development of the forces of production (this is, in general, the fundamental characteristic of long-term planning) and/or programmes which are more definitely determined by the actual economic situation (this is the method generally applied in the case of shorter-term plan programmes). Both kinds of programmes produce different shadow-price concepts. The more the state stresses economic efficiency, the more it assumes risks going together with more dynamic programmes (consequences in incomes policy and other consequences) and the more it heads towards the adoption of the plan variant of dynamic optimum. Whatever the state opts for, the shadow-price system of the *finally approved plan variant is the declared plan-conform price system.*

In drafting the plan a complicated method is applied in order to approach the plan-conform price. Prices (indices of price changes), which have to be taken into account in programming the national economy, are *determined by the direct method of price planning,* on the one hand, while shadow prices are obtained indirectly as a result of mathematical programming (as a secondary solution of programming), on the other. As a result of the necessity to take world market prices into account, *prices determined independently from programming* have also to be reckoned with. *World market prices* are given fundamentals of programming. This particularly refers to countries whose economic policy (foreign trade policy) can exert but a slight influence on international price formation. In the case of given prices, programming must start from the principle of *adaptation.* In such a case programming does not work out prices because the price is that particular *constraint* which produces the structure.

Social Utility

Now it will be possible to determine more closely the differing features of socialist and non-Marxist price theories. Non-Marxist price theories are designed to reveal the laws of the movement of market prices, while socialist price theories wish to discover the laws governing the movement of prices fitted into the economic control system of the state. Accordingly, in non-Marxist price theories it is the *market forms,* in socialist price theories the *systems of state control* that are in the focus of investigation. In non-Marxist price theories the price phenomenon is examined, depending on the number of persons (firms) operating in the market, in its relation to competitive, monopolistic and oligopolistic markets and, depending on the products marketed, according to standardized and differentiated products.[57] As against this, socialist price theories are based either on the acceptance or the criticism of the existing systems of economic control.

Neither do the non-Marxist price theories examine exclusively the existing market relations. An economist who advocates a free market and whose hypothesis of price theory holds only good to such market relations, will obviously criticize the monopolistic market, he will build into his price theory such economic regulators which ensure that practice can approach the assumption system of the theory in the best possible way. Nevertheless non-Marxist price theories are on the whole designed to illustrate the price automatism of market economy organized in a capitalist way. They focus their attention on the situation where the state is an exogeneous factor, where the market-price mechanism is the basic regulator of economic processes. It is from this fact that the *unity of economic equilibrium and efficiency arises.* This rests on two hypotheses. The first: equilibrium is an immanent part of the market-price automatism. The second: The determining feature of the rational behaviour of those operating in the market is profit maximiza-

[57] Chamberlin, E.H.: *The Theory of Monopolistic Competition.* Cambridge, Mass., USA, 1956. Robinson, J.: *The Economics of Imperfect Competition.* London, 1954.

tion. This is how, as a result of the theories of marginal utility, political economics has come to be identified with the logic of choices in the neo-liberal school.

In socialist economy the logic of choice is the *maximization of social utility interpreted within the socialist system of value.* This has to make itself felt by state planning in the last analysis. This value system cannot be approached by the rules of economic logic for it also includes humanistic values. For this reason the role of mathematical programming in the sphere of planning has to be determined more precisely.

The control of socialist economy asserts a priori social norms which are obligatory for the economic policy. Such are:

– constant economic growth (rise of living standards based on economic growth);

– full employment (freedom from fear of unemployment and uncertainty of existence);

– distribution according to work (this becomes possible as a result of the socialization of capital);

– social care for children and old people (this means an adequate co-ordination of distribution according to work and needs).

These norms are formulated by economic policy and are ranked among the economico-political objectives according to their timeliness. These objectives of economic policy *are constraints of mathematical programming, that is to say, of optimization* – in the sense of pure economic rationality. Political leadership does not judge all objectives within the context of economic efficiency. To take one example: it is possible that in case of optimum economic growth full employment cannot be brought about. When programming works out the optimum combination of the factors of production and labour force is available in abundance, it "sets aside" a part of the labour force. The political leadership, however, may turn down this plan and instruct programming to draft new plan variants which aim at optimization with the limitation though that employment is to be ensured in a definite way.

The economico-political system of aims is, so to speak connected as an "exogeneous" constraint to the mathematical programming. The latter is determined by the constraints on the factors of production.

Thus, when the concept of economic policy is developed the objectives must be differentiated dependent upon whether they are decisions "outside" programming and become in this way constraints of programming or are decisions "within" programming which have been determined as a result of programming. Economic policy's system of constraints can be expressed by clear-out instructions, in the form of minimum-maximum requirements and so on. The system of aims of economic policy consists of a tripartite structure, i.e.

– objective function,

– system of constraints (e.g. the number of workers to be employed) and

– programme (e.g. division of the labour force by branches); this is the systematical arrangement of the concept of economic policy. It is, of course, quite another question which notions are employed by the political leadership for *propagating* economic policy. This is a matter of popularizing the plan and getting it adopted by society. It is obvious that the development of certain industrial branches must be underlined in the propaganda campaign. The state, however, must be aware of the fact that those aims which have become objectives of economic policy as a result of rational programming may be subjected to modification whenever changed conditions justify the working out of a new programme.

Mathematical programming established the *theory of the optimum functioning of the socialist economy* by price planning.[58] This theory reveals the criteria of the maximization of social utility within the system of state planning of and control over the national economy; it starts from the assumption that one cannot place a sign of equality between social utility and consumer preference, neither between efficiency of the national economy and profitability of enterprises. This theory provides a more satisfactory answer to problems related to social-economic development because

– it represents the *relationship between state and economy* as it objectively develops in line with the unfolding of the forces of production and changes of social expectations;

– it does not start from the market but from social values hence, it is void of those speculative elements which, if the market model is idealized, originate from the existence of a non-perfect market and from that of a non-market mechanism.

[58] FEDORENKO, N. P.: Nauchno-tekhnicheskaya revolutsiya i upravleniye (Scientific Technical Revolution and Control). *Novy Mir,* No.10, 1970, Moscow. KANTOROVICH, L.V.: *Ekonomichesky raschot nailuchshego ispolyzovaniya resursov* (Economic Calculation of Optimal Utilization of Resources). Moscow, 1969. SHATALIN, S.: Nekotoriye problemy teoriyi optimalynogo funktsionirovaniya sotsialisticheskoy ekonomiki (Some Problems of the Theory of the Optimum Function of Socialist Economy). *Ekonomika i Matematicheskiye Metody,* No.6, 1970, Moscow.

3. State Regulation

Price in Regulation Based on Plan Directives

One can hold opinions based on theoretical reasoning about the price and its role, however, the price and its *genuine* role can only be determined dependent upon the economic ambience in which it exists. To begin with, let us consider the role of the price in regulating the economy by plan directives.

1. The regulation based on plan directives centres on the *breakdow of the plan and on a system of plan indicators of enterprises obtained by it*. By the breakdown of the plan to the level of enterprises planned development becomes concretized. The quantitative assessment of the plan fulfilment is measured by a comparison of the plan targets and factual figures of enterprises. The obligatory plan indicators of enterprises have a characteristic feature. A deviation from the plan does not entail punitive sanctions. Therefore, consequences attached to plan directives are considered in practice less from the point of view of responsibility to law than on the basis of material interest. *There are basic indicators and other kinds of plan indicators*. In case the basic indicators (such as: value of production of the enterprise and the per capita production value, cost level of the enterprise) are fulfilled or overfulfilled, the managerial group receives bonuses. Other kinds of plan indicators are attached to the mechanism of motivation, incidentally and differentially from branch to branch.

2. *State regulation based on obligatory plan indicators is realized through two channels*. In the regulation based on plan directives the state

– breaks down the plan of the national economy to enterprises and supervises their activity by setting plan objectives against factual figures;

– on the other hand, it provides the economic institutions with the relevant chapters of the national economic plan which is, hence, the compulsory norm in respect to commodity and money relations between institutions and enterprises.

State institutions (banks and trade organizations) maintaining commodity and money relations with enterprises strictly hold to the prescriptions of the plan in performing their functions. They are allowed to depart from the plan in exceptional cases and in a precisely determined manner only (e.g. in case of investment credits) whereas in every other respect it is the basis of operative management.

Plan indicators can only be deviated from if adherence to them would cause functional disturbances in the economy. The frequency of deviations from the plan indicators depends upon the extent the conditions prevailing in the operative plan period deviate from the hypotheses which were prevalent at the time the plan was prepared. Hence, the duality of plan directives and operative regulation is theoretically inherent in the two-channel system of regulation based on plan directives.

Both commercial and administrative methods are applied by state institutions in the operative regulation of the economy. For example, relations between the national material supply organization and industrial enterprises are based on commercial methods in case the former meets its obligations and makes the needed materials available in the required quantity and quality and only influences demand by prices. On the other hand, if the material supply organ also fixes quotas the relationship turns into an administrative one, for this is an administrative allocation of materials and not trade. The relationship between the organization of credit and industrial enterprises relies on commercial methods if the former fulfils solicitations of credits in conformity with customary banking services and influences credit demands by its policy of interest rates. This relationship is, however, an administrative one if the organization meets demands in accordance with the pre-established credit-quotas, and so on.

In the regulation based on plan directives the tendency prevails that state institutions prefer administrative regulations – that is, state directives – to commercial connections, in their commodity and money relations with enterprises.

3. The state makes regulation based on compulsory plan indicators effective by regulating the various economico-legal forms of the monopolistic organization. The prevalent tendency aims at organizing productive enterprises into sectoral units and at granting functional monopoly to state institutions. Accordingly, enterprises can organize production on a national scale, whereas state institutions are granted exclusive rights in their commodity and money relations with enterprises. Economico-legal stipulations and, in general, regulations pertaining to the conceptual field of market economy, which establish the compass of the economy, are in close connection with the aforesaid.

4. The sphere of economic functions is wider than what is subject to regulation in the operative system of commodity and

money relations. In the first place the basic indicators of enterprises (production value, productivity, cost level) cannot be regulated in an unambiguous way because of their complex character. For this reason the state makes enterprises financially interested in the fulfilment and overfulfilment of the basic indicators.

However, in the sphere of *financial interest* the state does not rest content in determining success criteria but also *includes in the field of administrative regulation incentive mechanisms*. The two most important manifestations of this are *state price and wage regulation*.

5. In the socialist society the government's activity in organizing the economy is not restricted to working out, sanctioning and breaking down the national economic plan. The government also performs *operative tasks directly*. This refers to the direct implementation of certain plan objectives of major importance, on the one hand, and to decisions making, on the other, with respect to important problems which emerge in the course of activities of state institutions and enterprises. Comprehensive problems of scientific and technical development are solved in a system of direct governmental regulations, inter-state economic agreements are reached by the government directly, and the obligations of branches and enterprises deriving thereof are also subject to direct government measures.

Regulation based on plan directives has raised a number of problems which the socialist countries have tried to overcome in different ways at the various stages of building socialism. In this context development in Hungary has taken place in three phases.

The first phase lasted up to 1953. This was the classical phase of state regulation based on a system of obligatory plan indicators. In this phase improvement of the mechanism relied on the hypothesis according to which *planning on the macroeconomic level relieves economy of problems while difficulties arise when the plan is implemented*. In view of this it was thought that the only solution of the problems was to bring to perfection the break-down of the plan and to consolidate plan-implementation discipline.

The main problems of planning and of the break-down of the plan were – in this period – the *internal contradictions among the various plan indicators*. Value indicators were inconsistent. There often were inconsistencies between the per capita value of production and the prime cost plan, between the production value and the prime cost plan, as well as between the production value and the estimate of the wage fund. There also were contradictions between plan indicators in physical terms and in value terms. Frequently the investment objectives were not in harmony with the available sum of money, and the foreign currency estimates of the international balance of payments were not in keeping with the indicators in physical terms of the foreign trade plan, etc. Attempts were made at that time to eliminate these inconsistencies by improving state planning of the national economy. The number of plan indicators was increased every year and more and more details had to be worked out. At the same time economico-legal rules were established with the aim to restrict or hinder every possibility of deviating from the plan.

In practice, economic processes could not be determined unambiguously from the point of view of central control even within the state sector of the economy. The state was unable to provide a production programme comprising all particulars. Nor could an all-embracing central distribution of materials be organized. It was not possible to establish all manufacturing technologies in an administrative way and it became particularly impossible administratively to regulate modernizing technological processes, etc. Consequently, in addition to obligatory plan indicators one had to depend upon the rational behaviour of enterprises based – in this model of control – *on the self-accounting system of enterprises and on material interest in the fulfilment of the plan*. Thus, productive units functioned as enterprises, and there existed commodity and money relations among enterprises which were influenced by material interest.

Under such conditions those plan indicators to whose fulfilment (overfulfilment) material interest was attached, *obtained a salient significance*. Enterprises aimed at an optimum situation from the viewpoint of remunerations even if this could only be achieved to the detriment of other plan indicators. At the same time they took good care to defend themselves against accusations for having offended against those plan indicators for the fulfilment of which a bonus was not awarded. Legal titles providing a favourable interpretation of the standpoint of enterprises proving that they worked according to plan could always be produced.

If material interest was attached to certain plan indicators, enterprises naturally became interested in obtaining easily executable plan objectives from the supervisory authorities. The most important function of the latter was to break down the plan indicators determined for branches to every single enterprise within the branch. Thus, opinions became prevalent according to which the *main problems originated in the sphere of execution*. The view came to be accepted: the administrative bodies do not divide properly the available resources between enterprises; enterprises offend against plan discipline, they deviate from the prescribed technology and do not achieve the planned savings, etc. There was always a possibility to point to a stock in scarce materials when it appeared that there was a shortfall in certain resources. If an enterprise proved that with the wage-fund allocated to it production according to plan could not be carried out, there always turned up an enterprise which had been granted a too large wage-fund and so on.

The second phase of regulation on the basis of plan directives was the period from 1953 to 1956. At that time the competent authorities recognized that certain problems of fundamental importance could not be solved by improving the planning methods and the break-down of the plan. *The market problem gradually came to the fore*. Economists started to investigate changes of demand which can hardly be planned ahead and/or the adaptability of production to changing demands. In this phase the question was raised in the following form: *how can state regulation based on a system of plan indicators be co-ordinated with the requirements of commodity economy*? Increasing the number of plan indices was considered detrimental and the intention was to change over from a system of many plan indicators to a system of fewer. It was assumed that by decreasing the number of compulsory plan indicators the independence of enterprises would increase enabling them to take into account market requirements in the operative organization of production. The particular field of economy best suited for independent management of enterprises had to be explored as well as the form of material interest established by which social interests assert themselves to the highest degree in case enterprises make decisions on their own.

In this period the main problem of planning and of the break-down of plans was the contradictory regulation of *obligatory plan indicators and economic incentives*. The obligatory plan indicators were based on the principle of plan overfulfilment, hence, *quantitative aspects* became prevalent in economic life. On the other hand, economic incentives stressed the qualitative *elements of the economy,* such as harmony between demand and supply, the modernization of production and products and the importance of economical management. The quantitative attitude often frustrated or even invalidated the realization of objectives instead of influencing their implementation according to plan, for example, by means of price policy. The decrease of the number of plan indicators in the regulation of economic processes increased the importance of contracts between enterprises. However, it appeared that the obligatory plan indicators were barriers due to which these relations did not develop according to the requirements of planned development.

The erroneous interpretation of the role of the price was particularly characteristic of this period; *effects were attributed to the price it really was not in a command of*. For example: (1) the state planned the profit-increment of enterprises every year, thus, the budgetary relations of an enterprise were laid on a new basis annually. Under such circumstances the intention of price policy to stimulate the interest of enterprises in striving for an improved quality or composition of the products by additional bonuses or in another way, was unrealistic. (2) The state prescribed the product and production technology by binding force and regulated the material supply accordingly. In this case incentive relative prices whose aim it ought to have been to influence enterprises in selecting more effective energy bearers or an improved material composition of products were futile.

The enumerated examples may have provided sufficient information making it clear that an ambitious socialist price policy has generally deduced the parameters of economic activity from the existence of market relations, however, all other kinds of regulation which have neutralized, and even thwarted the intention of price policy were equally ambitious. It is interesting to note that in the theoretical discussions on socialist economy the *suppositions underlying pricing were never disapproved of, on the other hand, intentions whose aim it was to make market relations effective were criticized.*

The third phase of state regulation based on plan directives were the years 1957–67. In this period *criticism focussed on the principle of the break-down of the plan and state regulation based on it*. The question to be answered was: is it possible at all to regulate the socialist economy in a system of obligatory plan indicators taking into account at the same time requirements deriving from commodity economy?

Three measures were adopted in this phase in order to ease state regulation based on the system of plan indicators: (a) in agriculture, the compulsory delivery of produce was discontinued and replaced by free state purchase; (b) in industry, the obligation to break down plan indicators by enterprises was lifted. Obligatory plan indicators were determined for every branch but the leaders of single branches had full powers to choose the methods to be applied in the running of enterprises; (c) the organic relationship between material interest and plan indicators of enterprises ceased. The bonuses of executives were determined from then on in every branch separately taking into account the characteristics of different trades. The profit-sharing system of workers was introduced on the stipulation that an enterprise maintained or improved its previous profit rate.

In this phase every branch had to overcome different problems in planning and in breaking down the plan dependent upon the regulation methods applied in the single branches. It appeared that those in charge of the branches could not emancipate themselves from the system of economic regulation they were subjected to. Thus, although, theoretically, regulation void of plan indicators had been introduced in the management of enterprises, in practical life there were scarcely any differences between the then state of affairs and the earlier one.

Experience has also shown that after the number of plan indicators had been reduced, it subsequently increased again. In a system of regulation based on plan directives this is generally induced by the enterprises in order to avoid erroneous judgements. This is quite understandable because, if excessively aggregated complex plan indicators are applied for the guidance and supervision of the management of enterprises, possibilities are greater to form false opinions on the work of enterprises when plan objectives are set against factual figures.

Plan and Planned Development

The opinion according to which the central planning of the national economy is closely connected with the break-down of the plan by enterprises has been prevalent for a long time. However, the experience of the socialist economy brought to the surface discussions about planned development. The requirement of planned development is expressed most comprehensively in the state plan of the national economy. The more truly the national economic plan reflects this requirement, the more precisely plan indicators approximate objective development processes. From this it also follows that the *concept of planned development is not quite in keeping with the system of directive indicators*, although in practical life it is understood that the implementation of planned development means the fulfilment of these indicators.

For example, if the plan envisages a 5 per cent increase of labour productivity, however, productivity has in fact increased by 7 per cent, this cannot be *considered deviation from planned development* for it shows that in the course of real development the reserves of socialist planned economy could be put to use to a higher degree than laid down by the plan objectives. It is, of course, also more advantageous if investments can be realized in a shorter time and with less expenditure than planned. Let us take, for example, two industrial branches: one, working hard to fulfil its production plan, turns out a lot of faulty products, while the other branch, say coal mining, falls below plan because the winter has been mild and demand has decreased; it is obvious that the activity of the latter branch has to be considered less disadvantageous for the economy.

On the other hand, it has to be considered a deviation from the plan if, as a consequence of tardy preparations and the lagging execution of investments, the latter take a longer time than envisaged and as a result new capacities start production with a delay; further deviations from the plan bring about expenditure exceeding the planned level, in consequence of which serious disorder arises in the supply of investment goods; furthermore, due to failures to achieve the reduction of prime costs by technical development as expected, the value of products does not decrease as required and sometimes even increases.

The fact that planned development and plan objectives *are not identical concepts* means that it may happen that deviation from the plan indicators does not upset planned development. If the requirements of the law of planned and proportionate development have not been taken fully into account when the plan was worked out and not all the reserves of economic growth were included in the plan, the economic process may reflect the above requirements to a greater extent than the plan. It can therefore be established as a general rule that deviation from directive plan objectives indicates in certain cases *higher* efficiency and in other cases *lower* efficiency than planned.

But how is it possible to qualify deviations in one or the other direction from directive plan targets? This is obviously only possible if there, *a priori, exists a system of criteria qualifying economic processes*. There is no doubt that such a system of criteria exists and therefore *plan objectives based on directives can only be conceived as means through which a determined degree of planned development materializes, from which practice can deviate in both a positive and a negative direction*. Better results than the planned ones represent a higher degree of planned development and, mutatis mutandis, poorer results than the planned ones represent a lower one.

Every variant that brings about faster economic growth than planned accompanied with improved efficiency and better adjustment to needs represents a higher degree of planned development than has been planned. Accordingly, planned development – as regards its economic content – can only be linked with directive plan tasks through this system of criteria.

But is there any possibility to bring about *maximum planned development*? As shown by efforts made to consolidate the scientific basis of planning there certainly is one. However, the optimum functioning of the socialist economy cannot be postponed to a future period when the up-to-date methods of state planning will have reached that stage of perfection which then will provide satisfactory efficiency. For the time being one has to reckon with the actual potentials of state planning. In addition one has to take into account those specific features which derive from the fact that the state does not organize the economy on the basis of a direct exchange of goods but on grounds of market relations. *Under such conditions maximum planned development is also quantifiable* because the criteria on the basis of which deviations from directive targets set by the plan are considered positive or negative are, at the same time, the criteria of planning.

Such criteria are: maximum increase of the national income: increase of the share of increased labour productivity in the growth of production; economic efficiency; adjustment to needs in production and so on. If an average rate of increase of 5 per cent annually is planned in industry this has obviously been decided in conformity with information according to which the probability of *only* this rate can be substantiated. On the other hand, if labour productivity increases at a faster rate (by, say, 7 per cent a year) this can be considered a positive phenomenon for it shows that in a given phase of development of the forces of production more resources were available for making the rising of the living standard and economic growth at a faster rate than planned possible.

More accomplished planned development *cannot be brought about merely by improved central planning*. In the economy there are elements, generally related to technology, which can *relatively easily be planned*. At the same time there are elements which can *hardly be planned*. It is characteristic of the latter that, in addition to lesser or greater margins of error, one has to be aware of the fact that events may take quite another turn in the future than expected at present. It is an eternal problem of central planning that *dynamic economy must be grasped in its complexity although planning can only rely on the knowledge of the present facts and depend upon certain empirical past trends of development*. Thus, the figures underlying the projection of certain elements of the economy are rough estimates only. These uncertainties are mainly related to the *planning* of changes of the market conditions. In the assessment of changing market conditions, planning and mathematical programming start from certain hypotheses. Shadow prices, obtained through mathematical programming and regarded the equilibrium prices of a long period, are, in fact, complementary to these hypotheses. In line with economic development, shadow prices become equilibrium prices in reality as far as economic life substantiates those hypotheses on which mathematical programming has been based upon.

The equilibrium price is the outcome of a synthesis of the producer's behaviour (supply price) and the consumer's behaviour (demand price). From the point of view of the *long-term supply price* changes in the conditions of production are of primary importance. Experiences gained hitherto show the extent a country's annual decrease of the cost level of production amounts to on the average. Professional planners know well that great errors can be committed in pre-determining changes of the cost level as a function of productive branches. The aim of mathematical programming is to plan an efficient economic structure. From this point of view the important factors are the relative changes ensuing in the conditions of production of the single productive branches and not the changes of the costs of production on the average of the national economy as a whole. It is precisely this that raises certain doubts whether the exactitude of the methodology is an unequivocal justification for the conclusions arrived at by the same methodology.

The situation is about the same in the case *of the long-term demand price*. In planning the programme of the consumption structure must be worked out in connection with the demand price which develop – in case of an economy in growth – at a higher living standard than the one of the basic period. This demand structure develops rather unequivocally in the system of technological interconnections, that is, in the sphere of the means of production. However, in the case of consumer articles programming leads us to the intricate field of the price elasticity of demand. It must be admitted that our theoretical knowledge about relationship between demand and price exceeds by far our faculty to reveal these connections by means of mathematical formulae in practice.

The aforesaid emerge in a closed economy only. Further problems arise if programming is to be worked out in a way which has to take into account a rational international division of labour. Yet, the economic development of a foreign trade-sensitive country can only be planned by forecasting the international division of labour. For this, one has to estimate the prospective development of the *price relations on the world market*. It is somewhat easier to draw up the plans of a country whose internal price relations considerably influence world market price relations. The situation is more difficult in the case of a country which has a negligible influence on world market price relations and has to co-operate in the international division of labour adjusting itself to world market prices which develop independently of it.

Since the value judgement of the market has penetrated into state planning one cannot identify the optimum functioning of the socialist economy with a plan drafted in complete alignment with a hypothetical market constellation. In the course of plan implementation, the actual market constellation may deviate, moreover it generally does deviate, from the assumed conditions which furnished the basis for planning. Therefore, planned development cannot be checked by comparing plan indicators and factual figures. Two factors get implicated in the deviation of facts from plan. One of them can be conceived as the impact of market conditions deviating from the hypothetical ones on the process of planned development. The other one can be considered disorders in the functioning of the market mechanism: reactions of producers and consumers deviating from rational suppositions. The first one shows that a phenomenon cannot be considered non-conform with the plan merely because it deviates from what was planned years ago; while the second one indicates that economic policy has not taken social reactions sufficiently into account. This goes to say that the optimum functioning of the socialist economy *does not depend exclusively upon state planning, for it is also the concern of the state control of the economy in a comprehensive sense*.

This also explains why discussions on *planned development have turned into discussions about the alternative models of economic control*. The different variants of the socialist economic model and discussions centering on it date back to the beginning of the fifties when, in Yugoslavia, directive regulation based on central plan indicators was discontinued in the industry, workers' self-management was introduced and the incentives by means of which the implementation of the social plan can be influenced in accordance with planned development, first of all by financial means, were worked out.[59] By the mid-fifties economics exerted considerable influence on the political leadership of all socialist countries aiming at the increased utilization of commodity and money relations. However, this was only considered as a perfectioning of the economic mechanism. This idea was contrasted with the two-model theory.

As a result of critical analyses of planned development, the opinion came to the fore that *socialist planned economy cannot*

[59] DOBIAS, P.: *Das jugoslawische Wirtschaftssystem.* Tübingen, 1969. KARDELJ, E.: *Drustveno ekonomski reforma* (Socio-Economic Reform). Beograd, 1966. MARSENIĆ, D. and PAVLOVIĆ, M.: Teorijski sporovi o privrednom sistemu SFRF (Theoretical Debates on the Yugoslav Economic System). *Ekonomist,* No.1, 1971. L'économie yougaslave au début de 1967, après dix-huit mois d'application de la réforme économique. *Problèmes Économiques,* 27 April 1967.

be confined to the regulatory system based on obligatory plan targets. It became clear that the more developed the forces of production are and the higher the living standard is, the more problems derive from that kind of central regulation which relies on the preliminary quantitative determination of every economic process.[60]

Objective processes have eventually focussed attention on the new trends. Until quite recently, disproportions between the rates of economic growth of industry and agriculture were characteristic of socialist countries. In agriculture the rate of growth generally fell behind the planned one. This was offset by the fast growth of industrial production in the fifties; in the sixties, however, the rate of economic growth decreased in general in most of the socialist countries as compared to earlier periods. A number of economists now think that economic efficiency can be improved and the rate of economic growth stepped up by transforming the economic mechanism. If economic growth lags behind and the economic structure deviates from the plan *economic distortions* may develop. One of the main deficiencies of the mechanism based on plan directives is that it makes economy inflexible rendering it more difficult for state economic policy to adapt itself flexibly to changing economic conditions in the course of plan implementation. Many economists hold the view that this deficiency of planned economy can be eliminated by improving the economic mechanism.

Price in Planned Market Regulation

The means of economic policy may be *classified* from different viewpoints. (1) Difference is made between production and distribution policy, price and incomes policy as well as financial policy. (2) Direct and indirect regulators are set apart. (3) Difference is made between selective and non-selective regulators. In developing the regulating system the main dilemma of the

[60] BOGNÁR, J.: A magyar mechanizmusreform két éve (Two Years of the Reform of the Hungarian Mechanism). *Közgazdasági Szemle,* No.1, 1970, Budapest. BRUS, W.: *A szocialista gazdaság működésének általános problémái* (General Problems of the Operation of Socialist Economy). Budapest, 1960. CSIKÓS-NAGY, B.: Gazdasági mechanizmusunk fejlesztésének főbb kérdései (The Chief Questions of the Development of Our Economic Mechanism). *Közgazdasági Szemle*, No. 4, 1970, Budapest. FRISS, I.: A szocialista gazdaság törvényei és az irányítás (Laws of Socialist Economy and Control). *Az MTA Gazdaság- és Jogtudományi Osztályának Közleményei,* Nos. 1–2, 1968, Budapest. NYERS, R.: *op.cit.* TIMÁR, M.: *op.cit.*

state is to decide which means it should have recourse to in order to achieve a certain aim and how the latter should be turned to account. In socialist planned economy this dilemma is also due to the fact that planned development cannot be ensured by a market conform economic policy.

The main point of market conform state regulation is the following: the state can avail itself of all means in order to influence market conditions but cannot restrict the price automatism. Simplifying matters one might say: the state can establish its price and incomes policy as well as production and distribution policy but cannot avail itself of direct price, incomes, production and distribution regulators. *Direct regulation has to take place within the market self-regulation system.* If the automatic market comes into collision with public aims, the state must influence market conditions partly by budgetary policy and partly by means available in the system of the monetary policy and ensure the functioning of the market in accordance with public purposes. *A market conform economic policy is economic policy narrowed down to financial policy*, ensuring – even in this sphere – only limited state activity. In the system of financial policy state decisions are limited by the assertion of the allocation function of the market price automatism. A market conform economic policy is a *non-selective economic policy*. The state cannot discriminate between different branches of production, nor can it put one group of consumers in a more advantageous situation than another one. Equal terms must be provided for and this can only be brought into effect in case of a *neutral* financial policy. Only in this way can it be achieved that the rational distribution function of the market should make itself felt in case economico-political means are applied.

In socialist economy, the problem of relationship between mechanism and price comes up in the case of non-market conform regulation; the question to be answered is in what manner the state restricts the market mechanism and in which fields and how it excludes the market. For objective reasons, socialist economic policy has to have recourse to direct means too, in addition to indirect ones, furthermore, the assertion of political preferences also requires the application of selective principles. Yet the *mentality of a market conform economic policy contains elements which are also acceptable from the point of view of market regulation according to plan.*[61]

In the first place, if one or another objective can be reached by indirect regulator this mode of regulation is to be given pref-

[61] CSIKÓS-NAGY, B.: *Socialist Economic Policy.* Budapest-London-New York, 1973.

erence to as against regulation by direct regulators. In the second place, if an aim cannot be realized by an indirect regulator it is not at all certain that a direct regulator can bring about the required solution. Market conform economico-political views draw attention to self-restraint justified in case of state regulation.

If it were possible to establish the *order of rank of economic regulators* it would appear that price and wage regulators are more expedient than regulators in physical terms, whereas budgetary regulators as well as the ones regulating monetary policy are more effective than price and wage regulators; in the sphere of financial regulators indirect regulators are more suitable than direct ones. If the state selects economic means in view of the above considerations, the regulating system will probably operate at the highest efficiency. It should, however, be added that in an economy with developed forces of production and where full employment and proportionate incomes are obligatory social norms of economy policy, the indirect regulators of budgetary and monetary policy do not provide complete solution to problems economic policy is bound to solve. It is not due to chance that, in our times, regulators of price and incomes policy are applied by economic policy of all industrially developed countries. The problem is not whether the regulators of price and incomes policy and regulators in physical terms can be applied or not, but far more how they can be applied so that they should not restrict the efficiency of financial policy to a greater degree than justified.

Some comments would not be out of place with regard to a *non-selective economic policy*. This view is devoid of reality if it concerns the customs, tax or credit system. Economic policy is necessarily connected with political preferences. Selectivity is the essence of the customs system which boosts national production by protectionism; if this were not so one would have to renounce customs as regulators for this aim could be reached – in a non-selective system – by regulating the rates of exchange. Export incentive policy has become a general practice within tax and credit policy for a long period now and it has been recently applied by a number of countries as a financial regulator in stimulating the development of economically underdeveloped countries.

However, the *non-selective economico-political view also contains positive elements*. In case economic means are applied in a differentiated way some questions must be cleared up. (1) How far does the effect of political preferences reach? (2) Which are its underlying criteria? (3) What is the extent of preferences determined by? The elucidation of these questions can protect us from making selections indiscriminately. To avoid this it is important that the market mechanism should be able to fulfil its rational distributing functions. If selective principles prevail in economic policy, the allocation role of the market is deprived of its rational content.

In the market mechanism regulated according to plan, the national-economic plan is a comprehensive regulator. The economic-political concept (system of aims) and the economic mechanism (system of means) are summed up in the national plan. The possibility of judging either of the means of economic policy per se is very limited. From the aspect of economic units *economic policy's system of means forms an integral entirety* which is scrutinized by the economic units from two viewpoints. First: to what extent does this system limit their freedom in decision making. Secondly: how does this system in its complexity influence their decisions. Economic regulators – in case of a lack of co-ordination – can neutralize each other or function contrarily. Every economic regulator depends upon an economic environment (medium) in which it can display the effects attributed to it. However, this often may lead to clashes with other regulators, moreover, it can happen that as a joint result of the means, a tendency of contrary reactions manifests itself. The requirement that economic policy be *consistent* also refers to the sphere of market regulation.

Consistency is a necessary prerequisite of the workability of all possible mechanism variants. In a market mechanism regulated according to plan, *consistency must come about on the basis of the plan concept*. This means that as a result of market regulation economic growth, structure transformation, employment, incomes relation, etc. must be realized as it was established by the political leadership in the plan concept. Therefore, the *comprehensive system of market regulators must be derived from the plan concept*. This is just as organic a part of planning as the shaping of the plan concept. The latter is a programme of growth which quantifies every element of the economy, at the same time, making the quantification of market regulators in accordance with the plan concept possible. The projection of economic growth directed in conformity with the plan concept renders it also possible to forecast

– the fields in which the regulation of economic processes can be put under market control;

– the indirect instruments by which the market mechanism can be aligned with the plan concept in case the market is the process regulator and

– the direct instruments by which the intention of the state can become effective in case the market must be restricted.

Planning must, nevertheless, be assessed realistically. Both the evolution of the plan concept and the *forming of the market regulators leads to sharp discussions*. Frequently one cannot give an unequivocal answer to the question whether new phenomena cropping up in the economy are to be considered positive or negative ones and, in the latter case to which element of the market regulation they are related to, consequently, in which way the regulating mechanism has to be changed in order to abolish negative features. Science cannot provide practice with ready-to-wear- solutions either in the case of the plan concept or in that of market regulation. The only thing science can do is to help reveal the inner consistency of the mechanism as well as the relationship between plan concept and market regulation. This, however, always provides sufficient orientation on how to approach the complicated questions of market regulation.

The plan concept determines the mode of market regulation, while the *approved system of the economic mechanism supervises the plan concept*. When the instruments of economic policy are derived from the plan concept, the possibility of how to adapt these instruments to the approved system of the economic mechanism is investigated at the same time. Discussions on this subject are in fact a critical analysis of the plan concept. The economic mechanism reacts in this way on the concept of economic policy. In the end a synthesis takes place in the planning of the national economy, which is performed – separately – within the sphere of targets and instruments on the one hand, and as an interaction of targets and instruments, on the other.

The application of market regulators raises the problem of the *frequent changes* they are submitted to. In respect to market regulators two requirements of equal importance have to be made. In the first place they must provide stability and, in the second place, they must adjust themselves to changing market conditions. Stability is an important condition showing positive reaction in respect to regulators. If the state continuously changes the regulators it impairs efficient market regulation at the most important point. In the micro-economic sphere that kind of safety must prevail which determines the situation and possibilities of the economic units on the ground of the results achieved by rational management, without contesting the results by post facto regulation or modification of the regulators. The "freezing" of the regulators must also be avoided because the development of the forces of production and the changing situation of the world market generally create new conditions economic policy cannot be indifferent to. Changing conditions cannot only bring about changes of the system of objectives, but it may happen that the same objectives can only be implemented by a changed system of instruments. *Economic policy has to derive the applied system of instruments from the contradictory requirements of stability and flexibility and has to re-examine and correct* it from time to time.

Structure – Market – Price

Thus, there is an essential difference between market economy and the mechanism of planned market regulation. As a result of state control, economic processes pursue a direction quite different from the course steered by market spontaneity. The question is, of course, unanswerable how the socialist economy would develop if the state did not have recourse to planned guidance. Anyhow, it is clear that the *socialist economy would be incapable of functioning as a free market economy.* Although planned market regulation reconciles plan and market on quite another basis than the mechanism based on plan directives, the allocating function of the market mechanism is restricted consciously and markedly in this case too.

If the two model variants of the socialist economic mechanism are to be distinguished from the point of view of market function, one could succinctly sum up the matter saying that in one of them distinctions are made according to the character of the products, and according to the type of decisions in the other one. The mechanism based on plan directives starts from the *non-typical commodity character of the means of production,* differentiating them from consumer goods on this basis. In the case of planned market regulation the *non-typically market* character of long-term decisions is taken as a starting point providing a basis of differentiation from short-term market decisions. Accordingly, enterprises can determine the manufacturing programme and material supply on a very broad basis while the determining role of self-financing is far slighter in shaping the macrostructure. Large investment projects and capital intensive research and development programmes are centrally planned and their construction is centrally directed. In other words: *the market mechanism plays an active role in developing the microstructure but it is not the main regulator of the macrostructure.*

This interpretation of the law of value in socialism deviates from *Stalin's* concept in that it sets aside – in view of two circumstances – Stalin's sharp distinction between consumer articles and means of production. In the first place, there are many means of production which also play a role in the supply of the population. In the second place, if consumption is the final purpose of production, the regulation of the production of the means of production and that of consumer articles cannot rely on radically different principles. It is therefore more correct to describe the functioning of the law of value in socialism starting from the regulation of the structure instead of products.

The question may arise: can there be a notion of the *microstructure* independent of the concept of the *macrostructure*? The answer is in the affirmative in view of the following: (1) the quantitative proportion of the *productive branches* of the macrostructure can be charactarized by the quantitative relations of *products* of the productive branches of the microstructure. (2) The concept of macrostructure is related to *expanded reproduction,* while that of the microstructure to *simple reproduction.* Decisions in investment matters belong to the former while the latter's concern is the programming of production. (3) In judging the degree of mobility of *production*, in one case the possible alternatives of the structure of production are examined in the given macrostructure, whereas in the other case investigation is interested in the kind of changes caused by the transformation of the macrostructure as a result of development, etc.

Naturally, one has to see clearly that all this does not provide an exact demarkation. The regulation of economic processes simultaneously refers to both the macro and the microstructure. Every investment decision transforms the macrostructure within a given product structure. Certain research, development and investment decisions primarily take place in the microsphere without essentially influencing the macrostructure. This shows that the dividing lines between the two spheres got blurred without touching upon the essentials. But from the point of view of practical economic policy the difference is very perceptible. One might even venture the remark that today the economic mechanism of countries with a market economy cannot be satisfactorily described without differentiating between the macro and microstructure. In our days there are no rules of universal validity with respect to the functioning of the economy; this is a necessary concomitant of the *socialization process of the economy.*

The alignment of plan and market, as it has been described above, *makes the most* of the possibilities *of the functioning of the law of value* (market law) as far as it can still be inserted in the framework of state planning. Therefore it is justified that in this system of economic control, the profit motive should assert itself on the side of production and consumer preferences on the side of consumption to the highest possible degree when the economy is organized. These are after all attributes of the producer's and the consumer's rational behaviour and are indispensable in a commodity producing society even if the means of production have been socialized. But they cannot determine by themselves the process of economic development which the state, starting from *social utility*, makes effective by employing planning and guidance based on the state plan.

In the socialist planned economy a *difference must be made between making use of the market mechanism and the price category.* Although the market is not the main regulator of the macrostructure, the state yet employs *the price category in planning economic development.* This means that the price also plays a role in regulating economic processes where the market mechanism does not function. This price, however, is not determined by the market for it is a *constructed price*, an economic evaluation system, which, dependent upon the nature of the decision in the sphere of the macrostructure, can be a *medium-term* (a) equilibrium (shadow) price, (b) world market price or (c) self-financing price. The common feature of all the three is that they do not express the actual market price but an expectable price tendency.

To form the macrostructure in the market mechanism and to rely on the price category in planning development are matters of different character. In the latter case *the country has an independent structural policy* and prices are only one of the criteria when all angles of the question are considered. This may also be expressed in the following way: the market mechanism also exists even here as the technical framework of process regulation but the principles underlying regulation basically differ from the ones the market model would suggest. In other words: structural policy forms prices and not the other way round; it is, not the market mechanism that produces the structure.

4. State Organization

The Profit Motive

In capitalism, the functioning of the law of value is based on the maximizing of the profit. In a capitalist market economy the dividing line between wages and the profit mechanism is clear-cut. In this kind of separation the price structure relies on an economic calculation where

– the components of the price are prime costs and profit,

– the components of prime costs are the costs of the factors of production (land, work and capital) and

– profitability is measured by the recovery period of capital (rate of profit).

However, the profit is not a comprehensive production regulator in capitalism. There are non-profit enterprises too. In farming carried on by small-scale producers, work performance and the assumption of risks is a one-man responsibility. This is due to the dual character of the small-holder peasant (both landowner and labourer). This also is characteristic of co-operative production, for the co-operative members are group proprietors at the same time. However, if the manual worker and owner are one and the same person, wages and profit merge and prime costs disappear. In such a case economic calculation relies on a price structure where

– the components of the price are costs of a non-wage character and the gross income,

– the cost components are amortization and the purchase price of materials bought and

– the result is measured by the per capita gross income of a labourer p. a.

These two systems of economic calculation express as a matter of fact, deviating principles of interestedness *characterizing capitalist production, on the one hand, and small-scale (co-operative) commodity production, on the other.*

The conditions indispensable for the functioning of the law of value can also be produced in the socialist commodity production. Labourers and employees get paid money for work performed and, theoretically, there is nothing to prevent the application of the profit motive. The state can provide a situation for enterprises in public ownership as a result of which their marketing activities are in the main in conformity with those of private enterprises. Enterprises can have a profit motivation and become independent. In this case the law of value continues to function, but the profit does not become a source of private property. Private capital having been socialized, socialist societies established the self-accounting system of state enterprises by making use of categories developed in capitalism (such as wages, prime cost, profit, etc.); gross income, the specific category of the small-scale economy and of the co-operative sector, also survived. *Thus, the two systems of economic calculation and the two forms of financial interest are also characteristic of the socialist economy.* It should, however, be added: in the state sector of the economy the criterion of success must be brought about by the state. This gave rise to the *discussion about profitability.*

In line with the unfolding of commodity production, the law of value includes the whole world of commodities into a uniform system. As a result, economic efficiency becomes a matter of alternative decisions through maximizing the profit. Yet, a number of Marxist economists believe that when establishing financial interest the socialist economy must go back to the pre-capitalist pattern; that is to say, profitability is a specific feature of capitalism.

According to this way of thinking, efficiency is *identified with thriftiness.* In organizing the economy prescriptions aimed at cutting down definite elements of input are often given. Experience quite often shows that if savings are started, a certain economic process is judged in itself detached from other processes related to it. However, *this kind of economizing does not always mean efficiency at the same time.* It is not at all certain that when an enterprise has saved a sum of money as compared to an earlier expense item, it has promoted the cause of more efficient production. It is possible that the enterprise would have acted more profitably if it had spent money "wastefully" in the case of certain costs. It is very important correctly to differentiate between economic efficiency and that of thriftiness as it is known in common usage. The delimitation of these concepts and the inferences derived from them may produce the conditions which enable the socialist state to lay its measures of economic management on firm foundations. Economic efficiency differs from thriftiness in that it approaches economic processes in their organic complexity and not as isolated phenomena; the correctness of one or another measure is considered on the basis of the favourable or unfavourable effect it has on all economic processes it touches. Thriftiness judged in itself conceals those losses through which savings could materialize at all. Efficiency investigations do not contain such hazards. This follows from the method and trend of efficiency investigations, which, first of all, compare all possible expenditure variants from the point of view of results and, secondly, only explore problems which can be judged in the light of the latters' relationship.

Should a subsequent analysis prove that economy has impaired efficiency, the fact remains that savings have been attained. Saving as such is justified if frugality becomes absolutely necessary e. g. for lack of a given material. Such problems can come about in a circumspectly organized economy, too. Experts know the situation called "impossibility of performance", that is, when irrational solutions have to be employed. In such cases economizing is justified because of poor circumstances. However, from this it does not follow that *exceptional regulations are to be raised to the level of general economic management.*

The supposition according to which in socialist economy (1) the per capita production (productivity) can be the sole success criterion of enterprise activity, and (2) bonuses must be based on the reduction of prime costs measured at constant prices and unchanged product compositions must also be considered in the light of the aforesaid. It is characteristic that discussions about profitability vs. productivity and/or those on the maximization of profit vs. the minimization of costs are questions that have given rise to much controversy as regards making economic efficiency relevant in socialism.[62]

Political considerations turn the scale in favour of productivity in the discussion about *productivity vs. profitability.* If the aim is to catch up with and overtake the industrially most advanced capitalist countries and this can only be brought about by raising work productivity to a higher level, then – in the view of many – this is the criterion of the good management of enterprises. From the point of view of the ideological representation of socialism it seems tempting to set productivity against profitability. In fact, however, this discussion derives from the confusion of ends and means. It is irrational to organize production by raising productivity at the level of enterprises because this *leads to differentiation of work performed inside and outside the enterprise.* If an enterprise is interested in improving the index

[62] BEHRENS, F.: *Arbeitsproduktivität.* Lohnentwicklung und Rentabilität. Berlin, 1955. Mrs. FALUS, SZIKRA, K.: A termelékenység növelésére ösztönzés néhány problémája (Some Problems of the Incentives for Increasing Productivity). *Társadalmi Szemle*, No. 2, 1971, Budapest. NYERS, R.: Problems of Profitability and Income Distribution. Parts I–II. *The New Hungarian Quarterly*, 1970/40, 1971/41, Budapest. PÉTER, GY.: *op.cit.* SEYMOUR, H.: *Decision-Making and Productivity.* Oxford, 1958.

of the per capita production value it is also interested in

– decreasing the average degree of labour intensity of the commodity pattern, that is, it gives preference to material-intensive products and

– in using commodities produced outside the enterprise wastefully, if in this way, it can save work which ought to have been performed within the enterprise.

Experiences of several socialist countries show the negative features of qualification based on the labour productivity of enterprises. Here the point must be borne in mind, that when the economy has, at the same time, to overcome disorders of equilibrium, neither the sale of products nor the production of unmarketable products causes problems. It is obvious that he who upholds the view of productivity of enterprises takes a stand not against profitability but against productivity on a national economic scale, that is he offends just against that principle whose cause he wants to advocate. On the other hand, the *category of the profitability of enterprises may be a yardstick which suitably synthetizes work in general, for it connects the work of an enterprise with work performed previously without which production could not have been carried out.* This is why profitability gives a notion in truer colours about the productivity of the national economy on a micro-economic level than the per capita production. Hence, in the discussion about productivity vs. profitability the question is not whether or not socialist society is interested in raising labour productivity to a higher level but how this can be achieved most purposefully.

In the discussion about *maximizing profits vs. minimizing costs,* political considerations have turned the scales in favour of the latter. This is so because, among other things, the increase of profits to the maximum is usually identical with a scramble for profit and this is regarded a typical manifestation of capitalism. However, *if profitability is the micro-reflection of the productivity of the national economy, the maximizing of profits is that kind of rational behaviour of enterprises which is able to optimize the productivity of the national economy.* To make it easier to understand the difference in content between maximizing profits and minimizing costs in socialist economy, let us start from the fact that enterprises cannot influence prices. In this case the maximizing of profits cannot be associated with the raising prices. This is a precondition of the minimizing of costs in socialist economy, for the decrease of the cost level is considered a yardstick for measuring the improvement of efficiency *within* the enterprise. In such cases the cost level is measured at an unchanged commodity pattern and at constant prices. Ensuing price changes are eliminated, on the one hand, while the comparable part of the production of an enterprise is separated from the non-comparable one, on the other.

Profit maximizing – if prices cannot be raised – implies that enterprises are free to decide the commodity pattern, the material input and the technology of production. They can therefore take into account the law of return when organizing production. In case of optimum capacity, utilization as well as an optimum structure of the commodities produced and materials consumed the enterprises can make maximum profit. Under such conditions the enterprise has asserted economic efficiency (productivity of the national economy) to the highest degree.

The principle of *cost minimizing in socialist economy* asserts itself if the compulsory plan indicators of the production volume, the commodity pattern and the material input structure prevail. If bonuses are tied up with cost minimizing, the enterprise will obviously attach marked importance to the latter and ignore – as far as possible – all other plan indicators. Enterprises will find most limitations in the choice of the material input because obligatory plan indicators are associated with the rationing of the means of production.

In a system of obligatory plan indicators, the rationality of cost minimizing depends upon the extent central organizations have succeeded to reach the optimum variant in production programming and in material allocation. However, this system takes it for granted that the central bodies know the optimum functioning of the factors of production of every enterprise at least as well as the management of each of the enterprises does.

Finally: the decrease of the cost level is measured by the profit increment, that is, the rate of profit is determined by comparing the price with the prime cost. As against this, in the case of maximizing profit, profitability is established as a function of the amount of profit and of the capital invested. The first statement gives an answer to the question to what degree the prime cost has decreased in the case of an unchanged commodity pattern measured at constant prices whereas the second case provides information about the recovery period of the capital.

The discussions about profitability vs. productivity have given place to the discussions about *profit vs. gross incomes* in the model of socialist economic control regulated by economic instruments. In these discussions economists mainly of Yugoslavia, Hungary and Czechoslovakia took part.[63]

[63] Csikós-Nagy, B.: A nyereségérdekeltség új vonásai (New Features of Interest in Profit). *Pénzügyi Szemle*, No. 5, 1965, Budapest. Horvát, B.: Contribution to the Theory of Yugoslav Enterprise. *Economcky Casopis*, No. 8, 1968. Pelikán, P. and Koconda, R.: The Socialist Enterprise as a Participant in the Market. *Czechoslovak Economic Papers*, IX, 1967, Prague.

Yugoslavia adopted the *self-management of workers* as the basis of socialist economy at the beginning of the fifties, that is, it made the quasi-co-operative form universal. By doing so it, in fact, eliminated the profit category, and income-motivation became the main economic regulator. In 1967, the Czechoslovak mechanism adopted income motivation, too, for a transitional period. The economic reform of 1968 introduced in Hungary the profit-sharing system. It would lead us too far afield if we were to discuss the social-political aspects of the profit vs. income discussions but it must be pointed out that different forms of socialist industrial democracy have come into being.[64]

Naturally, in case of profit maximizing the optimum commodity structure and capacity utilization work out differently from the case when the decision making of enterprises is governed by the maximization of incomes. In the former case production is organized by the optimal combination of the production factors. In the latter case the factors involved are only land and capital because wages, being an element of the income of enterprises, are raised to the level of an "objective function". It is a matter of course that in such a system the monopoly price becomes transformed – within socially tolerable limits – into "monopoly" wages, differentiation between wages of branches (enterprises) becomes strained. *B. Ward* rightly remarked that in the case of profit motive production, under the influence of the functioning of the market mechanism, rationally follows changes of supply and demand, and of prices in the case of incomes motive this automatism functions irrationally.[65]

Competition

Competition is an immanent element of the market. The existence of a market is concomitant with that of competition irrespective of the fact whether competition shows up in a perfect or imperfect form. From this point of view it is a matter of indifference who owns the means of production. However, in the case of public ownership it must be assumed that pure economic activity is exempt from exercising public law. A change of ownership alters the controlling role of competition if the state – in case it nationalizes the means of production – also restricts the sphere of action of the market.

[64] Csikós-Nagy, B.: Il Modello Ungherese democrazia aziendale, *CESES, L'Est*. No. 4, 1969, Milan.

[65] Ward, B.: The Firm in Illyria. Market Syndicalism. *American Economic Review*, Vol. XVII, No. 4, 1958.

In socialist planned economy the *tendency of "total" monopoly asserts itself.* This tendency is brought about by socialist property relations and centrally managed regulation. The principle of "total" monopoly makes itself felt (a) by organizational integration, when enterprises within certain industrial branches are merged so that finally a single enterprise or only a few represent a branch as a whole and (b) by assigning a special line of production (profile) to enterprises, when the state precisely determines the scope of activity of every enterprise connecting it with specialization. In a centrally managed economy specialization is not confined to economical-technical bounds. Specialized production programming expresses a tendency whose aim it is that every enterprise should eventually follow a monopolistic special line. In the specialization system enterprises organize production feeling – legally speaking – safe that they do not have to compete even if there exist enterprises which could turn out the same commodities they produce. The market restrictive policy is attributable to contradictions

– between *state planning* and *market spontaneity* and/or
– between *social utility* and *consumers'* sovereignty.

In the case of state regulation based on central plan directives, market relations become narrowed down to *consumer goods* bought and sold as commodities. Consumption is competitive in respect to products put on the market, however, the conditions of competition are considerably influenced by the price and incomes policy. In the sphere of production market relations do not exist but there is *emulation*. Enterprises compete with each other and within enterprises workers (workers' brigades) emulate. The work of enterprises is qualified on the basis of the obligatory plan indicators. This makes it possible to classify the enterprises. Centrally regulated task wages are the basis of emulation between workers (workers' brigades).

The situation is different if the socialist planned economy is organized within the system of *market regulation according to plan*. This relies on the idea that the concentration process of production is a normal development related to technical development and to criteria of economic efficiency. However, monopolies which came into being by legal dispositions diminish the efficiency of the mechanism. The state, however, must do everything to lessen the detrimental effects deriving from monopolistic organizations. In view of this a *limited competition* between both enterprises and products must be rendered possible. Thus, when the state regulates by economic instruments,

– the importance of the controlling role of the competition increases because market relations include trade as a whole and

– the role of consumer preferences in the direct regulation of economic processes intensifies; the value judgement of the consumer plays a more direct role in decision making in the sphere of production and in the formation of prices.

In his study "Power or Economic Law" *Böhm-Bawerk* distinguishes between "economic" and "social" power, as well as between power motives inside and outside the economy. From the viewpoint of "social" power he differentiates between social power making itself felt within the price law or against it.[66] These distinctions are also relevant in the socialist economy. In the legal system of the socialist economy, the determination of the form of ownership, the economic activities which can be carried on in various form of ownership and regulations determining the operational order of the economic units are of fundamental importance. In the socialist economy the content of state administration can be determined as a comprehensive system of

– economic control availing itself of *economic instruments*;
– *management of official character;* and
– *dispositions based on proprietary rights*.

From the point of view of the scope of the market and of the controlling function of competition it is important in what way the official functions of management and the non-official ones become separated from each other. Although the socialist state is not outside the economy, the economic reforms raised the necessity to *differentiate between the economy's external and internal sphere of management*.

In the socialist economy a serious problem is due to the fact that it is not always possible consistently to separate administrative and non-administrative spheres of authority. There are institutions (enterprises) which inevitably have a dual character: on the one hand, they possess spheres of activity assigned by the state, on the other hand, they establish commodity and money relations in a system of equal rights and obligations. State banks are, for example, mixed type organizations.

The deviating features of the control systems based on plan directives and/or economic instruments also manifest themselves in the legal system of *economy*. In the case of regulation based on plan directives administrative law comes into prominence. In such a case high standard sources of law (constitution, laws and decrees) are only a framework of statutory provisions; they do not regulate human behaviour but establish regulating norms for the state administration. State regulation based on

[66] BÖHM-BAWERK, E. V.: *Macht oder ökonomisches Gesetz?* Zeitschrift für Volkswirtschaft, Sozialpolitik und Verwaltung. Wien, Bd. XIII, 1914.

economic instruments observes another kind of interpretation of the law. In this case the state provides *legal safeguards for the autonomous management* of enterprises. Accordingly, administrative law is relegated to the background. State organizations can only intervene in the economy in an operative way in cases as prescribed by law. When the state directs the economy mainly by economic instruments, it naturally tries to assert motives outside the economy in conformity with economic laws and not contrarily to them. In such cases economic laws only regulate the mode of action supervising economic decisions in this way.

Two important questions arise from the point of view of supervising economic power by competition. *First:* does the state – when it decentralizes spheres of activity – grant independence to monopolies organized by productive branches or to enterprises working side by side? *Secondly:* does the economic mechanism oblige enterprises to strive for and keep up international competitiveness or does it provide enterprises total protectionism?

In the most important spheres of the economy *state monopolies* prevail. This refers – as a general rule – to the large-scale industry, to transport and communication, foreign trade, wholesale trade, banks and credit organizations. From the point of view of market relations and from that of the controlling function of competitiveness the main point is how state monopolies are to be regarded. State monopolies can be considered enterprises (institutions) carrying on activities in the form of monopolistic organizations with the right to exercise executive powers. However, state monopolies can also be considered organizations functioning in the form of state enterprises (or co-operatives) without having monopolistic rights and although they carry on their activities as representatives of the state they have no executive powers. The independence of enterprises, competition between enterprises, profitability as a regulator of export and competition in import are compatible with socialist economy. However, the system of constraints of the above must be determined in conformity with state planning.

When a socialist country first introduces a mechanism of plan directives and subsequently switches over to market regulation according to plan the interdependent questions of *monopoly and competition* come up in a complicated form. In the first place it is not at all easy to reorganize an organically integrated economy. Organizational integration has many obvious advantages. In small economies with a narrow domestic market it is characteristic of a number of productive branches that internal demand does not amount to the optimum size of productive units and that there are branches where production cannot be economically organized on a national scale. Competition increases the danger of the dissipation of energies; this must be prevented by a definite structural policy. Thus, organizational integration contains advantages mainly from the point of view of development policy.

However, organizational integration is not the outcome of an evolution process, but is carried into effect by state dispositions. In such cases centralization often manifests itself in petty bossing and concentration includes such branches of production which can efficiently function in a decentralized production pattern only, and in case of competition. It is difficult to grasp these elements separately. In case of a change-over from a mechanism based on plan directives to market regulation according to plan, the tendency continues to prevail to regard the control of the economy as an administrative function of the state, that is, control is identified with the giving of orders and the regulation of economic processes with measures taken by the authorities.

The *concentration of plants* also brings problems in its stride. In some socialist countries instead of building large-scale industrial units *in addition* to the existing small and medium-sized factories the latter were merged and large works came into being in this way. This caused a "vacuum" in the structure of productive units. The concentration and centralization process *did away with small and medium plants to a greater extent than justified*. Insufficiency of small and medium-sized factories is characteristic of the organizational structure of almost all branches. International experience shows that up-to-date and efficient large-scale industries can only function in the presence of a complementary network of small and medium-sized factories. The lack of the latter mainly shows that a flexible supply structure adjusted to demand can only be ensured in case of this kind of harmonious economic structure.

The functioning of the market mechanism *postulates a structure of productive units which is responsive to every kind of market signalling*. A large-scale plant is disinterested in the manufacture of a product even if it fetches a good price if its production does not fit in the plant's technological pattern. Only small and medium-sized plants can turn out certain products and perform certain services. Thus, if the structure of productive units is not up to the purpose, shortages will crop up due to objective reasons. However, a situation "tacitly allowed" in a mechanism based on plan directives has sooner or later to be solved in a system of planned market regulation.

This problem is due to the *statutes* of "state enterprises" or "co-operatives" simply because administrative requirements – often only formal ones – are considerable, particularly in case of state enterprises, but partly also in the case of co-operatives. If there is a numerous administrative staff because of great administrative demands, the tendency of developing the enterprise into a large-scale plant arises as a matter of course. In this case the management is disinterested in the manufacture of products or in services which are characteristic of small and medium-sized plants. An *organizational* form which ensures the functioning of viable small and medium-sized plants within the framework of socialist sectors poses a problem not satisfactorily solved yet.

Part III

Pricing

1. Price Planning

Content and Pattern of the Price Plan

The socialist state pursues an active price policy: it is not just a neutral onlooker but a regulator of price formation. In regulating prices the government makes use of both direct (regulating) and indirect (financial) means. Between individual socialist countries there are differences only in the forms of the manifestation of a *planned price formation.* In some socialist countries the *direct* role of the market factors in pricing is minimized, while in others a greater significance is attributed to the role of value judgements by the market, and therefore the planned influencing of the market factors is also considered an important part of effective price policy.

The government can solve the problem of planned price formation in a satisfactory way only by using appropriate *foresight*. Price prognostics is a precondition not only for value-oriented planning but is also indispensable in volume-oriented planning. Planning at constant prices does not necessarily mean the adoption of a "price freeze" policy. Even in the case of such a planning concept, several factors may make price changes desirable and even unavoidable. In other words, price plans are drawn up also in volume-oriented planning. The only specific feature is that a price plan is not organically intertwined with long- and medium-term plans, and its criteria are also different from those of value-oriented planning.

Price planning provides the institutional framework of planned price formation whose content and pattern adjust themselves to the general requirements of the national economic plan and, within it, to the criteria governing price policy. Accordingly, sectoral price plans are worked out for industrial producer prices, agricultural procurement prices and consumer prices separately. Similarly, plans are prepared according to the different plan periods. Thus, there are long-term (for 15 to 20 years), medium-term (for 5 years) and short-term (annual) price plans.

The price plan embraces all such elements of planned development which directly determine the socialist price system. In this respect, great attention is paid in price planning particularly to five interrelated problems:

1. *Price level (exchange rate).* Here, planning wishes to answer the question whether, owing to the movement (changes) of prices, the price level also changes or not, and if it does change, whether it rises or falls. In an autarchic price system, price planning is divorced from the movement of world market prices. If, however, a closer relationship is established between foreign-trade and domestic prices, the price level is associated with the planning of the exchange rate, with its envisaged devaluation or revaluation, depending on whether there exists a price gap ("price scissors") between domestic and foreign-trade price movements, and if it exists, of what direction it is.

2. *Price structure.* In this field, price planning examines whether it is justified to alter the price-forming factors, and if it proves to be justified, to what extent and in what direction they should be changed. The most important factors to be taken into account are

– taxes imposed on production costs, on enterprise profits and consumer prices;

– rates of depreciation, funds for technical development and guarantees, etc., and

– the profit rate.

3. *Foreign-trade financial bridges.* If there is an organic relationship between domestic and foreign-trade prices, the financial burdens imposed on imported and exported goods (duties, taxes, various dues, etc.), or financial preferences (import and export subsidies, tax allowances, etc.) are price-forming factors. They are designed to protect home production, and to set limits to competitiveness measured on an international scale. Price planning is aimed, in this respect, to answer the question if this mechanism should be maintained in an unchanged form, or if it is expedient and possible to change it.

4. *Relative prices.* This problem is examined in its interconnection with the socially necessary labour input, under consideration of the relationship between value and price. But where price operates as the regulator of commodity exchange, the price at which the planned supply structure ensures equilibrium is also analysed. It is exactly in this way that price planning exerts an influence on the planned development process (on the supply structure to be planned). If the equilibrium price substantially deviates from value, this may justify a modification of the development concept.

5. *Price mechanism.* Planning, in this respect, determines the changes that affect the general system of price regulation. Under the administrative price system, the way of regulating prices may change in the direction of both centralization and decentralization. Under a mixed price mechanism, however, planning

must reveal in what scope and under what conditions the price-regulating function of the market mechanism is permissible. This analysis extends to such questions as organization in price policy, price control and price law.

Sectoral Price Plans

The term "sectoral price" has been established in socialist price theory in connection with the forms of ownership. In the production sphere, state enterprises, co-operatives and small-commodity private producers are operating side by side. And the commodities produced and services rendered satisfy the needs of state institutions, social organizations and the population alike. Price policy takes into account the criteria that vary from sector to sector. This is why price planning has a sectoral character. Price policy meets this requirement in practice by drawing up the price plan in the system of industrial producer prices, agricultural procurement prices and consumer prices.

1. When planned price formation is interpreted in the context of the administrative price system, then the forms of manifestation of price planning with respect to *industrial producer prices* are the *price rearrangement* and price formation of *new industrial products*. An overall *rearrangement of industrial producer prices* is a highly intricate task as price relations have to be established for the undisturbed functioning of the enterprises' self-accounting system over a specified period of time, taking into consideration simultaneously the price-cost interdependences of the industrial productive organization. Its methods may be different.[67] Let us illustrate it by the methodology of the reform of industrial prices carried out in Hungary in 1959. When implementing this reform, the work was divided into *three main stages:*

(a) The enterprises prepared their price proposals in accordance with the calculation instructions received.

(b) The pricing authorities supervised the price calculations of the enterprises and approved them in this way, where the centrally fixed administrative prices were based on the enterprises' cost calculations.

(c) Price lists were drawn up.

[67] Csikós-Nagy, B.: *A szocialista árképzés* (Socialist Pricing). Budapest, 1961. Gordon, J.: O uporzadkowaniu systemu cen (Rearrangement of the Price System). *Gospodarska Planowa,* No. 3, 1960, Warsaw. Meisenberg, L. I.: *op.cit.* Turetsky, S. Ya.: *Ocherki planovogo tsenoobrazovaniya v* SSSR (Planned Price Control in the Soviet Union). Moscow, 1959.

The course of the price rearrangement was determined by the technological sequence (raw materials, semi-finished and finished products). Some difficulty was caused by the fact that the prices of certain products manufactured in a later production phase react on the cost of products manufactured in a previous phase. Thus, for example, changes in the price levels of machinery and construction projects determine the extent to which depreciation cost changes in the prime cost of products. Therefore, it was necessary already in the phase of fixing raw material prices to take into account the expected price level of machinery and construction.

Thus the principle of the price rearrangement process adapted to the technological sequence has to be correctly interpreted in such a way that first the prices of all primary raw materials are fixed, and then the prices for each of the individual industries are set separately in the appropriate technological sequence (e.g. spinning, weaving and finishing in the wool industry). At the same time, efforts must be made to set the phases of work in the various industries according to the requirements of the main price interdependences. The repercussions of the prices of products manufactured in a later production phase as well as the interrelations of industries give rise to certain difficulties but they can be eliminated by means of informative price-change indices.

Before the enterprises set about calculating their prices, the following prices and informative price-change indices were placed at their disposal:

– Prices of the most important raw materials.

– Foreign-exchange multipliers; supplemented by instructions needed to set the prices of imported raw materials.

– Indices of the re-valuation of fixed assets.

– Indices of the changes in freight rates.

– Profit margins for storing and trading enterprises.

Owing to the specific price relationships of allied industries, indices of expected price changes for industrial users had to be provided already at a time when the price lists had not yet been drawn up. Thus price modelling made it possible to provide the price-change indices.

The implications of the price rearrangement had been assessed before the reform was begun, and when it was put into operation, the enterprises had to give an account of their input-output price changes. For summarizing the national data, the following tables were used:

I. Balance of the Social Product at the former prices.

II. Input-output table of price changes.

III. Changes in budgetary relationships.

In the period between two price reforms the industrial producer prices do not change unless, owing to a substantial change in the conditions of production, a *partial* price revision appears to be necessary. On the other hand, the task of *fitting the prices of new industrial products* into the administrative price system has to be solved. Its technique may also be different, but its aim is to render profits proportionate.

The plan of industrial producer prices assumes the form of *price prognistication* if planned price formation envisages a *continuous* and not an intermittent consideration of changes in value relations. This change of form appears to be necessary if the industrial producer price turns from a self-accounting price into a self-financing one and, further, if the market value judgement plays a more direct role in price formation.

2. *The planning of agricultural prices takes place in the system of the regulation pattern of agricultural incomes*, with due consideration to the fact that some of the income-regulating factors can be influenced by direct, others only by indirect measures.

In influencing income distribution the government relies on various forms of both prices and taxes. Especially important from the point of view of receipts are contractual purchase prices and free market prices; from the point of view of *peasant*

The pattern of incomes from agricultural work

The structure of agricultural incomes		Factors of income regulation
Money incomes	Price receipts	Prices of agricultural produce
	Other money incomes	Government subsidies
Money expenditure	Machines, materials etc.	Prices of means of production produced in the industry
	State commitments	Income tax
Private incomes	Nominal income	Undistributed funds
	Real income	Prices of consumer goods

incomes, in addition to those listed above, taxes, prices of the means of production produced in industry and prices of consumer goods. Discounting what the peasantry consumes of what it produces a much greater share of its money income derives from sales to state enterprises (co-operatives) than from sales in the unorganized market. *Thus the direct regulation of agricultural prices exercises a more determining effect on peasant incomes than the free market prices.*

Peasant money income is a multiple of the taxes paid by the peasants to the government. If this ratio is, for example, ten to one, then it means that a 10 per cent change in the agricultural price level leads – assuming an unchanged volume of agricultural produce – to an income change corresponding to a 100 per cent change in taxes. *In other words, from the point of view of regulating peasant incomes, prices have a more important role to play than taxes.*

Peasants spend the bulk of their money incomes on buying industrial goods and various services in the state and co-operative network of trade. *Thus, from the point of view regulating peasant incomes, the consumer price policy of the government is much more important than the prices of private small-scale trade.*

The forms and methods of regulating peasant incomes must jointly be applied. When determining which of the forms of incomes regulation is expedient to apply first under the given circumstances, it is decisive to state for what reason the necessity of incomes regulation arises. To determine the effectiveness of price regulation, the following has to be taken into account:

(a) While regulating the income relations of the peasantry, the agricultural price policy of the government also exercises its influence on the scope of commodity production and the structure of agricultural production. By its purchase prices the government can either boost or restrict agricultural commodity production.

(b) Agricultural price policy is effective only if government purchase prices prevail. In this case free market prices are adjusted to them. Consequently, the unorganized market is only of a complementary character. Peasants sell their produce primarily to state enterprises (co-operatives).

(c) Agricultural price policy can have a bearing only on incomes derived from commodity-producing economic units. It has no significant influence on those working primarily in wage-earning jobs but doing at the same time secondary agricultural work, mainly to meet their own consumption needs. Furthermore, agrarian price policy is less effective for farming on household plots than for big farms as the former usually produces mainly what the peasants consume themselves.

Thus we come to the conclusion that the control of the price level of agricultural produce is the most effective tool of regulating peasant incomes. Socialist countries perform this task in *conformity* with the overall planning of the national economy. The price level of agrarian products is in harmony with the government plan of the national economy if the following conditions are met:

– It ensures, along with the envisaged production volume, the private income of the peasantry as foreseen by the plan.

– The price – in conformity with the private income planned – provides the financial means needed for extended reproduction by self-financing.

– It enables the peasants to fulfil their tax obligations.

3. *The planning of consumer prices is based on the household budget (money incomes and expenditure of the population). The living standard can be raised in a number of ways.* The socialist state can raise it by higher real wages or higher real incomes. In the former case it can increase the wages while keeping the prices unchanged, or decrease the prices while keeping the wages unchanged. In the latter case it can expand the scope and measure of social benefits etc. with unchanged wages and prices. A higher living standard can also be achieved in such a way that the already established income relations of the social classes and strata are either retained or altered. In the latter case the raising of the living standard may extend over the society as a whole, or may be confined to a given social class or stratum. It requires circumspect consideration to decide which way is preferable under the given circumstances. In any case, the principal requirement is to *put an end to*, or to diminish, *the disproportions* arising in the wake of the development of productive forces and the shaping of new production relations.

Both the rise and the abolition of *wage disproportions* is an unavoidable accessory process of socialist construction. In its income distribution policy the socialist state considers it as its most important task to provide adequate compensation for the work done by the masses of society, to ensure such living and working conditions which make it possible for them to lead a life worthy of man. The socialist countries are raising, according to a priority order, the real wages of workers engaged in the various productive branches and spheres. From this it follows that relative wages desirable at a given date will express a degree of disproportions at a later time, and therefore they must be changed.

There may also be disproportions in the system of social benefits. The interest of the society as a whole is satisfied by a system of social benefits which, on the basis of objective criteria, determines the scope of the eligible persons or the actual beneficiaries as well as the extent of benefits. Thus we are faced with a disproportionalities of social benefits when, owing to given limitations (e.g. lack of accomodation), *only part* of the eligible persons can partake of these benefits, or when their size is extremely *different*.

There may also be disproportions in prices. With the development of productive forces production conditions are also liable to change. Changes in the conditions of production find expression in the change of relative values. All this is due to the fact that the conditions of production do not change proportionately everywhere. Therefore it may happen that today the prices of two products still approximately reflect relative values, but they will deviate from them tomorrow. A disparity in prices may also ensue independently of that phenomenon. This may occur as a result of price regulations by the government, which aims primarily at ensuring a quantitative harmony between supply and demand. The greater price disparities are, the more the structure of supply deviates from the structure needed to bring about a harmony between supply and demand at prices approximating value. Nor can a conscious deflection of the price from value be identified independently of space and time. The raising of the living standard may also justify a revision of socio-political preferences. As a result of this, the question of prices approximating value will arise when the expansion of the material funds makes it possible to raise the living standard.

It is of crucial importance whether the socialist state wishes to use the raising of the living standard for the redistribution of incomes, or considers it merely as one of its policy measures. In the former case it resorts to a wage rise, in the latter rather to a price reduction. Price may also be an instrument of the policy of income distribution, but it materializes in an unambiguous and definite way through the wage policy only.

In choosing the appropriate price or wage measures, account must also be taken of the *pattern of goods on which a higher living standard is based*. It is obvious that if with a given living standard expanding production can create an abundance of only a specified group of products, and a higher living standard must be attained in such a way that the increased purchasing power should absorb these products, then either the purchasing power of those social strata (income categories) must be increased whose effective demand is presumably aimed at buying more of these products, or else the prices of the products in question must be reduced, in which case the demand elasticity of these products must specifically be studied.

In the last analysis, the consumer price plan must pay special attention to the *equilibrium of supply and demand.* But while in the administrative price system this is just one of the criteria of administrative price changes, it asserts itself in a more direct way wherever the market factors play a role in price formation. It is also a function of the market factors to what extent the retail prices of new industrial products are incorporated into the price system. In the case of an administrative price system the prices of new industrial goods are established by making prices proportionate to use value. In the case of free prices, market value judgements will help to fit the prices of new products into the price system of available products (related articles).

Long-, Medium- and Short-Term Price Plans

The national economy can develop on a planned basis if the main tendencies of the socio-economic processes are determined for a reasonably long period in advance, if the rate of economic growth and the socio-economic relations in which economic growth takes place are also predicted for several years ahead, if a sufficient number of facts are available for an operational economic policy to go by when making decisions which are consistent with them. These requirements cannot be met by any national economic plan. Plans for different periods of time are needed which constitute the components of a uniform *planning system.* Such considerations have given birth to a triple system of national economic planning whose components are

– *long-term plans* embracing a period of about 20 years, which in certain respects, may contain projections for 25–30 years or even for a longer span of time,

– *medium-term plans,* usually extending over a 5-year period,

– *short-term plans,* usually of one year's duration.

It is in the *long-term plan* that the main features of the government's economic policy find expression. *It is a perspective and not an action programme.* It becomes an action programme to the extent to which its elements are built into the medium-term plan. Long-term plans are needed – among other things – because medium-term decisions have their impact on a later period of time too, and therefore it is necessary to know how the perspective conditions of socio-economic factors will change. For this we must be in a position to delineate the perspective equilibrium state of the economy. Economic planning in itself is, of course, not sufficient, but it catches hold of a highly important factor, the changing conditions of material life. It is a *comprehensive and co-ordinated system* ensuring the harmony and joint feasibility of aims set in the various domains of social and economic life. But the complexity of the long-term plan differs in its very nature from the requirements that a medium-term plan is expected to meet. Long-term planning relies on the main features of economic and technical development and the basic changes in the socio-economic structure. The science of economic planning has not yet provided a more detailed definition of long-term planning, as even the socialist countries with their economic systems based on planning had until recently deduced the tasks of operational economic management largely from medium-term plans.

Medium-term plans are distinguished from long-term plans first of all by the *endeavour to be more concrete.* In this respect, a medium-term plan contains more targets, is manysided and envisages in greater detail the imagined path of future economic processes. This is all the more possible as with the knowledge of the present more facts can be predicted, and more unambiguously, for a medium-term (five years) than for a longer period of time. Five years is, of course, still a long enough period of time, and therefore it is hardly possible to project for that time all factors determining the rate and structural changes of economic development with absolute certainty. In any case, a five-year plan must be worked out so systematically and concretely that it may serve as a *foundation for a specific action programme.* A medium-term plan must contain, in addition to the assumed growth rate and economic equilibrium,

– all substantial features of the transformation of the economic structure,

– all such elements as, when deduced from the plan, render the determination of economic regulators of a long-standing character possible.

The short-term (annual) plan is the government's plan for operational measures. In operational planning a prominent role is played by mobile economic regulators i.e. by such elements of planned economic development as can be identified only in the knowledge of the actual market situation, and even thus the decisions of economic policy can be successfully solved only within an operational system.

The generally formulated principles of the planning system are reflected in a specific way in the system of *price planning.*[68]

[68] ARSENE, S.: Folosirea preturilor in conducerea planificate a economiei nationale (Using Prices in a Plan-Controlled Economy). Probleme de Pre-

The distinguishing features of price plans embracing longer or shorter periods of time are due to the fact that the freedom of decision-making is greater over a long period of time and the possibility to be specific is more limited. In the long run there is a much wider scope for the transformation of the macrostructure of production and for such technical developments as exert considerable influence on the conditions of production. At the same time, the accumulated information for long-term planning makes it possible to determine the planned development processes only in the context of branches and of certain priority products within them. Thus, long-term price plans can characterize price relations only through changes in the price proportions of the sectoral price level. The situation is just the opposite in the short run. Here, the determined character of the structure and the conditions of production are typical, and a change in relative prices can be characterized within the product system.

The theoretical questions of the long-term price plan are connected with the relationships between (1) foreign-trade prices and domestic prices, (2) industrial producer prices and agricultural purchase prices and (3) producer and consumer prices. From the point of view of the long-term price plan it is indifferent whether the accounting price of products within the sphere of the public sector is based on value, or on the "production price". A price reform (a rearrangement of industrial producer prices) which converts the cost-based accounting price into "value price" or even "production price" can be carried out at any time. On the other hand, it is only by means of long-term planning that an organic link can be established between

turi, *Institutul Central de Documentar Tehnica*, No. 4, 1969, Bucharest. Baum, H.: *op.cit.* Bugeanu, C. and Faifer, I.: Modelarea pretulirol cu amanuntul (Consumer Price Modelling). *Viata Economica*, No. 6, 1969, Bucharest. Komin, A. N.: *Voprosy perspektivnogo planirovaniya optovykh tsen* (Questions of Long-Term Planning of Producers' Prices). Moscow, 1970. Langer, K. and Maschke, R.: Aufbau der Preisprognose und perspektivische Industriepreisplanung. *Deutsche Finanzwirtschaft*, No. 5, 1969, Berlin. Marinescu, I.: Planificarea preturilor cu ridicate ale produselor industriale (Planning of Producers' Prices in Industry). *Institutul Central de Documentare Technica*, No. 11, 1969, Bucharest. Moldovan, R.: Probleme ale strategiei si tacticii planificarii pretulirol (Strategical and Practical Questions of Price Planning). In: *Contributii la dezbatarea problemelor teoretic ale economiei socialiste.* Bucharest, 1969. Porwit, K.: Problematyka cen w planowaniu dlugookresowym (Problems of Long-Term Price Planning). Warsaw, 1970. Szakolczay, Gy. and collaborators: Az ártervezés ökonometriai modellje. 1960–1970 (The Econometric Model of Price Planning. 1960–1970). In: *Árhivatali Kiadványok.* Budapest, 1973. Zavvelkov, A.: Voprosy perspektivnogo planirovaniya tsen (Questions of Long-Term Planning). *Planovoye Khozyaistvo*, No. 8, 1970, Moscow. Zekonski, Z.: Prognozy i alternatiwy zmian w strukturze konsumpcji (Prognoses and Alternatives of Various Consumption Structures). *Gospodarka Planowa*, No. 11, 1970, Warsaw.

domestic and foreign-trade prices and between producer and consumer prices. In the same way, only long-term planning makes it possible to create an identical price centre for both industrial and agricultural products.

The close relationship between domestic and foreign-trade prices presupposes that economic efficiency is identified with international competitiveness, and in this way price becomes a criterion of the development programme. A production structure based on the principle of international competitiveness cannot be created overnight. Even after an agreement has already been reached on the appropriate course of development to be taken, the transformation of the autarchic production structure will take a considerable time yet. The transition cannot be a "revolutionary" one. The productive units called forth by previous planning must not indiscriminately be excluded from production, the path of economic recession must not be embarked upon, the emergence of a crisis-situation is not tolerable. Such a "reform" would not be accepted by a socialist society. It is in the process of economic growth that those structural elements must be corrected which are formulated by a price concept different from the previous one as a critique of existing relations.

In this connection the inquiries of long-term price planning are concentrated on finding out to *what scope and extent state protectionism can be narrowed down.* It cannot of course completely be abolished. On the other hand, a price theory based on the principle of international competitiveness sets certain requirements for the *development policy.* The organic relationship between domestic and foreign-trade prices makes it necessary to pursue a *development policy ensuring technical development and an intensive type of growth along a wide front of production.* This is a development policy which continually expands the number of convertible products and thereby the freedom of deciding on the choice between selling them domestically or abroad, and, in the case of exports, among relations in which they are marketed. Since integration between individual productive branches is increasing, this aim can only be attained if there is a proportionate relationship between the share of social capital allotted to the development of preferred (progressive) branches and the share of capital placed at the disposal of the enterprises. And the price concept in itself is a "competitive" price. Considered in this sense, a long-term price plan is a plan of transition to the "competitive" price.

According to the traditional socialist price system, the prime cost is a compulsory criterion of price formation only for products within the public sector. In the public sector of the national economy it is the government that determines the wage levels. The prime cost thus obtained constitutes the basis of planned price formation. The case is different in *agriculture* (in the non-public sector), where private income is a function of price. The government's incomes policy asserts itself in agriculture – as a rule – in an indirect way, through its price policy. It provides, among other things, the possibility of price disparity (agricultural "price scissors"). Industrial-agricultural price disparity – if it exists – cannot be abolished overnight. In case there is an agreement on the practicability of creating a proportionate relationship between industrial and agrarian prices, its conditions must also be ensured by the development policy. The income parity of industrial and agricultural workers cannot be secured by averaging the income differential, by decreasing industrial wages. To achieve this it is necessary to envisage in the process of economic growth a temporarily faster increase of incomes in agricultural than of industrial work.

The *consumer price must function as an equilibrium price.* Consumer price relations greatly detached from value relations cannot be brought closer to relative values simply by a price reform. The preconditions for this must be ensured in the course of economic growth and in the process of an appropriate structural transformation. This means, at the same time, that in a socialist planned economy the relationship between value and price materializes through government planning. It is in the long-term price plan that an answer must be found to the question what socio-political preferences and "dispreferences" should be applied to approximate consumer prices to value.

If a socialist country has a long-term price plan, *the medium-term price plan* can be conceived as its more concrete formulation for the subsequent five-year period. When drawing up a five-year price plan, the essential processes influencing the structure and conditions of production are more or less unequivocally predetermined. In any subsequent five-year period only such new capacities will be applied the execution of which has already begun, or for which at least the necessary preparations have already been made. The new investments and large-scale technical development projects to be launched in the subsequent five-year period pave the way – with a few exceptions – for a long-term structural transformation. Although formulated in such a way this does not give an absolutely realistic picture, it may make clear that this price concept is on a more solid basis over a medium than over a long-term period. This makes it possible to plan in a more concrete way

– the rate of exchange (the foreign-trade price coefficient connecting external and internal prices),

– export subsidies and import duties,
– changes in producer prices,
– turnover taxes and budgetary subsidies determining consumer prices,
– the system of price regulation.

Thus a medium-term price plan specifies the tasks of price policy in forms corresponding to actual needs. In this way, it may also serve as a basis for assessing the concept of a price policy by which the price category can best fulfil its role in planned development.

The annual price plan is the plan of operative *price measures*. It is a summary of obligatory decisions for implementation. An envisaged measure does not mean at the same time a political commitment merely on the ground that it is a constituent part of the medium-term plan. The mechanism of a political decision does not completely adjust itself to the planning system. Party leadership and government make, on the one hand, general decisions on national economic plans and indicate, on the other, those elements of the envisaged development for which special confirmation is needed concerning their concrete interpretation and the date and way of their implementation. As far as price policy is concerned, this belongs, as a rule, to the system of annual plans.

Planning Changes in the Price Level

The most debated questions of price planning are concerned with changes in the price level. *Marx* set forth the diminishing tendency of value which is brought into effect as a consequence of the development of the forces of production and of the resulting productivity of labour. *Lenin* pointed out that the law of value is the law of prices. Starting out from this statement, many economists came to the conclusion that planned price formation in a socialist economy must manifest itself in a policy of reducing prices, it is changes in value relations that must be reflected by prices as faithfully as possible.[69] It was in this way that

[69] Ambree, K., Bösche, J. and Mathe, F.: *Objektive Grundlagen und Anforderungen für die Gestaltung des Preissystems im ökonomischen System des Sozialismus für den Perspektivplanzeitraum* 1976–1980. Berlin, Material vom 20. 2, 1970. Brettschneider, G.: Preisdegression für neue Erzeugnisse. *Sozialistische Finanzwirtschaft*, No. 6, 1970, Berlin. Pfütze, G.: Aufgaben und Maßnahmen aus dem Gebiet d. Kosten und Industriepreis bei der Verwirklichung des ökonomischen Systems des Sozialismus im Perspektivplanzeitraum 1971 bis 1975. *Die Wirtschaft,* No. 27, 1970, Berlin.

the view prevailing in the early 1950s connected the policy of price reduction with the labour theory of value.

Marx formulated the tendency of diminishing value, and thus of prices, too, as the generalization of the experiences of commodity production in a free-market economy. The historical period from which *Marx* drew his experience was the classical period of capitalism characterized by partial unemployment and regularly recurring crises. However with the introduction of an anti-cyclical economic policy a new situation has evolved; in the market economies the price tendency has changed. Price rises have become constant attending phenomena concomitant with capitalist economic development[70] and finally, in the 1970s a sharpening of inflationary tendencies can be observed.

It would obviously be senseless to refer to inflation as evidence of the law of value no longer working under capitalism, and especially of the labour theory of value having lost its validity. What in fact is involved here is that, as a result of an anti-cyclical economic policy, first the tendency of an increase in money value has been curbed, followed later by the deterioration of the latter. Thus what is decisive from the point of view of the assertion of the labour theory of value and of the working of the law of value is not whether prices show a rising or falling tendency; the latter can only be defined as a function of money relations. The value of the product may diminish while its price rises, simply because the value of money decreases. Thus it is justified to ask why exactly the price tendency of the free-market system of the last century should be regarded as decisive for the socialist economy when the socialist societies organize their economies on the basis of full employment and regular economic growth.

Strangely enough, the policy of price reduction was generally applied in the first half of the 1950s, that is, in a period when most socialist countries disrupted the equilibrium of their economies by forced industrialization. Thus, in formulating the

[70] ANDREW, CH. F.: *The Control of Inflation.* CED/Problems of United States Economy, Development. Vols. 1 and 2, 1958, New York. BALOGH, T.: Productivity and Inflation. *Oxford Economic Papers,* No. 2, 1958, Oxford. CLARK, J. M.: *The Wage-Price Problem.* The American Bankers' Association, 1960. HOCH, R.: Piaci egyensúly és az árszinvonal változása a szocializmusban (Market Equilibrium and Changes of the Price Level in Socialism). *Közgazdasági Szemle*, No. 9, 1965, Budapest. LUMER, H.: The Problem of Inflation. *Political Affairs,* No. 1, 1958, New York. MACHLUP, F.: Another View of Cost-Push and Demand-Pull Inflation. *The Review of Economics and Statistics,* No. 2, 1960, Cambridge. SAMUELSON, P. A.: *America's Most Important Economic Problems. Threat of Inflation.* New York, 1957. THORP, W. L. AND QUANDT, R. E.: *The New Inflation.* New York, Toronto, London, 1959.

policy of price reduction, market laws had no chance to play any role. On the other hand, in socialist economic policy the *state was attributed the same faculty that Marx had assigned to the laws of the market.* It was the prevailing view that, while taking enterprises into social ownership, centrally organizing production, allocating the resources of production as well as determining prices and wages, the state also curbs the market. The categories of commodity production survive, but become means of a planned regulation.

It is possible to create really a *high-level state of organization in the price policy of a socialist economy.* The state can go a long way towards centrallv regulating price relations. In principle, in the field of prices no change can take place without a political decision on it. It is possible to think like this: if the cost of a product rises, the price need not be raised, it can even be decreased. The difference between price and cost can be equalized by the budget. This in itself does not cause any problem if the general cost level of social production falls. If all enterprises are state-owned, the social aggregate product can also be conceived of as "one" product, and input need not be refunded in the price-receipt of every single product separately; in the financial relations between enterprises and the budget all problems of price differentiation may be solved.

We have now followed a train of thought that is in contradiction with all that we have explained so far about the relationship of value and price. *This contradiction can be demonstrated both in socialist price theory and price policy.* When the regulation of economic processes is approached from the angle of economic efficiency and equilibrium, the role that price plays as a signalling system for economic decisions, and as an equalizer in demand–supply relationship seems to be natural. Looked upon from this side, it appears a matter of course that the price function has to be limited in the interest of society. It must be interpreted as a deliberate obstacle to market mechanism.

Somewhat separated from it exists the *price-level hypothesis.* When examining the regulation of economic processes from this point of view, the principle of price reduction, price stability, or relative price stability, as a general requirement set for price policy, is formulated in a different way in the various socialist countries. It follows from the nature of things that the less economic policy is in a position to bring the real processes it has sparked off into alignment with setting the price level, the more the signalling and equalizing function of the price is bound to weaken.

All this also implies that in most socialist countries the price level would be higher if the governments did not apply price regulation. In other words: such are money relations that their price-raising effect can only be prevented by price fixing. Under such circumstances the question also arises *what, in fact, the limits to the efficiency of such a price policy are.* In works dealing with comparative analyses we can often encounter views according to which the inflationary process that assumes open forms in the capitalist countries takes place in a "hidden" way in the socialist countries. Thus inflation should be a world phenomenon different only in its forms of manifestation. Put in this way, however, this statement does not hold water. If in commodity turnover the state is able to ensure sale and purchase at administrative prices and prevents the rise in prices (the redistribution of incomes attached to this price rise), then the situation is basically different from that when the state regards price formation as a matter of market mechanism. In the same way, it is also natural that government price regulation has its limitations, its negative concomitant phenomena.

Let us assume that prices for all products and services are determined and kept frozen by the state. What changes in price relations can ensue under such circumstances? *Is a hidden price-level change possible, and if so, what forms may it assume?* If there is such a possibility, then it is, in the judgement of society, the same as if the government had openly changed the prices of single products. Moreover, a hidden change in price relations is, in its effect on society, different from an overt price change. A hidden rise in the price level is generally more unfavourably received by society than an open one. This can be explained by the fact that an open price rise can be taken account of, and its control by society is possible. A hidden price change, however, cannot be measured and cannot even be taken account of.

A change in the price level, with prices remaining unchanged, *can take place for three reasons.* First, because the assortment of goods may change with unchanged prices. Secondly, because the quality of goods may change with unchanged prices. Thirdly, because the assortment of goods is replaced or expanded, and the prices of new products are set in such a way that they are no longer in harmony with the prices of industrial goods already in the market.

Changes in individual and average prices are different. The movement of average prices is of the same direction and measure as that of individual prices only if production or the structure of production remains unchanged, or if all individual prices in it change at the same time, in the same direction and to the same extent. In all other cases the movement of average prices deviates from that of individual prices. In practice, the deviating movement of average and individual prices is typical. The movement of average prices is made recurrent by changes in the economic structure. Thus average prices are subject to changes even if individual prices remain unchanged. If the weight of lower-priced products increases within the overall volume of products, average prices decrease while individual prices remain unchanged. In the reverse case, they will rise.

If the consumer finds the products he wishes to buy at unchanged prices in the market, he justly considers the price level stable. If e.g. the average price of footwear rises because the proportions within the assortment of footwear shift at the expense of shoes and in favour of boots and high boots, but otherwise shoes are available in a sufficient quantity, the consumer does not see any change in prices. But the judgement of the consumer will change when he finds that the article he wishes to buy is not available and he is compelled to buy a substitute for it.

How does the question arise from the point of view of the national economy as a whole? If social restratification takes place in the direction of the higher income brackets, average prices are bound to increase with individual prices being unchanged as in the changed consumption pattern the demand for more expensive sorts of goods will rise and for cheaper ones will accordingly decline. Unchanged individual prices, rising average prices with an ascending living standard, this is the natural relationship between unchanged individual prices and the movement of average prices in a state of the national economy in which there is not only a global equilibrium between the commodity fund and the purchasing fund, but there is also an internal equilibrium between supply and effective demand. But the rise in average prices may surpass the extent determined by the rise in the living standard. This may happen in the case of imbalances when the production of cheap goods is prematurely discontinued, or decreased to an extremely low supply. In such cases society becomes aware of a scarcity in the assortment of cheap goods. And if the rise in average prices takes place in the inelastic demand sphere of life, the consumer finds himself in a state of emergency; *he unjustifiedly considers the phenomenon that in reality arises from a discrepancy between the patterns of supply and consumption, a price increase.*

The quality of industrial products may change with their prices being unchanged. When doing his shopping, the consumer may experience that the same prices refer to products with specific properties either superior or inferior to those they had before. In the former case he is faced with a hidden decrease in the price level while in the latter with a hidden rise in the price level. The price level changes in concealed forms because changes in quality are not pursued by the price index, in which these changes are not expressed.

Owing to changes in the level of technical and technological development, the quality of products has, as a rule, to improve. Thus, under normal circumstances, the living standard of workers should register a greater improvement than that shown by the real-income index formed by means of the price index. In reality, however, the quality of products may not only improve but also deteriorate. This is due primarily to two factors. The first one is that in manufacturing certain products, materials with inferior specific properties may be used. The other is that in processing the product, certain operations affecting quality are either curtailed or omitted altogether. The improvement of quality and the reduction of costs do not always go hand in hand. The possibilities of reducing costs by deteriorating quality instead of technical development are greater, and what is even more important, they can be put into effect immediately, while cost reduction by technical development and improved quality require reorganization and investments, and make their favourable effects felt considerably later.

Changes in the composition of the raw materials of the product may lead to cost reduction especially in such product groups in which the basic material is of inferior specific properties and therefore cheaper, and does not increase the material input per unit of product (e.g. mass products of the iron industry). Moreover, quality deterioration manifests itself in a decreased specific material input (e.g. in products of the textile and clothing industry). The possibility of quality deterioration is therefore less in the case of product groups where materials of inferior quality increase specific material input (e.g. in the furniture industry), or may even lead to the absolute uselessness of the product (e.g. in the case of pharmaceuticals). Changes in the technology of production may result in great cost reduction in such product groups where production requires a high labour input and the worker does not accord the product the necessary processing (as in the wood-processing industry), and especially in the case of such technologies where quality control during processing constitutes a substantial part of the input and is therefore omitted. The possibility of quality deterioration is less when mechanized or fully automatic technologies are applied.

Changes in the assortment of industrial products in use raise a specific problem: what happens, *if the assortment is replaced or expanded, that is, if new industrial products are put on the market?* In such cases individual prices already known are complemented or replaced by new individual prices. The principle of price stability includes the requirement that the prices of newly marketed products should be in harmony with the prices of industrial products already in the market. Prices set for new industrial products cannot justify changes in price relations determining the general price level. Yet the very fact that in the case of a new product the price has to be established for the first time, involves the possibility of a hidden change in the price level through new pricing. The possibility lies in the fact that the price of the new product is set higher than it would follow from the price level determined by the industrial products already in the market, and that perhaps the old product is no longer manufactured at all. In such a case there is a hidden rise in the price level, as these differences do not appear in the price index in the construction of which only comparable actual industrial articles are taken into consideration. The prices of new products can be included in the price index only if they have already been manufactured for a sufficiently long period. But their initial price is always taken into account on the assumption that it cannot exercise any influence on the price level. Apart from its effect on the consumption pattern, the new industrial product shows a change in the price index only if its individual price has been changed.

In case there is abundant supply of goods in the market, trade exercises a strict control over the prices of new products. Since in the administrative price system the proposals for the prices of new products are made by the wholesale enterprise ordering them, and they are approved by the Ministry of Home Trade, it appears to be organizationally ensured that the introduction of new products cannot cause any hidden price rise. However, if the goods in question are in a relatively short supply, the price-regulating role of the trade cannot function effectively enough. Under such circumstances it occurs that trade not only tolerates quality deterioration of the products in short supply but also condones their higher prices. The greater the commodity shortage of a given product group in the market, the greater the dependence of trade on industry. Thus, seasonal disequilibria of supply and demand find expression not only in quality deterioration but also in higher prices through the introduction of new products.

Opinions widely differ in assessing such tendencies in the price relations of the socialist countries. There are economists who maintain that such a price policy does not follow the Marxist way and is therefore wrong. Obviously, it can also be interpreted in this way: it is not consistent enough, not strict enough, unable or unwilling to prevent hidden price rises, which are indirect *manifestations of the enterprises' price policy*. Or another possible interpretation: the economic mechanism is wrong because it weakens the chances of a planned price formation and tends to make the enterprises interested in price rises.

A hidden price rise is in fact a form of manifestation of the law of value working under the conditions of commodity production. This form particularly sharpened in the early 1950s. It also played a role in the fact that several socialist countries revised their price policies and substituted the principle of price stability for that of price reduction.

Looked upon in the long run, the price level in some socialist countries rises and does not fall although price reductions of single products are carried out from time to time. In price rises in individual countries different factors are at work, that is to say, the individual factors exercise their effect on the price level with different weights. In retrospect, *the rise in the procurement prices of agricultural products* was the most decisive factor, and the budget subsidizing of foodstuffs was the typical method applied by most socialist countries to prevent, or to vigorously limit, the spreading effect of higher procurement prices on the consumer prices of foodstuffs. The unfavourable experiences of a rise in the living standard by means of price reductions and, consequently, the *coming into prominence of wage rises* as a tool of the living-standard policy have already brought up, now with a more general claim, the possibility of a deviating development of the input of labour time per unit of output on the one hand, and of the wage bill on the other, and have made it necessary to raise from time to time industrial producer prices in certain branches of production. In our days it is especially three factors that are exerting, though to different extents in different countries, a price-raising effect: (1) Inflation in the world capitalist market. (2) The specific rise in research and development costs. (3) Commodity supply not adjusting itself flexibly to demand.

The socialist countries are trying to counterbalance, or *at least limit the spreading effect of inflation in the capitalist world market.* In such countries where prices are regulated under an autarchic system, the import of inflation is virtually eliminated, but, in the interest of maintaining the terms of trade, even these countries are endeavouring to offset the more expensive imports by raising their export prices. The indirect way of the inroad of capitalist inflation of the world market into the socialist economies is the contractual-price system as applied in the economic co-operation of the CMEA countries. When revising (adjusting) that price in each five-year period, it is the world market price stripped of its cyclical, etc. elements that is taken as a basis for setting the contract price. Differences in this respect between socialist countries derive from the fact that the foreign-trade sensitivity of the individual national economies is different and, as a function of the latter, there are also differences between them in the necessity to take into account the international value (world-market price) in pricing.

A rising tendency is displayed by inputs required by research and development, as well as by environment protection. For this reason, and also for others, *the introduction of new production techniques* increases *the costs of production.* Owing to differences among the financial systems of socialist countries, this factor has different impacts on pricing. In socialist countries where the government finances research and development in an institutional system organizationally separated from enterprises, and, further, where the state budget places the financial resources of investments at the disposal of enterprises free of charge, price, too, may display an indifference towards these processes. In other countries, however, the new technology is reflected, at least partly, in pricing. Let us add to it right now: it is being increasingly realized that these progressive elements are organic components of value-creating labour, consequently, their separation from the price distorts the enterprises' self-accounting system.

The price level as characterized by prices expresses the value of money if *commodities demanded can be bought at these prices.* A combination of use values needed to maintain an undisturbed supply, ensures an adequate commodity supply in a given commodity structure. Looked upon from the aspect of money, this is its legal tender function, and from the aspect of price, it is its distribution function. If an adequate commodity supply is not a requirement set to the price, then a "discretionary" price (price level) can be formed. The equilibrium of demand and supply is not determined economically even if it rests on emergency purchases or emergency savings. Characteristic of all socialist countries is the fact that they ensure, with a few exceptions, the allocation function of price in the sphere of consumer goods. The disturbances of commodity supply, however, have become typical of individual countries to a varying extent. Price stability or price reduction can be applied with more safety by a country which tolerates scarcity than by another one, where price stability and undisturbed commodity supply alike are criteria of the price policy.

All this sufficiently explains the *differing features* of price plans drawn up in the socialist countries. This manifests itself first of all in the fact that while certain countries are planning, on the medium term the lowering of the price level in the sphere of industrial producer prices, or at least in the maintenance of the price level in the sphere of consumer prices, other countries take into account a possible rise in the price level.

2. Price Regulation

Direct and Indirect Price Regulation

Any state intervention in the economy has a bearing on the exchange of goods and, consequently, on prices, too, as price constitutes the core of the market problem. There is no economic policy without a price policy. Prices are, for objective reasons, effected by state interferences. This also applies to "free-market prices". The market price mechanism does not exclude, but rather conceals those factors of price formation which can only be deduced from the relationship between state and economy. It is for this reason that justified doubts may arise about the realistic nature of any debates on whether the state must be considered as an exogeneous or an endogeneous factor. With the development of the productive forces, the relationship between state and economy undergoes, of course, certain changes and also develops differently according to socio-economic systems. But in any economic formation the state is, for objective reasons, an endogeneous factor.

Why must we lay special emphasis on this? Because no unambiguous answer can be given to the question of prices in a social environment without taking into account the existence of the state. Without it there can be no economic rationality in practice. That is why a price theory without a policy cannot have any realistic content. *In other words, price as an economic category must also be defined in terms of the economic relationship between state and economy.* This is exactly what we have done by demonstrating the two models in a way applied to socialist relations. These models determine the role of the government in controlling the economy in two different ways, which means, at the same time, that the laws governing a socialist economy can assert themselves in different systems or regulation. Though these alternatives arise within a socialist planned economy, from the point of view of price theory, there are substantial differences between the two.

We have characterized market regulation by the government as a manifestation of the production and distribution policy, of price and incomes policy, as well as of fiscal and monetary policy. All this can be conceived *as a sum total of direct and indirect government measures of price regulation.* The state exercises a direct sort of price regulation when it sets prices or controls price formation. Price regulation is indirect when it regulates or influences market conditions. Indirect price regulation may conform, but direct price regulation *necessarily* does not conform to the market. Indirect price regulation may be market-conformed if considerations of the economic policy are confined to the financial policy, if it applies only indirect financial measures without any selective principles.[71] Such an economic policy is so speculative and unrealistic that in the following we can entirely leave it out of account as a possible alternative.

If, however, the more practicable alternatives of indirect price regulation are confronted with the alternatives of direct price regulation, the resulting differences are *often overestimated.* Market prices are usually identified with competitive prices and administrative prices with autarchic ones. Indirect price regulation may have forms, in which prices operate as autarchic prices and administrative pricing may create competitive ones. Without setting even one single price, merely by taking indirect measures, economic policy can, on the one hand, establish and maintain such price relations which do not differ very substantially from the price relations established by government price regulation. On the other hand, in the system of direct price regulation, the government may apply principles which divert prices from their "natural" state only to the extent dictated by social interests. In this way, they assume a flexibility enabling them to adapt themselves to the changing market conditions.

It may be argued, of course, that the government does not set prices with the aim of simulating the market mechanism. And if it does, why does it resort to direct price regulation when the national interest can also be satisfied by indirect price regulation? The question is justified, but here we only want to place on a realistic foundation the charateristic differences of the two systems of regulatory instruments applied by direct and indirect price policy. In whichever way price policy asserts itself, *we must invariably interpret it, from the point of view of price theory, as the manifestation of socio-political preferences.*

In the following we want to concern ourselves primarily with the system of these regulatory instruments. To do this, we avail ourselves of three models of price regulation:

- indirect price regulation,
- the administrative price system and
- a mixed price mechanism.

[71] RÖPKE, W.: Die Gesellschaftskrisis der Gegenwart. Erlenbach–Zürich, 1942.

In order to reveal the entire body of knowledge of socialist pricing, we need all the three models because the government also resorts to the use of indirect price regulation when otherwise it adopts an administrative price system, because, further, a socialist economy can also be operated in a mixed price mechanism, and, finally, because certain elements of a mixed type of price mechanism can also be found in an administrative price system.

Indirect Price Regulation

We understand *indirect price mechanism* as direct government influence upon demand and supply prices, as well as on the market. In this respect supply, demand and equilibrium prices are expressions of the producer's, the consumer's and the market's behaviour respectively. The first is the expression of the producer's, the second of the consumer's market value judgement, while the equilibrium price is a synthesis of the two. The terms "demand price" and "supply price" were coined by *Marshall,* who wanted to indicate thereby that demand and supply can be considered as determined only when they are related to a certain quantity or price.[72] Therefore, demand and supply prices in themselves do not mean prices, but only demand or supply at certain given prices. Even though they are not real prices yet, when used as categories they make it substantially easier for us to clarify the mechanism of indirect price regulation.

Private, producers' and public consumption are summarized in social demand. Public consumption presupposes that the state and other institutions possess money incomes which they come by in different ways: by imposing taxes on private and enterprise incomes, by drawing off, in the form of credits, accumulated money incomes, by increasing the circulation of banknotes, i.e. by issue operations. In other words, the state acquires its own capital resources by restricting consumers' and producers' effective demand. But this means, at the same time, that demand and supply prices are liable to be influenced by the government's income distribution policy. By centralizing and redistributing a part of the surplus value created in the production process, the *government performs an active and a passive function of effective demand regulation.* The government (public institution)

– plays, on the one hand, an active role in that it purchases goods and services,

[72] MARSHALL, A.: *op.cit.*

– and, on the other hand, creates, supplements, restricts and channels consumers' and producers' demands.

Active and passive demand control by the government (public institution) finds expression in fiscal, capital, credit and foreign-exchange policy. The socialist state performs the function of organizing the economy. The state lays the foundations of this function by its expenditure and revenue policy in which, in compliance with the national economy, market regulation is also being exercised. The more consciously market regulation asserts itself, the more economic elements are included in the fiscal policy, and the more effective forms of co-operation come into being between the government and the banking organizations.

The way of restricting consumers' and producers' demand finds expression in a *specific tax system.* The government acquires its capital resources not just by one, but by several channels of income deduction. We are faced, in fact, with an intricate tax system whose interconnections with price relations are often not quite clearly apparent. In general, the government imposes taxes on incomes in two ways. First, it taxes money incomes and, second, real incomes. In the latter case, it withdraws a certain part of money incomes in the process of transforming money incomes into real incomes. It is on these two possible ways of income deduction that the *distinction between direct and indirect taxes is based.* It is for this reason that direct taxes are also called residual, and indirect taxes price taxes. *The former decrease the nominal amount of the income, while the latter the real value of the nominal income.* The basis of the distinction between direct and indirect taxes is provided by the hypothesis that

– direct taxes decrease the incomes of persons paying taxes,

– while indirect taxes are shifted over by the taxpayers, they eventually appear in the market price and diminish, in fact, the real value of the consumers' money incomes.

The government converts part of the centralized income into private incomes, and creates, guarantees and supplements consumers' demand. All this is reflected in the fiscal expenditure policy. The state budget controls private incomes in the *system of direct and indirect regulation, in the gross and net accounting system* in the following ways: (1) It exercises direct control over the personal outlays of government institutions (budgeting organizations). (2) By making use of the accounting system based on annual balance sheets as well as of the income-redistribution schemes, the state budget can exercise indirect control over enterprises' and personal outlays. (3) By supporting social institutions, it may regulate, partly directly, partly indirectly, social –

so called fringe – benefits (i.e. other than wages). (4) By granting budgetary subsidies it may let consumer preferences assert themselves.

A part of the government (public) funds created by tax revenues and credit operations which is not used for income redistribution is *spent on purchasing goods and services.* It is in this way that the undisturbed operation of public institutions is ensured, defence, cultural, social, economic and development objectives are attained. The government (public institution) appears as an agency in the market and creates demand for goods and services. We usually distinguish between two forms of the market created through the agency of the government: state-monopolized market and competitive market. Characteristic of the first is the fact that it is only the government that creates (can create) demand, and of the latter that state (public) demand is in competition with producers' and consumers' demand.

There is substantial state demand for goods and services which constitute at the same time the objects of enterprise (public) and private demand. In connection with this, two questions must be answered: (1) What is the role of state demand in forming market prices? (2) Has public demand price elasticity?

If the state budget is rigid, and its outlays do not follow the changes in market prices, then the price elasticity of state demand is equal to one. If the government performs its economic activities under conditions of changing market prices and on the basis of unchanged budgetary outlays, it will buy more or less of the given products than originally planned, depending on whether their prices have dropped or risen. But the government may pursue a budgetary policy which adapts its expenditures to changes in price relations. In this *case the price elasticity of state demand is equal to zero.* The more a given objective of the government is determined by a certain quantity of product, the more the movement of its budgetary outlays follows the movement of prices. Therefore, state demand, when considered separately, has not the same regular price elasticity based on the characteristics (specific features) of the product as private consumption has. All this is regulated, in the last analysis, by fiscal budgetary policy.

Wishing to carry out an effective market regulation, the government cannot assess its demand *independently of general market conditions.* If e.g. the government decides on a certain course of action in its economic policy concerning market price relations, it must conform to this course in its fiscal policy, too. Consequently, the government must assess its purchases with due consideration to their effects on price relations. It must restrict, or even suspend, its purchases if at the given (desired) price an equilibrium can only be maintained in this way, while it must step up its purchases if it appears expedient from the point of view of the equilibrium position. It is here that the basic difference becomes apparent between the regulation of state (public) demand adapting itself to the requirements of a conscious market regulation and the satisfaction of private demand subject to specific laws.

Supply prices are based on economic calculation. Therefore, if the government wishes to exert influence on the supply price, *it must influence these very economic calculations.* There are three regulatory systems suitable for this purpose:

- production costs,
- profits and
- prices.

The government can influence production costs by *levying taxation on the production process.* The method most commonly applied for this purpose is *import duty* levied on the means of production. Thus, import duty has two aspects: it promotes the unfolding of the productive forces and also makes production more expensive. For an enterprise that sets about manufacturing a given means of production, import duty makes production more profitable, while for an enterprise using this means of production in its manufacturing process, import duty adds to its production costs. With a view to judging export profitability it may be at the same time expedient to exempt from import duties such materials (parts, etc.) as are used in producing export goods.

The application of the system of *selective custom duties* leads to a differentiation of the supply price. Production costs vary depending on whether the products are sold in the domestic or the world market. Export calculation differs from a general type of economic calculation. In such a system, the enterprise can offer a foreign buyer cheaper prices than those it can fetch on the home market. The difference between a high domestic supply price and a relatively low international supply price is a general tendency created by the customs policy and further developed by the enterprises' business strategy in accordance with their interest in expanding the market.

A less widely applied method is the *taxation of the production processes* (phases). Where it is applied, the enterprises are compelled to pay taxes on their turnover and by them they will burden the prices of their products. The rate of the turnover tax applied in the productive sphere can be either uniform or selective, and certain productive branches can even be exempt from paying this tax. The rate of tax may be related to the value and to the value added. In the former case the materials and components processed and embodied in the end product are taxed in a multiple way as the tax is imposed on the product at every phase of the manufacturing process. In the latter case taxation taxation is not cumulative as tax is imposed in each phase on the value added only.

The government may impose taxes not only on the production process as a whole but also on the individual factors of production separately. Concessions granted for exploiting natural resources or *wage-tax* to be paid on the wage bill are well-known cases in point.

Control of the supply price by the government based on the regulation of enterprise profits is related to the system of profit tax. Profit tax is usually considered as a neutral tax with no direct bearing on price relations. When taxing profits, the government centralizes its revenues only where and to the extent to which market prices realize profits. Yet, profit tax may contain several elements which the enterprise cannot leave out of account when making its economic calculations. The government levies taxes primarily on a substantial proportion of total profits. The latter are composed of two parts: profits before taxation (gross profit), which is separated from the profit after taxation (net profit). In its economic decisions the enterprise aims of course, at maximizing its profits in a way which *ensures an optimum situation from the point of view of net profit.* Though not a cost element, profit tax is, nevertheless, a loss in price from the point of view of the enterprise. In the last analysis, profit tax is also a burden on price, and it is only the conditions under which the tax must be paid that are basically different from classical price taxes.

The most effective way for the government to influence the supply price is the one *in which, by directly subsidizing certain productive branches (enterprises), it disrupts the organic relationship between cost and supply price*. Thus the government supplements, as it were, the enterprise's price income, refunds part of its production cost, which otherwise could not be realized in the commodity exchange. State subsidizing of production is an income-redistribution process financed from the budget. This is resorted to because otherwise certain productive branches (enterprises), whose operation is deemed necessary by the government, could not survive, or, because the unfavourable conditions of production would result in such market prices which the government does not consider expedient. Thus, considerations on part of both production and price policy have a part to play in the matter of government subsidies.

Side by side with its budgetary policy the government can influence the supply price by using different *means of monetary policy.* In this respect the most important instruments are given by the foreign exchange policy (e.g. by determining the rate of foreign exchange), and by the credit policy (by determining the rate of interest and, more generally, by the conditions of credit in a selective way).

Direct Price Regulation

In most socialist countries prices are set and changed by a price authority. There are some exceptions, though. The terms "organized" and "unorganized" markets are meant to point to the possibility of market relations (for example trade between agricultural producers, or products sold directly by agricultural producers) in which the application of the administrative price is not obligatory. It is possible, therefore, for a given product simultaneously to have both an administrative and a free price. This duality, however, is confined to a relatively limited nomenclature of products. Therefore, it is justified to call this system *an administrative price system.*

The price authority includes the prices in a list. This price list is not simply a source of information. The inclusion in the list of the price of a product is a legal action. In principle, no product can be left out of the list, and in practice products not entered in the list cannot be put on the market. A new product cannot be manufactured or sold until its price is set. This price is, as a rule, a *fixed* one, no deviation from it either in an upward or downward direction is permissible. The administrative price is intended to protect, on the one hand, the consumer (against price rises), and on the other, the net income taken into account in price formation, and finally the state budget (against price reductions).

When fixing the price, the state *either sets the price directly, or just certain elements of it.* The former is the more effective form of price regulation. Since the enterprises are only concerned with price application, it is relatively easy both for the price authority and the users to control it. The control of price application in the case of state regulation affecting individual price elements is already somewhat clumsier, especially if the price has to be formed out of its elements in an intricate mechanism. Nevertheless, both ways of setting prices administratively meet the requirement which price-fixing by the government involves, the difference between them being only in the way it is done.

What is essential in the fixing of price elements by the government is that out of these elements the price may be calculated unambiguously, that is, that no so-called non-regulated factors appear which enable for the enterprises arbitrarily to include costs in the price. What is in fact involved here? Some products are manufactured in medium and large batches on a mass scale, regularly and in a recurrent way, others again are turned out in varying qualities and forms of finish. Some needs are satisfied by standard products, which are rarely, if at all, replaced by others in the production process. Other needs are met by regularly changing types of products which, though identical in their principal technical-specific qualities, are different in certain properties also affecting their prices.

State regulation is of course more effective in the case of medium and large batches of mass-produced industrial goods than in the case of *individual, custom-made machines, industrial services, installation, repairing and construction work*. In the former case, the fixing of prices does not cause any major difficulty, and the only thing that needs special attention is to see to it that the chosen form of price-fixing should meet the requirements set by the technical qualities of the product group subject to price regulation. In the latter case, however, owing to the individual character of the products, enterprises must be allowed to make their own price calculations, the prices thus formed being the ones that are to be realized unless they are subject to approval by the price authority.

In forming prices regulated by cost calculation instructions, the socialist countries follow different methods in so far as the prices set by them are to be submitted to the price authority for approval or not. Price regulation in the case of construction projects is usually conducted in the course of a banking procedure, in connection with investment financing. With engineering and installation work, however, previous approval of the calculated price by the price authority is usually required only above a certain value limit.

In order to *consider the administrative price of a given product as unambiguously determined*, three price-influencing factors must be clarified:

– the technical parameters, in which the product in question differs from all other products in respect of price,

– price parity, which determines the relationship between the price system and the terms of delivery for the product,

– and, finally, whether the fixed price is applied independently of the quantity of the product ordered or, depending on the quantity ordered, a surcharge or an allowance is made.

With a view to the workability of the administrative price system it is important to clarify *what exactly must be considered as a product from the point of view of price*. The product nomenclature of the enterprises is necessarily more detailed than the one with which the price authority is concerned. The product which is priced administratively comes into being in the various manufacturing phases of the production process. What is considered by the price authority as an "unfinished" product, is treated by the enterprise, depending on the self-accounting system applied, as an "independent" product. The prices of products that one plant or one shop passes on to another for further improvement within an enterprise, must somehow be evaluated. The most appropriate way of evaluating part of the work performed is *the "accounting price" within the enterprise*. The "enterprise accounting price" is beyond the competence of the price authority, and can be looked upon as the manifestation of the enterprise's price policy. Thus, the administrative price system may be characterized as the price system of products *to be traded with*. This is a good characterization even if we take into account that the price authority fixes the prices of the so-called "typical" semi-finished products (e.g. pig iron, steel, etc.), irrespective of whether they are sold or further processed by the enterprise.

It is due to the divergence of the *total* product-mix from the product-mix *on sale* that the price list of the central authority containing, say, several million items, may be complemented by perhaps ten-twenty million items on the enterprises' accounting list. It has not even come up in any serious form that the price authorities should extend their activities to the sphere of the enterprises' accounting prices. This, on the one hand, would not be technically feasible, and, on the other, would infringe upon the organization of production and work within the enterprise, which is an enterprise responsibility even under a directive system of planning. At the same time, the price authorities may start from the hypothesis that, when fixing the prices of the products on sale and of the typical intermediate products, they exercise regressive regulatory influence on the enterprises' accounting prices of the product nomenclature comprising what are called unfinished products.

Now we can also understand that the relationship between administrative price and enterprise accounting price primarily depends on what the *structure of the productive organization* is like. If the socialist country carries out an organizational integration, and especially if, as a result of consolidating enterprises, vertical productive units come into being, then this will result in a decrease in administrative prices. The situation is different if industrial production develops by way of specialization. Under such circumstances the role of administrative prices will increase as a result of the expansion of the sphere in which the production process is organized in the system of commodity and money relations.

From the point of view of the operational power of the administrative price system, *we also have to clarify what must be regarded a new product.*[73] Within certain limits, the enterprises are entitled to decide independently whether they turn out their products with unchanged or modified technical parameters. Modification of the technical parameters does not change the intended use of the product, but improves or deteriorates its use value. *Changes in qualitative factors* do not necessarily ensure the marketing of the new product. Characteristic of a wide range of products on sale is the fact that when a given product is marketed in a non-standard quality, the administrative price will be modified either by a surcharge or a price allowance.

In setting the administrative prices of new products a difficulty arises first of all from the fact that the current prices were originally set according to the productive conditions of a previous period. The price formation of new products must be effected in a systematically developing national economy when the scope and pattern of production are in a process of change, when new productive branches come into being, new enterprises join in production and others are reorganized.

One possible solution starts from the distinction between *products for a new purpose and those widening the assortment*. In the former case technical pre-calculation, in the latter *differential technical pre-calculation adjusted* to specific characteristics differing from those of related products constitute *the basis for price formation*. In the first case, the price is made up of the individual prime cost, in the second, of the prices of related current products by way of a proportionate calculation. If an enterprise turns out a product for a new purpose it may charge its actual prime cost and, under certain conditions, extra profit. It is on the producer price thus formed that the consumer price is based. If an enterprise turns out a new product widening the assortment, it must conform to the prices of related products, which means that it is not to get either into a more or into a less favourable situation than when it produced the old varieties. And if the enterprise turns out such products for the first time, a differential calculation must be applied, by which the enterprise compares its own price calculation with that of an enterprise

[73] Csikós-Nagy, B.: *A szocialista árképzés* (Socialist Pricing). Budapest, 1961.

regularly manufacturing the related products. Consequently, if the conditions of production for the enterprise starting the production of such goods are below the average level, the price cannot cover even the enterprises' prime costs.

In order to apply such a price formation system, it is necessary to specify the *criteria of qualifying the new product*. This is no difficult task. The following may be qualified as products for new purposes: (a) goods that create or satisfy novel needs, in the initial period irrespective of the quantity or value planned to be produced, (b) durable consumer goods which are substantially different in their design from those produced domestically, (c) products intended as substitutes for imported goods to be manufactured in large batches or on a large scale for the first time in the country, (d) natural or synthetic raw materials not yet used in production, (e) first varieties of goods manufactured from synthetic raw or intermediate materials not yet used, (f) means of production which, regarding the technical standard of the industrial branch concerned, are new, etc.

The following may be qualified as *new products widening assortments*: (a) varieties of products already manufactured before, which differ from current varieties in the quantity or quality of the material embodied in them, or in size, (b) varieties conforming to fluctuations in demand, whims of fashion or seasonal changes, varieties which differ from those already in use in their finish (style, decoration, etc.), (c) varieties which, as a result of changes in the materials used (components, accessories), in the technology applied in production or for similar reasons differ in respect of modernity and utility from comparable products already in circulation.

What accounts for the different methods of price formation for products for new purposes and new products widening assortments? Primarily the fact that in the case of the former products there are no related products with which unambiguous cost accounting comparisons could be made. This is only possible if the product in question has already been regularly imported before. But this price does not generally provide a reliable basis for comparison because it is usually too high. It is only natural that a retail-price policy sets relatively high prices for typical imported goods, in the case of which imports are justifiable because domestic production has not yet attained in a given branch the development level necessary to produce the product for which there is a social demand. A high consumer price serves here the aim of preventing the formation of price relations in which the product in question can only be manufactured domestically at a loss.

But the *consumer also reacts differently* to the prices of new purpose and new-assortment products. In his judgement, products designed for the same use but of a different variety must conform to the already known price relations, and he considers it as a hidden price rise if the price of the new product shows an upward deviation from them. The same applies to new purpose products if related products have already been imported regularly. And if this is not the case, the price relations become known when the price of the new product is set.

Moreover, the effect of prices on the manufacturing enterprises must be taken into account differently in the case of new purpose and new-assortment products. In the former case, owing to the lack of production experience and many other factors, temporary extra costs will arise, and it is reasonable to stimulate their introduction. The situation is different in the case of new assortment goods. It must be prevented, on the one hand, that the established and regulated order of production should be "distorted" by products of a new assortment, and enterprises with relatively unfavourable production conditions should increase their returns by introducing new varieties. On the other hand, it would not be wise to put at a disadvantage those enterprises which are compelled by commercial orders to change their accustomed product-mix. The method of differential cost calculation also makes it possible to take into account the production conditions in pricing new varieties in the same way as in setting the prices of all other products.

There are *certain differences* in the practice applied by the socialist countries in the price formation for new products. There are differences in two respects between socialist countries adopting an administrative price system:

(a) in defining the concept of a new product and

(b) in the time of the validity of prices set for the first time. For a product to be qualified as new, *stricter or looser* criteria may be set. If price policy starts from the requirement of *price stability*, it is designed to prevent, by detailed specifications and formulations, that the tendency of hidden price rises and of changes in the product-mix meant to increase prices may arise. In such cases attention is paid not only to confining the introduction of a new variety to changes approved by the consumer too, but also to limiting the special interest of enterprises in introducing it. Looser criteria are applied by countries where changes in the *product-mix are regarded as a matter of reaction to technical development and to changes in fashion*, where a special interest in effecting these changes prevails as a general principle. The concomitant speculative motive of product replacements is considered as a tolerable phenomenon which resolves, to some extent, the rigidity of the administrative price system and improves the regulatory function of price.

The price of a new product set for the first time may be regarded as (a) a *temporary price* to be established on the basis of costs measured in mass production, (b) an *initial price*, in which case the prices adapted to the various stages of the life cycle of the product are fixed in advance, (c) a *final price* which, integrated into the price system, changes within the limits of a general (or partial) price rearrangement. The latter is the method that can best be generalized in practice under an administrative price system. This is so because it may give rise to various contradictions if prices of certain goods within the group of related products are frozen while the prices of others are subject to changes. Therefore, the practice is increasingly adopted that goods which are technologically obsolete or out of fashion are sold out at a discount.

Fixed price is not the only possible manifestation of a state administrative price system. *Price formation may also be regulated by administrative price forms of a looser nature*. Worth mentioning are among them, maximum prices, protective prices and guiding prices.

1. *Price maximization* is applied, as a rule, in the interest of price stability. It is assumed that, unless price movements are stopped, the inflationary tendency will gain momentum, and this process can be put an end to by maximizing prices. It is for this reason that maximized prices are often called "stop" prices. And that is why price-stop measures are considered price freezing. This, however, is at best a tendency but not the whole truth. *It is price fixing that means price* freezing because it makes price changes impossible unless by way of state regulation. But a maximized (stop) price can change only downwards. However, can a stop price decrease if its very introduction is aimed at preventing further price increases? Yes, it can. It is not only in principle that price maximization makes price reductions possible. Even in a national economy faced with equilibrium difficulties there may arise situations which can be brought into alignment with demand only by price reductions. We only need to think of rapidly perishable foodstuffs, industrial articles exposed to changes in fashion and to technological obsolescence. If the producer wants to evade the risk of freezing his stocks, or wishes to solve the reorganization of production by a rational utilization of his productive capacities, he is necessarily interested in selling his old products at a discount.

In general, it must be emphasized: if direct administrative price regulation is needed in order to curb inflation, price maximization is a more suitable method of doing this than price-fixing. Inflation is not simply a price increase, a rise in the price level is *accompanied by a regular change in relative prices*. The market revaluates the products day by day not only at an unchanged but also at a rising price level, in the system of inter-product relations. The market sustains, on the one hand, the equilibrium of supply and demand, and, on the other hand, orientates economic decisions by means of changes in relative prices. This is market rationality, which must be made use of under a socialist system of economic management. Inflation weakens market rationality but does not put an end to it. Therefore, efforts must be made to ensure *that state price regulation takes up the struggle against inflation by preserving, to the greatest possible extent, the role of price as a signalling system*.

2. *Protective price is a means of stopping price movement in a downward direction*. Here it is not price stability but *production stability* that is the governing principle of price policy. Several considerations may lead the government to apply a *protective price* in the interest of production. A classical case in point is the protective price set for typical market products of *agriculture*, a price by setting which the government wishes to provide security for the producer. *Price guarantee* creates specific relations between the producer and the state budget depending on whether the protective price does or does not set the lower limit to market price movements. There may arise a market situation in which the market price is lower than the protective price. Such situations can only be prevented if the government does not simply undertake price guarantees but also regulates demand by its intervention purchases. To put it in other words: the government (or the marketing board acting on its behalf) does not make purchases below the protective level, or, in the case of oversupply, it limits its purchases to the extent which ensures that the price does not drop below the protective price level. However, price guarantee in that sense presupposes that the government is able to realize the volume of commodities thus purchased in its productive and trade organizations. It is a simple compensation for the price loss from budgetary funds if the government does not intervene in the market or cannot, or does not want to, prevent the market price from falling below the protective price.

The two possible ways of providing price guarantee also make it clear to us why the consumer reacts positively to a pure price guarantee, and negatively to state interventions aimed at maintaining prices. In the former case, the consumer enjoys the advantages of low market prices which, in the latter case, are cancelled out by additional state revenues. But, in fact, state purchases made in the interest of price maintenance give protection to the producer at the expense of the consumer of "to-day" so that he may also buy products "tomorrow". When making purchases explicitly with the aim to protect production, the government comes into the possession of stocks which it temporarily does not need. It makes use of the stocks thus obtained (stocks that can be stored, preserved and processed, etc.) to ensure that it may protect tomorrow's consumer against the producer in case the changed market situation favours the supply side.

Three forms of the protective price as generally applied in *industry* are worth special attention: (1) Owing to the limited competitiveness of production, *protection against the competition of imports* to be effected by import levies and, occasionally, by taxes complementing them. (2) The lower limit of certain industrial articles, which *constitutes protection for producers against trade*. Here the lower limit is meant to indicate that every time the trade wants to conclude a contract for a given variety of a product group with a wide assortment only at a price below the protective price, then the producer may refuse it. In a socialist society this has primarily a moral importance. Protective price means here the limit below which a price may oust a variety from production. (3) When the government subsidizes consumption, that is, sets deficit prices for the consumer, it also fixes the price *which is justifiable for the producer*. This can also be regarded as a sort of protective price since the government wishes to prefer consumption, in a way that supply and demand should be in an equilibrium position at the subsidized price. This, however, makes it necessary for the producer to be given price protection, which makes him interested in maintaining and even expanding production.

3. *Guiding price is a specific instrument to limit market-price movement in the interest of price stability*. Its possible variants are the following:

– price maximization specifically affecting the representative (preferred) products within a product group. It is based on the assumption that fixing the prices of selected representative products (basic, guiding, master products) will exercise an impact, within the given product group, on the price level of those products for which otherwise no direct price-fixing is applied;

– fixing the price level of product groups renders the free price movement of actual products possible on the assumption that a levelling out will eventually take place;

– fixing the price level of individual products, which makes it possible to change seasonally the price of a given product on the assumption that in the turnover of a given period the guiding price will assert itself as an average price.

Mixed Price Mechanism

Now we have come to discuss a novel and not sufficiently clarified problem of planned price formation. What should (or rather could) be the system of price regulation in a socialist economy if economic policy wishes price to be a *signalling system* in economic decisions? Obviously, such a role can be played by price only in a mechanism in which it acts as an economically determined equilibrium price. Therefore, we are focussing our attention now on a price regulation system conforming to a planned market control.

The problems of planned price formation in the mechanism of a directive system are easy to define. Its aim is to put into effect an administrative price regulation on the widest possible scale. To attain this aim, price administration is ready to go to all lengths of formalities. It even regulates, by issuing price lists, such service fees (e.g. flat maintenance) whose observance or violation cannot possibly be checked. Yet, what is clear here is the expectation of a price policy deduced in a logical way from the requirement system of economic management.

But what is the exceptation of price policy in the model of a controlled market economy? With absolute certainty only two statements can be made: (1) Expectation of a price policy cannot be met in the system of indirect price regulation, market price automatism cannot be reconciled with the social norms compulsory in a socialist system of economic management. It is for objective reasons that direct price regulation is needed. (2) Under the conditions of a controlled market economy, the administrative fixing of prices follows not from the essence of the system of economic management but from the expedience of a given market situation. Consequently, administrative regulation of prices is compatible with a controlled market economy but an indiscriminate application of the method is not.

The body of knowledge provided by *non-Marxist price theories* may prove very useful but is by far not sufficient for solving the problem satisfactorily. These theories based as they are on the hypothesis of balanced development and dependent, in the system of market forms, on the number of those operating in the market, or on the nature of commodities placed on the market, only reveal the peculiarities of price movements. We can get acquainted with those features that are the concomitants of competitive, monopolistic and oligopolistic markets, resp. of the market of standardized and differentiated products.[74] It was in reliance on this body of knowledge that among the economists of the socialist countries the view took shape that the principal requirement of creating an economically determined price under socialism is to ensure such market relations in which the market "disciplines" the enterprises. This requirement was formulated as follows: competition must be institutionalized, and the sellers' market must be changed into a buyers' market, such relations must be brought about in which demand lags somewhat behind supply, where, therefore, marketing does cause difficulty.[75]

However, the substitution of a "mixed" price mechanism for the "administrative" price system is meant to be a reference to it that market price mechanism is no realistic alternative to an overall administrative price fixing; the former cannot be brought into alignment with the requirements or planned development. We must be aware, among other things, of the following: (1) In an economy with high foreign-trade sensitivity, where the domestic market is narrow, the alternatives of buyers' and sellers' markets arise under peculiar conditions because, when production substantially exceeds domestic demand, the market situation in relation to actual products can only be determined as a function of exports and imports. (2) In price regulation it is impossible to ignore such tendencies of planned development which are expressions of production tensions in fields that change as a function of time. (3) In socialist economic policy there are elements which find expression in concrete prices, when, consequently, it is exactly the essence of economic policy to prevent, or allow changes in the price of given goods only on the basis of a political decision. (4) Price stability is regarded as a basic issue by the socialist countries. They can only accept a price policy which provides the guarantee that the price movement is kept within limits previously planned.

Thus, in relation to the transition from an administrative price system to a mixed type of price mechanism, the question arises first of all *how far reliance can be placed on monetary regulators in the field of price stability*. It is hardly questionable how great an importance is attached to an appropriate budgetary and monetary policy under the conditions of a planned market

[74] Bain, J. S.: A Note on Pricing in Monopoly and Oligopoly. *American Economic Review*, No. 2, 1949. Enke, S.: Profit Maximization under Monopolistic Competition. *American Economic Review*, No. 2, 1941. Kaysen, C.: Dynamic Aspects of Oligopoly Price Theory. *American Economic Review*, No. 42, 1952. Morgenstern, O.: Economics and the Theory of Games. *Kyhlos*, No. 4, 1949. Robinson, J.: *The Economics of Imperfect Competition.* London, 1954.

[75] Péter, Gy.: *op.cit.*

regulation, nor is it disputable what a significant role the exchange-rate policy plays in stemming the import of world-market inflation. If given an appropriate role in state regulation, financial regulators may ensure a relative stability of money value. But *price stability and the stability of the currency are not identical concepts*.

Though the measure of increase in the price level is the principal indicator of the deterioration of the value of money, but the *permissible* measure of a rise in the price level is not entirely independent of the products (services) it affects, and of the degree of its dispersion (changes in price relations). What must clearly be understood is simply this: when a price rise is constant, it becomes a general, national affair and gains, as such, a meaning detached from financial policy. Not only money but *price, too, has its own laws of movement*. These laws of price movement operate by means of credit expansion and are known as the characteristics of the inflationary process.

We may start, in principle, from the consideration that while the government regulates incomes in accordance with the requirements of equilibrium, there is no need for administrative price regulation beyond the extent required by the assertion of the government's incomes policy. *In practice, however, the administrative control over market prices must be effected to such an extent and in such forms as required by price stability*: If we consider relative price stability an annual increase of the price level by a few per cent, the starting hypothesis will also objectively regulate the time-table and direction of putting into practice government price policy. When the government pursues such a price policy, then it considers expedient and even objectively necessary all price-fixing measures that, in its judgement, are needed to prevent an inflationary tendency. By reacting to such situations, this price policy prevents, on the one hand, the danger of the emergence of such tendencies and, on the other, becomes a system of information needed to supervise economic policy. When, in order to prevent an inflationary tendency, market prices must be controlled administratively, this will necessarily lead to disequilibria in the commodity relations of the market. This is easy to understand, as in such cases prices will prevail which are not applied to meet the requirements of maintaining an equilibrium, but to assert the principle of price stability. This may lead to a partial shortage of commodities, to quality deterioration of products and difficulties in distribution. But these problems, if they temporarily arise, are easier to bear and overcome than the weakening of the process of exercising control over inflation.

Looked upon in this way, administrative price regulation, adopted with a view to countering inflationary tendencies, can also be regarded as an objectively necessary concomitant of a controlled market mechanism, which is applied, as the case may be, in more or less intensive forms. This ensures for economic policy a higher degree of stability and, first of all, makes it possible to solve the tasks of economic development by mobilizing the forces of production more effectively. Thus, what is involved here is simply the fact that the *demand-expanding policy of the government*, even if applied with a due consideration to the market equilibrium, *necessarily brings about a demand pressure on the market*. This pressure must first be warded off by price regulation, then by an increase in supply or by a certain constraint on demand to restore an equilibrium situation. This is, by the way, the *problem of bottlenecks*, which every rapidly developing country is faced with, and in which an adequate solution can only be provided by government intervention at appropriate points of the economy, among other things, by intervention in price formation. It is for this reason that a conscious attempt to abolish bottlenecks is the essence of any stabilization policy. Without this, all measures can be effective only temporarily.

We have come to the conclusion that, under certain conditions, the government must also resort to directly controlling prices even under a controlled market mechanism, that it must apply the methods of a direct administrative price regulation. To put it in another way: a vigorously developing national economy necessarily has a *mixed type of price mechanism*, in which price movements can only take place within limits that are set in an administrative way. The administrative limitation of the market price can take effect in different systems of price stabilization. It was the debate on this question of the Hungarian economic reform of 1968 that analysed most extensively the problems of a mixed type of price mechanism.[76]

Some of the economists started from the assumption that, in the interest of attaining the desired degree of price stability, *it is expedient to apply, in the lowest and highest phases of social production, control over price formation by methods of administrative price regulation*. They deemed it desirable to maintain fixed administrative prices of the most important industrial raw ma-

[76] Preparing the 1968 Hungarian economic reform, a committee, headed by the author, elaborated the "guiding principles for transforming the price system and the price mechanism". Bakonyi, A., Erős, Gy., Esze, Zs., Fenyő, I., Feszler, L., Gadó, O., Hoch, R., Jávorka, E., Kainer, Gy., Madarassy, A., Mikósdi, Gy., Sándor, S., Somhegyi, N., Tarnóy, L., Vallus, P., Vigh, H., Wessely, V. contributed to the committee's work.

terials or intermediate products in the lowest phase of production as well as of prime necessities in foodstuffs. In the highest phase, that is, in the case of industrial finished products (manufactures) it was considered expedient to ensure administrative price regulation in the form of maximum prices. This means that the only binding factor governing the commodity relations of the industrial and non-industrial sectors – except the necessities of life (primarily foodstuffs) – is the setting of an upper limit to price formation below which the price is a matter of agreement between producer and consumer. According to this, price formation for intermediate industrial products and component parts manufactured on a co-operation basis, etc. can be allowed without any government intervention since the activity of the pricing authorities can be confined to cases when pricing problems cannot be settled in a normal way within the system of commodity relations. A distinction between the forms of regulating the prices of raw materials, intermediate and finished products is based on the following considerations:

– The stability of the price level should be established through fixed prices of raw materials. Changes in value relations of the extractive industries producing these goods are slower, and taking them into account at irregular intervals does not cause any substantial disadvantage;

– Maximization of the prices of industrial finished goods (manufactures) arises out of the principle of consumer price stability, and provides in fact an assistance to trade in its price negotiations with industry;

– The substitution of calculation guidelines for the administrative pricing of semi-finished products (semi-manufactures) – which is usually taken into account when decisions are taken on price questions – makes it possible to prevent price rigidity from putting obstacles in the way to co-operation within the industry, and to create all possible conditions for the organization of production by rapidly and independently adapting it to new, modern processes; it helps the industries to adjust themselves appropriately and immediately to rapid changes in value relations, that is, that economic calculations are always made in accordance with the prevailing circumstances.

Other economists held the maximization of prices of the end products not to be an appropriate method. They thought that in the case of a "scarcity economy" maximized price functioned as a fixed price. In addition, the price maximization of the end products might lead to serious difficulties as the effect of the price movements of semi-finished products could not be taken into account for the price setting of finished products. In their view, it would be sufficient to fix prices administratively only in the lower phases of the economy, in the field of strategic raw materials, while in other phases of production, and in the case of the end products, the free movement of prices were allowed. The fixing of raw material prices would ensure the desirable price stability, while free price formation in the phases of intermediate products and the end products would promote the emergence of a production pattern better suited to actual necessities.

There were again economists who maintained that the *fixing of raw material prices was not desirable, at least not in respect to imported goods*. Conceivable, in their view, would be a system in which the price of basic materials was fixed only if the reasons for it were given (domestic production with a relative cost stability, imports fixed over a considerable time both in volume and price). If these conditions did not prevail, it would be expedient to fix the prices of the products of the manufacturing industry instead of freezing the prices of basic materials. It ought to be stipulated, they said, that changes in the world market prices should have a bearing on domestic demand. The effect of world market prices should assert itself in the lower phases of production.

There were economists who said that the *stabilization of the prices of end products was not sufficient*. They argued that in view of the monopolistic organization and the scarcity character of the economy, the free prices of raw materials and semi-finished products would unavoidably undermine the stability of the price system of the end products.

Accepting the requirement of a more flexible consumer price formation and wishing to prevent the rise in the consumer price level, some economists suggested that *several varieties of poor-, medium- and good-quality products should be selected in each product group.* Their prices should be set administratively, and the producers should be compelled to fully satisfy the needs of the domestic trade at all times in respect to the products selected in this way. They supposed that the fixed prices of selected goods of the product group would also affect the prices of other assortments as the consumer would not buy at too high prices such products the demand for which could satisfactorily be met by comparable products that are available at prices set at a lower level.

From the Hungarian debate on prices the following statements on a flexible price mechanism have emerged as a majority opinion:

(a) A flexible price mechanism presupposes the reaction of industrial producer prices to changes in production and market conditions. However, in the interest of a relative stability of the price level it is necessary to limit price movements. This can, in general, be solved by fixing prices. But if price-fixing is not to render the price system too rigid, then it should be carried out within a relatively narrow sphere. If the prices of raw materials are fixed, then administrative price regulation will operate within a relatively narrow sphere, but its effect on price stability will assert itself in practically every production phase. Therefore, it *is reasonable to fix the prices of crucial raw materials* in all fields where the production costs remain, as a rule, relatively constant.

Another group of raw materials, whose inputs change comparatively more frequently, needs a different evaluation. Enterprises using these raw materials are interested in experiencing, through their production costs, the input changes of these raw materials, and they should take these experiences into consideration in their decisions on utilizing them. On the other hand, it would not be desirable if changes in these raw material prices brought about large-scale changes in industrial prices.

Therefore, it is correct to let the changes in raw material inputs be transmitted in the form of price changes into those production phases in which the use of these raw materials is of basic importance. But the price must be fixed in the particular phase from which the raw material already processed is channelled into many enterprises of several industrial branches, or where it gets into the production cycle of some processing enterprises only as a subsidiary or auxiliary material. In such cases it is not desirable that changes in raw material prices should weaken price stability.

A deviation from administrative price regulation may be allowed in the case of raw materials which are neither in the lower nor in the upper production phases significant factors of production.

(b) For products used within the sphere of production, i.e. *designed for further processing, it is desirable to apply free prices*. This makes it possible to attain that price rigidity does not put any obstacle in the way of realizing production co-operation, to adapting prices automatically to new, modern methods, to changes in value relations taking effect immediately. The price-level raising effect of the free-price mechanism introduced in this sphere is obviously restricted, on the one hand, by the fact that the monopolistic character of manufacturing these commodities is more limited, allowing even a certain degree of competition, and, on the other hand, that the prices of the end products set, to a certain extent, limits to their price movements.

(c) Depending on the character of products, a differentiated price mechanism must be formulated and applied for *industrial end products*. From the point of view of the form of price regulation at least the following types of end products must be distinguished:

– products for public consumption,

– products for productive and non-productive investments,

– products not to be further processed in the productive sphere (goods for renewal, products for labour safety purposes and for social benefits, etc.) and goods for the consumption of public institutions,

– export products.

In forming the mechanism of producer prices for *consumer goods*, we must start from the fact that the turnover of these products has a genuine market character, but the requirement of a more flexible consumer price mechanism does not preclude a broader interpretation of price stability or the fixing of the price of consumer goods which decisively determine the living standard.

For products designed to be used for productive and non-productive investments, a freer price mechanism can safely be applied.

In respect to the *material consumption of public institutions and products not meant to be used for further processing in the productive sphere,* account must be taken of the fact that state enterprises and public institutions may create a substantial demand without reacting sensitively to the effects of a possible price rise in the free market and causing thereby a serious competition with the private purchases of the population. From the above statements the conclusion must be drawn that in this field administrative pricing can and must be made use of on a large scale.

Selective Price Policy

With the economic reform introduced in Hungary in 1968, part of the fixed prices have changed into maximum prices, and the movement of prices beyond or within certain limits has also been made possible for a fairly large number of goods and services. With the transition from an administrative price system to a mixed price mechanism, planned price formation is *ensured by a selective price policy*. It is perhaps, for the most part, the Hungarian model which renders a closer examination of the underlying principles of this selective price policy possible. At the beginning, the *choice of price forms* was about the only method of enforcing this selective policy. In other words, price relations under this mechanism were formed as a joint result of central administrative decisions and market factors. It was clear already at the preparatory stage of the economic reform that the planned development of production (structural policy) and the planned allocation of consumer goods (living-standard policy) were conceivable only by pursuing an active price policy. Identifying the *strategic points* at which price formation was to be released, partly or wholly, from the effect of market forces was considered the only task. In this respect three main hypotheses were developed:

1. *Administrative price regulation must be applied to a greater extent to consumer goods than to the means of production (capital goods).* The price forms in the sphere of consumption were chosen with a view to ensuring guaranteed prices for such goods and services on which a consumer with an average income spent 50 per cent of his total expenditure. Projected on living costs, this meant a price guarantee for 70 per cent of total consumer outlays.

In this decision, in addition to the primary interest in *consumer price stability*, another factor also had a role to play. Analyses preparatory to the economic reform, revealed a wide gap between consumer prices and inputs. It was stated that only *about 10 per cent of the commodity fund of the population was marketed at prices near the actual value.* In about 30 per cent of the consumer commodity fund consumer prices realized a substantial turnover tax, while about 60 per cent of the commodity fund was marketed below cost, or realized a net income below the average. In general, the prices of such products were low (or below cost) which constituted a substantial share in the consumption structure of people in the low-income brackets, and only the prices of such commodities were high which had no direct bearing on subsistence. Under such conditions, the economic reform of 1968 could not set the objective of placing consumer prices on a value basis. It was the idea that – with consciously observing the principle of price preferences – *input-proportionate consumer prices could be introduced within 10 to 15 years.* Consequently, a consumer price mechanism had to be created which unambiguously ensured that any price increase affecting living conditions could be effected only by central decisions, within the framework of a comprehensive living standard policy.

2. The second hypothesis was based on the idea that *administrative pricing should be applied on a wider scale to the sphere of co-operative agriculture than to the state industry.* The arguments put forward were as follows:

– The production pattern of industry is determined by the already existing plant structure, the process of a transformation of the macro-structure is largely regulated by the development policy laid down in the national plan by means of central control. Agriculture, on the other hand, is characterized by the specific structural feature that micro-economic decisions provide ample possibility to transform its production pattern. Following the abolition of compulsory deliveries, experiencies gained in the years 1957–1967 provided the evidence that an active price policy supplemented by financial regulators proved an extremely effective method of a plan-based control of the agricultural structure.

– The basic wages of industrial workers are guaranteed by the government even if a given enterprise works unprofitably. The income relations of agricultural workers, on the other hand, are regulated virtually by prices and taxes. Thus, for achieving production security, a *security of prices* is also needed, that is, that the desired price elasticity and price stability should exist side by side, in harmony with one another.

– A considerable proportion of agricultural produce is sold directly or indirectly on the world market. Apart from a few products, exports are marketed at a loss and need budget subsidy. Under such circumstances the formation of agricultural prices is of crucial importance also from the point of view of the state budget.

3. The third hypothesis required that in the *public sector of the national economy*, apart from transport and communications, market value judgements should take effect to the greatest possible extent, particularly in the *material improvement processes.* It was for this reason that the strategic points of administrative price regulation were specified in the state industry, in the spheres of power and basic materials. At the same time the starting point was the assumption that prices formed in industrial co-operation were regulated retrospectively by the prices of the end products.

These hypotheses have been practically confirmed by actual experiences. A supervision of the price forms was necessitated only by certain *structural equilibrium disturbances.* It has been realized that a structural disequilibrium – such as caused e.g. by overinvestment – cannot be eliminated under the socialist control system simply by price movements subordinated to the effect of market. Since the *transformation* of production at the macro-structural level is a matter of government planning and central distribution, and the allocation function of the price is limited, the *effect-generating mechanism of prices* cannot be endowed with non-existing features.

As also evidenced by experience, planned price formation cannot be ensured by price forms alone. From the very outset, the reconciliation of cyclical and inflationary price movements in the world market with price stability has compelled enterprises to create import price funds, and the influencing of free prices at *sensitive points* has necessitated *any price-rising intention to be* reported in advance to the authorities (early warning system). But all this did not prove sufficient to maintain price stability. The seller's advantage, i.e. price increase, also asserted itself if domestic orders did not engage the available capacities. In such cases enterprises either switched over to export production or offset their higher production costs by price increases. That is why it seemed to be necessary to lay down legal norms for enterprise behaviour in pricing.

Enterprise independence does not mean *unlimited* freedom. Governments, primarily for socio-political considerations, tried already at a historically early time to put obstacles to the practice of a business policy making use of the sellers' advantage in the market. Unjustified price rises, price usury in a war economy, and unfair competition in a peace economy have long been in the limelight of interest. "Fair price", "*reasonable profit*" have become economic categories as a result of social expectations, which compelled governments to enact appropriate legislation and determined the criteria on which the price policies of other countries were based. In today's capitalist countries this is laid down in the "restrictive trade practices acts", "antitrust laws", etc.[77]

Unjustified price rises, unfair profits are relevant categories in such socialist countries where price – within a limited range of products – can be formed in contractual agreements between enterprises. In the *administrative price system everything is subject to considerations* of price policy. Administrative prices contain in one case a loss, in another a profit well above what is called "reasonable". If the government fixes (freezes) the price, and makes the enterprises interested in reducing their costs, the profit rate becomes a yardstick to measure the efficiency of the enterprise. This is anyway a system of economic management in which price only finances simple reproduction, while the bulk of net social income realized in the price is centralized by the state budget, from which the needs of society as a whole are financed.

The situation is different if the socialist state activizes market mechanism, if the role of the market factors in price formation becomes effective and strengthens. Under such circumstances

[77] Meznerics, I.: *A gazdasági verseny jogi szabályozása* (Legal Regulation of Economic Competition). Budapest, 1965.

legislation in needed for regulating market competition and its conditions.[78] Legislation must promote competition, the taking of risks and of responsibility. But all this cannot justify an enterprise economy contrary to socialism and violating social interest. *In Hungarian legislation this is summarized in the system of the criteria of "unfair profit"* which says: Unfair is the profit if it is obtained by a price formed by *unfair practices*, that is, if the economic organization gains unfair profit by methods directly and seriously damaging social interest and violating the principles of socialist economy. It is worth noting that in determining unfair profit, the *magnitude of the profit itself realized in the price* can be a criterion. Thus, unfair profit can be established on the basis both of the way it is obtained and also of the rate of the profit itself.

Independently of the magnitude of the gain, unfair profit can be determined especially in the following cases:

– The productive unit itself brings about an unbalanced economic situation which makes it necessary to set higher prices. Thus, if the productive unit itself creates a monopoly position making possible a one-sided setting of prices by violating trade regulations, or by eliminating certain distribution channels or in any other way, or if the productive unit enjoys a monopoly position which prevents competition from unfolding, enabling it to charge exorbitant prices for its products meeting vital social needs.

– The productive unit chooses its assortment in such a way that the earlier lower-priced product demanded by the consumers disappears and instead of it the enterprise launches on the market another product at a higher price. The same applies to the case when it hampers the supply of relatively cheap but good-quality products or cheap mass consumption goods, or raises the prices of the latter without sufficient economic justification.

– The productive unit introduces to the market products of inferior quality, make-up and packaging at unchanged prices.

– The productive unit regularly reacts to any lasting rise in input prices (including foreign-trade prices) or costs by raising its selling prices, but does not react to a permanent decrease in its input prices (costs). Equally unfair is the surplus profit gained by the productive unit which sells its products at unchanged prices even if the prices of raw materials and components have

[78] GERBERDING, U.: Wirtschaftsvertrag zur Sicherung der planmäßigen Preisentwicklung. *Vertragssystem,* Nos. 1–2, 1969, Berlin. LIBÁNSKY, V.: Zmeny cen a hospodarske smlouvy (Price Changes and Economic Contracts). *Arbitrázni praxe,* No. 8, 1969, Prague.

dropped, though earlier, taking advantage of the spill-over effects of price rises, it always raised its selling prices.

– The productive unit sets or maintains a price by fraud, by misleading its customers, including the case when it deceitfully calculates a price or publishes false figures for its price formation in order to gain thereby illegal material advantages.

– The productive unit maintains an unchanged price, or does not decrease it proportionately though it enjoys a subsidy granted by central decree designed to protect the price level, or when its costs have decreased (owing e.g. to a tax allowance), including the case when the prices of state-subsidized products realize a high profit.

– The productive unit counterbalances a decline or loss of expected export receipts by increasing its domestic prices.

– The productive unit forms its output prices with due consideration to an announced rise in input prices and keeps them unchanged even if the price rise has not materialized.

– In the case of buying its materials and products at different prices the productive unit, disregarding the allowed or usual "price mixing" of the branch, sets its prices according to the highest input prices.

The productive unit pays out employee remunerations which greatly surpass the personal incomes usual in the trade concerned, or offsets its surplus costs arising from unused capacities by arbitrary price rises.

– The prices charged by the productive unit violate the normatives or guidelines concerning the method of price formation.

The productive unit sets or raises its prices by taking advantage of an emergency situation caused by an unforeseen disaster.

Price formation may result in unfair profit when the price of the product realizes a profit exceeding the rate of justifiable gain in such a way that an exorbitant price is set or asserted, the measure of which is in no proportion to the value or use value of the product. This may happen when setting the price of a new product, or raising an existing price.

A price is regarded as exorbitantly high if it is in no proportion with the utility and value of related or substitute products, and if it does not fit into domestic and international relations.

The profit realized in the price cannot be regarded as a gain surpassing the rate of justified profit in the following cases:

– If a product is put on the market at a price realizing higher than justifiable profit in order to provide funds for maintaining or reducing the prices of other products (price levelling).

– If this profit is realized in the price of a product manufactured as a result of an effective *investment* aimed at shaping an economical production structure.

– If it results, with price remaining unchanged, from *technical development*, management and production organization, or from other cost reductions without deteriorating of quality.

– If a *more up-to-date product* representing a higher level of technical development is produced, and if the customer is allowed to have a share in the economic result achieved.

– If the product *satisfies special requirements of fashion.*

– If the product meets *special* requirements of the buyers (finish, out-of-turn production, etc.) and no surcharge system is adopted in the trade concerned.

– In the case of *small-batch* production.

– If the productive unit operating at lower running costs realizes a high profit in its products, but sells them at competitive prices, that is, markets them at lower prices than those at which competitive products of inferior utility and use value are sold.

– If the profit derives from savings as against the normatives applied in forming administrative prices.

– If the domestic price of a product, which is also in demand abroad, is formed with due consideration of the export price, with a profit content higher than the usual average profit level of the trade concerned.

3. Price Supervision

Operative Market Supervision

Socialist price policy is aimed at a degree of organization which makes it possible both to supervise the observance of legal prescriptions and of the functioning of prices. All this finds expression in a price supervision interpreted in its widest sense.[79] The former is the *legal*, the latter the *economic* aspect of price supervision. The related tasks are solved by *operative market supervision*.

Market supervision can be defined in the following way: *a system of top-level measures or their preparation needed for the planned development of market processes in the knowledge of short-term factors influencing demand and supply as well as prices.* The content of market supervision is determined by the concrete system of economic control. *In the directive type of management system* price supervision extends, in the sphere of products circulated within the sector of state ownership, not over market relations, but over the observation of administrative prices and the functioning of the enterprises' self-accounting system. But even in the case of products circulated outside the sector of state ownership, market relations are paid special attention to in this system of control. *In the system based predominantly on economic instruments*, market supervision embraces commodity exchange as a whole.

Market supervision – as interpreted e.g. in Hungary – is *markedly distinguished from the planning activities of the national*

[79] DERGACHEV, N.: Sovershenstvovat kontroly za tsenami (Perfectioning Price Control). *Sovetskaya torgovlya*, No. 5, 1969, Moscow. JANCAR, V.: Ceny potrebuji kontrolu. Ucty mistniho a druzstevniho stavebnictvi ped lupou (Prices Demand Supervision. On the accounts of local and co-operative construction). *Hospodárské noviny,* No. 46, 1969, Prague. KUZNETSOV, A.: Ukreplyat gosudarstvennuyu distsiplinu tsen (Strengthening State Price Discipline). *Ekonomicheskaya Gazeta*, No. 24, 1970, Moscow. LIBÁNSKY, V.: Kontrola cen a dusledky peruseni predpisu o cenách (Price Control and Consequences of Unfair Behaviour). *Arbitrázni praxe*, No. 9, 1970, Prague. LIBERMAN, F.: Neobkhodimo Soblyudat gosudarstvennuyu distsiplinu v ustanovlenii i primenenii tsen (State Discipline to be Observed in Setting and Applying Prices). *Soyuznaya yustitsiya*, No. 23, 1969, Moscow. PETROV, G. V.: Kontroly za tsenami v torgovlye (Price Supervision in Commerce). *Ekonomika*, No. 77, 1969, Moscow.

economy, or the supervision of plan implementation. Not included in market supervision are

– the analysis of medium- and long-term factors, or of the related decisions, further, even in their short-run aspects, such factors as

– investment and development policy,

– labour and wages policy and the resulting questions of the living-standard policy.

Performing the tasks of market supervision, however, requires that the organizations concerned should be adequately informed about the medium- and long-term decisions including the questions of investment, labour and living-standard policy. Furthermore, in the course of the examination of the short-term factors, and of the market processes in general, problems may arise which can only be solved by measures with effects extending over a longer period of time. As regards these problems, market supervision is confined to fact-finding, expert opinion and recommendations. Thus, in carrying out market supervision, the effects are examined that development policy, labour policy and living-standard policy exert on demand and supply and on price formation. From this it follows that the agencies of market supervision have the task to feed back the information gained from the market processes to the directive organizations with powers to decide on these questions.

Market supervision expresses the endeavour of economic policy to overcome the disturbances emerging in the course of planned development by *influencing the market factors, and not by a market-eliminating policy.* It is, after all, real processes that underlie the price problem. Prices only reflect them. The elimination of the market does not resolve the disturbing phenomena, only diverts them to fields that are difficult to control. It is market supervision interpreted in this way that makes us clearly understand the controlling function of the market in a socialist economy. It is, after all, the need for a planned price formation reconciled to market equilibrium that makes it imperative to introduce the continuous supervision of the short-term decisions of economic policy.

For the purposes of market supervision all kinds of information are equally important, which it evaluates on grounds of the effect the relevant economic phenomenon exercises on prices. The *peculiarity* of its information system lies in the way it approaches the problems. There are three hypotheses underlying that system: (1) Any price (administrative or free) functions as an equilibrium price unless its allocation function is suspended; this applies, for example, to rents, as in most socialist countries the turnover in flats is regulated by a central allocation system.

(2) All the information needed to prevent any "unplanned" price movements is available at the right time. (3) "Non-planned" price movements may be recognized in their concrete forms, and measures can be taken to overcome them in the short run.

In assessing the role of market supervision two circumstances must be taken into account: (1) Price stability is a *strict* political requirement. (2) Foreign trade cannot be liberalized *completely*. Transition from a mechanism operating with plan indicators to a system of management based on economic instruments takes place under circumstances when economic development is accompanied by disequilibria, and hence any planned price formation can only be ensured by effective price regulation. Consequently, in many cases it is only within the sphere of authority of economic policy that decisions can be taken by which unfavourable tendencies can be prevented, or the disturbing phenomena already in existence can be overcome.

In carrying out market supervision *it is necessary*, in the first place, *to be able to distinguish between the planned course of economic processes and the disturbances rooted in spontaneous market processes.* The possibility of meeting this requirement is provided by the system of indicators of the state plan of the national economy worked out on the macro-level. Yet, the two processes cannot be considered identical. Market supervision does not examine plan implementation, but the way in which demand-supply equilibrium can be maintained under planned price formation. Therefore, it also takes into account the development of processes deviating from centrally set plan indicators, or even promotes these processes by operative decisions if an equilibrium position reconciled to price stability can only be maintained in this way.

Market supervision makes use especially of two elements of the system of central plan indicators: *stock normatives* and *price-change indices.* This follows from the fact that in preventing market "irregularities", market supervision regards *stock analysis* as the main method of preparing the decision-making process; the same role is played by *price analysis* in qualifying already existing "irregularities". These are, of course, *not rigid rules.* The information system of a well-organized market supervision operates in such a way that price analysis – at least for products which are essential for price formation – can already be carried out at a time when prices are still in the process of planning, but such factors have already emerged which, without appropriate measures being taken, might start a price formation deviating from the plan, or which might cause supply shortages. Furthermore: stock analysis – apart from specific cases – is associated with price analysis, and vice-versa. Specific is, for example, the case when stocks decline because, owing to extraordinary weather conditions, deliveries are temporarily suspended. This case is not motivated by price changes, though it may give rise to price problems. Specific is, further, the case when the price of a typical import product rises in consequence of a rise in the import price. In such a case a decision can only be taken on whether a higher import price should be allowed to be transmitted, or import should be restricted.

Thus, for market supervision to be carried out in a purposeful way, *sufficiently detailed normatives of stocks and price plans are needed.* If all these preconditions for market supervision exist, the "irregularities" can be identified by comparing standardized and actual stocks in commodity turnover, and planned and actual price changes in price formation. Here we have arrived at a point where it is of special importance to *clarify* terms. An economy, if somewhat developed, has to do with millions of price items. This enormous number of prices is due to the great variety of products and, within each product group, to the range of assortment by size and quality, to the prices of the same sort of product differing according to the various relations in which they are marketed. The prices thus obtained are prices of definite products. It is these prices that are directly attached to the product materialized in a concrete form with a certain use value. Exchange in the sales process is effected by them. They determine the receipts and the payments to be made in a business deal. Legal disputes that may arise between the sellers and buyers are concerned with these prices. Price regulation is aimed at, and finds expression in setting such prices.

The commodities to be distinguished according to prices of definite products have, in the first place, to be *systematized.* This task is solved by an *uniform product list.* Products can be classified according to various viewpoints. Their systematization can be effected according to the origin of the materials used in the production of the goods to the use that is made of the product, and the way it is processed. Though the product lists of the various socialist countries are not of the same structure, but the principles applied in drawing them up have many features in common. The *Hungarian* product list arranges the products, within their classification according to the materials used in their manufacture, primarily on the basis of *production considerations,* of the similarity in their production technology, in the sequence of the stages of processing. Consequently, the products of a given branch of production follow each other in the product list in the sequence of the production or processing phases. Within individual groups, first *the products of a relative-*

ly simple technological processing, then the semi-finished, and finally the finished products are listed. The product list breaks down each product into individual products or varieties, according to quality and size.[80]

The uniform product list enables state planning to determine product and price movements. Products, the number of which runs into millions, cannot, of course, be handled centrally. Planning and statistics apply the method of aggregation. *They determine and analyse economic processes in the system of product groups and selected products.* It is the character of the individual product variety that determines at what depth of the decimal system of the uniform product list the "product group" can be found. The selection of concrete products is based on the consideration that certain products have a preferred significance from the point of view of product and price movements.

Thus, planning in physical terms sets up product-group balances, and within them balances of selected products. Similarly, the price plan is concerned with average prices, and within them the individual prices of selected products. It is on this that market supervision is based. Market supervision, however, cannot ignore individual phenomena. Even with a generally satisfactory stock of coal available, serious troubles may develop owing to the lack of certain sorts of coal since there is demand not for a product in general but for a certain variety in particular, and substitutability may have absolute and relative limitations. The same applies to *prices,* too. A change in the average price measured in an unchanged commodity structure may take place with individual prices changing in a different direction and to a different extent. A change in price relations is the natural concomitant of equilibrium price. In certain cases, however, it is exactly this that can give rise to irregular processes.

This means that *the analytical methods of market supervision are more sophisticated than those of planning.* The comprehensive planning of the national economy makes it unavoidable to use averages. Within the framework of market supervision there is a possibility of deeply analysing concrete interrelationships, as market supervision always concentrates on the "weak" points of the national economy; in its analyses, information both at macro- and micro-levels are synthesized in a timely form.

[80] Kürthy, P.: *Útmutató az egységes termék- és árjegyzék felhasználásához* (Guide for Using the Unified Product and Price List). Budapest, 1954.

Stock Analysis

The harmony of demand and supply is realized by the permanent movement of commodity stocks. Stocks of certain products increase from time to time, while those of others decrease. Thinking of emergencies, the government usually also keeps iron reserves of vitally important materials. This, too, contributes to the undisturbed commodity supply in such cases when demand exceeds supply, and it takes some time before production catches up with demand to meet actual needs, or before imports can be realized. Demand for certain sorts of products may also lag behind the targets envisaged, which will lead to a rise in stocks. Stocks smaller or greater than normal are equally worth attention. Low stocks may hinder continuous supply and involve the risk of shortages that may crop up sooner or later. Excessive stocks superfluously tie up economic resources and may lead to the danger of unsaleable products.

Disclosing the causes of changes in stocks calls for a thorough analysis. Stocks are determined by the character of intermittent production (e.g. in agriculture) and its seasonal nature (e.g. in the food-processing industry). But the intermittent character of consumption (e.g. fuels) and its seasonal nature (e.g. in clothing articles) are also decisive. A production drive is followed and a consumption drive is preceded by a natural stock build-up, while a production drive is preceded and a consumption drive is followed by a natural reduction of stocks. This is usually the case in countries which satisfy demand for such products not from well-phased imports, but wholly or primarily from domestic production. As in the latter case lower stocks do not involve the danger of commodity shortages, in the former case higher stocks do not mean overproduction. Therefore, stock changes in themselves do not mean anything. An investigation must be meant to separate natural stock changes from cases when there are irregularities behind the changes.

To carry out market supervision, the data of planning in physical terms and of materials statistics alone are not sufficient. *Enterprises usually signal the danger of expected commodity shortages* at a time when stocks are still sufficiently high and the commodity shortage can be prevented by appropriate measures (expansion of production or, in case this should not be sufficient, by imports). The system of recording delivery times, the fulfilment of contracts as well as of giving notice of expected delivery delays, etc. is the basis on which production is checked and adequate information is provided for a concerted decision-making mechanism of undisturbed commodity supply.

A decrease of stocks may develop from time to time in different fields and to a different extent either because supply lags behind the planned level, or because demand exceeds it. In respect of the planned expansion of *supply,* in the socialist countries most problems are caused by investments. Owing to the slow execution of new investment projects and to the delay in the reconstruction of plants, supply lags behind demand mostly where and when the plan reckons with new capacities starting to operate at a planned point of time. In such cases, the equilibrium of supply and demand can mostly be ensured only by increased imports; domestic equilibrium can possibly be established only in association with international disequilibria. It depends on the adaptability of supply whether *demand exceeding the planned target* causes a problem or not. Market supervision regards supply as adaptable if it can reach the level of demand in a few weeks or months, at any rate within a period of time in which the differential between smaller commodity supply and higher demand can be equalized by reserves. But even in the case of less elastic supply, imports may bridge the gap.

A commodity shortage cannot always be prevented by the rapid expansion of production or imports. Even with a good commodity supply there might be commodities which are temporarily either a complete lacking or of which there is a shortage of certain varieties. In such cases price measures or other steps of economic policy are taken depending on what need is met by the commodity in question, of what nature the shortage is, and to what causes it can be traced back. The measure of price policy to prevent an expected commodity shortage, i.e. a price rise, cannot be applied indiscriminately. An administrative price cannot perform the function of a daily equalization of supply and demand. Greater stability is desirable even in the sphere of free prices. The daily price movement of seasonal, rapidly perishable foodstuffs is rather an exception to the rule.

A sizable rise in the usual demand may be of a transitory character. If e.g. the population thinks that the government intends to take measures to restrict consumption, it will increase its purchases. It does the same if e.g. it anticipates a general or partial price rise or a devaluation of money. In such cases the normal course of market supply is disturbed not only by the fact that the consumers spend their incomes in a way different from the normal but especially because they may also use their savings, to a greater or lesser extent, for commodity purchases. But experience has shown that even though such phenomena do sometimes occur, they are usually short-lived and can be effectively offset if adequate stocks are available before the general symptoms of a commodity shortage make their appearance. It is obvious that the government, in order to counteract such phenomena, cannot apply price measures or other steps of its economic policy unless it had planned them anyway. Different from this in character is a temporarily high demand which emerges because a product is placed on the market which was *not available over a shorter or longer period.* Temporarily, there is an increased demand for such a product, and it takes some time before the demand is stabilized at the usual level. It would not be correct if the government resorted even to a temporary price rise in order to curb demand.

To raise the administrative price or to set limits to market price movements is justified only if the demand-supply disequilibrium seems to be a lasting one, or when, on the basis of the national economic plan, it can be predicted that the demand for a given product will surpass supply. But even then it is advisable to exert a restrictive influence on demand by the modification of the assortment and by a corresponding *price stratification.* In such cases the government does not take administrative price measures but leaves it to the enterprises to apply a price policy which is adjusted to the ruling market relations. But a change in the commodity assortment and the related price stratification do not always yield the desired results. This policy is successful only in the case of commodities the demand for which is decisively influenced by different varieties in the assortment. Moreover, it presupposes that the expected or already existing shortage is not of a very great extent. Otherwise, the commodity shortage can only be eliminated by a price rise or, more exactly, by changing the relative prices in favour of substitute products. Price stratification also involves a change in relative prices. While, however, the former applies to the varieties of a given type of product, the latter is used in the case of substitute products.

Stocks may increase either because the level of output surpasses the target envisaged in the plan, or because demand lags behind the planned level. In case production exceeds the plan target, or demand lags behind the plan, the government usually deliberates the possibilities of *exports.* The volume of commodities that is released from domestic demand does not usually cause any difficulty if it can be exported directly or in a modified assortment. The case is different, however, if the commodity, or the type of commodity that can be produced with the capacity thus released can only be converted at a great loss or not at all. Then the nature of analysis will change since the case may be an instance of uneconomical production.

Demand may assume smaller proportions than normal if the consumers believe that their purchasing power may grow. They take this course of action if they expect on a price cut. But this alone does not justify a price reduction unless the government really plans to take such a measure. Insecurity may also cause certain consumer strata to reduce their purchases to a minimum and rather to increase their savings in order to weather temporary income losses or income restrictions.

Different from this in character is the *temporarily low demand for a new product.* With the expansion of his social knowledge, the consumer makes use of his consumption fund differently from how he did at an earlier stage of his knowledge. Investigations have shown that the share of new products, especially those differing in their use from the old-established products, is smaller in the pattern of demand than it will be later when its utility has become generally known. Consequently, the unambiguous relationship between a commodity and price presupposes that the consumers are sufficiently knowledgeable about the utility of the given commodity. If this knowledge is not yet general, even with prices remaining unchanged, demand may substantially increase in the future. This increase may be especially great if society considers that commodity more suitable and relatively cheaper than those which it bought earlier, or if it recognizes in the product the possibility of meeting a need in the interest of which it is willing to restrict the satisfaction of other needs.

The government may deem it expedient to maintain the production level of such industrial goods the demand for which has lagged behind supply for a considerable time. In this case, however, the prices have to be cut.

The measures of economic policy taken in connection with increasing stocks have rested so far on the assumption that the government wishes to maintain the equilibrium between supply and demand, while leaving the purchasing power of the population unchanged, or, at least, without increasing it considerably. The situation is different when the government makes preparations to carry out a general or partial price reduction or an increase of wages. *In the time preceding such a course the build-up of stocks is a usual process.*

The case is again different in character, though – at least temporarily – identical in its effect on purchasing power, when the government allows outmoded or *outdated* stocks to *be sold at reduced price (*sales). Owing to changes in consumption patterns, fashions, technology, etc., it is unavoidable that goods without any defect in qualitity, yet difficult to sell are accumulated in the warehouses of trade. Though as far as their utility is concerned these goods represent full value, yet this value cannot be realized because, owing to new varieties, the demand for them has decreased or completely ceased. But the indifference of demand for these outmoded and outdated articles manifests itself only at a given level of consumer prices. As soon as their prices are reduced, the demand for them will get a boost. It is on this peculiarity of demand that the method of government price regulation is based, which promotes demand for unsold commodities – the production of which is discontinued – by setting reduced prices for them.

Price Statistics

Price statistics plays an important role in price supervision. At their conference held in 1973, the presidents of the price offices of CMEA countries discussed the questions of price statistics and the application of electronic computers in price statistics.[81] From their discussions the conclusion could be drawn that the notion of price statistics as used in the socialist countries is different from its interpretation in the market economies. This also follows from the fact that price statistics has to adjust itself to the requirements of planned price formation. In this connection it appears to be worthwhile to point to two features of price statistics: (1) Price statistics adjust itself to *categories* established in planned price formation. Such are: industrial producer price, agricultural procurement (purchase) price, price of capital goods, consumer price, foreign-trade price. (2) In the system of price categories not only changes in prices, in average prices and in relative prices are paid attention to, but investigations into the *price structure* (cost, profit, price) are also performed.

For the time being, price statistics cannot yet fulfil the requirements that it is expected to meet. In price statistics there are still "blank spots", that is, areas where prices and their changes are not registered. Here the question arises what the criterion is by which the existence of these "blank spots" can be determined. Obviously, this criterion can only be the construction of a general deflator, that is, of an *impilicit price index,* which presents a comprehensive, synthetic picture of price movements taking place in the national economy.[82] In certain

[81] RÁCZ, L.: Árstatisztikai módszerek és az elektronikus gépek árstatisztikai alkalmazása a KGST országokban (Methods of Price Statistics and the Use of Electronic Machines in Price Statistics in the CMEA Countries). *Statisztikai Szemle,* No. 2, 1974, Budapest.

[82] COPELAND, M. A.: *A Study of Money Flows in the United States*. National Bureau of Economic Research, New York, 1952.

socialist countries the elaboration of such a statistical indicator is in its experimental stage.

There are economists who deny the validity of a synthetic price index. In their view, price formation cannot be characterized by a comprehensive index.[83] We do not want to go into a detailed account of this debate. We are convinced that the practical use of an implicit price index can hardly be questioned, at least in one respect. This namely raises the demand, that various types of prices and prices in various sectors should be synchronized. And really one of the main deficiencies of today's price statistics lies exactly in the fact that representation in the various grades, and weights in the various phases, etc., are different. Therefore, it is impossible unambiguously to conclude from price statistics the effect on one another of import prices and domestic prices, producer prices and consumer prices, etc. To reveal the interconnections, special analyses, occasional surveys, etc. are needed. Thus, what appears to be perhaps most important is the creation of complexity in order to improve of price statistics.

In choosing the commodity pattern underlying the calculation of the price index three methods are generally applied. In the *Paasche* index the commodity pattern of the periods surveyed is taken to be decisive.[84] In the *Laspeyres* index changes in the price level are calculated by the weights of the base period.[85] The *Fischer index* is the geometric average of the two indices of different weighting.[86] These methods yield different results depending on changes in the commodity pattern. The use of all three methods is fruitful just because they make the examination of changes in the commodity pattern possible. When price statistics is used as a tool to supervise planned price formation, it is obviously the commodity pattern constituting the basis for the price plan that has to be used. If, however, emphasis is placed on the quantification of socio-economic effects, then the Paasche index gives the best information since it characterizes price movements in the current commodity pattern.

[83] ERDŐS, P.: *Adalékok a mai tőkés pénz, a konjunktura ingadozások és a gazdasági válságok elméletéhez* (Contributions to the Present Capitalistic Theory of Money, of Cyclical Fluctuations and of Economic Crises). Budapest, 1966.

[84] PAASCHE, H.: Über die Preisentwicklung der letzten Jahre nach den Hamburger Börsennotierungen. *Jahrbücher für Nationalökonomie und Statistik*, No. 23, 1874.

[85] LASPEYRES, E.: Hamburger Warenpreise 1851–1863 und die kalifornisch-australischen Goldentdeckungen seit 1848. *Jahrbücher für Nationalökonomie und Statistik*, No. 3, 1864.

[86] FISCHER, I.: *The Making of Index Numbers*, Boston and New York, 1927.

Quite understandably, the consumer price index is in the focus of interest in the system of price statistics.[87] At an experts' conference held in March 1973 under the auspices of the European Economic Committee questions of the statistical integration of the price and volume index were discussed. At this conference the view was voiced that in the coherent system of value, price and volume index consumption cannot be characterized satisfactorily. According to this view, the rise in the volume of consumption is accounted for partly by an increase in the *quantity* of goods consumed, partly by the way the *quality* pattern of consumption changes, usually in such a way that the share of higher-quality, more expensive products increases. The former can be called the quantitative, the latter the qualitative component of the increment in consumption. Therefore, if we are to characterize changes in the volume of consumption, it is expedient to keep quantitative and qualitative factors apart. After this conference, the Central Statistical Office in Hungary carried out this calculation for the period 1955–1972. Its calculations were based on the fact that

– the *quantitative index* of the volume index is the quotient of quantitative figures representing the consumption in different periods of time of groups of products comprising quantities expressed in terms of a common unit of measure and put to the same use,

– and its *qualitative* index is the change in pattern taking place among products with differing qualitative parameters.

And further, the starting-point in its calculations was the recognition that changes in average prices jointly express

– the price change (change in the prices of products placed on the market) and

– the qualitative change in pattern which takes place among products treated independently in the price index.

Consequently, the qualitative index is the quotient of the average-price index and of the price index. Interpreting the qualitative price index in this way, we get the following picture:

[87] BURGEANU, C.: Teoris indicilor si sistemul de indici si preturilor in economica tarii noastre (Index Theory and the System of the Price Index in the Economy of Our Country). *Probleme de Preturi*, No. 9, 1970, Bucharest. HESKE, G.: Die Weiterentwicklung des Systems statistischer Informationen über die Dynamik der Industriepreise ab 1971. *Statistische Praxis*, No. 10, 1970, Berlin. SERBAN, G. – DUMITRESCU, V. V.: Preturi si indici de preturi (Prices and the Price Index). *Revista de Statistica*, No. 3, 1970, Bucharest. SLAVOV, D. – MEDNEV, K.: Nyakoji problemi na indexite na cenite na debro (Some Problems of the Consumers Price Index). *Statistica*, No. 5, 1969, Sofia.

Rise in the volume of per-capita product consumption by components

Items	Annual average growth rate (percentage) of per-capita volume				
	1956–1960	1961–1967	1968 1971	1972	1956–1972
Rise in volume					
owing to a rise in quantities	4.9	2.8	3.9	2.6	3.7
owing to a change in quality composition	0.6	0.6	1.6	0.5	0.8
Total	5.5	3.4	5.5	3.1	4.5
The role of change in quality composition (percentage)	11	18	29	16	18

In Hungary, since 1968, the measuring of the consumer-price level in several product groups (where the assortment is wide and product replacement is fast) has been based on the average prices of product varieties being in a relationship of close substitution, on the so-called narrowed-down (I.) average price. In addition, the Central Statistical Office also keeps track of the qualitative changes in average prices in their wider sense (II.). Here are a few examples illustrating the deviations that the range of products interpreted in a narrower or wider sense may cause in the movement of average prices:

Changes in the average prices of selected related articles

	Average price index in 1970	
	I.	II.
Cheese	102	104
Bakery products	100	105
Cotton fabric	99	101
Woollen and man-made fabric	101	112
Silk fabrics	96	102
Men's suits	103	113

In the case of mass products regularly replacing one another in production, and also of single goods produced in a sequence, it is extremely difficult, almost impossible, to assess to what extent the price ratio can be reduced to differences in use value, and to what extent it may express a change in the price level. We cannot exclude the possibility that, when prices rise as a result of general economic conditions this tendency also asserts itself with single products and product replacements which generally cannot be taken into consideration by the measuring of the price level. In this the assumption is also expressed that the rate of the rise in the price level is somewhat greater, and therefore the annual growth rate of the national product, as well as the rate of improving living conditions is smaller – perhaps on a world-wide scale – than indicated by statistics.

The price index is needed for *price analyses conducted to achieve various aims.* Their most important fields of application are the *exchange rate, "price scissors" and real income calculations.* Such analyses set specific requirements for price index calculation, primarily because it must be carried out in a commodity pattern that is in line with the aims concerned.

The socialist countries carry out exchange rate computations in a differentiated system. Its typical manifestations are the *foreign-trade price co-efficient and the purchasing power parity.* The former is an index of foreign-exchange earnings measured at producer prices in the export commodity pattern, the latter is an index measured at consumer prices in the pattern of "diplomats' basket". Some socialist countries also measure currency parity at producer prices in the *production structure,* and in addition to purchasing power parity, they also measure *wages parity.* In the first case, they seek an answer to the question how average efficiency measured in the export commodity pattern relates to the average efficiency measured in the production structure. In the latter case, they investigate what the divergence from purchasing power parity is if the national currency is measured in the consumption pattern of the working people. In such a case, house rents are substituted for hotel prices and food prices (charges for public catering), for restaurant prices, and account is also taken of the social benefits that every citizen of the state is entitled to.

The choice of the commodity pattern in the case of purchasing power parity takes place in a specific way. There is a definite relationship between consumption (consumption pattern) depending on production conditions and other economic factors, on the one hand, and relative consumer prices on the other. Generally, those products which have a great share in total consumption are relatively cheap in a given country. This accounts for the peculiar phenomenon that the purchasing power parity of the national currency of a given country gives the best results from the point of view of this currency when it measures the differences in international price levels in its own consumption pattern. The purchasing power parities of the currencies of two countries – measured in the consumption pattern of one country or the other – show the greater deviation, the greater the difference in the consumption pattern of the two countries is.

Typical manifestations of price scissors are foreign-trade price parity (terms of trade) and the agrarian (industrial) price scissors. Price scissors in their classical sense provide the answer to the question what shift has taken place, in relation to a selected period (base period), in "opposed" interest relations determined by price relations. This is measured in foreign trade relations by the shift of the export-price level compared to the import-price level. In the relationship between industry and agriculture the price-level difference is examined which exists between the selling prices of agricultural produce and the input prices of industrial products used as means of production in agriculture.

However, price scissors can be measured not only as a function of time but also in the price structure. When, for example, evidence is needed to prove that commodity exchange based on international value carries out a redistribution of national labour between productive and less productive countries, i.e. that in the division of labour between two countries, the country with a higher labour intensity and productivity enjoys an absolute advantage over the other, it is not the classical foreign-trade price scissors but the commodity pattern that reference is made to. In such a case, the main point is, that the profit realized in the export commodity pattern of the developed country considerably surpasses – assuming a balanced foreign trade – the magnitude of profit realized in the export commodity pattern of the developing country.[88] Similarly, agrarian industrial price scissors can be measured by comparing the net profit realized in average industrial and agricultural prices.[89]

Price scissors provide a general method of price analysis. This is applied when, for example, shifts in input-output prices (cost-price-profit), incomes redistribution among various industries (production stages), changes in the price level of capital goods as against changes in the consumer price level, etc. are analysed. Changes in the price proportions of various types of

[88] Kohlmey, G.: Karl Marx, Theorie von den Internationalen Werten. *Jahrbuch des Instituts für Wirtschaftswissenschaften*, Bd. 5, Berlin, 1962.
[89] Csikós-Nagy, B.: *Szocialista árképzés* (Socialist Pricing). Budapest, 1961.

substitute products, or, within the same type of product, of related products, can also be expressed in terms of price scissors.

In computing real incomes (real wages) it is equally important to quantify the changes in living conditions as calculated on a social average, and to find out the different extent to which they affect the various social strata. To base the consumer price index calculated as a social average on a commodity pattern causes no special difficulty. Much more difficult is it to form those specific commodity patterns that must be considered in establishing the implications for the various social strata of this method of computation. This makes it necessary to analyse by product groups *the effects that different incomes exercise on the consumption pattern.* In assessing this problem, account must be taken of the fact that the socialist state applies an extremely sophisticated normative system in its living standards policy, that price measures – if they are designed to raise prices – are always based on the assumption that they cannot cause a decrease in the living standards of any significant stratum of society. Since, in the case of a price rise in the necessities of life this requirement – without harming the primary interests of old age pensioners, families with many children, low-income workers, etc., – can only be met by socio-economic measures under specific circumstances, a highly sophisticated information system is needed to prepare these steps. This information must be provided by household statistics.

Part IV

Producer Price

1. Agricultural Prices

Characteristics of the Natural Factors in the Price System

Marx's rent theory manysidedly reveals the special features of *primary production* based on natural endowments. Agriculture, within primary production, *rests on biological processes.* Owing to the fertility of soil, the substances put into the earth produce, by means of physical and chemical processes of decomposition, new materials. Thus in agriculture the law of physical metabolism is in operation, controlled by agrotechnology, but its conditions are determined by natural endowments (climate and soil). Consequently, the peculiarities of the agricultural price are closely connected with the role of natural factors.[90] The interconnections of natural factors and the agricultural price system deserve special attention for three reasons:

1. *The different climatic zones create, on the one hand, favourable conditions for growing certain plant species, or, on the other, make it impossible to grow them.*

Agrarian policy and agrarian price policy have different possibilities where the soil and climate provide the conditions for creating a varied pattern of agricultural production from those where natural factors do not allow such a production pattern to evolve. Price is, of course, a much more effective regulator of production policy in the case of an *oligo-cultural* (multi-crop) production pattern than in a *mono-cultural* (mono-crop) one.[91] Yet, even if the agriculture of a given country has a mono-cultural character, the possible function of the price is essentially decided by the particular structure of agriculture, which may be determined predominantly either by natural conditions or production decisions. A given country may have a mono-cultural production pattern and also such natural edowments as provide the possibility of evolving a diversified agricultural structure. In

[90] *FAO, An Enquiry into the Problems of Agricultural Price Stabilization and Support Policies*. Rome, 1960.

[91] Dantwala, M. L.: Rapporteurs' Report on Price Policy for Agricultural Development. *Indian Journal of Agricultural Economics*, No. 1, 1962. Abel, W.: *Agrarpolitik*. Göttingen, 1958. Heady, O.: The Supply of US Farm Products under Conditions of Full Employment. *American Economic Review*, Vol. 45, No. 2, 1955.

the latter case, there can hardly be any doubt about it that the government is in a position to radically transform the production pattern.

Apart from a few exceptions, the mono-cultural pattern of agricultural production may also conceal a general *economic backwardness.* Historically, mono-cultural (one-crop) economy has come into being as a result of colonization or capital export, and means one-sided dependence on the world market. Under such a production pattern, a great number of goods are imported, while only one single or a few agricultural products are produced mainly for the world market. Yet the transformation of the agricultural pattern constitutes a dilemma for the government. Though it is fully aware of the harmful effects of a one-sided reliance on the world market, it also needs the foreign currency earned by these exports. If the agrarian structure is one-sidedly world market-oriented, the government cannot pursue an independent agricultural price policy. A price policy designed to transform the pattern of agriculture threatens, on the one hand, the foreign-exchange position of the country, and requires, on the other, substantial capital inputs.

An autonomous agrarian price policy alone can only create material motivation for the transformation of the agricultural structure considered desirable. Here we interpret motivation as effective demand (in a sense, as a self-financing price). But if there is no supply of capital goods, or if it is not in equilibrium with the effective demand, such a price policy will not promote the intensive development of agriculture, but will lead to inflation.

We have come to the conclusion that it is easier to pursue an effective price policy in a diversified production pattern than to abandon mono-culture. *In an oligo-cultural production structure,* in which the government wishes decisively to influence the structure of production, it starts from a coherent analysis of the given price relations and the existing production pattern, bearing in mind the general formula according to which, with all the other product prices being unchanged, *a price rise of a given product has an output-expanding effect and its reduction an output-contracting one.* And really, over a reasonably long period of time, those factors of the price movements of agricultural produce which directly or indirectly affect the government's price policy, provide the evidence that nearly all movements can be traced back to this simplified formula. Agricultural production generally reacts proportionately to changes in relative prices.

It is primarily by means of the incentive prices of products grown or to be grown in the largest volume that the government can create a material motivation for realizing the objectives of its production policy.[92] Whether a given country has an agricultural price policy of its own or not, can best be judged by the assertion or the degree, if there is any, of the principle based on the stimulating effect of prices on production. Most markedly comes this principle into effect in an agricultural pattern in which the government selects a few crops for the cultivation of which it wishes to ensure primary material motivation. These are, in certain European socialist countries, *wheat* and *milk*. In these countries it is the highest degree of profitability of the production of these products upon which agrarian price policy rests. Consequently, it is the prices of these two products, which are mostly detached from world market prices, and require the highest government subsidy. This price policy is built on the production policy aiming, on the one hand, at increasing the intensive character of agriculture through cattle breeding, based virtually on an imported fodder basis, and, on the other hand, at ensuring the highest possible supply of bread grain.

The relationship between production pattern and relative prices is not a *static* one. The same production pattern may make desirable different relative prices in different periods of time. This follows from the fact that *the prime costs* of different agricultural products *change differently*, and this is of primary importance from the point of the reaction of agricultural producers. At the same time, the *supply and demand relations*, the identical utility and substitutability of individual products must also be taken into account. The problem to be solved is often extremely intricate and complex.[93]

[92] MEISENBERG, L.: *op. cit.*

[93] BAJLOV, F.: *Ravnishtshe i s' otnosenie na izkupnite tseni na selskostopanskite prozvedeniya* (Price Level and Relative Prices of Agricultural Products). Sofia, 1970. LEWANDOWSKI, J.: *Ekonomiczne problemy polityki rolnej* (Economic Problems of the Policy of Agriculture). Warsaw, 1969. MLADENOV, B.: Osnovni nasoki za ponatat' snoto us'v' rshenstvuvane na izkupnite tseni na selskostopanskite proizvedenia (Chief Directions of a Further Perfectioning of State Purchase Prices of Agricultural Products). *Co-operativno Zemledeliye*, No. 6, 1970, Sofia. OKUNIEWSKI, J.: Warunki produkcji a koszty i ceny produktiw rolnych (Conditions of Production, Inputs and Prices of Agricultural Products. Book, entitled: Political Economics of Socialism.) In: *Ekonomia polityczna socializmu*. Warsaw, 1969. RADULOV, A.: Osnovy formirovaniya tsen na produktsiyu selskogo khozyaistva (Bases of the Pricing of Agricultural Products). *Mezhdunarodny selyskokhozyaistvenny zhurnal*, No. 6, 1970. RASINKI, J.: *Ceny dechodowosc, oplacalmo[illegible] w gospodarce rolnej* (Prices, Profitability and Recovery in Agriculture). Warsaw, 1970. TERENTEV, M. L.: Nekotorye voprosy tsenoobrazovaniya na selyskokhozyaistvennuyu produktsiyu (Some Questions of Agricultural Pricing). *Voprosy Ekonomiki*, No. 3, 1958, Moscow.

2. *The natural factors bring about differential land rent No. I, which is created on land of better quality than that of the worst cultivated land, or on farms near the market, provided the price is in line with the conditions of farming on poor-quality soil or on land far from markets.*[94] The withdrawal of differential land rent No. I would be, in principle, the task of a *land tax*, but no tax system exists which could solve this problem satisfactorily. This accounts, partly, for *income dispersions* within agriculture, which are limited today mainly by some elements of the price system.

If the prices of agricultural products are set by the government, and even if they are not, but it is in a position to exert influence on *the price level* by indirect regulators, it is within the competence of agrarian policy to judge to the production capabilities of what units the price level should be adapted. Heated debates are being carried on upon this question in the socialist countries.

Some economists taking part in the debates in the Soviet Union disapproved of the view that agricultural prices should be set according to the worst production conditions. This principle is valid, in their view, only under capitalist conditions, and even there only if the formation of agricultural prices is spontaneous. It has no validity, however, in a socialist economy, where it is expedient to regulate prices according to average conditions.[95] Czechoslovak economists have adopted a practically identical view on that question.[96] The Czechoslovak collective of economists discussing the basic questions of the price system refer to *Marx* who, in the third volume of his "Capital", publishes a computation concerning the production prices of a quarter of wheat grown on different soils. According to this, all wheat grown on any soil is sold at the cost incurred in growing wheat on the poorest soil, namely for 60 shillings, irrespective of the fact that the production price of a quarter of wheat grown on soils of with good qualities is 24 shillings. Thus, capitalist farms register an income two and a half times higher than the average production price of wheat.

Marx calls the difference between the market price and producer price of wheat *false social value*, which ensues from the private ownership of land, from capitalistic competition and the

[94] MARX, K.: *op. cit.*

[95] TERENTEV, M. L.: *Sebestoimost kolkhoznoy produktsii* (On the Costs of Kolkhoz Production). Doklady T.S.N.A. Brochure 1, 1957, Moscow.

[96] BARTUNEK, J., KLECATSKY, K., KNÁKAL, J., KOHOUTEK, M., KORALKA, J., LOBNAROVA, A., PÁCHA, J. and PROUZA, B.: *Novy ceskoslovenské republice* (The New Method of State Purchase of Agricultural Products in the Czechoslovak Republic). Prague, 1959.

enormous power of market relations. To this *Marx* adds: if capitalism ceases to exist and society is organized as a conscious and planned association of people, it is apparent that society will not pay for this product of land two and half times the labour expended on it. If the prices were set according to the conditions of the best or worst farming co-operatives, in the opinion of Czechoslovak economists, their effect would be limited and would give rise to undesirable discrepancies. If the prices were based on the costs of co-operatives run below the average level, this would lead to a significant increase in the price level and would not stimulate the majority of co-operatives either to increase their agricultural output, or to reduce their prime costs. If, however, the prices based on the costs of the best co-operatives were too low, they would not be suitable to ensure the conditions of expanded reproduction for most co-operatives. In both cases prices would be in contradiction with the requirements set by the principle of material interest.

A lower or higher agricultural price level *cannot, of course, change the difference existing between the production conditions of individual productive units.* But when the price level is adjusted to medium conditions, farms with the best endowments cannot realize part (say, half) of the differential land rent. *It is precisely in this way that price-level policy may become a means of restricting differential land rent.* But this restriction can materialize here only by the marginal productive units becoming economically "bankrupt". This economic "bankruptcy" is partly solved by ensuring lower personal incomes for the marginal farms than for the most advanced ones. At the same time, the government must also subsidize the marginal farms as the national economy needs their products. And indeed, the methods other than pricing for providing government subsidies to farms operating under the worst production conditions is widely applied in several socialist countries. A further restriction of the differential land rent *can be realized by the regional differentiation of prices.* Prices may not be diverted according to farms but according to regions. The agricultural price system of the Soviet Union is based on the system of regional prices.

The "average" and "worst" production conditions need a closer investigation. In the debate held in Hungary on the rent problem, the following statements were made: (1) In approaching the price problem, it is not the input relations *in general that are decisive, but the production conditions on those farms* where certain plant varieties are grown regularly. This is a *substantial difference*. What is decisive is that the various crops must generally be produced on *soils suitable for them.* And price policy may take into account economic efficiency by adjusting prices to the conditions of production specified in this way. (2) In forming state purchase prices, different factors have to be taken into account, depending on individual product groups. Prices must be set differently if the government wishes to purchase the whole volume of the products grown (state monopoly products, e.g. tobacco), if it wants to purchase only the commodity part/or the major proportion of the total production (e.g. in the case of bread grain), and finally, if it has a demand for only a relatively small fraction of the total commodity supply (as in the case of maize).

An adjustment of prices to lower than average-quality lands can only arise in the case of state monopoly products. But here too, land rent as a price factor must be raised or lowered depending on the intention of the government to expand or to diminish the production of the crop in question. Presumably, the expansion of the acreage of a given crop is possible only on lands that are less suitable for that crop, and the profitability of its production must be ensured by a price rise. And, in limiting the size of the area under cultivation, it is desirable that new crops are introduced on lands which are more suitable for their production.

Non-monopoly products have to be judged differently. The government purchases a substantial part of the commodity supply of bread grain. But from this it does not follow at all that the price must generally be adjusted to the production conditions of the poorest soil. Price formation cannot leave out of account that part of the area under bread grain cultivation which is not used for regular commodity production. Bread grain is grown on co-operative farms and household plots even if it were more profitable to grow a different plant. This is simply because here farmers produce primarily what they consume themselves.

Hence price restricts land rent but does not eliminate it. When with price applied as a regulating factor, land rent is limited, then differential land rents No. I and No. II are jointly restricted. Therefore, much circumspection is needed when price is used for such purposes. But there is a pricing measure which is specifically designed to skim off only differential land rent No. I, and is therefore often applied. The price systems adopted by the socialist countries largely *neutralize land rent because of the different distances of farms from markets*. Since socialist procurement trade has an extensive network, it is practically possible to form prices excluding freight, or, apart from normal short-haul deliveries, a special allowance is made for justified freight.

3. *Owing to changes in weather, agricultural yield fluctuates year after year even on lands of the same quality*. In industry, if

work is done and the necessary inputs are made in a controlled system of technological processes, output is predictable with a fair certainty. The case is different in agriculture. Here there is no unambiguous relationship between input and output. Or more precisely: inputs as regulated by agrotechnology constitute a precondition for outputs but, as a consequence of natural factors, the results actually achieved may be more or less favourable than expected.

The resulting peculiarities for the price system are most conspicuous in the case of typical market goods (vegetables and fruit) because they cannot always be stored, and lose their use value within a short time. Under such circumstances the demand-supply relations determine price formation in flexible forms and create early, seasonal and end-of-season prices. In addition, seasonal prices may also vary depending on average crops and the duration of the season. In case the yield is good and the season short, prices may be established at such a low level that the producer allows part of the crop to get lost and, if possible, will not grow the same plant in the following cycle of production. This is why protective prices are applied in agriculture to provide a measure of production security. Crop fluctuation caused by weather demands anyway a *flexibility* of price policy.

In connection with any comprehensive agricultural price policy, three questions must be answered: (1) What *price level* should be considered satisfactory? (2) On the basis of what *relative prices* should the desirable price level be approached? (3) What *schemes* are deemed suitable to realize the desired price relations? These questions can only be answered in the light of the objectives of the government's agrarian policy. The agricultural price level is not independent of the government's incomes-distribution policy, nor are the relative prices independent of its production policy. Price formation schemes, on the other hand, virtually determine the mechanism in which the government's agrarian policy operates.

Price level and relative prices are as closely interconnected as incomes and production policy. Can price be equally effective both in its incomes- and production-influencing role? Incomes relations can be influenced by prices only through the given production structure. If the producer does not turn out a product whose price changes, his incomes will not be affected by price movements. And as far as the product he turns out is concerned, any price change will affect his incomes to the extent of the share of that product in the farm's total output. It constitutes one of the problems of the state regulation of agricultural prices that whenever the government modifies prices in order to bring about incomes-redistribution, it can never be sure whether the measure taken will really result in the intended incomes-redistribution, or in a change in the production structure. A price measure will work in both directions. But which will prove stronger? In principle, the possibility is never excluded that the agricultural producer will neutralize the incomes-redistribution effect intended by the government by a transformation of his production structure.

All this satisfactorily explains that, wherever the government interferes in the process of agricultural production, this policy is never confined to considerations affecting incomes-distribution only, but is supplemented by production policy measures. The government endeavours to realize its incomes policy while shaping at the same time a specific production structure. It wishes either to maintain a production structure which otherwise, without its interference, and with the unlimited assertion of the market price automatism would basically change, or it wants to change it, which, in its judgement, has been diverted in a wrong direction by the spontaneous market processes. Thus, the state has a very important role to play in forming, maintaining and changing not only the general price level of agricultural produce but also those relative prices on which the general price level is based.

The relationship between the role of price in influencing incomes on the one hand, and production on the other, may also be problematic from another point of view. There are economists who approach the problem in this way: *only prices determined in the full knowledge of production can effectively regulate incomes, but an effective regulation of production presupposes the declaration of prices well in advance.* From this the conclusion may be drawn that price should serve the aims of production policy, and that the government should regulate incomes not by prices, but by other means, e. g. by taxes. In brief: all price changes that keep production and demand in harmony should be maximum, while all changes that do constitute to an adjusment of production be kept at a minimum. In this case, all stimulating price changes should be declared when the productive forces may still adapt themselves to these changes.

Agricultural Procurement System and Price System

Urban and rural economic relations can be organized by the socialist state in different systems. It is according to these systems that the agricultural price system is formed. Our investigations are based on three models:

– compulsory delivery,
– planned government procurement and
– free government purchase.

In the first post-war decade varieties of the first system were employed in the European socialist countries. Most socialist countries have already switched over to the second system, but e. g. Hungary is applying the third one. As a method different from those listed above is usually considered the *contractual form* of the state purchase system. In reality, however, the contractual form does not determine the content of urban and rural economic relationship, it only gives it a legal form.

The different forms of agricultural procurement presuppose different *price systems*. But whatever the method of procurement and the related price system, material motivation cannot be excluded. If the price system applied in compulsory delivery does not sufficiently take into account material motivation, then the latter will break through the barriers set up by official measures.[97] In Hungary, in the period 1950 – 1955, the structure of agricultural production developed not according to the state plan of the national economy, but in the way it was determined by the material interest of small-holders. The state plan of the national economy envisaged the maintenance of the acreage of bread grain and a somewhat diminished area under maize. In fact, however, the bread-grain area was decreased by 20 per cent, while that of the area of maize increased by more than 10 per cent. This deviation from the plan was due to the fact that the government wished to maintain the previous production level of bread grain by obligatory delivery and by sowing instructions, and thought it could achieve this even if the price level of grain deliveries was kept low, and considered compulsory decrees sufficient substitutes for material incentives. By contrast, the government stimulated the producers to increase the output of fattened pigs by raising the price of live pigs. This created material interest in expanding the area sown to maize. This incentive proved stronger than any instruction, and led to a decrease in the area sown with bread grain. Thus obligatory delivery cannot be differentiated from delivery according to planned targets simply by saying that the former "liquidates" the base for the latter.

[97] Gaponenko, G. and Gorodsky, M.: *Novaya sistema zagotovki selsko-knozyaistvennoy produktsii v kolkhozakh* (The New Method of State Purchasing Agricultural Products in Kolkhozes). Moscow, 1959. Sághy, V.: A mezőgazdasági termelés tervszerű fejlesztéséről (On the Planned Development of Agricultural Production). *Társadalmi Szemle*, No. 3, 1957, Budapest.

Nevertheless, obligatory delivery was suitable for the adoption of an opinion according to which this method need not be reinforced by material incentives. In the socialist countries, especially in the 1950s, instructions were largely interpreted as substitutes for material incentives, and efforts were made to ensure in this way the financial contribution of agriculture to meeting the needs of society as a whole. In practice, obligatory delivery solved two, entirely separate problems. It ensured, on the one hand, the organized public supply of the urban population, and laid the foundation of an agricultural price policy which attributed to price the exclusive role it could play as a means of redistributing the national income. If, however, the system of free government purchases is allowed to assert itself, the government reckons with the planned influencing role of prices, price policy being one of the main instruments of exercising this influence.

Under the *obligatory delivery system,* the state prescribes for each hectare of the area under cultivation the composition and quantity of the produce to be delivered. In no socialist country did the system of obligatory delivery comprise all crops grown in agriculture and the total quantity of products subject to compulsory delivery. In general, only such products fell under the compulsory delivery system which were consumed regularly and in large quantities by the urban population either in their raw or in their processed forms, and such as could be produced by each farm. These products, then, were such as were considered, on the one hand, of vital importance for public supply, and, on the other, suitable for making it compulsory for all farming units to grow them. The government did not abolish the title of the producers to the total quantity of commodities produced by them and subject to obligatory delivery, but it did abolish their title to a specified part of the surplus commodity.

The socialist countries generally made every effort that the producers should meet their obligations even if they happened not to grow the product to be delivered in the envisaged quantity. They were allowed to deliver substitutes, but sometimes they were also compelled to buy produce on the free market to meet part of their obligations.

Since the producers were allowed to dispose of their surplus products on the free market when they had discharged their deliveries, the government wanted to make them interested in boosting commodity production by stabilizing the obligatory deliveries, and set quotas per hectare for several years ahead. They were paid considerably higher prices for crops in excess of discharged deliveries. *Thus the dual price system became an organic part of the system of compulsory delivery of agricultural produce,* and the delivery price set well below the free government purchase prices became the method of skimming off value, which proved a more important device from the point of view of the national economy than agricultural taxation.

Delivery quotas and the dual price system constitute the main pillars of the obligatory delivery system. Yet, they do not comprise all characteristic features of this system. It is further characterized by the government's endeavour to get hold of the commodity fund in a number of other ways, too. Thus, e. g. producers were compelled to pay in kind in settlement of various government services (use of machinery, milling, etc.). Socialist governments exercised influence on production not only indirectly, by delivery obligations, but also wished to ensure by direct plan instructions that agricultural producers realized a crop structure and livestock population by hectare, etc. as envisaged by the state plan of the national economy. The decrees governing the scope and conditions of the operation of the peasants' market were also important concomitants of the compulsory delivery system. These legal decrees determined, in the last analysis, to what extent the commodity producers have free choice in selling their products. Direct government regulation was also extended to produce the farmers consumed themselves. With products subject to delivery this was done by means of obliging farmers to render reports to the authorities. Ban on slaughtering, or the permission of local authorities to slaughter livestock for domestic needs, are well-known methods of this policy.

Along with the progress made in the socialist reorganization of agriculture, the dual system of compulsory delivery and free government purchase coupled with the related dual price system posed more and more problems in the countries building socialism. Problems cropped up in the fields of incomes distribution, of the planned influencing of production and the development rate of the forces of production alike, and they were in many respects closely connected with price formation.[98]

Planned state purchase is a special variety of compulsory delivery. The basic difference between the two methods lies in the fact that while under the system of compulsory delivery obligations must be met according to nationally (regionally) unified directives, the planned state purchase system adapts itself to the individual product-mix of producers. This is done by planning.

In Hungary, the state contract and free purchase system as evolved in 1957 follows as its main guideline the practice of confining directive regulation basically to the government (co-

[98] BARTUNEK, J. et al.: *op. cit.*

operative) purchase, trading, credit, etc. organizations, and exercising through them the planned control over agriculture. By production contracts it ensures that the basic technical raw materials of agricultural origin (fibre, plants, tobacco, sugar beet, seeds, vegetables, etc.) are available to the industry at the right time and in right quantities, that the export of such crops as can be crown in the given area under favourable conditions is maintained and further developed. By contracts for fattening livestock the state wishes to lay on firm foundations both the meat supply of the urban population and meat exports, and by stockbreeding contracts to promote the development of animal husbandry. The system of production contracts is supplemented by a contractual marketing system. The latter applies primarily to free-market products (fruit, poultry, eggs, etc.).

The commitments based on delivery contracts are, in the relationship between government and producers, obligations of a novel nature entirely different from those undertaken in the compulsory delivery system. Compulsory delivery is a forced commitment, while contractual delivery is, legally, a voluntary obligation. This system acknowledges only one sort of obligation as legal: the producers' free undertaking to deliver to the state, in the case of monopolized products, their total output, and, in the case of non-monopolized products, either the output volume for which the contract was signed, or the produce harvested from the area specified in the contract. This system is based, theoretically, on the producers' free determination to conclude or not to conclude a contract with the government in compliance with the provisions of the plan, and therefore the government has to pay increased attention to the producers' material interest when organizing public supply.

In the case of obligatory delivery the producer is not free to deliberate which way of marketing ensures him the greatest benefit. He is simply bound to meet his obligation. It is exactly this which makes it possible for the state detach, in a sense, the price relations of the organized market from free-market price relations. When, however, the producer is free to decide to sell his produce to the state or directly to the population, he makes his decision dependent exactly on the prices he can obtain for his produce. The free state purchase price can, of course, be lower than the market price since the producer can sell large quantities on the organized market and often only small lots on the free-market. However, the more free state purchase prices are diverted (in a downward direction) from market prices, the smaller quantities the state is able to purchase.

Qualitative Price Systems

The prices of agricultural products are given for units of quantity (kilogrammes, pieces, litres, etc.). From this, however, it does not follow that there is no relationship between price and quality. And socialist countries make use of price regulation to stimulate the production of quality products.

Agriculture turns out products which directly or indirectly serve the satisfaction of human needs. Some agricultural products are bought directly for consumption, others are processed as industrial raw materials and placed at the disposal of the consumers as products of the food, chemical, textile, etc. industries. Thus, the useful properties of one part of the agricultural products are appreciated by the consumers, and those of another part by the industry. In grading agricultural products state price regulation relies on the findings of agrotechnology or on scientific grading methods. Price categories with respects to grading as applied by the socialist countries are as follows:

- weight price,
- specific price,
- class price,
- species price,
- regional species price.

In several socialist countries *weight price* is applied to a greater extent than desirable. In this connection reference is usually made to the following facts:

(a) Grading agricultural products usually calls for special technical equipment, instrument, etc. If the purchasing agencies, field organizations, have not got the necessary equipment – if the objective conditions of grading are missing – quality price is either not applicable in practice, or will give rise to such subjective methods which may be extremely disadvantageous for the producers.

(b) The differentiation of agricultural products by quality is often a very sophisticated job, while its practical use is not very significant. Certain aspects of quality control and grading methods are not yet satisfactorily well-founded scientifically, or the varied use that an agricultural product can be put to, the availability of main and by-products, or dual products may make debatable the practice of limiting the grading method to a given main product only. For this and other reasons, the socialist countries fix the purchase price of the same product in different quality-price systems, and the system used in the case of consumer prices is not always reflected in the system of purchase prices.

For deciding whether the price of agricultural produce is set according to weight or quality, it may be regarded as a general rule that the products must meet *basic quality requirements.* Thus, whether the prices of agricultural products are set in the system of weight or quality prices, grading concerning basic quality requirements will take place in any case, which may lead either to a refusal of taking delivery or to the devaluation of the product. Disputes arising from grading are regulated differently in the various countries. It is a general practice that such disputes are locally decided in the case of perishable products. For other agricultural produce (e. g. seeds, etc.) national organizations set up specifically for this task are competent.

Specific price is a quality price in which the evaluation of the agricultural product by the industry finds primary expression. Industry evaluates a given raw material of agricultural origin according to its processing cost per unit of industrial finished product. Wheat – for instance – has a specific price. The quality stratification of bread grain prices reflects the consideration of its effect on the cost of flour and bread. It is a requirement that the prices of bread grain with different specific properties should be equalized in the prime cost of flour-bread. According to this, the content of valuable substances of bread grain is jointly determined by the hectolitre weight (gluten content), purity and moisture content of 100 kilogramme net weight. It is these factors that determine the quantity of flour or bread that can be gained from 100 kilogramme net weight of bread grain.

Class price is a variety of specific price, in the application of which the product is classified, according to quality, into several (2–5) categories, and the prices are set accordingly. Prices are determined in this system in the case of fibre plants, red pepper, tobacco, hops, onion, certain vegetables, beef cattle, mutton sheep, etc. Class price is a qualitative, graded price system most widely used in agriculture. Its use is generally preferred for its easy applicability in practice. Differences between the individual quality categories are well defined and easy to check. When accustomed to this price system, the producer will know well in advance the category the requirements of which his product offered for sale will meet.

One form of incentives is the *stimulation to choose the right species.* The productive capacity of different species shows a wide range of deviation. If the various plant and animal species are differentiated by their productive capacities – and the aim is that agriculture should be geared to the cultivation resp. breeding of species ensuring the highest yields – then there is no point in stimulating the introduction of these species also through prices. This follows from the economic law that the cost, with approximately identical inputs, will be higher or lower depending on the measure of yields, and the yield in turn is determined, among other things, by the productive capacity of the species chosen. Assuming a uniform price, the higher the yield specific to the species chosen by the producer, the higher the profit he can attain. But the application of a uniform price is justifiable only on certain assumptions:

(a) If there is no substantial difference in quality between the various species of a given product. This exactly makes it possible to use quantity as the basis of price.

(b) If there is a substantial difference in quality between the various species of a given product, but it is not reflected in consumer price relations. From the point of view of the consumer this difference is immaterial, or is not significant enough to induce him to pay a higher price for the better quality. Therefore it is reasonable, also with regard to the producer price, to make quantity the basis of price.

(c) If the difference in quality between the various species of the given product is reflected in consumer price relations, but, for the producer price, this differentiation can duly be taken into account in the uniform price system even by applying specific or class prices. Therefore, it is not necessary to divert the price of a given product directly by species.

But in many cases prices have to be regulated under conditions differing from those outlined above. In the international market e. g. the so-called Dunghan Shali rice species is known as an established and excellent quality. This rice species is easy to cultivate industrially and can also be marketed easily and profitably. With certain oil seeds, for instance, there is such a great difference in oil content between the various species that, in the final analysis, it is the species that determines the oil-content ratio. The producer can influence the oil content of the same species only to an insignificant extent.

These few examples will suffice to make it clear that a given product cannot be reduced, in respect of price, to a common denominator merely on the ground that is satisfies the same need. Furthermore, owing to different properties of the various species, the question of species cannot be evaluted with all products on the basis of productive capacity, or of productive capacity only. Here we must also consider that a *high-quality product is not necessarily characterized by a high productive capacity.* On the contrary, with certain products, productive capacity and quality are in an inverse proportion. Thus e. g. in wine-growing, the yields of better-quality grape-vine species are less than those of poorer-quality grape-vines. The former are harvested at a time when optimum quality and not when the highest quantity can be obtained.

These are the reasons which require that in the case of a few agricultural products a price system is applied which stimulates the production of better qualities by prices set according to species. It is only in the light of the specific production conditions of individual countries, their historically established consumption habits and the resulting relative consumer prices and, finally, of the relations established in the international trade of their agricultural outputs that it can be determined in the case of what products and in what way it is expedient to stimulate by pricing the choise of the right species.

There are agricultural products in the *case of which natural endowments play such a determining role that they can only be grown in specific areas.* Commonly known are the excellent properties of the Brazilian Santos coffee or the Parana coffee, the Israeli Jaffa orange or the Hungarian improved wheat seeds of Bánkút. Every country makes, of course, efforts to introduce species that are most sought for and possess the best properties. Thus e. g. in the 1930s, when the world demand for light Virginia tobacco species increased more and more, several countries switched over to growing Virginia tobacco.

When species known for their excellent properties are introduced, the producers usually cannot immediately grow the equivalent product. Species of certain agricultural products yield very different results under different natural endowments, or in different environments. The specific properties of certain products can only be ensured in certain regions of the country. In the case of agricultural products, with a close relationship between species and the cultivation area, or properties of quality and cultivation area, it seems desirable to stimulate the establishment of appropriate growing conditions through the price system.

Agricultural Price Scissors

An economically backward country – especially a country with no capital import or just an insignificant one – raises the material funds needed for industrialization primarily by withdrawing part of the value produced in agriculture. Thus, from a historical point of view, industrial protectionism is the first manifestation of the national development of productive forces. This is easy to understand: when there is already a relative abundance of foodstuffs, but still a great shortage of manufactures, then, owing to demand-supply relations, the manufactures are necessarily overestimated as compared to agrarian products. This overestimation provides the possibility to pay higher wages for industrial labour, which exercises at the same time an absorptive effect on manpower, and attracts to industry the labour only partially employed in agriculture. This industrial protectionism, while free-market world economy still rested on a classical basis, was brought about and maintained not by the government but by market relations, by the law of supply and demand. Later on this was changed into state protectionism by the system of protective customs.

But even now, when the forces of industrial production are already well-developed in a great many countries, the question may be raised whether the state subsidies granted to agriculture are not due, at least partly, to the fact that the world market prices of agricultural products, being, as it were, subordinated to the economic laws of industrialization, are too low. In any case, there are economists who regard government subsidies granted to agriculture not as the protection of agriculture but as a social injustice. We do not want to dwell on this problem, yet we think that merely to raise the question may be useful in one respect. If we consider the "conflict" between industry and agriculture in its historical perspective, we can more realistically assess the economic policy of the socialist countries, too.

Following the Second World War, the socialist countries set their agricultural prices below the world market prices, and ensured the assertion of these prices by introducing the compulsory delivery system. At the same time, the industrially advanced capitalist countries set their agricultural prices above the world market price level. *Many looked upon this phenomenon as a typical difference between socialist and capitalist agrarian policy.* In fact, however, what was involved here was rather the fact that the socialist societies were formed in countries relatively backward in industrial development. It is not necessary and even not justified to defend the agrarian policy of the socialist countries in all its aspects. It is sufficiently obvious that oversized industrialization in these countries had its repercussions on agricultural development. The one necessarily follows from the other. But all this cannot be regarded as a characteristic of socialist agrarian policy as such. *The crucial thing is that, for objective reasons, industrialized and industrializing societies assess and solve their agrarian problems differently.*

Looked upon historically, agrarian protectionism dates back to the period of the Great Depression,[99] which especially gravely affected agriculture. In this situation, the capitalist countries established a whole system of state intervention in order to put

[99] *ECE – European Agriculture in 1965*. Geneva, 1960. *FAO – Towards a Capital Intensive Agriculture*. Geneva, 1961.

an end to depression and to stabilize agriculture. It was not difficult to form a public opinion supporting all administrative interference which curbed the fluctuation of agricultural prices and an automatism leading even in the case of a relatively slight increase in supply to a substantial price decrease and undermining thereby all entrepreneurial initiative.

Until about the middle of our century we could still think that all that had been started by the Great Depression and maintained and further developed by the war preparations in the second half of the 1930s and later by a war economy would, sooner or later, be discontinued after the Second World War. In the industrially advanced countries, agriculture recovered after the Second World War in a relatively short period of time. The general level of production reached its pre-war level already in 1949–1950. By the early 1950s, the causes that had given rise to protectionism had practically disappeared. Still, the agrarian policy of protectionism in which the most important role was played by the governments' price policy, survived and even deepened. Evidently, new elements emerged which formerly had not been in prominence. It was primarily in agriculture that the general sharpening of the market problem raised especially intricate questions. Here it became quite obvious that spontaneous price automatism would make it impossible for agriculture to develop, and even the production level already reached could not be maintained as the world market price in West Europe would not even cover the reproduction cost of labour. It was under these circumstances that the decision on maintaining agrarian protectionism was taken.

The same problem came up in the socialist countries partly in the 1950s and especially in the 1960s. Agrarian protectionism had already been applied by the socialist countries earlier, too. The budgets of the socialist countries have always assigned substantial sums to financing agriculture. But formerly, this was done with low delivery prices under the system of state purchase and compulsory procurement prices kept below the level of world market prices. Consequently, agriculture could not enjoy, on the one hand, even the incomes ensured by world market prices, but, on the other, it did enjoy the material support of the state aimed at maintaining the production process, or the realization of the development objectives laid down in the national economic plan. After the great change in agrarian policy, the state protectionism of agriculture began to assume real forms.

One of the principal motive forces of agrarian protectionism is the endeavour to bring into line agrarian and industrial incomes. This comes objectively into effect with the development of the forces of production. While the reserve of agricultural labour supply is substantial, it might appear natural that the incomes of agricultural labour and their ratio to industrial wages, and agrarian-industrial relations in general should reflect the differences in productivity, should be adapted to market price relations. The situation changes completely when the industrial bases are established, the reserves of labour supply get depleted, the labour-absorbing effect of industry makes itself strongly felt, and the retaining (typing up) of rural manpower constitutes a major problem. Under such circumstances the existing difference between the pay for industrial and agricultural work emerges as the problem of *incomes disparity,* and special attention is focussed on gradually eliminating the gap between industrial and agrarian incomes. The related price and wage movements are in many cases effected by means of the government's price policy.

The fact that the agrarian-industrial incomes ratio is treated as a matter of the government's price policy may give rise to the belief that the government is in a position to bring about arbitrary income relations by avoiding the market problem.[100] This problem is worth a more detailed analysis as the worker-peasant incomes ratio is one of the key problems of incomes policy. *What is at the bottom of the rural-urban incomes ratio is the so-called agrarian "price scissors" problem, and this needs to be cleared up in its historical context. The agrarian-industrial price gap as evolved in the course of history has a double content, which expresses:*

– First, that wages paid for agricultural work are lower than those paid for industrial work causing a disparity between agricultural and industrial incomes,

– Secondly, the prices of agricultural produce as against industrial products do not provide the possibility of adequate self-financing, causing a gap between the prices of agricultural and industrial goods.

But what should be the yardstick to be applied in respect of these disparities and their liquidation? There are economists who think of the traditional calculation method. They evaluate the agricultural price level on the basis of changes that it has undergone in relation to the industrial price level during a specified period of time. Thus they think of changes in *agricultural and industrial price proportions* while also taking into account that agricultural prices have to be compared not with in-

[100] SIMON, S.: Az ipar és a mezőgazdaság kapcsolata az árak tükrében (Connection between Industry and Agriculture in the Mirror of Prices). *Statisztikai Szemle*, No. 6, 1965, Budapest.

dustrial prices in general, but with the prices of industrial goods bought by the rural population. If the price level of these articles increases to a greater extent in relation to the industrial price level or decreases to a lesser extent than the agricultural price level in an earlier period of time chosen, then the price gap widens (the "price scissors" open) to the detriment of agriculture. In the case of a contrary movement of price proportions, the gap widens to the disadvantage of industry (industrial "price scissors").

In reality, however, the *low or high agricultural price level is not identical with the agrarian or industrial price scissors as interpreted above.* The fact itself that the price relations during two periods of time change either to the advantage or disadvantage of agriculture, does not involve any danger. A lower or higher agricultural price level is of course not independent of the agricultural-industrial price ratio, or of changes in that ratio. But the price policy may find the agricultural price level too high even if price relations have changed compared to an earlier time period to the disadvantage of agricultural prices, e.g. because the farm outputs were significantly high. And conversely, the price policy may consider the agricultural price level as too low if the price relations have changed in relation to an earlier period of time to the advantage of agriculture. This is the case when e.g. farm outputs are poor, or when agricultural prices were too depressed in the base period. The difference between a low agricultural price level and agrarian "price scissors", or between a high agricultural price level and the industrial "price scissors" must specifically be emphasized as they are often mixed up in practice. Comparing the various changing price levels and drawing conclusions from this comparison is debatable if only because of the arbitrary choice of the base period.

It may be suggested that the problem of the *agrarian "price scissors" should be approached from the angle of the net income realized in the prices.* It is fully possible to get to know the value levels of agricultural and industrial products and thus the disparity between these price levels. But several objections can be made to approaching the problem of proportionate agricultural and industrial prices in this way. One part of the net income is used in the branch concerned, while another is used to meet social needs. Thus, net income consists of *profits and taxes. The relationship between industrial and agricultural prices must be analysed not only on the basis of prices but also on the basis of incomes after taxes.* The position of individual branches in the national economy is characterized by price relationships. *Hence, when the problem of price parity is raised, the problem of tax parity should also be raised.* The approximation of prices also includes the approximation of the price structures. The price structure is also closely connected with the given price level. If price formation in agriculture were solved on the basis of the approximate coincidence of price and value, then that part of the social net income realized in agriculture which is needed to meet social needs should be drawn off by taxation. But it is not absolutely necessary to form prices at the level of value. *The withdrawal of value can be effected either by taxes or by prices.* The withdrawal of value by taxation presupposes a price which realizes a higher net income than what can be left with the owner of the commodity. If the price level can be reduced to a level at which costs can be refunded, and the net income left with the producer is realized in the price, then taxes in agriculture should be maintained only to restrict differential land rent. And we can really experience in most socialist countries that the tax form of the withdrawal of agricultural value is substituted mostly by its price form.

In the debates on the agrarian "price scissors", the following over-simplification can often be heard: with price parity established, state subsidies to agriculture could be put an end to, and indeed, agriculture could be compelled to contribute to social costs in a proportionate ratio to industry. *But can agricultural subsidies be transformed into price and can price rises be combined with a new kind of taxation?* These are very intricate questions, as part of the value produced in agriculture is sold directly or indirectly on foreign markets, and exports need budgetary support exactly because of depressed world market prices. This means at the same time that the state subsidy granted to agriculture cannot simply be regarded as a technical question of accounting. It is at most its form that can be changed. Furthermore: the price subsidy of agriculture has, as we have seen, its specific features, which are concomitants of the natural factors. And finally: the proportionate taxation of the productive branches is not merely a question of decision. It is not accidental that in most countries an *industry-oriented system of taxation* has historically evolved. Historically, taxation took, of course, into account the relations prevailing in a fragmented, small-commodity type of agricultural production at a time when the conditions for assessing the tax base and the organized accountancy needed for taxation were hardly available in agriculture. Yet, even in our days the practice is still applied which involves agriculture in bearing the burden of social costs not in a direct but an indirect way.

In considering the question of agrarian price scissors, *the existing difference between the productivity of industrial and agricultural labour cannot entirely be ignored.* If income parity is established at a relatively low productivity of agricultural labour,

– agricultural exports can be maintained only by considerable government subsidies,

– food prices have either to be raised significantly, or to be subsidized.

What must clearly be seen is the following: the complete liquidation of price and income disparity is a *historical process,* which takes place under definite objective circumstances. This process is closely connected with the integration of agriculture into industry, with the higher standard of cultivation and the intensive development of agricultural production. This means that rural living conditions get closer to urban living conditions not only because industrialization strengthens the material position of the urban population, but because the conditions in which agricultural work is done are improving considerably. Worker-peasant income parity can be achieved not by maintaining the old, primitive rural conditions, but by their radical transformation. This process can be accelerated by economic policy and stimulated by price policy. Those who handle this problem exclusively as a question of political decisions, commit a serious mistake: they single one element out of the context in which it can be interpreted on its merit.

2. Industrial Prices

Characteristics of the Industrial Production Pattern in the Price System

When characterizing industrial prices in general, it is appropriate to start from the peculiarities of industrial production. The organizational structure, the technology of production and the product mix of industry are carriers of the peculiarities of the price system. It is worthwhile to deal with them in greater detail.

1. The relationship between the macrostructure and microstructure of production is quite different in industry from that in agriculture. It is typical of the agriculture of the European socialist countries that the production structure of productive units can substantially be changed. As far as individual productive units are concerned, animal husbandry can either be developed or reduced; the structure of plant cultivation, depending on climatic and soil conditions, can be transformed. By contrast, in industry *the structure of the productive units virtually determines the macrostructure of production.* A shoe factory cannot manufacture iron, and iron works cannot produce bricks. Development in agriculture takes place, as a rule, within the framework of the existing production organization. In industry, however, the state can also transform the macrostructure independently of the existing organization of production. It can link up new industrial establishments with the foundation of new enterprises. Thus, though investment policy is an organic part of production policy, the former can be handled more appropriately in an autonomous system in the industrial than in the agricultural sphere.

When discussing *structure-market-price* relationship, we emphasized the following: when the government achieves planned economic development by making use of the market mechanism, price plays an active role in shaping microstructure, but it is not the main regulator of the macrostructure. Though this statement claims general validity, agriculture and industry cannot be *equated* in this respect. In *transforming the macrostructure, price function cannot be circumvented in agriculture.* This follows exactly from the close interconnection between the macro and microstructure of production. Industry provides more possibility of restricting the price function.

If the government centrally plans, finances and executes structural investments, price policy cannot, of course, be expected to be the regulator of structural transformation with adequate industrial producer prices. If central decision is consciously substituted for the price function, it is exactly in its interest that the allocation function of price should be restricted. The resulting difference in nature between agricultural and industrial price policy can be made clear in the following way: If in agriculture a productive branch is declared progressive, it can be taken for granted that price policy for this particular branch must be brought into line with economic policy by means of increased material interest in production. In industry, however, price policy is expected rather *to ensure the undisturbed marketing of the products of the progressive industrial branches appointed for preferential development by prices stimulating consumption.* Thus it is almost certain that progressive branches in industry will not be placed first on the list of profitability; on the contrary, they may need, at least temporarily, a subsidy from the state budget.

Price policy stimulating consumption is a general attendant phenomenon of the development of *new industrial branches* in the socialist countries. Well known is the decisive influence of large-scale industry on consumption habits. The spread of mass products is taking place parallel with the gradual ousting of the products of the handicraft industry. The consumer reacts to the price difference which results from the difference between the prime costs of the mass products of large-scale and the individual products of handicraft industry. We must lay a special emphasis the role of price policy in changing consumption habits because the latter cannot be changed overnight, and therefore it is inappropriate to take administrative measures which make it practically impossible for the consumer to buy products of the handicraft industry. It is, however, entirely justified that consumer prices should reflect not only differences in prime costs, but also that the government should realize higher social net incomes in the prices of top-quality handicraft products than in the prices of related goods produced by the mass production methods of the large-scale industry.

The deflection of the relative prices of custom-made single products and of the related mass products from relative values is in harmony with the policy of industrialization, which ensures that the industrial branches that have not – or not sufficiently – developed under capitalism, i.e. those that have practically remained within the scope of handicrafts, can grow at a relatively high speed. Under the conditions of socialist construction, the point that must be emphasized is that, owing to the massive growth of social needs not only production has to be raised to a large-scale level in almost all branches, but that artisans gradually join co-operative associations, which inevitably results in establishing forms of medium-scale production in the interest of raising labour productivity. These two factors together (rapid development of state-owned large-scale industrial production and the organization of medium-scale production by artisans joined in handicraft co-operatives) change the structure of supply more rapidly than demand is able to adapt itself to these changes if the relative prices reflect cost proportions. That is why price policy has to support this process. It is mainly with the products of the clothing, footwear and knitwear industry as well as the furniture industry.

The fact, that we have referred only to a few branches of the consumer-goods industry should not make us believe that this peculiar feature of industrial price formation is effective only within a limited scope; it also applies to the production of capital goods. When, for example, the expansion of the production capacities of synthetic materials was put on the agenda, several socialist countries set the price of the plastics powder deliberately at a low level. This made imports rise temporarily, but the underlying idea was that demand should reach the level of supply by the time new capacities have been put into operation.

This will perhaps suffice to make clear the difference in nature between agricultural and industrial price policy. To put it briefly, *agricultural price has a role to play directly in the transformation of structure, while industrial price has the function to adapt demand to structural transformation.* All this is an *oversimplified* explanation of process regulation. Agricultural price exercises its effect on the determination of structure together with other regulators. In the same way, price, too, has a role to play in determining the structure in industry. But this does not change what is essential, namely that the allocation function of price is much stronger in agriculture than in industry. In addition, price policy must allow this function to operate differently in industry and in agriculture.

Agricultural price policy is *product-oriented.* A price policy in the conceptual framework of the agrarian policy is unambiguously determined by the envisaged development tendencies. When, for example, in Hungary, in the second half of the 1950s, criticism was levelled at the policy which gave preferential treatment to self-sufficiency in bread-grain growing in plant cultivation and pig fattening in animal husbandry, and an agrarian policy concept was accepted which gave priority to cattle raising in animal husbandry and emphasized self-sufficiency in producing fodder grain in plant cultivation, then the price policy to be adapted was easy to formulate. Price policy may regard a conceptual change in agrarian policy as a matter of relative prices. It is in this fact that the product-oriented character of agricultural price policy finds expression.

A conceptual price policy has to approach the problem of industrial policy in a different way. *In our days, even a national industry at a medium level of development is extremely diversified, and there is a close interdependence among the various industrial branches.* Both specialization and production co-operation create special tendencies. In the manufacture of final products the assembling (handling, packaging, etc.) activities are increasingly coming to the fore. In the preceding manufacturing phases standarized mass production is pursued. The "assembling" industries rely on an ever-widening network of contributory plants supplying components. This network comprises the productive units of the various industries.

Owing to the central control of structure-determining industrial investments and the inter-dependencies among industrial branches, the allocation function of industrial prices can only be *project-oriented.* Let us take as an example of a possible government programme the development of the use of natural gas. From this point of view, chemical industry is a progressive industrial branch. The development of the use of natural gas demands, in turn, that a number of industries, practically from metallurgy on, should be developed according to this programme. If the development of the utilization of natural gas is a central programme, its direct investment needs are financed partly or wholly from the state budget. But if the management of the national economy is based predominantly on economic instruments the complementary (related) investments have to be financed by industry. It is price policy that is expected to meet the requirement of ensuring the necessary self-financing capability of industry.

2. In industrial production, considered from the point of view of prices, a distinction is to be made *between mining and manufacturing industry.* Mining is a branch of primary production. In mining natural factors are determinant with the difference that they manifest themselves in other forms than in agriculture. The resulting specific price problem is less conspicuous in a free market economy as the development of productive forces takes place in conformity with historically established market price relations. The situation is different in a socialist economy where the extraction of raw materials is carried out in a planned, state-controlled way, and planning itself in the socialist countries – in the sphere of basic raw materials – is determined by the endeavour to ensure autarchy.

If the industrial price system is interpreted as a cost system, then it is not impossible to set such raw material prices as cover the inputs. In certain cases, however, this method results in getting unreasonably high prices. Input-related raw material prices are particularly high if they are based on the inputs of marginal mines. Whether average cost or marginal cost is the basis of price formation, a solution must be found to the problem which arises out of the fact that the inputs of individual mines, owing to different natural endowments, vary to a great extent. This is especially conspicuous if we relate inputs not to the unit of quantity but to the unit of utility value. And, as far as raw materials are concerned, they, as a rule, do not lend themselves to weight prices. Price can only be related to average quality, when individual price is determined according to the specific properties of the commodity. Taking into account the substitutability of varieties of raw materials, the specific features of the price formation of raw materials become apparent.[101]

3. The industrial product mix in general must also be characterized from the point of view of industrial price policy. An *up-to-date industrial commodity structure* is characterized by

– a wide assortment of commodities,
– a quick product replacement and
– a comprehensive complementarity and substitutability.

With the widening of the commodity assortment, the question of price relations of allied products (substitute products) is gaining increasing importance. The great multitude of products has virtually resulted in the fact that the prices of the different goods are in a mutual relationship with one another not in respect of concrete product prices but of prices system. Given this industrial structure, the tendency that evaluation based on the utility principle should have a role to play in making the prices of related products proportionate, is becoming stronger and stronger. The utility of the product, its evaluation according to its properties deemed important from the point of view of the consumer (user) are attributable to the fact that the consumer is willing to pay more for one product than for the other if its utili-

[101] Avrukh, A. Ya.: Problemy sebestoimosti i tsenoobrazovaniya v energetike (Problems of Costs and Pricing of Energetics). *Energia*, Moscow, 1970. Brent, A. D., Nikolashkin, A. K. and Petrenko, A. A.: O vozmeshcheniyi zatrat na geologorazvedotshnye raboty v sebestoimosti i tsenakh (Returns of the Input of Geological Research Work in Cost and Prices). *Gazovaya promyslennost*, No. 3, 1970. Lipcsey, M. and Vécsey, A.: *Árpolitika és árszabályozás a bányászatban* (Price Policy and Pricing in Mining). Budapest, 1964. Némethy, K.: Energetikai árrendszerünk alapelvei és továbbfejlesztésének szempontjai (Basic Principles and the Points of View of the Further Development in Our Price System of Energetics). *Energiagazdálkodás*, No. 10, 1969, Budapest

ty is superior to that of the cheaper product. Thus, an up-to-date commodity pattern gives rise to a certain rearrangement of product prices, new criteria come into being, which integrate the products by a given industry (related products) into a uniform price system.

The development of product prices into an intricate price system can also be witnessed in the *extracting industries,* caused here by steadily increasing needs and a variety of utilization. Rising demand expands the range of the raw material varieties extracted. And the varied use they are put to creates a closer relationship between quality and price through a more accurate grading. What can be observed already in the extractive industries, takes effect to a much greater extent in the *manufacturing industries.* The expansion of assortment is a natural concomitant of the rising living standards and of the mass demand for more sophisticated consumer goods. The same process results, in the case of producer goods, from improving working conditions and modern production technology.

Wide assortment in the manufacturing industries is coupled with a *rapid product replacement.* This is due, primarily, to technical development and changes in fashion. *Technical development* is accompanied by the introduction of new products and new varieties. Thus, owing to inventions, partly new-use products (television sets, tape recorders, etc.) come into circulation, which create a sense of new needs (wants), and, on the other hand, owing to technical research and development, improved varieties of already existing products are placed on the market, a process which changes the value judgement of the consumers concerning the old varieties, and may even completely terminate the sense of want for some of them. The same situation is brought about by *changes in fashion.* The higher the living standard, the larger the field of the commodity world in which fashion becomes a criterion of market value judgement, and transgresses the traditional limits of the so-called fashion goods. In this sense, fashion is a criterion governing material and commodity structure, colour and form alike.

Under the conditions of technical development and changes in fashion attention is focussed on the *life cycle of commodities,* which is determined by the changing position of the given product in the realm of commodities.[102] The commodity first appears on the market as a new product. Later when its utility has

[102] BRETTSCHNEIDER, G.: Preisdegression für neue Erzeugnisse. *Sozialistische Finanzwirtschaft*, No. 6, 1970, Berlin. SOPNIEWSKA, H.: Analiza Zasad ustalania cen na nowe wyroby w niektórych krajach socjelistycznych (Analysis of Pricing Principles in Different Socialist Countries). *Prace Zakladu Badania Cen*, No. 7, 1970, Warsaw.

been successfully put to test, it becomes an established product. Finally, it reaches a stage when the market is saturated with it. The demand for new products is generally not large. It is only later that there may be a massive demand for them. And when the market gets saturated, the demand is determined by the consumer's need for replacement. The prices of new products are high. With demand (and production) assuming large proportions, the prices will decline. And with a product becomig obsolete it is, usually not price reduction, but quality improvement, product development that will take place.

With technical development *substitutability and complementarity come increasingly into prominence.* In a modern economy, there is practically no variety of material for which no substitute could be found.

Accountancy, Cost Calculation and Pricing

Planned price formation is based on the guidelines of accountancy, cost calculation and pricing. *We shall discuss these guidelines* and the related questions of industrial price formation under *the conditions of the administrative price system.* Following that, we shall point to the differences that can be met in the transition to the system of a mixed price mechanism.

The foundation of a planned price formation *accounts for the differences that exist in many respects between socialist enterprise accountancy and capitalist enterprise accountancy.* In the accounting system of a socialist enterprise the cost calculation of the productive process is in the centre of book-keeping. Accounting is closely connected with cost calculation and its principles are also valid in book-keeping. Book-keeping is organized in such a way that it virtually solves the tasks of an aggregated cost calculation. It is exactly for this reasons that the socialist countries regularly improve the organization of their accounting systems.[103]

If enterprise accounting is of such a structure, the enterprise production budget can be drawn up, from the book-keeping records of the period determined by two different stock-taking dates. This in turn makes it possible to calculate the production costs directly or indirectly. An enterprise production budget can provide a basis for calculating the prime costs of production for the following reasons:

[103] WILCSEK, J.: *Az önköltség tervezése és ellenőrzése* (Planning and Supervision of Prime Costs). Budapest, 1952.

(a) It compares not the expenses, but the costs of the enterprise with its sales receipts. Costs cannot be equated with expenses. Expenses will not always became costs, and costs do not necessarily involve expenses. If, for example, an enterprise buys some material for further processing, however, for some reason does not use it in the production process, but sells it instead, then though the expenses have already been incurred, they do not cause any cost inputs. Some items' computed costs, however, have the common feature that they do not represent actual expenses. But expenses cannot be equated with costs also for a further reason: expenses are incurred at the time of making the actual payments, while costs arise at the moment the production inputs are made.

(b) An enterprise production budget does not contrast total money receipts with total costs, but only the sales receipts of the enterprise with its production costs. At an industrial enterprise various receipts and expenses connected with trading activities, with the maintenance of welfare institutions, etc. may also arise. The latter do not result from the enterprise's productive activity, and the related cost inputs are not production costs. Socialist enterprise accounting adopts calculation principles when it separates these expenses and receipts outside the sphere of production from the production budget.

(c) The production budget confronts the adequate production costs with sales receipts. Book-keeping takes into consideration cost calculation directives when it carries out a "piecemeal" accounting of the costs burdening the production processes of a longer period of time (e.g. the costs of producing a prototype). Thus, these cost are represented in the production budget in the proportion of the volume of products turned out over the given period of time. Such costs will, on the one hand, burden the production budget even if they were actually incurred at a point of time proceeding the given period; on the other hand, they will be taken into account only proportionally even if they were wholly incurred during that period.

Sales receipts compared with the production costs recorded for a given period may be unjustifiably high (if the volume of semi-finished products decreases) or may be unjustifiably low (if the volume of semi-finished products increases). In the former case, the enterprise can also market products the production costs of which have already partly arisen in the preceding period. In the latter case, part of the production costs of the enterprise will only be refunded in the following period. The resulting distortions in the enterprise budget are eliminated by modifying the production costs by the difference in the volume of semi-finished products.

We have only pointed to the most important facts in the relationship between cost calculation and book-keeping. The relationship of book-keeping and cost accounting is very varied, since it is based on the very comprehensive system of book-keeping by cost types and cost centres. The accountancy instructions are supplemented – in this sense – by the regulations relating to prompt payments, and the prohibition to grant inter-enterprise credits (credit monopoly), by which it can be ensured, among other things, that the enterprise sales receipts during a given period reflect the quantity of commodity outputs for the same period. In this way, though in production cost accounting actual price (sales) receipts are set against production costs, price receipts can approximately express gross returns relative to production costs.

According to the directives of the authorities, the enterprises prepare *pre-* and *post-calculations.* The compulsory system of *cost-calculation* is set up according to the peculiarities of the individual industries. If the prime cost of the product cannot be determined from the overall production costs of the enterprise by division-calculation (or by gradual division-calculation or division calculation by equivalents), if, therefore, additional calculation is needed, the directives start with the allocation of overhead costs (which cannot be directly assigned to particular products) from the fact that these costs must be borne by the products proportionately. The sectoral characteristics (specific to individual industries) find expression in the allocation of overheads in the determination of the *basis of allocation* (direct wages, direct material expenses, direct expenses, etc.).

Enterprise production cost becomes, with certain qualifications, the basis for price formation. *The guidelines of price calculation* lay down what costs cannot be taken into consideration in price formation, and they also determine the normatives which regulate the measure in which the costs can be refunded by the price. This is, therefore, a *normative-calculation system.*[104] In allocating direct costs, the time normatives of the centrally approved production technology and the norms of specific material consumption are of a decisive character. Over-

[104] Gozes, H. and Vasilev, V.: Nyakoyi problemi na formiraneto na normativnata sebestoynost v promislenostta (Some Problems of Setting Industrial Normative Cost). *K-t po tsenite, tseni i tsenoobrazuvane*, No. 2, 1970, Sofia. Kolomiets, R. A.: Opredeleniye normativnoy tsenovoy sebestoimosti na osnove primeneniya korrelatsionnykh metodov (Setting Normative Factory Costs by Applying Correlation Methods). *Ekonomika i organizatsiya prom. proizvodstva*, No. 5, 1969, Kiev. Staneov, D.: Normativna sebestoymost i tsenoobrazovanetov (Normative Cost and Pricing). *Ikonomtcheska misl*, No. 8, 1970, Sofia.

head costs are allowed to be charged according to a given burden rate which, assuming a planned utilization of capacities, coincide with actual costs. Partly within the direct, partly within the overhead costs, there are costs of the character of funds (depreciation, technical development fund, risk fund, etc.). The way in which they can be charged is regulated by special directives.

For the price to absorb prime cost on a social scale, it need not be adapted to the prime cost of each enterprise separately. Cost may be refunded by the price in two ways. Either the price is adapted to enterprise prime cost, or social costs are taken account of in forming the price. In the latter case, we obtain *uniform prices.* The administrative price system brings about the tendency of creating uniform prices, and develops price formation methods meeting this requirement.

Though not independent of enterprise prime costs, social costs eliminate individual, enterprise-bound differences, and can thus be regarded as a socially justified magnitude. By social costs – assuming a rational utilization of the existing production conditions of the given industrial branch – we understand production costs per unit of output. Its determination raises intricate problems.

The social costs of industrial products are often mixed up with the so-called *weighted average costs of the industrial branch concerned.* But the latter can only be regarded as just one of the approaches to social costs.[105] Undoubtedly, it is an important method, which is of special importance from the point of view of the unification of prices. *But in a planned price formation it is in reality two problems that have to be solved.* Individual enterprise costs have to be reduced to a common denominator, and the prices of related products have to be made proportionate to value. By applying the method of calculating the weighted average costs of the industry concerned, the first task can be solved, but not the second. For the purpose of price proportioning let us assume that a given enterprise manufactures a given product all by itself. In this case social costs will coincide with enterprise costs. But only under certain conditions! A distinction must be made depending on whether this monopoly position is due to natural-technical factors, or to production-political measures. If production is based on one single iron ore deposit, it is this natural endowment which accounts for the monopoly position of the enterprise engaged in extracting that ore. In this case, the production cost of the enterprise equals social costs. The

[105] Jávorka, E.: Az ipari árrendszer egyes kérdései (Some Questions of the Industrial Price System). *Közgazdasági Szemle*, No. 2, 1957, Budapest.

monopoly position of a foundry-coke plant may be attributable to the technical factor if the country has not got any other plants with adequate coking equipment. But the monopoly position of an enterprise manufacturing wintercoats is the result of a state policy measure if the production of wintercoats is concentrated in a single enterprise.

Uniform and proportionate prices can be attained when prices are based on social costs. Social costs coincide with the prime costs of an enterprise if the given product is manufactured by an enterprise enjoying monopoly position, and in case the monopoly position is due to natural-technical factors. Social costs coincide with the average costs of the industry concerned if several enterprises turn out the same product, as their combined monopoly position is based on natural-technical factors. In the case of related products, the task of price formation must be solved by taking into account the cost proportions of related products. In this case, neither the one, nor the other method of price formation alone provides the desired solution. *Then social costs can best be approximated with the help of normatives by industrial branches.*

Price calculation can be based on normatives by industrial branches in such industries in which wide range assortments are produced from materials of the same type. This provides the possibility of setting the standards of material consumption as well as the time and wage standards of the individual assortment of production.[106]

A distinction is made between completely closed and not completely closed price calculation by sectoral normatives. A completely closed cost calculation by sectoral normatives is a system in which all cost factors are determined by calculation directives.In a not completely closed system there might be cost factors which are not fixed, but the enterprises are free to include them in their actual magnitude in their calculations. In the former case, the sectoral cost normatives (standards), prescribed or formed, provide the costs serving as a basis for the determination of the producer prices for all products of the given industrial sector. In the latter case, these sectoral cost normatives (standards) do not make up the full price, since certain cost factors or cost elements are calculated, according to central directives, by the enterprises themselves. The completely closed calculation by normatives (standards) of industrial branches

[106] Hungarian economists (Sternfeld, A., Németh, P., Korponai, N., Balogh, J., Rácz, L.) were the first to introduce normative pricing to industrial branches. Its practical method, applied to cotton grey goods, was elaborated by a large group of specialists.

results in such price proportions in which allowance has been made for the effect of differing production conditions of the various enterprises.

Normative (standardized) costs by industries can be used in relatively few industries (usually in the light industries only). But to form proportionate prices, other methods can also be applied. Such is, for example, the construction of *the cost equivalent index.* The enterprise's equivalent index is used when calculations for product groups are made in order to identify the costs by size and quality of products. Group calculation provides the cost for the master type. The enterprise equivalent index is the master type of the product group, and fixes the cost proportions between the other size (quality) varieties. It is by these two methods (group calculation and equivalent indices) that the costs of the varieties of the product group are obtained.

It follows from the foregoing that, when price-proportioning for related products must be made on the scale of industrial branches, the enterprise equivalent index can be of the greatest help. If in a given product group the bulk of production is concentrated in a single enterprise, then the equivalent indices based on the post-calculation figures or the technical calculations of this enterprise can also be used as the basis on which the price list of the whole product group can be built. In such a case, the equivalent index for a given industrial branch can be obtained by the methods of extrapolation or interpolation.

Prime cost equivalents cannot be worked out for every product group. The adaptation, however, of price proportions to social labour-input proportions cannot be narrowed down to calculating the enterprise normative costs of industrial branches and enterprise equivalents. This requirement has brought parameter pricing into prominence.

The parameter price formation of engineering products is the method by which cost is synthetized with consumer evaluation.[107] With the development of the price calculation methods, the requirement has increasingly been emphasized to make *price* interdependent of the jerky changes in enterprise prime costs, and *to base it instead on the technical level of products.* This makes it possible to determine those straight lines – or rather curves – (parabolas, hyperbolas, circles, exponential

[107] HANUS, V.: Otázky plánováni a tvorby tsen ve strojirenstvi (Price Planning and Pricing in the Engineering Industry). *Planovane Hospodarstvi*, No. 6, 1957, Prague. MYNÁR, A.: Nekolik problémü tvorby á uschovania urovne velkoobchodnich cen (Some problems of Setting Wholesale Prices and of Maintaining the Price Level). *Podnikova Organisatce*, No. 5, 1957, Prague. SZABADITS, D.: *Paraméteres árképzés* (Parametric Pricing). Budapest, 1965.

curves, etc.) which, within the sphere of related products, characterize relative prices. If we adequately illustrate the prices of related products obtained by enterprise price calculation, we can experience that prices are dispersed around the ideal price curve based on technical (technological) considerations. It is exactly these dispersions that are eliminated by parameter price formation.

Parameter price formation can primarily be applied to products which have some important characteristics in common, and differ from one another only in size, quality, capacity, etc. (intermediate materials, alloys, screws, synthetic materials, mass articles, etc.). Therefore, it is not accidental that parametric price formation was first applied to component parts. The price system of components exercises a decisive influence on the prime costs and producer prices of engineering end products. This has given rise to the requirement to base proportionate prices of the end products also on the parameter price formation of components, and of basic units. The technical-economic price parameters of these products manufactured at the low production phases of engineering ensure a cost level within the group of varieties, and determine the price proportions of the different varieties on the basis of the technical-technological data of the products concerned (material, dimensions, etc.). Thus it is predominantly the size and workmanship (finish) that constitute the basis of price formation, which is related to prime costs in a certain way, since the quantity of material and of man-hours needed determines the inputs, too.

Much more difficult is the application of parameters to composite, more sophisticated products. These products are made up of different components and basic units, and thus the output varieties do not provide an unambiguous relationship between changes in technical characteristics and changes in prime costs. Therefore, they can only be characterized by several technical parameters, and it is almost impossible to find out which should be taken as a basis for forming the correct price proportions. It is also important to consider that a given product may be regarded useful by different users in different respects. In the case of a lathe, for example, for one user it is accuracy, for another the length or the diameter of the workpiece to be processed that is the most important technical characteristic.

Accountancy, cost calculation and price formation undergo a certain degree of modification if the government activates the role of the market in price formation, and retains, as a consequence, administrative price regulation only in relation to fields of crucial importance. Under such circumstances, *the primary requirement to be set for accountancy is not to register faithfully the economic processes that have taken place, but to provide the necessary information for rational economic decisions*. Thus, enterprise organization cannot be taken to be equal exclusively to production organization. Accountancy cannot follow solely the requirements of the closed, internal life of the enterprise, but must reflect the enterprise's relationship to the outside world. In Hungary, for example, at the time of the transition from the administrative price system to a mixed-type of price system, accountancy was required to provide appropriate information both for the national economy and for the given enterprise. The fulfilment of this double task should be ensured by regulating, in a compulsory way and according to uniform principles, the scope of data supply meeting the information needs of the national economy. At the same time the accounting instructions relating to the data supply and registration needed for the internal information system of the enterprises should provide the possibility for the enterprises to make use of their capabilities and to meet their obligations.

The system of *cost calculation* will also change. Given the system of enterprise independence based on profit motivation, cost and price calculation systems are an active organizing factor of production engineering and product programming. Therefore, enterprises must be free to develop the cost and price calculation systems which best suit their possibilities and successful business policies, and, in allocating fixed (overhead) costs among individual products, to take into account the cost-bearing capacities of various products. The government only compels the enterprises to have the system applied by them in their cost calculations put into written regulations so that in the case of a price control the data supplied can be verified.

The guidelines for price calculation and the systems of price formation remain in force under a mixed price mechanism in a specific way. They provide, on the one hand, the foundations for a planned price formation in the sphere of administrative prices, and serve, on the other, the aims of an effective price supervision. This is a consequence of the fact that the obligation to prepare price calculations based on the principles of cost calculation also applies, as a rule, to free prices. Furthermore, when the government restricts the market movement of price by setting limits to it, then the systems of price formation (prices computed by normative calculation by industrial branches, etc.) regulate prices, from which actual prices may deviate within the limits set.

In addition, the various price formation systems continue to survive as non-compulsory but purposefully used mechanisms in shaping an enterprise's price policy. Thus, for example, *parameter price formation can also be conceived as a modern calculation method of enterprises which can well be utilized in the field of manufacturing individual engineering products.* Parametric price formation – including its decentralized form – can be regarded as an aid ensuring substantial labour saving, providing the possibility of making price offers within a short time. If we consider the price parameter from this point of view, then the scope of its application and its role in the operational activity of the enterprise will expand on a large scale. This is bacause it gives, in this case, information on the expected costs or the initial price. It can be stated, in general, that in parameter price formation based on technical-economic relationships, the special knowledge of the *enterprises'* experts, the information unaccessible to any outside organization, will be of increasingly crucial importance. This must be specifically emphasized because the rigid application of parameter prices may lead to a *perpetuating* effect. It may perpetuate the direction of technical development as any parameter price formation will place emphasis, depending on technical properties, on different factors, creating thereby interest in developing the product structure in a way which is favourable from the point of view of the price parameter.

Relationship between Industrial Prices and Technical Development

Industrial price is also expected to meet a quality requirement: to promote technical development, to stimulate the growth of labour productivity. Price alone cannot, of course, be expected to produce such an effect. But if the government creates material interest in profit, it is really the price relations on which depend the direction and order of priority of the measures of a technical and organizational nature taken to improve production results. The criteria of industrial planned price formation to comply with this requirement were formulated differently at the different stages of socialist construction.

1. In the period of the formation of the socialist world economic system, the most serious problems were raised by *how to ensure full employment* in the majority of countries. Before the war, in today's socialist countries of Eastern Europe, a considerable part of the population of working age found no jobs. The bulk of the employed worked in agriculture, but they, too, could work only seasonally or occasionally. In the light of this fact it can be realized what immense social pressure was exerted, following the introduction of the socialist system, by the

demand for full employment. Therefore, *to create as many new jobs as possible outside agriculture had to be regarded as the main direction of planned development*. This made it imperative to adopt an extensive type of industrialization. This is how *the low price of the means of production* became, in a given historical period of time, the main criterion of planned industrial price formation.

According to what is essential in this view, in order to stimulate industrialization, the prices of means of production have to be determined at a lower level than what their production really costs the national economy. This view of price policy was regarded as a guiding principle by almost all socialist countries. This accounts for the fact that in the 1950s the extractive industries of basic raw materials and the high-priority material-processing industries were state-subsidized. Though it was commonly known that in this way cost relationships were distorted by the industrial price structure, the effect exercised by the price system on industrialization was deemed to be superior to any other consideration.

In a socialist economy, the government determines, regardless of the price system, how much of the national income it allocates to consumption and accumulation, and how it distributes, within accumulation, the investments among the various sectors of the economy. But the effect of the price system on industrialization can hardly be questioned. Price-cost relationships have an important role to play in determining the enterprise policies of a technical-organizational nature. Several of them are put into force by the enterprises in their own sphere of authority. Even under the directive planning mechanism, the state plan of the national economy does not specify small investments individually. Furthermore, in certain socialist countries, the enterprises may draw so-called prime cost-reducing investment credits directly from the credit organizations. And finally, in preparing the perspective and annual plans of the national economy, the central authorities also make use of the project plans of the enterprises, which, in turn, also attach importance to profit considerations. As a result, the low prices of means of production cannot be dismissed simply by declaring that they attribute to price an effect that it does not have under a directive planning mechanism.

On the low (deficit) prices of the means of production many critical remarks were made already in the second half of the 1950s in several socialist countries.[108] Looked upon from the angle of the possibilities of the national economy, the question

[108] STRUMILIN, S.: *op. cit.* MALISHEV, I. S.: *op. cit.*

is this: should the expansion of production be effected under the circumstances of a relative abundance, or a relative scarcity of materials. A country richly endowed with natural resources can pursue a policy of low-priced materials. This can be justified by the bottleneck of manufacturing capacities. Under such conditions, it is in the interest of society to expand material processing at a rapid rate even if it is accompanied by wasting materials to a certain degree. But if it is raw materials the country lacks most, such a price policy cannot be expedient as it regularly gives rise to conflicts between factors stimulating the waste of materials and administrative policy measures aimed at saving them. In certain cases, however, it is exactly through high raw-material prices that enterprises can be urged to make increasing efforts to economize on materials.

2. By extensive industrialization the industrial production of the socialist countries increased at a more rapid rate than that of the capitalist countries. At the same time, the difference in the technical level of industrial production and, consequently, in the level of labour productivity did not decrease, on the contrary, it increased. It was partly for this reason, but in the first place because of the gradual depletion of the reserves of extensive development, that it became necessary to change from the extensive to the *intensive stage* of economic development. It was under such circumstances that the tasks of technical development and, in compliance with them, the criteria of planned industrial price formation were revised.[109]

Several socialist countries built into their economic calculation systems a "*technical development fund*", and raised from time to time the rates of depreciation. As a rule, these are

[109] Berea, A.: Reciprocitatea influentei dintre progresul technic si formarea preturilor (Connection between Technical Progress and Pricing). *Economic Probleme*, No. 3, 1969, Bucharest. Cezik, J.: Vedesketechnicky pokrok a ceny (Scientific-Technical Progress and Prices). *Svetové finance*, No. 17, 1969, Prague. Kosuta, A.: Novaya tekhnika i problemy tsenoobrazovaniya (New Technology and Problems of Pricing). *Ekonomicheskaya Gazeta*, No. 22, 1970, Moscow. Levtrinsky, T. and Vasilenko, G.: Tsenoobrazovaniye i tekhnichesky progress (Pricing and Technological Progress). *Planovoye Khozyaistvo*, No. 11, 1969, Moscow. P. Ritter, J. and Német, I.: A műszaki fejlesztés és az árrendszer (Technical Development and the Price System). *Pénzügyi Szemle*, No. 5, 1972, Budapest. Rozanova, L. I.: Tekhnichesky progress i tsenoobrazovanie na produktsiyu mashinostroeniya (Technical Progress and the Pricing of Engineering Products). *Vestnik Mashinostroeniya*, No. 3, 1970. Sica, G.: Preturile cu ridicate – pirghie pentru promovarea progresului tehnic (Producers' Prices – Incentives of Technological Progress). *Viata Economica*, No. 5, 1970, Bucharest. Veica, M. and Zaman, G.: Stimularea prin pret a progresului tehnic (Encouraging Technological Progress by Prices). *Viata Economica,* No. 26, 1969, Bucharest. Wolter, W. and Krüger, E.: Die Rolle der Preisbildung im System der Überleitung neuer Ergebnisse der Forschung und Entwicklung in die Produktion. *Die Wirtschaft*, No. 17, 1969, Berlin.

handled as funds, together with the guarantee costs. The treatment as funds of the sums accumulated for the purposes of *depreciation and technical development* is connected, partly, with the fact that a specified proportion of them is centralized by the budget. The centralized part of the depreciation fund serves new investments, and the centralized part of the technical development fund serves the purpose of financing centrally subsidized technical development projects. Their fund-like treatment is connected, on the other hand, with the endeavour to prevent the depletion of the financial resources earmarked for renewal, product and production development. Otherwise, the management of an enterprise may raise wages at the expense of technical development, or increase enterprise profits in the interest of higher rates of profit sharing. *Guarantee costs* treated as a fund serve the purpose that in case the costs of free repairs and commodity replacements within the time of guarantee is smaller than the calculated sum, the savings can be used to develop servicing.

In the sphere of *price formulae* connected with technical development, the following points are worth noting:

– *Price formulae effecting the material structure of industrial products*. In this respect, it is the price proportions of substitutable large-volume energy sources and intermediate materials that affect industrial pricing policy. The price proportions of energy sources exert a substantial influence on the energy pattern, which is undergoing significant changes in our days. It was in the 1960s that carbohydrates began increasingly to be used, which was made possible partly by newly discovered gas and oil resources, partly by co-operation agreements between CMEA countries. Under such circumstances, however, the relative prices must regularly be analysed, and the interests of the users and the changing supply structure must be reconciled from time to time. In utilization, substitute products appear as a problem in almost every industry.

– *Price formulae influencing the quality (assortment) pattern of industrial products*. This is, in reality, the price proportion problem of related articles. Though related products are generally evaluated in the case of capital goods and partly in the case of consumer goods by the market, material interest in manufacturing up-to-date, that is, high-quality products must be ensured by administrative price formation. This manifests itself in measures regulating the price formation of new industrial products, the system of class prices, the system of surcharges and allowances, etc.

3. The interrelationship of industrial producer prices and technical development came into prominence with the

economists of the DDR in the early 1970s, primarily in connection with the *dynamization* of industrial producer prices. The preconditions for this were provided by the wide application of price planning. The arguments may be marshalled like this: If the tasks of technical development and their effects on the productivity of labour can be specified perspectively or in the medium-run by taking into account the mobilizable material resources, the changes in the cost relations of production can also be conceived of as normative requirements. State planning, then, identifies, on the one hand, the objectives of technical development, and controls, on the other, whether the enterprises have implemented the measures taken with a view to carrying out the planned technical and organizational development, or to determining whether, as a result of these measures, the planned improvement of economic efficiency has taken place.

Price can be instrumental in carrying out this supervising function through price change normatives. According to this idea to set such normatives is, generally, the task of middle term price planning. Thus the dynamization of the industrial producer price has emerged as a counter-measure to the earlier price freezing policy. The assumption is here that industrial producer prices must decrease in proportion to the productivity of labour improving as a result of technical development. The normatives of price reduction are determined in such a way that under a planned economy the initial profitability is stabilized. If, with decreasing prices, profitability deteriorates, or the enterprise incurs a loss, this is an indication that either the directives for technical development have not fully been carried out, or the expected improvement of efficiency in these directives has not yielded the planned results.

4. It is a view prevailing primarily among Hungarian economists that the stimulation of technological development is a matter of general economic regulation rather than of price policy itself.[110] The essence may be summed up as follows: *A situation must be created in which the users are the principal regulators of technical development enabling them to bring about a producers' behaviour which provides the stimulus to carry out economic development*. In this approach, viewed from the angle of the price category, the orientating role of the market value judgement and a *flexible price mechanism* making that role possible, seem to be of basic importance; a further requirement is the strengthening of the self-financing capacity and thus the adaptability of enterprises to changing demand conditions.

[110] Balázsy, S.: Pénzügyi szabályozó rendszerünk a műszaki fejlődés szemszögéből (Our Financial Control System from the Point of View of Technical Development). *Közgazdasági Szemle*, No. 12, 1972, Budapest.

3. The Price of Marketing

Commercial Profit Margin

The production process does not end with the manufacture of the product. In the case of further processing, the commodity must be transported to the place where it will be processed, and, in the case of consumption, to shops accessible to the consumers. Depending on its nature, the commodity must be graded, packed and brought into a state in which it can directly be processed or be placed at the disposal of final consumers by retail trade. Accordingly, production costs are composed of manufacturing and sales costs, the latter comprising transportation and commodity-handling costs. The latter again contain costs relating to warehousing, material handling, packaging as well as to natural wastage.

Thus sales costs are not merely the inputs of marketing, but are also the expression of *losses* resulting from the sales process. In the sales process, the commodity's volume may decrease and its quality deteriorate. The *quantity of the commodity* may decrease during warehousing, transportation, unloading and sorting. Natural wastage may be caused by shrinkage, evaporation, dispersion, etc. *Qualitative value loss* is due mainly to deterioration, fashion changes and technological obsolescence. In the case of perishable foodstuffs, the loss of use satisfaction value, and in the case of fashion and technical articles, changes is consumer preferences may bring about a situation in which the value of the commodity is less at the time of marketing than anticipated by trade when having bought it. This is one element of *trade risk*.

Producer price (price receipts of industrial and agricultural plants) generally covers the costs of producing the commodity while the commercial profit margin in covered by the mark-up. Just as the components of the producer price are prime cost and profit, the mark-up too falls into two components: the one covering marketing costs and the other covering profit.[111]

[111] Tsenoobrazovanie i torgovye skidki (Pricing and Trade Allowances). *Ekonomika*, Moscow, 1970. FALL, L.: Vállalati árpolitika a kereskedelemben (Enterprise Price Policy in Commerce). *Közgazdasági Szemle*, No. 4, 1969, Budapest. FENYŐ, I.: *Árpolitika és áruk a kereskedelemben* (Price Policy and Goods in Commerce). Budapest, 1971. SIMKOVÁ, M. and SLIVO-

According to the provisions of the delivery contracts between industrial and agricultural enterprises (co-operatives), wholesale trade buys the commodities and passes them on to retail trade. Sales costs emerge both in wholesale and retail trade and fall into categories of wholesale and retail mark-ups. Wholesale input price (producer price) supplemented by the wholesale mark-up yields the wholesale price. Retail input price (wholesale price) supplemented by the mark-up of retail trade yields the retail selling price, which equals the consumer price. Producer price – wholesale price – consumer price: it is this triple segmentation that expresses the successive processes of production, the manufacture of the commodity, its wholesale distribution and retail sales. These are the processes to which the cost inputs are attached, and consequently, on which the structure of the consumer price is built.

The structure of consumer prices as out-lined here in general terms asserts itself in real life with many exceptions. (a) There may be a direct relationship between the producer and the consumer either without any trade organization in between, or the productive plant itself performs the marketing. (b) It is also possible that one single trading organization establishes relations between the producer and the consumer (demi-wholesale trade). (c) There are fields where commodity sale is transacted not in the dual system of wholesale and retail trade but of the 3-5-channel system of purchasing and distribution. (For example, in vegetable and fruit trade.) (d) Finally, there may be cases when the activity of the trading enterprise also extends to manufacturing (improving) processes.

These intricate relations are, of course, also reflected in the price mechanism; in certain cases, sales costs are included in the producer price, or production costs in the mark-up. It is, in practice, the *system of specific conditions of delivery* that make it possible to distinguish between the contents of producer price and mark-up. In their delivery contracts, the manufacturing and trading enterprises specify in detail delivery obligations, lay down their division of tasks in the processes of commodity handling. These contracts also provide for the price surcharges or price allowances to be made in case the commitments stipulated in the contracts are not fully observed. When e.g. carrying out transportation instead of the contractually obliged partner, the other contracting party is entitled to a freight refund, etc. In

←

vá, B.: Nekolik poznámek k rizikovému fondu v obchode (Some Comments on the Risk in Commerce). *Socialisticky obchod*, No. 8, 1969, Prague. Sós, J.: Árpolitika a kereskedelmi vállalatoknál (Price Policy with Commercial Enterprises). *Kereskedelmi Szemle*, No. 3, 1969, Budapest.

the case of free prices, all this is the responsibility of the enterprises. If, however, the state fixes or maximizes the producer price, and/or the commercial profit margin, distinguishing between manufacturing and sales costs, forming the specific delivery conditions is more or less the responsibility of state price regulation. All the more so as fixed or maximized prices can only be interpreted if the delivery conditions are laid down unambiguously. *The characteristic features of the difference between the mark-up as formed in the free-market system and the administrative price system can be summed up as follows*:

1. The sales cost per unit of commodity differs by product groups and, within them, even by product varieties. As a rule, the higher the *sales-cost intensity* of a given product, the greater the share of transport costs in the production inputs. With the majority of products, sales costs account only for about 10 to 20 per cent of the production inputs, but for example with certain construction materials (sand, gravel, etc.), sales costs amount to a multiple of the costs of extraction. Generally, sales-cost intensity is especially substantial with raw materials. In regulating the mark-up, state price regulation takes these objective differences into account. It is in harmony with them that the government differentiates the mark-up according to product groups.

Though the sales-cost intensity of a commodity as a factor determining the mark-up also plays an important role in the autonomous price policy of enterprises, here it is primarily the *trade risk* that is of decisive importance. Moreover: in its price policy the trading enterprise does not narrow down the risk element to the qualitative or quantitative losses in value sustained in the course of commodity handling. The trading enterprise also weighs the risk by considering whether the product can be sold in the volume ordered, or what consumer-price relations are needed for an adequate trade to be made in that product. Therefore, in addition to the sales-cost intensity of a commodity, the trade also takes into account the *cost-bearing capacity* of a product. It places certain products on the market with a minimum mark-up if it can assume that it will give rise to an added turnover in products whose prices are set with a high mark-up. Thus, in the price policy of the trading enterprise an important role is played by "price mixing", while the mark-up in the market-price system is higher than the mark-up that can be accounted for in the case of state price regulation.

2. If the mark-up is determined by the state, a special significance is attached to *the regulation of transport costs*. What, in the first place, must be decided upon is this: should transport costs be taken into account in forming the mark-up as they are actually incurred, or only according to standards, and, further,

whether the freight rates of any transport branch or just of specified transport branches should be applied. If the consumer price is fixed, the transport costs too can be charged only according to standards, that is, in such cases the *system of average freight costs* is applied.

Owing to transport being made in different relations, the *so-called average distance needed* provides the basis for determining the average freight cost. For transport costs to be charged for an average distance, the freight rates of that transport branch is applied which transacts the bulk of transports economically. This stimulates to organize transports rationally, that is, to carry out transports between the place of production and the place of destination in the shortest possible way, and to increase the share of transit transports within toal transports, and to endeavour, in general, to carry the commodity without delay to its destination. It is justifiable, in exceptional cases, for the government to establish a central *freight-equalizing fund* which undertakes to refund the differences between average and actual transport costs. Such a fund is usually created with freight-intensive goods when uniform consumer prices are applied within the country (a region). If transport costs are high and the price is uniform, enterprises usually dislike transporting their products over long distances. This makes it necessary to establish a freight-equalizing fund.

3. The mark-up can be determined in two different systems: either in the *rate system or the system of itemized mark-ups*. The rate system (gross profit margin) can be formed again in two ways: either by way of calculating it back from the current consumer price, or by basing it on the wholesale input price. The system of the mark-up as applied by the trading enterprises in their price policy, rests on considerations of expedience. If, however, the mark-up is regulated by the government, the question arises, what effect will be exercised by this or that system of the mark-up on the business policy of enterprises.

It is commonly experienced that if (a) the consumer price and within it the mark-up is fixed, (b) the market is a sellers'market, (c) the employees of the trading enterprises receive bonuses in proportion to the profit of turnover made, (d) and the government regulates the mark-up in the system of gross profit margins, the tendency may assert itself for the trading enterprises not to be interested in low purchase prices or in buying varieties with a mark-up whose profit-covering part is unfavourable for them. Since in the conditions outlined above the trade cannot pursue a price policy, it asserts its endeavour to maximize turnover (profit) by its *commodity purchasing policy*. Thus, the state regulation of the mark-up brings into prominence the conflict of interests of the basic aim of the government's price policy (price stability) and of the interest (profit maximization) of the trading enterprises.

This conflict of interests can be mitigated. Itemized mark-ups can also be set, but their application in absolute terms has its limitations; in the case of product groups with wide assortments, it makes accounting very complicated, etc. This mark-up system is suited rather for foodstuffs and industrial mass articles. In addition, it is possible to develop for the employees of trade a system of material interest which somewhat mitigates the antisocial features of the system of turnover or profit interest. Experiences, however, evince that the problems arising, as a result of the state-fixing of prices, already in the production sphere, will further be sharpened in the sphere of trade. Therefore, it is not accidental that when socialist planned economy is developing in the mechanism of a planned market regulation, the attempt is made to resolve, first of all, the rigid stipulations concerning the mark-up.

Commodity Freight Rates

The setting of commodity freight rates is a task of the central authorities even if the socialist state approves of free price movement in a wide range of commodities. Price policy has to solve intricate problems in the field of transport. *A commodity freight rate system* has to be elaborated in which care is taken that all commodity items are carried to their destination by the means of transport most appropriate to them and in the most economical way. For the majority of commodities the most adequate way of transport is unambiguous. There are cases, however, where this is a *matter of choice*. It is exactly this problematic part of the physical movement of commodities that can set special requirements for commodity freight rates.

With the development of the forces of production, the technology of transport is also making progress, and a marked differentiation of transport is taking place. Thus the economic considerations underlying correct decisions in this field, have to be ensured in an increasingly intricate system of transport. A system of commodity freight rates ensuring a rational combination of the various branches of transport has got a pattern generally applicable. It has to be formed by each country with due consideration to its peculiar economic-geographical conditions, the developmental level of its transportation network, and of the possibilities of further developing a modern system of transport, and also of the rate of progress at which the investment policy envisages its implementation.

In Hungary, in compliance with the above considerations, the main task of forming a commodity freight rate system has been specified in the following: it has to ensure the *separation of the functions of rail and road transport and the co-operation of these two branches of transport with the highest possible degree of economic efficiency.* [112]

The commodity freight rate system is based on the following principles: it must

– reflect actual inputs;

– promote an optimum distribution of the carriage of goods among the various branches of transport;

– make both carrier and consigner interested in the better utilization of the means of transport in all branches of transport;

– stimulate a maximum sectoral efficiency in each individual branch of transport;

– make possible, by its simple set-up, the reduction and mechanization of the administration of transport;

– ensure a continuous, comparative analysis of individual branches of transport.

These requirements can best be met by a uniform, nationwide commodity freight rate system in which the *freight rates of individual transport branches reflect the input proportions*. It is not an easy task to create such a system of commodity freight rates, since the cost calculations underlying freight rates rest on conditions widely differing according to transport branches. In rail transport – as already mentioned – the maintenance of the railway track constitutes part of the prime cost. In river and road transport, however, the corresponding item being covered by the state budget, is separated from carriage costs. The freight rate system must also take into consideration that the input per

[112] CZÉRE, B.: A közlekedési ágazatok koordinációja érdekében végzett kutatások (Research to Co-ordinate Branches of Transport). *Közlekedéstudományi Szemle*, No. 3, 1962, Budapest. GUREVICH, G. and ZAGALSKY, E.: Tarify na perevozki exportnykh i importnykh gruzov (The Transport of Goods in Export-Import). *Morskoy Flot*, No. 3, 1970. KREMER, E.: *Die Gütertransportpreise im ökonomischen System*. Transpress VEB., Berlin, 1969. KREININ, A. V.: Sistema tarifov i khozyaistvennykh razchot zheleznykh dorog (Railway Tariff Systems and their Self-Accounting. Book entitled: New System of Planning Economic Incentives in Railway Transport). Moscow, 1969. NESKUBO, B. I.: Voprosy sovershenstvovaniya tsen na transporte gaza v usloviyakh novoy sistemy khozyaistvovaniya (Perfectioning the Prices of Gas Transportation under the Conditions of a New Economic System). *Ekonomika, organizatsiya i upravleniye v gazovoy promyslennosti*, No. 11, 1970. SULYMAN, A.: Effektivnost avtomobilynogo transporta i tarify (The Efficiency and Tariffs of Road Transportation). *Avtomobilyny transport*, No. 12, 1969, Moscow. TEICHMANOWA, E.: Tranzyt przez Polske w taryfach kolejowych (Railway Tariffs of Polish Transit Traffic). *Handel Zagraniczny*, No. 8, 1969, Warsaw.

ton-kilometre varies with the distance, and shows different peculiarities according to transport branches.

Road transport is the only mode of transport in which the goods can be carried from door to door without unloading. With all other means of transport the goods have first to be carted to the dispatch station (harbour, railway station or airport), and from there to the place of destination. All this involves unloading. The share of this added cost is naturally smaller in the case of long-distance transport. The freight rate system must, of course, also reflect this peculiarity of cost formation so that rational economic decisions can be made by comparing individual freight rates.

Historically evolved freight rates generally take into account these peculiarities and also other factors. In several socialist countries rail transport is still the main means of long-distance haulage and of carrying bulk goods. Suitable for river (canal) transport are generally such mass goods whose places of dispatch and destination are situated along the waterway concerned, and where the dispatching and receiving stations are separated from each other by a long enough distance. Lorries can economically be used for the carriage of goods which require rapid transport and are sensitive to unloading. The upper limit of distance for economical road transport is around 30–50 kilometres. Air transport is especially suited to carrying goods over long distances.

Worth noting is the possibility of establishing freight rates based on averages and of eliminating the contradictions arising out of individual circumstances. Freight rates calculated on averages may show wide dispersions. Obviously, water transport is cheaper downstream than upstream. The cost of railway carriage is different if the track is flat or graded, since in the latter case it is necessary to use and maintain special equipment. It is with due consideration to all these peculiarities that a uniform freight rate system can be evolved. This is not always possible. It may be necessary to apply specific provisions to adapt freight rates to concrete circumstances or possibly to particular consignments.

It is one of the characteristics of the freight rates of rail transport that the rates conforming to transport inputs are differentiated according to commodity varieties. Goods are divided, on the basis of various considerations, into freight classes. The underlying idea of the *ad valorem rate system* is the fact that the costs of railway transport have to be recovered in a global way as the railways as a whole must be profitable. On the other hand, considerations of the transport policy, stimulation, etc. come into prominence when a decision has to be taken on the share of individual products in bearing total cost. In our time of increasing rail transport the idea asserts itself that freight rates must adapt themselves to the cost-bearing capacity of the product carried. Since it may be assumed that a commodity representing a higher value can bear a higher burden of cost, the classical basic form of freight rates is the cost of carriage proportionate to the value of the products transported. It is in the latest decades that the concept has come to the fore which requires that forwarding costs have to be covered not only in a global way *but also by each product separately*, that is, each product has to bear the cost that its carriage involves. The transition from value (ad valorem) rates to input rates simplifies commodity freight rates because when the factors of primary importance for the cost of carriage of individual products (the type of railway truck needed, the specific weight of the good transported, the measure of handling they need, etc.) are accepted as the basis for forming the rates, this can be expressed with relatively few commodity classes. The railway freight rates currently in use in most socialist countries are of a *mixed type* in which the elements of both input and value freight rates are intermingled.

Commodity freight rates must also create interest in *the maximum utilization of the means of transport*. The means of transport are utilized to the maximum extent when the good are carried with an adequate use of the loading-weight capacity and when the time of demurrage is minimized. Hungarian freight rates provide stimulation – in several socialist countries – for the economical loading of vehicles by the systems of weight standard rates and of so-called sub-class freight rates. In the case of the application of the weight standard system, freight has always to be paid according to the carrying capacity of the vehicle concerned (loading weight, tonnage of the railway truck), or according to the minimum weight specified. In applying the sub-class system, the freight adapts itself to the quantity of the consignment, but the freight rates will grow progressively if the quantity of the goods consigned does not reach the loading weight. The sub-class system is used indiscriminately in the rail transport rates, while the two systems are applied alternately in the shipping, road transport and cartage rates.

The observance of a *minimum time of demurrage* is stimulated by the time allowed free of demurrage and by charging a penalty in case this time is transgressed.

Railway freight rates must adequately express the peculiarity of carriage costs, namely that *the cost of carriage per one kilometre varies with the distance of transport*. The railway freight rate system takes this characteristic of cost formation into account by determining the ton-per-kilometre charges specified for the various commodity classes according to the distance of transport.

Just as in the case of grouping the products into different freight rate classes and of establishing appropriate rate proportions between them, considerations of the transport policy also assert themselves in differentiating the freight rates according to the distance of transport. One of these considerations is the *principle of minimum transport distance*. If, for example, goods are to be carried by the railway over a distance of less than 30 kilometres, it is always the freight rate for 30 kilometres that is charged. In the principle of minimum transport distance the transport-political consideration finds expression that in carrying goods over a short distance the use of road transport vehicles should be stimulated. And in determining a rational *maximum distance*, the transport-political idea asserts itself that goods should not be transported beyond a specified distance at all, and a stimulus should be given in this way to a rational location of industrial plants.

Rational Transport and the Terms of Delivery

When examining the issue of economical forwarding not from the point of view of the agencies of transport, but of those making use of their services (the consigners), the following two requirements must be set: 1. The consigners should not overburden the transport system by commodities that cannot be transported economically. 2. The economically transportable goods should only be carried over distances that are absolutely needed. This problem receives a very strong emphasis in the case of raw materials, especially those the greater part of which incorporates value-creating labour provided by transport.[113]

The more the weight of a given raw material exceeds the weight of the end product, the more important it is to process the raw material locally and to transport the finished product only. It is not economical, for example, to transport sugar-beet over a long distance, as 70 per cent of the weight transported is water, and only 17 per cent is sugar. Transported unprocessed timber by rail is also uneconomical as nearly 50 per cent of its volume is waste material. Therefore, it is wortwhile to have it first sawn. Sawn timber is economical to transport without further processing, and not in a manufactured form as furniture. Therefore,

[113] TURETSKY, S.: Problemy raspredeleniya i tsenoobrazovaniya (Problems of Distribution and Pricing). *Voprosy Ekonomiki*, No. 4, 1963, Moscow.

furniture factories are economically located near consumer markets and not near sawmills. In the majority of cases, raw materials are partly utilized locally, partly transported over shorter or longer distances. There are power stations located near coal mines, and factories manufacturing concrete panels located near the extraction places of construction materials, etc., but the bulk of coal and a substantial part of the construction materials get to the place of utilization through the transportation network. This shows that value relations underlying price relations do not exclude in most cases the transport of carriage cost-intensive products; they only ensure them an advantage for local manufacturing.

There are product varieties whose market value adapts itself to the cost of local handling processes, and thus they cannot bear transport costs. This is the general characteristic of products that in the world of commodities are usually referred to as *by-products*. Products having a low market value can gain transport-worthiness if special freight rates are set for them. Such a freight-rate policy can be applied especially in agricultural development or soil amelioration programmes.

It is often in consequence of inadequate organization of commodity distribution, that the principle of economical transport may not fully assert itself. When the principle of efficiency consistently asserts itself in transport, superfluous transports are eliminated, or kept at least within tolarable limits. Such are cross transports, transports over unduly long distances, empty haulage, re-transports, etc.

Economical transports cannot be ensured by freight rates alone. This is connected with a large number of factors that are outside the scope of price formation. In a specific way, price formation too can, of course, exercise a certain effect on commodity freight rates. Therefore, it is worth examining more closely *the relationship between the price of products and their transport costs*. Here we have to answer two interrelated questions: how is the cost of carriage realized in the price of the product, and at whose expense is it to be covered? When we want to be informed about the price relations of products, it is not enough to know their prices, it is also necessary to be informed about the *terms of delivery* (Incoterms), that is, the place in relation to which the price has its validity. From this respect, product prices fall into two groups: to the first belong prices which include the costs of transportation to the place of utilization, and to the second the prices that do not include these costs.

Where prices are regulated in the administrative price system, the principle of a uniform price, in the case of products belonging to the first group is also uniform from the point of view of users (consumers). With products belonging to the second group, however, uniform prices are valid only at the parity of the place of production. Products belonging to the first group can be obtained at the same price in any part of the country, however far the place of purchase should be from the place of production. At the parity of the user, a uniform price may be differentiated in practice. Sometimes the user bears part of the costs of transporting the products to him from the station nearest to him (place of destination). In the same way, it is possible that, with products belonging to the second group, the manufacturing enterprise bears those costs of transportation that arise during the carriage of products to the station nearest to it (place of dispatch).

Making allowance for different distances in transport aggravates *the evaluation of the economical location of new plants*. Within individual branches of production, differences in the conditions of production should also manifest themselves in the more advantageous position of plants located near natural resources. If the cost of further processing does not indicate the distance that the material used in production has covered, an indifference to creating the most economical location conditions will develop in economic organization. Therefore, in such branches of production where one of the main determinants of economical location is closeness to the basis of natural resources (e.g. coal mines in locating electric power stations) and, further, where the enterprise can exert influence on forming its own basis of material resources (e.g. the foodstuff industry by means of production contracts), it is advisable for the industry making use of these materials also to include in its prime cost those transportation costs which emerge between the place of production and the place of utilization.

Including the cost of carriage may also be justified in forming the consumer price (e.g. with construction materials). With these and generally with products whose manufacture can only be organized in a decentralized way – and whose transport charges constitute at the same time a significant proportion of their prime cost, it is expedient to set the price without the cost of transportation, and to support from the state budget the price fixed in this way by the actually incurred cost of carriage.

Part V

Factory Costs and Retail Prices

1. The Price of Capital Goods

Characteristics of the Price System of National Wealth

Part of the goods produced for the satisfaction of wants serve the *future*, part of them the present *needs* of the population. It is in this way that we can distinguish between capital goods and consumer goods. Price policy treats them independently since social property and the population's consumer-goods fund display different characteristics in the price system.

In characterizing investment price policy, we start from the concept of national wealth. In the socialist countries, the principle prevails that *national wealth is the accumulated national product*, which only comprises material goods produced by human labour. Regarded from this angle, national wealth is – if we disregard the personal property of the population – the total of social fixed and working capital. This can also be considered social capital. It is true that assets become capital goods depending on the role they play in production, yet it does not follow from this that social capital should be identified with fixed and working capital *directly* tied up in material production. The relationship between the production of national product and the capital required by it can only be determined if capital is interpreted in a wider sense. Moreover, in analysing investment price policy, social property has to be interpreted in a still wider sense, so that it also includes land. Considering social property in this sense, the main feature of its price system can be summed up in the following way.

1. *Land and capital are necessary for human labour to create value*. Land as a factor of production, is a productive force carrying and storing water, containing mineral resources and representing the scene of production. Capital is the totality of fixed and working assets engaged in production. In a socialist economy, apart from the private plots of citizens and generally from the private property of small-commodity producers, land and capital can only be in state or co-operative ownership. The state may put land and capital at the disposal of its enterprises free of charge. The same is not possible in the case of co-operatives because this would make the existence of the two forms of socialist ownership questionable. But co-operative do not need free land and capital in order to carry on simple reproduction as

they realize production through the integration of the land and capital of their members. But if a form of co-operative ownership does exist, this sector too must play an active part in the planned development of the national economy. It must be able to carry out expanded reproduction.

Thus, the two forms of socialist ownership have necessarily led to the dual *price functions*. State enterprises may operate in the *self-accounting price system* covering the costs of simple reproduction, while co-operatives are viable only in the *self-financing price system* covering the costs of expanded reproduction. Formerly, the socialist countries regarded co-operative self-financing an obstacle to planned development (the central allocation of investment resources). Therefore they endeavoured to separate the capital required to expand agricultural production from co-operative ownership. It was for this reason that they prevented agricultural co-operatives from buying major machinery. They established for this purpose state-owned tractor stations. However, it soon became evident that this put obstacles in the way of intensifying production.

In our days we can rather witness the tendency *that self-accounting in the state sector of the national economy, too, is developing in the direction of self-financing*. An industrial producer price is increasingly required to ensure the financial cover of a planned expansion of production, or to provide funds for the repayment of credits raised for this purpose, and for paying interests. In addition, in most socialist countries *there is a charge for the use of state-owned land and capital*.

2. The outcome of any investment activity is a *single product*. Thus it has no pre-determined value even under an administrative price system. The price of investment has invariably to be calculated under the consideration of individual circumstances, and this differs in its very nature from usual price calculations. The planner (contractor) of an investment project draws up a *cost estimate* which takes into account the characteristics of the investment technology. The investment estimate comprises all elements of investment activity (planning, organization, construction, installation) as well as the related inputs (wage bill, cost of materials, money value of the machinery and equipment installed). The calculation of net costs supplemented by surcharges yield the price of the given investment project. Exception to this are projects produced according to standarized designs, but even in this case account must be taken of individual circumstances requiring local adaptation.

An investment project is, at the same time, a *totality of use values of which some have a price independent of the investment, others have no price since they are produced specifically for the investment*: services (planning, organization, assembly on the site), individually produced machines and equipment geared to the requirements of the investor. Materials, standard machinery, vehicles, etc., however, have prices independent of the investment.

3. The part of the national product earmarked for accumulation *is tied up directly in material production, while the other part increases the capital stock of the non-productive branches* (state administration, social organizations, cultural and health institutions, etc.). Thus there are institutions directly serving commodity production, and others which only indirectly join in commodity production. It is on this basis that a distinction is made between productive and non-productive investments.

Non-productive investments are financed by the budget, and they add to the wealth serving socially organized consumption. The value of non-productive investments (schools, hospitals, etc.) can only be concluded from the *actual* inputs made on them, as these outputs do not change into commodities; they are public goods. Though the price of such establishments can be regulated by normative calculations, it is mostly the method of *tenders* that is suitable to ensure that actual inputs should adapt themselves to inputs that are socially necessary.

The situation is different with *productive investments* because they become commodities. But they are specific commodities because they serve future consumption. Their use value lies in the fact that they create the conditions for productive work, that is, that in them commodity production can be carried out. From this follows as a natural conclusion that the socially necessary input of productive investments and the actual inputs of the establishment may differ from one another, and indeed they do differ in most cases. The *socially necessary inputs can be identified only in an indirect way, by means of the cost and price relations of the products (as commodities) produced in the establishment concerned*. If the inputs of the products turned out by the new capacity are higher than in the case of most of the already operating capacities, then the investment input, or its part, is not justified, it does not become a part of value. From this arises perhaps the most important task of investment price policy: the quantification of socially justifiable investments. It is for this purpose that in the preparatory phase of investment decisions calculations of the economic efficiency of the investment are made.

The Price of the Investment Project and its Efficiency

The first step of the preparation of investment is *planning*. Its usual course is this: specification of the objective, planning of the technology to be used, planning of the activities of specialized trades (building, equipment, installation of machinery, etc.) and their co-ordination (plan documentation). The technical designs of construction are usually prepared by the designing offices. The task of the designers is to prepare such a plan documentation as realizes the desired function of the investment project with an optimum use of space, economic and up-to-date installations, and in a quality meeting the requirements set by the function of the investment. The economic efficiency of the construction depends in the first place on the activity of the designing offices as the choice of the elements making up the construction is the designers' task.

The remuneration of the designing activity is determined by special designing rates. In the sphere of construction projects the socialist countries apply different rate systems. Depending on the basic methods of determining the fees of designing, these rate systems can be grouped into four categories:

(a) *Base-value systems*, in which the amount of the designing fee is determined as a percentage of the total construction cost of the project.

(b) *Fixed-rate systems*, in which the designing fee is calculated as a fixed amount of remuneration for a given performance or its physical units.

(c) *Lump-sum systems*, in which the designing fee is fixed in advance by an agreement between the investor and the designer.

(d) *Input-related systems,* in which the designing fee is determined subsequently, according to the actual inputs of designing.

The fee rates of technology-planning determine the planning fees mostly for physical units, for data of capacity, or are of a post-calculation nature.

Already the fee rates of designing raise problems that have a decisive role to play in the price regulation of the *construction-installation work. When the enterprise forms the price by the method of cost calculation, it attains the so-called overhead price.* The term "overhead price" is used to imply that the price covers all costs arising in the course of performing some work, and does not take into account how these costs would have emerged if the execution of the investment project had been done rationally, with the most appropriate organization of work. This distinguishes overhead prices from fixed prices. In the case of fixed prices, the actual output of production is expressed in terms of production value in such a way that the totality of the use values produced (the weight of products, their number, etc.) is multiplied by the price. If the price is fixed, the production value does not reflect the actual inputs but only those which, projected to the unit of product, are recognized in the price. In the case of overhead prices the measure of output is expressed in terms of production value in such a way that prices are formed on the basis of inputs actually made to produce the various goods, and the products turned out are multiplied by these prices.

If the price is formed by the enterprise cost calculation, the previous statement of the price constitutes an essential part of the delivery contract. This price is the tender price and the party placing the order makes the conclusion of the contract subject, among other things, to the *tender price.* The latter must be distinguished from the contractual price, which is the calculated price fixed for a given product. In the case of an overhead price, the contractual price is a preliminary price, a guiding or orientation price. As the overhead price takes into account the costs according to their actual incidence – and such a price can only be determined by means of post-calculation –, the contractor (supplier) reserves in the contract of execution the right to change the price.

It is self-evident that investment accounting on the basis of overhead prices disturbs the planned fulfilment of investments, because if the planned financial resources needed for the construction as envisaged in the national economic plan must substantially be increased in the course of implementation, this ties up more money, more material funds than taken into account by the plan. Therefore, the socialist countries made efforts relatively soon to eliminate overhead prices. In this way, the basis-value system has become the principal form of the remuneration of designing work. This accounts, further, for the fact that in the field of construction installation work, overhead price has been limited to the repair and maintenance of existing flats and buildings, or to investments made in constructing new buildings of minor value. In the sphere of construction installation work, there are *several possibilities to eliminate overhead prices.* These are:

– the introduction of cost calculation standards in the building industry,
– the application of standardized designs in constructions,
– price formation based on cost averaging,
– the principle of a previous agreement on prices.

It was as early as in the 1950s that several socialist countries began to introduce *standarized designs, and worked out the basis-price system of standardized construction projects.* The underlying idea was that more and more buildings would be constructed in this system requiring only a *design of local adaptation,* by which the price of construction would be the sum total of the cost estimate of the standarized design concerned and the cost estimate of the differential design. This idea, however, has not proved realistic. The assumption that deviations from the original standardized design would be insignificant, has turned out to be illfounded. Owing to the progress made in technical development, to changes in the principles of urban development, to modified demands made by those commissioning the construction work, the standardized design had to undergo substantial re-designing so that the measure taken with a view to simplifying matters has made the situation even more intricate.

Rapidly developing technologies call for the standardization of construction elements and for standardized dimensions, which can also be applied without any further difficulty to individually designed buildings. Therefore, attention is increasingly being turned toward methods *of cost calculation standards, or cost averaging in the building industry.*[114] The former method was used in the 1950s. The socialist countries first based cost calculation and price formation on a uniform basis in the building industry. Later they introduced the materials standards for the individual construction elements (1 m^3 wall, 1 m^2 plastering, 1 m^3 earth moved, etc.), time standards and machine performance standards. Then the various standards were supplemented by fixed unit prices for the construction elements.

Experience later led to the realization that administrative price regulation cannot be effective without applying the

[114] CISAR, J.: Ceny a stavebni vyrobe (Prices and Production in the Building Industry). *Hospodarske noviny*, No. 5, 1970, Prague. DZIEWOLSKI, L. and ZIOLKOWSKI, M.: System can w budownictwic na tle nowych zasad gospodarowania (New Price System of the Building Industry in the Mirror of New Economic Principles). *Inwestycje i Budownictwo*, No. 11, 1969, Warsaw. FILIPOV, J.: Techniko-ikonomitcheski parametri i tseni na stroitelnite materiali i gotovata stroitelne produkciya (Technical Economic Parameters and Prices of Materials and Completed Products of the Building Industry). *M-va na stroezhito i architecturata*. Sofia, 1969. KRÖHL, W. and ALTMANN, R.: Probleme der Preiskalkulation bei General- und Hauptauftragnehmern. *Die Wirtschaft*, No. 32, 1969, Berlin. MALYUGIN, V. I.: *Puti dalneyshego sovershenstvovaniya tsenoobrazovaniya v stroitelstve* (Ways of a Building Industry). Moscow, 1970. NADOMA, M.: K problémum regulace cen ve stavebnictvi (On Problems of Pricing in the Building Industry). *Finance a uver*, No. 6, 1969, Prague. REZNIKOV, A. I.: *Tsenoobrazovanie v stroitelstve* (Montazhnye raboty). [Pricing in the Building Industry (Fitting)]. Moscow, 1969.

methods of cost averaging. It is true that the price when formed by the method of cost averaging – leaving individual circumstances out of account – is unjustifiably low in one case, or unjustifiably strained in another. But in the opinion of the socialist countries this drawback is less than the benefit that can be derived from the abolition of overhead prices. When the price is to attain a high degree of local and individual accuracy, it undermines enterprise initiative and the endeavour to achieve economic efficiency. The contractor enterprise is stimulated to organize materials supply, development of construction equipment on the site, etc. economically if it is not told in advance how, with what vehicles the supplies have to be effected, how the deployment of equipment has to be organized. In the case of ensuring cost averaging, savings will add to the profits of the enterprise. It will make efforts to achieve the most economical type of mechanization if it is not prescribed what technology of mechanization it has to apply to organize the execution of the project. In creating the price system of the building industry, the main role is played, as we have seen, by considerations aimed at price stability.

The future belongs to assembly-type construction. Its realization calls for a wide application of new building methods, for the development of a novel industry producing (prefabricated) construction elements and of the assembly (installations) industry. These requirements can only be met by such a flexible price mechanism which does not hamper the transformation process but stimulates it. This process, however, can hardly be reconciled with the *rigid price system of the building industry.* The standards set for materials, wages and transport are difficult to bring into harmony with the regular changes that technical-technological conditions, wages and costs of transportation undergo. In Hungary, for example, in order to ensure price stability, cost calculation was regulated until 1968 down to its minutest detail with calculation standards set for about 8,000 sorts of work and construction elements. The number of unit-price varieties, depending on the materials used, amounted to about 28,000.

The Hungarian price system of the building industry introduced in 1968 started from the assumption that *placing contracts against tenders might be made general in such construction activities as can be performed with convertible capacities.* In this sphere, cost calculation standards and other aids of price regulation only perform the function of orientation. It is only in the field of *non-convertible* building activities that cost calculation standards and other aids of price regulation should be made of compulsory. Here, the centrally determined prices should be regarded as maximum or orientation prices, from which actual prices may deviate within certain limits.

The price mechanism of the building and installation industries ensures this flexibility by dividing the unit prices of the building industry into two parts: those that are independent of market relations, and those that follow the development of the market situation with a certain degree of flexibility. In the first part account is taken – on the basis of the socially necessary input proportions or the cost calculation standard of the building industry – of live-labour, machine-work and overhead costs of manufacturing the construction elements. The costs of the technically necessary materials needed for the construction elements are formed on the basis of current prices.[115]

The *price of the installation or assembly work on the spot* is also based on a cost estimate. In preparing this cost estimate reliance is made on a collection of unit prices comprising norms of materials and assembly dues. By using this collection, the so-called net estimate sum is attained, which, supplemented by a surcharge, results in the price of assembly work on the spot. The directives relating to the price formation of assembly work on the spot take into account assembly work carried out under continual and normal conditions. In the case of unusual conditions, the resulting surplus costs are agreed upon in a contract concluded between the investor and the contractor. Unusual are the conditions in which e.g. the installation must be done at an operating industrial plant or in an establishment where the assembly work has to be discontinued in certain phases of the working time.

In the case of *international tenders* a fixed price must be set for the project, the payment for the obligation specified by technical parameters being unambiguously determined by the price stipulated in the contract. The conditions for any deviation from that price are laid down in advance. The resulting risk is borne by the principal contractor signing the order. In several socialist countries examinations are under way to find out how this principle could also be applied to domestic relations. It is the regular transgression of investment-cost estimates that makes this justified. It is practically impossible to tell precisely how far this results from a change in technical designs while work is in progress or from taking advantage of the inevitable deficiencies of normative cost calculation. This is the reason

115 KEREKES, O.: Az épitőipari árak alakulásának lényegesebb tendenciái és problémái (The most Important Trends and Problems of Price Formation in the Building Industry). *Épitésügyi Szemle,* No. 9, 1970, Budapest. TARNÓY, L.: Az épitőipari árak újraszabályozása (New Pricing in the Building Industry). *Pénzügyi Szemle*, Nos. 7–8, 1973, Budapest.

why the disequilibrium of the investment market and competition are increasingly regarded as important preconditions for a planned formation of investment inputs.[116]

If the cost of the investment is given, then the *economic efficiency of the investment* can also be determined. For its determination the socialist countries have worked out a number of methods.[117] They have one thing in common, namely, that all of them are designed to find such an "efficiency indicator" which makes it possible to apply a method of appraisal fitting the national economic approach. For this the total net income accrueing from the investment must be determined and related to the investment cost. This must be an index number which expresses, by means of a uniform rate of interest regarded as a minimum annual return, how many times the inputs of the investment are returned within a uniform time horizon chosen, by the net social income thus created. Since the realization of the net income and the cost inputs of development are effected in different years, they must be related to one another by means of compound interest calculations (discounting).

In the index number applied in Hungary the uniform rate of interest is 12 per cent, and the time horizon 15 years from the beginning of execution (implementation). In determining the index number, depreciation is taken to be a profit, but the costs of complementary investments are taken into account as factors diminishing net income. Owing to the foreign-trade sensitivity of Hungary's national economy, the competitive products and the costs of the capacities to be established are calculated at the actual (or expected) import resp. export prices of the realistically possible foreign-trade relation, and the non-competitive products are computed at actual (or expected) domestic prices.[118]

[116] KURZMANN, E.: Die Beeinflussung von Angebotspreisen auf Bauleistungen durch Konkurrenzdruck. *Die Bauwirtschaft*, März, 1969. Wiesbaden-Berlin.

[117] In June, 1958, the Institute for Economics of the Academy of Sciences of the Soviet Union staged a conference in Moscow to discuss the questions of the economic efficiency of investments and of the introduction of new technologies. Three questions were debated at the conference. (1) The significance of indexes in terms of value. (2) Problems of the price system. (3) The limits within which the normatives for completing the construction projects are to be applied. KHACHATUROV, T. S., STRUMILIN, S. G., KLIMENKO, K. I., ATLAS, Z. V. and others took part in the debate. For a summary of the debate see: FARKAS, I.: Vita a beruházások és az új technika bevezetésének gazdasági hatékonyságáról a Szovjetunióban (Debate on the economic efficiency of investments and the introduction of new technologies in the Soviet Union). *Közgazdasági Szemle*, No. 2, 1959, Budapest.

[118] RABI, B.: A beruházások hatékonysága mérésének néhány népgazdasági szintű kérdése (Some Questions of Measuring the Efficiency of Invest-

Charge on the Use of Land and Capital

It is becoming an ever-widening practice in the socialist countries to levy a tax on the *use of land.* Its principal forms of manifestation are taxes withdrawing part of the rent income (land rent, tax on mineral oil, etc.) charges on the use of industrial sites, on the use of water, etc.[119] In the same way, charges are to be paid for the use of capital engaged in production, and interest has to be paid on credit-financed invested property.[120]

←

ments on a National Economic Level). *Gazdaság*, No. 3, 1971, Budapest. BARTA, I.: A népgazdaságszemléletű beruházásgazdaságossági módszer továbbfejlesztéséről (On Further Developing the Method of the Efficiency of Investments, Reflecting the State of the National Economy). *Gazdaság*, No. 4, 1972, Budapest. HUSZÁR, I. and MANDEL, M.: A beruházási döntések rendszeréről (On the System of Investment Decisions). *Közgazdasági Szemle*, No. 6, 1972, Budapest.

119 BOCHNIARZ, Z.: Przeglad opinii o roli ceny ziemi w rachnunku ekonomicznym (Survey of Opinions on the Role the Price of Land Plays in Economic Calculation). *Zeszyty Naukowe SGPiS*, No. 72, 1969, Warsaw. CHOLAJ, H.: Cena ziemi jako kategoria ekonomiczna w socjalizmie (The Price of Land as an Economic Category in Socialism). *Zeszyty Naukowe SGPiS*, No. 72, 1969, Warsaw. FILIPIAK, P.: Cena ziemi w gospodarce PGR (The Price of Land in the Economy of State Farms). *Gospodarka Planowa*, No. 8, 1970, Warsaw. GABYSHEV, K. E.: Economicheskaya otsenka prirodnykh resursov i rentnye platezhi (Economic Evaluation of Natural Resources and the Payments of Rent). *Vestnik MGU* (Moskovskogo Gosudarstvennogo Universiteta), Seria VII, *Ekonomika*, No. 5, 1969. HORNIECZKY, Z.: Ceny nemovitesti a problematika ocenováni nemovitosti (Prices of Real Estate and the Problems of its Evaluation). *Finance a uver*, No. 7, 1969, Prague. KOBAKHIDZE, L. P.: O tsene razvedannykh zapasov poleznykh iskopaemykh v nedrakh (On the Prices of Explored Natural Resources). *Sov. geologiya*, No. 2, 1970. RABINOVICH, B.: Gornaya renta i effektivnost proizvodstva (The Rent of Mines and the Efficinecy of Production). *Ekonomicheskiye nauki*, No. 5, 1970. SCHROEDER, G.: *Waldbewertung und Rohholzpreise als Gegenstand und Instrument volkswirtschaftlicher Planung in ihrer Verbindung mit der wirtschaftlichen Rechnungsführung in den Staatlichen Forstwirtschaftsbetrieben*. Hochschule für Ökonomie. Berlin, 1969.

120 BOTKIN, V.: Plata za fondy i puti povysheniya tse stimuliruyush chey roli (Charges on Capital and the Ways of Increasing their Role as Incentives). *Planovoye Khozyaistvo*, No. 12, 1969, Moscow. IVANCHENKO, V.: O kategorii i funksiyakh platy za fondy (On Categories and Functions of the Charge on Capital). *Voprosy Ekonomiki*, No. 3, 1970, Moscow. MAKSIMOVA, M.: Dan'ka v'rhu proizvodstvenite fendove i tsenoobrazuveneto (Charge on Capital and Pricing). *Tseni i tsenoobrazuvane*, No. 2, 1970, Sofia. P. RITTER, J.: Az eszközhasználati díj (Charge on Capital). *Pénzügyi Szemle*, No. 9, 1963, Budapest. STALE, R.: Procentowanie srodków trwalych (Charge on Capital). *Wiadomosci Narodowego Bankh Polskiege*, No. 1, 1969, Warsaw. TSUROV, YU., KOZLOV, V. and SUMBATOV, V.: Plata za proizvodstvennye fondy (Charge on Capital). *Ekonomika stroyitelystva*, No. 6, 1970.

From the point of view of price theory, the charge on the use of capital (in short: capital charge, charge on assets) is worth special attention. In this connection we must point back to the debate on value price versus production price. In the case of the classical price types (value price, production price) there is no income realization problem, as the state detracts income through "one channel": as wage tax in the case of value prices, and as charge on capital in the case of production prices. In the former case the measure of the wage tax can unambiguously be determined by the relationship of the wage cost of the national economy to accumulation, and in the latter case the measure of the charge on capital by the relationship of the total value of capital engaged by the enterprise to accumulation. The situation is different when a *multi-channel system* prevails. In this case the problem emerges what should be the proportion among the various forms the state applies in siphoning off incomes, to what extent should the state open this or that channel. This will, evidently, be the characteristic of the mixed-price type, and this will also determine how the price performs its function in economic calculation.

It is especially Hungarian economists who are concerned with the basic questions of evaluating the factors of production. Thus explanations should be based upon the Hungarian price model.[121] But in order to make the essence of the intricate problem clearer, we want to simplify that model. The cost is refunded in the product prices of our price model, while the state withdraws the net profit from the enterprises through two channels, in the forms of the wage tax and of the charge on capital. Let us first consider the charge on capital, in its varieties of 5–10–15–20 per cent. Before letting these varieties come into play, prime cost corresponds to real prime cost as it contains no net income even indirectly. Thus, when these varieties are not taken into consideration, cost proportions roughly express value proportions. With charges on capital coming into play, however, the *value proportions are modified*. The greater the size of the charge on capital the more the price level will rise compared to the level of real cost, and the price proportions will further change in proportion to the capital-intensity of the product.

(See the Table on page 266.)

Which is the point that expresses the production price? The one at which the size of the charge on capital coincides with the coefficient of accumulation and capital value on the national economic level. The point of intersection in the price model is at

[121] Csikós-Nagy, B.: *Eszközgazdálkodás és árrendszer* (Resource Management and the Price System). Budapest, 1964.

The value-modifying effect of the charge on capital

(Calculated from the consolidated input-output table of the year 1959)

Branch of production	Charge on capital as a percentage of real cost in the case of a rate of charge of 5	10	15	20
	per cent			
Heavy industry	26	61	109	184
Metallurgy and engineering	24	56	99	167
Light industry	19	44	79	133
Food industry	17	39	70	118
Building industry	16	36	65	109
Agriculture	11	26	46	77
Transport	34	80	142	239
Trade	30	71	127	213
National economy as a whole	18	41	77	124

a *15 per cent value of the charge on capital. It is here that the modification of the value price coincides with the production price.* But this also means that in the "two-channel" price model the charge on capital must be less than 15 per cent, or else it would be impossible to withdraw incomes in the form of a wage tax, too.

Now we shall let the wage tax (payroll tax) – without the charge on capital – come into play, in its varieties of 25–50–75–100 per cent of the wage cost. The tax is again built on real prime cost as it contains no net income even indirectly. With the wage tax entering the scene, the level of real prime cost will rise, but the price proportions will stay unchanged because, when we add a net income in proportion to the wages, we always arrive approximately at value proportions. At which point do we find the value level? Where the wage tax coincides with the coefficient of accumulation and the wage cost on the national economic level. *The point of intersection in the price model is at a 75 per cent. It is here that prices coincide with value prices.* But this, again means; that in the "two-channel" price model the wage tax must be less than 75 per cent of the wage cost, or else it would be impossible to withdraw incomes in the form of a charge on capital. The above expositions enable us to make some statements:

(a) In the two-channel price system – on the assumption made – the charge on capital must be less than 15 per cent and the wage tax less than 75 per cent.

(b) Every 1 per cent of the charge on capital raises the price level by 1.1 per cent, so that it modifies at the same time the value proportions. The larger the rate of the charge on capital, the greater the extent to which the value proportions are modified.

(c) Every 5 per cent of the wage tax raises the price level by 1.2 per cent, without changing the price proportions.

Thus the real questions is this: what rate of wage tax and charge on capital should be jointly applied so that the price system helps to make correct economic decisions? Our present knowledge is not sufficient to answer this question. We do not know yet if the different varieties of the wage tax will be indifferent in relation to the real prime cost if we apply them in the case of real prime cost supplemented by the charge on capital. Looking upon the question superficially, we might think that the wage tax will partly offset the price-modifying effect of the charge on capital, and thus it depends eventually on the proportion of the two supplementary factors how the price proportions of the two-channel price model deviate from value proportions. The relevant examinations have provided the mathematical evidence that the varieties of the wage tax cannot influence price proportions even in the case of real price cost supplemented by the charge on capital.[122] *The wage tax, even in the case of real prime cost adjusted by a definite amount of charge on capital, has only an effect on raising the price level.* How can this fact be accounted for? The wage tax increases prime cost to the extent of the wage level, but the value (price in money terms) of capital tied up in turning out the product will rise accordingly, as now this value (price in money terms) consists of nothing else than the total wage cost of the national economy supplemented by the wage tax and the charge on capital taken into account appropriately (i.e. making allowance for its spill-over effect).

Now the starting point might be clear: in the two-channel price model the charge on capital raises the price level and changes price proportions. The wage tax, however, only raises the price level. But if this is the case, why does the wage tax come in at all? Under such circumstances this is obviously justified only if the desirable modifying effect of the charge on capital asserts itself at a lower level than the value. In this case it is namely necessary to apply a form of income withdrawal which raises the price level but, is neutral as a factor shaping the price proportions. This form is – as we have seen – the wage tax.

Why is it of any importance that, in applying the charge on capital, a contradiction may arise between the value level and

[122] RÉVÉSZ, G.: *Az Országos Anyag- és Árhivatal részére készült dokumentum* (Document Prepared for the National Office of Materials and Prices). Budapest, 1968.

the rate of this charge desirable from the point of view of its modifying effect on value proportions? This can easily be understood if we consider that in economic calculation capital cost (which can be determined by the rate of the charge on capital), wage cost (which depends on the wage bill and the rate of wage tax), materials cost and depreciation (as real prime cost increased and modified depending on the price type used) constitute to a certain degree competing costs. It follows from these peculiarities of economic calculation that the rate of the charge on capital can be determined on its merits only in the knowledge of the modification of value proportions. And the rate of the wage tax is connected with the value level.

The debate on the measure of the charge on capital put the *growth process* into the focus of attention. According to this, the charge for the use of capital should be determined

(a) in proportion to the average annual growth rate of the national income, or

(b) in proportion to the average annual growth rate of productive capital, or

(c) according to the ratio of national savings used for the expansion of productive capital to the volume of productive capital.

The charge according to (a) was 5–6 per cent, to (b) and (c) between 8 and 10 per cent. Thus the conclusion has been reached that in shaping an appropriate price system it is expedient to calculate with a ten years' return on capital. All this is summarized in the price models shown in the table below:

Withdrawal of incomes in the price models

(Calculated from the input-output table of the year 1958. Percentages)

Price type	Measure of the net income realizable in product prices related to the corresponding base of projection	Percentage of net income realized in total price
I. *Value price*		
Wage tax	75.0	100.0
II. *Production price*		
Charge on capital	15.4	100.0
III. *Mixed price type*		
Wage tax	26.6	35.8
Charge on capital	10.0	64.2

It was not possible, however, to incorporate a 10 per cent charge on capital into the prime cost, since part of the return on capital has to be realized as *enterprise profit*. This part of the return on capital realized as profit cannot be uniform, since the differing economic efficiency of the branches of production must find expression exactly in the dispersion of profits. *The charge on capital accounted as enterprise cost can only reflect the lower margin of profitability, which has been fixed at 5 per cent, in compliance with the average annual growth rate of the national income measured over a long period of time.*

The Price of New Technologies

In our days, the rise in labour productivity is taking place in the context of the scientific-technical revolution. This is related to the price category in the system of research-development-investment. Basic research – and budget-financed technical development in general – has no direct bearing on prices. Nevertheless, the specific need for the technical development of production shows a rising tendency. It would seem natural that improving labour productivity through technical development leads to decreasing prices. It is, after all, in this field that the efficiency of technical development should be manifested. In practice, however, this is not always the case. *Technical development rapidly accelerating in our days is coupled with the tendency of a price increase in several countries.*

In the debates in Hungary it is usually regarded as a majority opinion that can briefly be formulated like this: *labour is cheap, new technologies* are expensive.[123] In this view, the new technology raises the prices not because it increases real inputs but because it becomes dear "artificially" under the current price and financial systems. Therefore, the enterprises, enjoying the freedom of decision-making, prefer an extensive type of development to an intensive one. It is because of this considera-

[123] Antal, L.: Az élőmunka és a lekötött eszközök költségterhének szerepéről (On the Role of Costs of Labour and Charge on Capital). *Pénzügyi Szemle*, No. 12, 1973, Budapest. Kunvári, A.: Korszerűség és jövedelmezőség, elméletben és gyakorlatban (Modernity and Profitability in Theory and Practice). *Közgazdasági Szemle*, No. 11, 1971, Budapest. Megyeri, E.: A vállalati alapok optimális kihasználása és a hatékonyságmérés néhány problémája (Optimal Utilization of Enterprise Funds and Some Problems of Measuring Efficiency). *Közgazdasági Szemle*, No. 10, 1973, Budapest. Vincze, I.: Gondolatok a vállalati adórendszer egyes elemeinek jövőbeni módositására (Thoughts on the Future Modification of Some Elements of the Taxation System of Enterprises.) *Pénzügyi Szemle*, No. 5, 1971, Budapest.

tion that they suggest the cheapening of new technologies (primarily by decreasing the charge on capital) by a simultaneous rise in the wage tax.

All these critical comments have one characteristic in common, namely, that they seek a solution to the evaluation of the factors of production not on the basis of *growth theory* but of *production theory.* They only differ in emphasizing one or the other aspect of the same approach. Depending on these differences, they criticize the concrete system of cost calculation either on the basis of the principles of the return on capital, of substitution or of equilibrium.[124] Thus, according to the views represented in the debate

– the wage tax should be raised to a level which ensures that wages and the wage tax cover the *reproduction cost of live labour,*

– the charges on capital should be lowered to a level which ensures that the ratio of the sum total of wages and of the wage tax to the charge on capital corresponds to the *substitution ratio of labour to* capital, and finally,

– both the wage tax and the charge on capital should be set at a level at which they can *ensure* the *equilibrium of the labour market and the investment market.*

As we have seen, in a consistent price system the wage tax is a *neutral* factor from the point of substitution decisions. Nevertheless it appeared expedient to revise the appraisal of the factors of production and quantify them in mathematical models.[125] But what really matters is not what proportions (say, 40 to 3) are shown by one or the other mathematical model as against the current ratio of 25 to 5 of the wage tax and charge on capital. What is essential is the debate on whether the problem of extensive-intensive industrialization in a socialist economy can be reduced to the system of cost calculation, and, if cost calculation is a relevant factor, wether the *ratio* of the wage tax to the charge on capital should be regarded as decisive.

The hypothesis "cheap labour and expensive new technologies" is worth attention not from the point of view of the charge on capital but of *the marginal cost of enterprise investment.* If the budget withdraws *the profits* of enterprises but places at their disposal, without any obligation of repayment, the funds needed for investments envisaged in the state plan,

[124] Szakolczai, Gy.: Az erőforrások értékelése (Evaluation of Resources). *Közgazdasági Szemle*, Nos. 4–5, 1973, Budapest.

[125] Rácz, L. and Vissi, F.: Az erőforrások lineáris adóztatása vagy korszerű ár- és jövedelemszabályozás (The Linear Taxation of Resources or an Up-To-Date Regulation of Prices and Incomes). *Közgazdasági Szemle*, No. 9, 1973, Budapest.

the introduction of new technologies is primarily a matter of state planning. The situation, however, changes at once if the enterprises' self-accounting system changes into self-financing, if the budget does not withdraw enterprise profits, but imposes a tax on them, if along with structural investments financed or subsidized by the budget, there also exist decentralized investments by enterprises. Enterprise investments can be realized in reliance either on their own capital (depreciation and enterprise profit) or on foreign capital (bank credits, joint undertakings). Under such circumstances it must be really examined what conditions are necessary to ensure the *expansion* of the capital supply of enterprises.

Let us see the conditions prevailing in Hungary. The *burden of capital* remains within reasonable limits if the enterprise finances investments at given prices from the *development fund* retained after taxation and financial dues paid. Such investments are liable to a 5 per cent charge on capital. Investments financed by *bank credits* are more expensive. If we consider that, apart from a few exceptions, a bank credit is granted with a repayment obligation in 5 years at most, and only to enterprises having a specified amount of capital of their own the burden of capital is, inclusive interest payment, an annual 30–35 per cent. The real problem arises when the enterprise wishes, for example, to expand its development fund by raising the selling price of its products. It has to pay 40 per cent of the depreciation into the budget, 30 per cent of the technical development fund will go into the centralized fund, finally, the part of the enterprise profit allocated to development is burdened by a tax of 60 per cent. From this follows that one per cent rise in enterprise capital is possible only at a 6–7 per cent increase in the price level. Thus the marginal cost of enterprise development is extremely high.

But here the marginal cost of development is regulated not by the law of returns but by the fiscal withdrawal of profits. This is why the marginal cost of development can only be interpreted in the context of the development policy. The financial regulators derived from the five-year plan serve the planned execution of the development policy. If a substantial part of the social savings has to be concentrated on investments financed and supported by the budget, it is only natural that considerable resources have to be withdrawn from the enterprises, and that the terms of investment credits must be very strict. The planned course of development makes it imperative that enterprise development should be kept within reasonable limits by *prohibitive* financial regulators and a selective credit policy. From this it logically follows, on the other hand, that when an enterprise wishes to gain additional financial resources by price rises, it can achieve this end only by an irrational price rise. Thus, what appears at first sight the *expensiveness of development,* is in fact a *shortage* of *capital supply.* Capital is expensive where the ideas of development have not an adequate material backing. And the sense of expensiveness is nourished in the first place by the endeavour to make *over-investments,* i.e. by exaggerated investment activities.

Thus the hypothesis "cheap labour and expensive new technologies" is questionable. This applies to the case when we examine the price of new technologies from the point of view whether the ratio of the wage tax to the charge on capital can exercise an effect on the enterprises' decisions. Looked upon separately, the price of new technologies is definitely very relevant. Of the possible alternatives of updating production and product technology, the enterprise is likely to prefer the one which ensures the most favourable return on capital.

But how can the rise in the indicators of the specific costs of technical development be accounted for? It might be due, among other things, to the fact that the scientific-technical revolution is taking place in a poly- (hetero-) centric world economy. In the last century, world economy developed under the conditions of conflicts and struggles between a few industrially developed countries. Economic development was controlled by monopolistic organizations or their international amalgamations on a world scale, and they also exercised influence on technical development. They stimulated, but, at the same time, also restricted this development according to the interests of their business policy. They introduced new technologies to production with regard to the return on the capital concentrated on the technical methods applied.

There are fewer possibilities of doing this in a poly- (hetero-) centric world economy, where the conflicts and struggle between the different socio-economic system often manifest themselves in a sharp competition. In such circumstances the introduction of a modern technology is usually governed not by the return on the capital invested in the technology applied but by the parties' requirement of preserving their competitiveness. Thus the adoption of a new technology also implies the risk that part of the capital concentrated on it will be lost. *That is why accelerated depreciation has come to play a prominent role in economic calculations,* a process which has also been made possible by new taxation measures in many countries.

The new economic policy of the government of making the enterprises interested in using their funds for the purposes of research, development and investment to an ever-increasing extent, in the interest of preserving their competitive position in the world market, has only strengthened the formation of self-financing prices. This price is connected with value in its dynamics, with the difference that it tends to incorporate into the price the capital needs of research-development-investment and not just the actual capital inputs. In the accelerating process of technical development it appears as a tendency of rising-prices.

Thus the impact of new technologies on prices must realistically be taken into account. International experience seems also to suggest that the new technology results in certain cases in price-raising tendencies. It is adopted not only when it is cheaper, but also when *the old technology is simply impossible to maintain,* or when the old and cheaper technologies *cannot keep pace with increasing demands.* It is also natural that product development and the improved service of the population require additional inputs. It is irrealistic to expect of the industry and the distribution trade to ensure all this at the price of the old product. In addition, we must also bear in mind that in the engineering industry, owing to the sharpening of international competition and the acceleration of technical development, the obsolescence of machinery and equipment has got speeded up, and the demand for research and development of modern technologies has greatly increased. Nevertheless, *there are specific cases when the high prices of technical development are socially unjustifiable.* Here are some of the most typical instances:

1. *Surplus investment cost.* Surplus cost – at unchanged prices – usually emerge because the project is not completed by the date envisaged by the plan, because the project is carried out not according to technically approved parameters but according to higher quality standards, with reserve capacities, etc., and because, in the hope of obtaining approval, the socially necessary inputs of the investment unit have been underplanned.

2. *Diminished profits (lucram cessans).* If an unreasonably long span of time elapses form the time when the decision on a state investment is taken until it is implemented and put into regular operation as a productive unit, the chances are that the market conditions will change substantially (i.e. not in the way anticipated by the plan). The lost time often amounts to 3–4 years. Since in the transformation of the structure a prominent role is played by the progressive industrial branches which exhibit a rapid technical development, it may happen that by the time the new plant starts operating, its technology is no longer up-to-date, and it is impossible for its products to fetch on the world market the price calculated when the decision on the investment was taken.

3. Most socialist countries have small-scale economies. Therefore, a *variety of investment projects are executed on a scale considerably smaller than the optimum.*

4. The state plan of the national economy *allocates so many material resources to the attainment of a few top-priority objectives of development that insufficient resources are left to other development aims.* Thus, enterprises are unable to devote sufficient material resources to development in a large field of production, resources that would be needed to keep pace with international technical development. This finds expression in the financial mechanism whose essence it is that the budget withdraws from the enterprises the larger part of their gains, and leaves only a part of the depreciation fund with them. This reacts on the production conditions of the progressive industrial branches. If the industrial background lags behind in development, the new technology created in a concentrated form does not yield the expected results.

2. The Retail Price of Consumer Goods

Direct and Indirect Political Preferences

In a market economy the consumer price fits organically into the general price structure; it is only in a relatively narrow sphere that the state budget incorporates, as a rule, the turnover tax into the consumer price, or subsidizes the consumer price. Consequently, general price theory also offers a satisfactory explanation of the consumer price. By contrast, in the socialist price theory the consumer price must be interpreted in an independent way. This is because in a socialist planned economy the *living-standard policy* lends the consumer price specific characteristics. The socialist state regards the consumer price as a specific category and *accords the consumer-price system a separate treatment.* This manifests itself in the following:

– The consumer price is separated from the producer (foreign-trade) price by the turnover tax (or budgetary subsidies).

– Changes in the producer (foreign-trade) price – apart from a few exceptions – do not automatically affect the consumer price, the consumer price changes as a result of special measures of price policy.

– Owing to deviations in the time, dimension and direction of changes in the producer (foreign-trade) price and consumer price, the consumer-price policy asserts itself by a continuous rearrangement of the turnover tax (budgetary subsidies).

Hence, the separate treatment of the consumer price in *reflected in the turnover-tax and subsidy system,* therefore the theoretical debates on the consumer price rest on the critical analysis of taxes and budgetary subsidies.[126] In Hungary, these

[126] CIAS, B. and CHUDZYNSKI, S.: Podatek obrotowy (Turnover Tax). *Zycie Gospodareze*, No. 47, 1968, Warsaw. CZERWINSKY, E.: Ceny, koszty i podatek obrotowy (Goods, Costs and Turnover Tax). Ruch Prawniczy: *Ekonomiczny i Socjologiezny*, No. 4, 1969, Poznan. LIPINSKI, J.: System cen srodków konsumpeji a reforma podatku obrotowego (The Price System of Consumer Goods and the Reform of Turnover Tax). *Ekonomista*, No. 1, 1969, Warsaw. MARYAKHIN, G.: K voprosu o naloge s oborota (On the Question of Turnover Tax). *Planovoye Khozyaistvo*, No. 7, 1970, Moscow. ZABIELLO, N. and ZABKOWICZ, L.: Role i moejsce podatku obrodowego. (The Role and Place of Turnover Tax). *Zycie Gospodarcze*, No. 24, 1969, Warsaw.

debates began in the late 1950s between experts of planning and trade, on the one hand, and financial and price specialists, on the other.[127] The most consistent separation of the producer price system from the consumer-price system as well as a taxation policy ensuring that separation are advocated mostly by planning experts many of whom take a stand, on a rigid producer-price system and on a consumer-price system which adapts itself to changing market requirements, no matter how these consumer prices are related to actual inputs. It is namely in this way that the producer price as a planning instrument and the consumer price as a demand-affecting factor can be used simultaneously. According to this view, what really matters is to ensure the separation of the producer price from the consumer price. This view also denies the existence of an objective relationship between consumer price and value under the conditions of a socialist economy.

Most price experts are endeavouring to create a closer relationship between the two price systems. They attach importance to the producer price not as a pure instrument of planning but of labour input, consequently, they regard the adequate formation of changing cost relations as essential. And they are convinced that the consumer price – apart from a few conscious exceptions – has to follow the producer price simultaneously or with some time lag. It is mostly specialists of finance who emphasize the necessity of putting an end to the separation of the producer-price system from the consumer-price system, and to limit the diversion of the consumer price from inputs to a restricted range of products.

A distinction is made between the systems of rated (percentage) turnover tax, itemized (per-unit) turnover tax and differential turnover tax. *In the rated turnover-tax system,* the tax inserted between the producer and consumer price is expressed in an a priori determined tax rate, either in an upward direction built on the producer price, or in a downward direction, starting from the consumer price. The rated turnover-tax system separates the producer price from the consumer price by rate differentials. The more the rates deviate from one another, the greater the difference between the lowest and the highest tax rate, and the more characteristic is the dispersion of consumer-price proportions. We want to repeat: it is not the institution of the tax in itself but the differential tax rates that separate the two prices. It stands to reason that if producer prices consistently adapt themselves to the cost proportions of outputs and further,

[127] HOCH, R. and RÉDEI, A.: A fogyasztói árképzés fő kérdései (Chief Questions of Setting Consumer Prices). *Közgazdasági Szemle*, No. 1, 1957, Budapest.

if the turnover tax is uniform, we get value-related consumer prices. It is the differences between tax rates that ensure the diversion of the consumer price from value.

But two more conclusions can be also drawn from the above expositions. First: in the sphere where it is uniformly charged, the rated turnover tax separates the producer price from the consumer price only in relation to other products (for which the rate is differentiated). Within this sphere, it brings about an organic relationship between producer and consumer price proportions. Here it ensures – given the specified conditions – the adaptation of consumer prices to value relations. Secondly: The consumer prices of products for which the turnover tax is formed by an average tax rate may be called not only value-proportionate but also approximately value-representing – granted the above conditions. It is, namely, exactly a rate higher than the average that raises the price above value, and, conversely, a rate lower than the average brings the price below value.

In the *itemized tax system,* the turnover tax inserted between the producer and consumer price is determined in absolute terms. This tax, too, could be expressed by a tax rate, and such a conversion is in fact carried out if such questions are to be answered as in what direction and to what extent the consumer price of the product thus obtained deviates from the value level. Itemized turnover tax is applied to homogeneous bulk commodities (sugar, mineral, oil, etc.).

In the *differential tax system* the turnover tax inserted between the producer and consumer price is also determined in absolute terms. Thus its form of manifestation exhibits characteristics not unlike those of the itemized tax. This tax system is applied to such product groups where the assortment is extremely wide, where product-replacement is frequent, and consumer prices should be made proportionate from the point of view of the commerce. It is precisely this fact that accounts for the essential differences between the itemized and differential tax systems: the small resp. large number of items, on the one hand, and the stability resp. instability of the tax. All differential taxes already determined represent stable tax rates in the sense that they unambiguously determine the tax realized in the price as long as the assortment in question is produced. All differential taxes already determined are unstable in the sense that they are usually set for assortments that are produced only for a relatively short period of time and need therefore a re-adjustment as soon as they are replaced by a new assortment.

The essential difference between rated and differential taxes must also be emphasized. When the producer price is separated from the consumer price by different tax rates, it also expresses the endeavour to preserve a certain relationship between the producer and consumer price. When, however, the two prices are separated by the system of differential tax, a complete separation of price proportions between the product groups is generally ensured. The differential tax system also presupposes that the producer and consumer prices are different within the product groups. The former adopts the principle of cost, while the latter – within the product groups – the principle of utility (use value).

The state can sell a product not only at a price which is higher than its cost of production and of retail sale but also at a lower price. It is self-evident that the aggregate consumer price must realize a net income that is needed to cover total social needs. But if we admit that the consumer price may be higher and lower than value, we must also admit that the consumer price may be lower than cost. If the consumer price is lower than the producer price, the turnover tax is replaced by a price subsidy. *Consumer-price subsidy is in fact a kind of negative turnover tax.* From this it follows that the rated, itemized and differential systems can also be used in the consumer-price subsidy. Therefore, all that we have said in connection with the turnover-tax system, also applies here, but with a negative sign. Price subsidy links up producer and consumer prices in an opposite direction.

When producer prices in the sphere of related products are set according to the cost principle, and consumer price proportions according to the use value principle, it is obviously impossible to set a uniform tax rate for a product group. A necessary concomitant of relative prices formed according to different principles is the different measure of taxes connecting the two prices. This is the form of the manifestation of the separation of producer prices from consumer prices, which would also prevail if we renounced the application of the use value principle. But the use value principle sharpens and institutionalizes the stratification of the tax. The more intricate the taxation system, the more work is involved in its administration, and the more difficult it is to exercise a central control over the correct payment of taxes. And it is not only the intricate nature of the tax system that may cause difficulties. The simultaneous existence of the cost principle interwoven with individual elements, in the case of producer prices and of the principle of proportionality interwoven with subjective elements in the case of consumer prices works towards the abolition of the price-forming function of taxes.

It is in the relationship between producer and consumer prices that we can attach a price-forming role to taxes, but we can also disregard this role. In the former case the tax has a definite weight in price formation and determines the producer price starting from the consumer price, or determines the consumer price starting from the producer price. In the latter case, the tax is the "residual" sum within the price, a sum which still can be included into the consumer price, in addition to the producer price and the mark-up.

The role that tax plays depends not on the taxation system, that is, not on whether the tax connecting the producer and the consumer price is determined in percentage or absolute terms. Generally speaking, the producer and consumer-price system, being in a closer relationship with one another, rely on the rated taxation system, while the producer- and consumer-price systems, being in a loose relationship with one another, rely on the differential taxation system. But the relationship of the two prices can also be loosened by an excessive proliferation of different tax rates, just as a closer relationship between producer- and consumer-price formation can also be realized under the system of taxes expressed in absolute terms. What really matters is what role we want to assign to taxes.

Nevertheless, the following is worth noting: if in the socialist price policy the tendency of a complete separation of the consumer-price system asserts itself, then the turnover-tax system applied is, as a rule, differentiated in the depth of the assortment (i.e. it is a differential tax system), and the tax has not a price-regulating function but is of a residual character. This practice of price policy in the socialist countries was created by another tendency, namely that of changing the prices of products in the sphere of state ownership. We may argue like this: if the prices (changes in prices) of products within the sphere of state ownership have no bearing on consumer prices, any price revision in the sphere of producer prices made desirable by the better operation of the enterprise self-accounting system can be carried out.

The improvement of the enterprise self-accounting system has led in most socialist countries to an occasional increase in the producer-price level, to the approximation of the producer-price level to the consumer-price level. Simultaneously, the turnover tax realized in consumer prices has declined from time to time, and several consumer prices, embodying no turnover tax or just an insignificant part of it, have become deficit prices. Thus, on the one hand, the occasional re-adjustment of producer prices, the raising of the producer-price level based on changing relative prices and, on the other hand, the endeavour not to change consumer prices have changed the turnover tax realized in consumer prices (the proportions of this tax according to various product lines), or the range of deficit consumer goods, and the size and proportions of budgetary subsidies.

It is precisely this fact that makes it difficult for us to interpret budgetary subsidy or turnover tax unambiguously as conscious political preference (discouragement). Under such circumstances the preference (discouragement) is determined as a function of the accounting system applied to the sphere of production, and it is the main motivation for stabilizing consumer prices once they have been established. It is on such a basis that a distinction can be made between *direct and indirect political preferences.* The first was evolved consciously by the socialist state, and the second was created by the principle of frozen consumer prices. But just this makes it doubtful whether the socialist state interprets the consumer price in the most appropriate way. This can be answered, however, only in the light of the living-standard policy.

The Taxation of Incomes and Products

In a market economy the interpretation of social utility based on consumers' sovereignty makes it possible to equate producer and consumer prices. The content of social utility is basically different in a socialist society. Here social utility is formed in the synthesis of political and consumer preferences. It is these questions of content that we are going to analyse now.

The state can perform *income redistribution* in two ways: by taxing (complementing) *incomes* and by taxing (subsidizing) *products.* The first can be characterized as a *production-oriented (efficiency-oriented) model of income redistribution.* Why is it justified to endow this model of income redistribution with such characteristics? Because if the state does not restrict price and wage movements in the market,

– the market creates, with respect to prices, identical conditions for all, and differences between people can only be reduced to income relations;

– the market brings about an organic link between consumer-price relations and cost relations, income proportions are formed according to efficient contributions to production.

We must also directly circumscribe the *criteria* which ensure the optimum assertion of economic efficiency. These are: relative incomes adjusted to relative performances and relative prices to relative costs. If relative prices are related to relative values and relative incomes to relative performances, then the national economy has the greatest possibility of ensuring both the effective operation of the factors of production and their optimum development.

In this model of income redistribution the state is a passive on-looker of the formation of price and income relations, only to carry out a subsequent *correction* of the incomes evolved as a result of the operation of market forces by taxing the incomes. Income tax is a *passive* income regulator because it does not play any role in shaping relative incomes. This tax is not a predetermined magnitude, it only appears where the income is already realized and it differentiates realized incomes according to their tax-bearing capacity. At the same time, the income tax is also an *active* income regulator in that only taxed income constitutes demand.

The problem proper of taxing incomes is of a dual nature. (1) What incomes qualify as incomes liable to taxation? This question is connected with subsistence incomes, and is, therefore, related to the elements of incomes policy derived from social policy. (2) How does the tax-bearing capacity change with changing incomes? The proposition generally accepted is this: the tax-bearing capacity of a larger income is greater, hence the income tax should be *progressive.*

Now let us *substitute turnover (purchase) tax for income tax in the model of income redistribution.* Prices and incomes will also be regulated by the market, but the state corrects the income proportions not directly, but by modifying relative consumer-prices. This takes place in such a way that the government levies extremely heavy taxes on certain goods (services), while taxes on other goods (services) are lower, and there are also tax-free products (services) and even such which are subsidized by the state (negative turnover tax). What are the criteria for making these distinctions? It will suffice to refer to the four most important ones:

1. Income distribution is not completed by the members of society acquiring incomes. This process will be completed when the *beneficiaries of incomes buy commodities and make use of services.* In this realization process money income represents a quantity of commodities, exactly as much as can be bought for money income. This depends on the price. This is how money value is connected with the process of income distribution. And household statistics is the system in which the real value of money income, the changes in real incomes are measured. In household statistics the population as a consuming economy, and the beneficiaries of incomes as consuming units behave according to their peculiar consumption patterns.

2. The state regards *demand* not simply as the demand of the population but as the *aggregate demand of high-, medium- and*

low-income consumers, of single individuals, childless families and families with children. The state is well aware of how widely the consumption habits of the various social strata differ. It also knows exactly how differently consumers of different incomes behave with respect to wants. The consumption pattern of a low-income consumer is different from that of a high-income consumer.

3. With the selective application of turnover taxes and budgetary subsidies the *proportions of nominal incomes are expressed in different proportions of real incomes.* In other words: In the market-price system modified by turnover taxes (subsidies), the money incomes of the various social strata with high, medium and low incomes will change into different real incomes. For them money has a differentiated value, and its magnitude depends precisely on differences in consumption habits.

4. Considering all this, the government can not only levy heavier taxes on incomes with higher tax-bearing capacity, but *it can also carry out income redistribution in favour of those in the low-income brackets.* The former procedure takes place when the turnover tax is applied mainly to such products (services) which are significant in the consumption pattern of strata with lower than average or lowest incomes. When the turnover tax is associated with the budgetary support of consumption, then the explicit idea is that part of the tax realized in one product finances the deficit price of another product. Or to put it in other words: part of the cost of a product bought by a consumer is paid by another consumer. The money income of the former is revalued in an upward direction; while that of the latter is devalued.

Thus, we have to do here with a consumption-oriented model of income redistribution which restricts economic efficiency. Turnover taxes (subsidies) applied to a wide range of products disrupt the organic unity of consumer-price relations and production cost relations, greatly diverts relative prices from relative values and creates thereby irrational consumption patterns.

Formerly, the prevailing idea was that income *redistribution adjusted to the requirements of production policy was typical of capitalist countries, while income redistribution adjusted to social-political requirements was characteristic of socialist countries.* Thus these two income patterns were set against each other as one of the characteristics of the basis difference between the two socio-economic systems. This could become a dominant view because in a certain historical period the socialist countries formed their income policies mostly according to socio-political considerations. Such a price policy blurred the basic difference between social equality and egalitarianism, and between distribution according to work done and according to needs. Thus, the tendency as realized in practice is not the objective consequence of a social order brought about on a socialist basis. On the other hand, the socialization of the means of production undoubtedly increases the possibility of a large-scale redistribution of net incomes realized in production.

At the same time it would be a gross mistake to regard the incomes policy of the socialist countries applied in a historical period as an immanent element of socialist income distribution. The difference between the income structures characteristic of the socialist and capitalist countries is partly a consequence of the *fact that, generally, the socialist societies did not come into being in the industrially advanced countries.* And if the society of a country carries out a socialist revolution at a relatively low level of the productive forces, socialist production relations require by necessity the adoption of a consumption – oriented incomes policy. This makes us understand the difference that is unjustifiably identified – at least partly – with the difference between socio-economic systems. *Socialism and social policy are two different things.* Approached realistically, incomes policy is always formulated in the unavoidable dilemma of considerations of the nature of production-policy on the one hand and of social-policy synthetized in the living-standard policy on the other.

Living-standard policy is formulated in the organic relationship of the following *four* factors:

– *Employment policy;* its tasks are specified by the socialist state on the basis of the principle of *full employment*.

– *Wages policy;* determined by the socialist state on the basis of the principle of *distribution according to work done.*

– The *policy of social benefits,* regulated by the socialist state on the basis of the principle of *distribution according to needs* as asserted in the sphere of social welfare policy.

– *Consumer-price policy,* approached by the socialist state on the basis of *social preferences.*

Employment Policy and Consumer Price

What position should we adopt on the issue of income redistribution by the state? A closer investigation of the problem will convince us that there is a *kind of interrelationship between the state of development of the forces of production and the system of income redistribution*. A country at the initial stage of industrialization, especially if capital inflow plays no role, or just an insignificant one, and the savings of the population are negligible, can hardly start capital formation without setting up customs barriers and levying turnover (purchase) taxes. The former creates revenues for the state and favourable price relations for industrialization, the latter ensures the conditions for financing the economy from the state budget. In such a socio-economic structure the taxation of the value created in agriculture has a special significance, and this is realized in most countries in an indirect way, by the channels of the food industry and wholesale trade, that is, by turnover (purchase) taxes.

At the initial stage of industrialization there is no full employment, and unemployment is characterized by a high ratio of the rural population. The right to work of the population of working age is ensured by the constitution in the socialist societies. Thus it is evident what a great social pressure is exercised by the demand for full employment after the transition to socialist order. This provides the explanation of the fact that, when socialist transformation is carried out at a low level of industrialization, the *maximization of new jobs* outside agriculture is regarded as the main target of planned development. With this we have already *specified the principal criterion of the living-standard policy of the socialist state under the conditions of partial employment*. This criterion is the creation of full employment which gives rise to two tendencies:

– *Rapid industrialization*, consequently the endeavour to accumulate the largest possible proportion of the national income in the interest of developing the forces of production.

– *The extensive mode of industrialization*, that is, the endeavour to invest in such a sectoral structure and such ways as ensure the new labour-absorptive capacity of industry according to the expectations of society.

Extensive industrialization leads of course to restricting the assertion of economic efficiency. Under such circumstances the rising number of the employed is the main source of industrialization and not the improving productivity of labour. The quantity of commodities consumed by the population rises more slowly than the national income, and the distribution of the annual increment of the consumption fund must be effected by taking account of the increasing number of the employed. To put in other words: Social restratification, and parallel with it the shift in the ratio of wage-earners and dependants, become the main characteristic of the living-standard policy. In such circumstances, however,

– in the *wages policy* the tendency of egalitarianism asserts itself; extremely low wages can only be paid for unskilled work; from the point of view of wages no suitable distinction can be made between simple and sophisticated work as would be justified with regard to labour, responsibility and contribution to the national income;

– in the policy of *social benefits* a relatively wide scope must be allowed to asserting the principle of distribution according to needs; basic social care is to be provided, as much as possible, by social benefits;

– in the *consumption policy* the low level of the costs of living that is, the social preferences of the basic necessities and communal services must be regarded as high-priority tasks.

This is, then, a living-standard policy in which relative wages deliberately deviate from relative performances, in which social benefits consciously restrict the distribution function of the market, and the consumer price performs a planned income redistribution. *In the living-standard policy it is possible to determine the socio-political considerations*: the position of the low-income wage-earners and old age pensioners, as well as the living conditions of large families are in the centre of attention. If unskilled manual work is poorly paid, and there are not too great differences in the remuneration of the various occupations, *the greatest difference in the living conditions of workers and employees is due to the differing numbers of wage-earners in families, or the divergent ratios of the gainfully employed to dependants*.

In the case of wage and salary earners real income is determined by the average income per occupied person, per head and per family. Changes in per-family income are especially important because of their effect on the structure of production. If family real incomes rise because in certain families the number of wage-earners increases, this will give rise to a change only in the living conditions of the families in question. The case is different if the number of wage earners per family is unchanged, and family real incomes change in line with real earnings. In this case the living conditions within a social stratum change proportionately.

Real wages may be favourable, and family real incomes low, because the family is large and the ratio of wage-earners to dependants is unfavourable. The distribution of per-capita real income in the living-standard policy under discussion follows not so much the dispersion of real earnings but is rather connected with the size of the family and the ratio of wage-earners to dependants. *This is exactly the point made by the socialist state in its consumer-price policy*. Given this situation, it is not indifferent to society under what conditions people live who perform unskilled manual work and are paid according to the lowest eage category, and what the positions of a worker doing sučh work becomes if he gets married and rears children. Therefore it is not accidental that in this concept of living-standard policy preferences determining consumer-price relations are *tied to the costs of living in the context of the family problem*.

When we consider relative prices prevailing in the market mechanism, we can experience that the so-called *children's articles* are relatively expensive. This finds its explanation in relative inputs. In the socialist societies, however, we can see that these children's goods are inexpensive, high-priority articles. Their low prices are ensured by the state in certain cases by reduced turnover tax rates compared with those of related products by tax exemption or budgetary subsidies. Under market-price conditions, a process of regularly rising prices of *foodstuffs and services* can be observed. By contrast, in socialist societies they are usually subsidized by the state. Thus a deficit consumer price is a typical manifestation of the consumer-price policy of socialist countries. Consumer-price policy lowers the cost of living below the level of the production cost of use values embodying subsistence wages, and also performs a function which, otherwise, is the task of the family allowance.

The situation changes basically when full employment is realized, and the *conditions of a transition from the extensive to the intensive stage of economic development have been created*. Under such circumstances, only a rise in labour productivity can be the main material basis for industrialization, which calls for a more effective wages development and a more rational consumer-price structure. It also follows, however, from all this that the prevailing wage and price relations cannot be evaluated in their static state as they reflect verifiable conditions only at the *given stage of the development* of the productive forces. With their development, these conditions are subject to re-valuation.

The intensive mode of economic development requires, of course, a *living-standard policy different from that pursued in the case of an extensive economic development*.

In the former case *economic growth is much more closely connected with increment in real wages*. The less the living-standard policy is able to perform at the right time and in the right way a switch-over required by the intensive mode of economic development the more pronounced forms the contradictions between the available supply of manpower and the demand for it will assume.

Wage Policy and Consumer Price

The two aspects of the satisfaction of needs: production and consumption are synthetized in price. Working people produce value, on the one hand, and consume products, on the other. The relationship of workers to economic policy is determined

– in their *value-producing capacity* by the development and production policy,

– and in their *capacity as consumers* by the living-standard policy.

This relationship of a dual nature is expressed in a specific way by the price, this being *one of the characteristics in which the nature of price under socialism becomes apparent.*

Price under socialism is not simply a market equilibrium price but, at the same time, a category reflecting the value system of socialism. We can ascertain the truth of this statement if we consider more closely the enterprises' self-accounting system. Thinking superficially, enterprise self-accounting *only* means that in carrying out the planned process of production and distribution, price covers costs and also realizes some profit. This in itself does not mean anything particular as the refund of costs is the natural concomitant of the continuity of production. *The specific feature of self-accounting shows itself in the content of inputs, in wage costs.* This differs in its very nature from inputs under capitalism, where market regulates both employment and wages.

Let us first consider wages as a nominal magnitude. In the socialist economy *this is built into cost as if from outside.* The pay workers get for their productive labour is determined not by the market value of products but by the wages policy. Hungary is one of the socialist countries which have gone furthest towards activating the market mechanism. But the price reform of 1958 founding this economic reform introduced such new prices (price system) which were in alignment with the wage relations established by the state incomes policy. This price reform ensured, in the interest of the living-standard policy, the continuity of production in an already established structure. Out of similar considerations, wages were specifically guaranteed by the state in case prices should not cover costs, or an enterprise should prove submarginal. In the interest of a better assertion of efficiency, this economic reform was designed to establish a more organic relationship *between enterprise profit and wage increment.* But it was clear from the outset that this relationship too could only be established by making allowance for exceptions, as the position of individual production branches (enterprises) is different in respect of increasing labour productivity. At the same time, the requirement of "equal wage for equal work" or of proportionate wage development is such a basic principle of socialist economic control which is independent of its economic control.

Let us assume, as a first approach to the problem, that the prices of products are regulated by their market value. In this case the following formula will arise: price is determined in an "upward direction" by the market value of the product, and in a "downward direction" by the government's wages policy. When price is regulated by the market and wages by the incomes policy, a contradiction may, of course, develop between prices and wages. It is possible that for some productive work such wages must be paid which will never be realized in the price of the product. And yet production must not be discontinued as society needs that product. In this case, the contradiction is resolved by budgetary price subsidies.

Let us now consider the amount of wage as a definite amount of use values. The protection of the real value of wages is an integral part of the living-standard policy. The state sets out from the requirement that higher wages should reflect a better economic situation. Consequently, the price-wage spiral should not reverse the intended rise in the living standard and in income distribution. This criterion sets such requirements to price as often can only be met if the price as a market category is restricted. The state is in a position to restrict market-price movements even without disrupting the organic relationship between price and market value. If the price is given (fixed), then price will have an orientating function for the decisions of economic policy. In this case the task is to create a supply which, either by the expansion of production or stepping up imports, ensures an equilibrium position at the given price.

Looked upon in the interrelationship of wages and prices, the living standard may rise, with an unchanged consumer price level, owing to rising wages, or, with unchanged wages, owing to a fall in the price level. In the fifties it was the prevailing view that prices must decrease with the rise in labour productivity, that is, that the reduction of consumer prices must be regarded as the main measure of rising living-standard policy. The preference-discouragement system in itself does not hamper such a living-standard policy, it sets, at most, limits to the price reduction of goods sold at deficit prices. If this is the main course of the living-standard policy, it must be assumed that the price gap between sufficit and deficit products will narrow, and this will take place to the extent and where – with unchanged wage rates – prime costs will fall owing to the improvement in labour productivity, or where the government, in view of that improvement, will decrease consumer prices.

When discussing price stability, we analysed the causes that may give rise to difficulties in a socialist economy to implement a policy of price reduction. When the equilibrium of the national economy encounters difficulties, and the government lowers consumer prices, it is always possible that a commodity shortage develops in product groups that either cannot be centrally controlled or only with extreme difficulties and the social savings intended to be ensured by the price reduction are offset by hidden price rises. These experiences were bound to exert an influence on the living-standard policy of the socialist countries. Wage rises came into prominence, and price reduction became just one element but by far not the most important one of the policy of raising living standards. This new course of the living-standard policy coincides, as a general rule, with the realization of full employment, and with the transition from the extensive to the intensive stage of development.

The more intricate questions of the transition from the extensive to the intensive type of development *arise from achievements recently attained in economic efficiency*. In this case, those disproportions have to be eliminated which were built deliberately, for socio-political considerations, into the price and wage system at a lower level of the development of the productive forces. Therefore, what is involved here is not merely the requirement that wages should rise with prices remaining unchanged, or, when prices rise, wage increases should substantially exceed the price rise, but also the requirement that relative wages should adapt themselves better than before to relative performances, and relative prices to relative value. The transition from the extensive to the intensive stage is associated with *the revision of the wage and price systems*. The transformation of the wage and price systems is an intricate task because eliminating disproportions always implies an income redistribution with a negative sign, incomes must be redistributed always in favour of those who are better off anyway, but not to the extent justified by their proportionate performance.

Now we have arrived at the point where the *differing principles of distributing the incremental rise in living standards in the extensive and intensive stages are easier to define*. In the extensive phase, a relatively large proportion of the incremental rise in living standard is tied up by the increase of social benefits in addition to wages as well as by the additional wages fund resulting from the higher number of the employed. Consequently, comparatively little is left for raising the wages of those already employed. By contrast, in the intensive stage a substantial proportion of the incremental rise in living standards can be devoted to wage increases. It is exactly this fact that provides the possibility of a more vigorous differentation of wages increments. Looked upon from the *side of the price*, the same can be formulated as follows: in the extensive stage, the socialist state wishes to serve its socio-political considerations most effectively by deficit prices and by price-fixing extended possibly to all commodities. In the intensive stage, however, the more dynamic wage development gives price policy a wider scope in creating a rational price structure.

Social Benefits and Consumer Price

Working people are remunerated for their labour by wages, but they are also entitled to fringe benefits in addition to wages. The main principles of a socially organized consumption have already been discussed. Now we are going to investigate the elements of social benefits connected with consumer prices.[128] Let us take the situation when wages account for 60 per cent, social benefits for 40 per cent of the population's incomes, and within the latter category represent benefits 25 per cent in money and 15 per cent in kind. Under such circumstances 85 per cent of private consumption takes place within the framework of the market mechanism, and 15 per cent is governed by socially determined wants. In other words: the commodity exchange – and thus the distribution function of the consumer price – is wider than the proportion of incomes distributed according to work done. Social money benefits in addition to wages (old-age pension, sick pay, etc.) adapt themselves to socially determined needs, but the benefits themselves are only designed to ensure *solvency*, and the *satisfaction* of needs is not socially determined. This distinguishes this sort of benefits from benefits is kind (education, health services, etc.). It is for this reason that, from the point of view of the consumer price, attention can be limited to benefits in kind.

Benefits in kind are partly *free of charge* and have partly to be paid for. In the latter case, the *rate of payment is always a reduced one,* emphasis being laid on the requirement that *prices should not prevent the satisfaction of wants*. This distinguishes

128 JÁRVORKA, E.: *A fogyasztói árak és dotációk* (Consumer Prices and Subsidies). Budapest, 1967.

the consumer price from the price applied in the system of benefits in kind. In the exchange of commodities it is the price that has a selective function and establishes the demand-supply equilibrium by exclusion. In the sphere of benefits in kind the price is assigned no selective function, the primary means of regulating consumption being the determination by the government of the eligibility for them. This is quite obvious in the case of products that do not take part in commodity exchange. (Certain life-saving medicines etc.)

Benefits in kind influence income distribution if they are available only to certain social strata, if the subject of these benefits is a saleable product, a service available to everybody, and if the difference lies in the fact that in the system of benefits the product (service) in question is available free of charge, or at a price that is substantially lower than the consumer price. A case in point is, for example, long-distance or city transport: some members of society (transport employees) make use of this service free of charge, others (for the purpose of reaching their workplaces) at reduced rates, others again, or the latter on occasions other than specified, pay full rates of fare. Under such circumstances the satisfaction of the same volume or similar kinds of needs absorbs in the case of one consumer no amount of income or only a very limited one, while in the case of an other consumer the satisfaction of this need is possible only in the exchange of commodities, at a consumer price.

Under the conditions specified above, we have to do with a *duality of the consumer price*. The dual character of the consumer price (dual consumer price) must be distinguished from the deficit consumer price. In the former case, a definite range of *consumers*, in the latter case that of *products* is accorded political preference. In the former case, the state redistribution of incomes rests on the system of benefits, in the latter case on the consumer price. In subsidizing the consumer price from the budget, the state starts from the realization that the consumption pattern is different according to the high-, medium- and low-income categories, and it wishes to redistribute incomes in favour of those in the low-income bracket. In the case of dual consumer price, however, the state is led by the intention to prevent that, under certain circumstances, the amount of incomes should have the function of regulating the consumption pattern in a specified range of products (services).

This makes us understand why only a relatively insignificant proportion of the budgetary inputs related to benefits in kind is covered by payments made by the beneficiaries of these services. In Hungary, for example, contributions paid by the population to the costs of the benefits of social insurance amount to 18 per cent, while the payments of the population account for 15 per cent of the costs of health services and social care, education, cultural and communal services. 85 per cent ot the input price of pharmaceuticals and medical supplies is paid by the state, and only 15 per cent of the sales price burdens the population. Persons making use of the services of organized holidays pay only 25 per cent of the actual costs. Of the payments made by the population for the services offered by the various institutions of public education, it is only the radio and television licenses which are significant.

In socialist societies, *income per head of population generally increases faster than the wage per head of active earners*. This directly follows from the fact that there is a year-by-year increase in (a) the number of wage- and salary-earners, (b) the number of pensioners as a result of rising life expectation, (c) in the costs of operating educational, social and health institutions due to their extension and modernization, etc. *In the judgement of society, however, wage is regarded* as the real measure of the living standard. Such a narrowed-down interpretation of the living standard is easy to understand. One can argue like this: though the material situation of the newly employed is improving, it does not affect the living conditions of other working persons, or it affects only those families in which, as a result of this improvement, the wage-earner-dependent ratio has improved. Only families with children are entitled to family allowance. The increase in the pensions burdening society cannot be felt by those who are still working. And he who retires from work, usually complains that he is worse off than he was when still working. There are many who seldom or never make use of the services of social insurance, and those who do, often raise objections to the quality of medical care, and are not aware of the enormous costs of operating and developing these institutions.

In other words: *working people* weigh up their living conditions from their narrow individual or family points of view, and appreciate a general improvement only if they are directly affected by it. *The government*, however, can develop a general welfare only by considering all objective conditions. Yet social judgement concerning the living standards has its bearing on the living-standard policy of the socialist state. In the transition from the extensive to the intensive stage of development, several socialist countries have come to realize that *social benefits granted in an extremely wide scope, and especially their highly centralized forms, do not lead to the desired effects*. At any rate, they have not the same stimulating force as wage incomes. This provides the reason why there is a change of two directions in the matter of social benefits.

(a) The tendency is coming to the fore that payments from the state budget should be confined to the sphere of basic social welfare policy, that is, to benefits that constitute the basic factors of the reproduction of manpower.

(b) The tendency asserts itself that social benefits closely connected with labour should be regulated in a decentralized way. Among the enterprise funds there are also social and cultural ones. Their importance is gradually increasing, which implies that such benefits always vary from enterprise to enterprise, depending on their profits.

Part VI

Foreign Trade Prices

1. Financial and Price Mechanisms of the CMEA

The Principal Features of the CMEA Mechanism

In the system of socialist world economy, which was established after the Second World War, eight European countries (Albania, Bulgaria, Czechoslovakia, Hungary, Poland, the German Democratic Republic, Romania and the Soviet Union) brought into being the Council for Mutual Economic Assistance (CMEA). Although not officially seceded from the CMEA, Albania has not taken part in its work for a considerable time. Mongolia joined it in 1962, and Cuba in 1972. Yugoslavia has since 1965 been participating in the work of some of its Standing Committees, and Finland signed a treaty of association with the CMEA in 1973. This socialist economic integration represents a substantial power.

The CMEA is not an autarchic association, its market cannot provide all material preconditions for the economic development of each of its member countries. Thus, although to varying degrees, each CMEA country transacts lively business activities on the capitalist world market. Although the European socialist countries rely on an extensive international division of labour in the development of their national economies, their *principal market* is the CMEA. This is noteworthy, since prior to the Second World War these countries maintained rather loose trade relations with one another. Before the war, the economies of most CMEA countries developed as integral parts of the West-European economy. In this way, the CMEA *came into being as a result of a radical economic re-orientation* and as a natural outcome of socialist revolutions after the Second World War. Account must also be taken of the fact that in the initial period of socialist transformation the capitalist countries used every conceivable means of discrimination to drive the economies of the historically West-oriented and thus vulnerable, non-socialist economies into an impasse.

Relying on its own resources alone, no European socialist country could have parried these attacks of the capitalist world. To preserve the socialist achievements, economic co-operation became indispensable, and for this primarily the economic endowments of *the Soviet Union provided the necessary basis*. It was the economic relationship established with the Soviet Union which permitted the consolidation of the productive forces heavily damaged in the war, and the implementation of large-scale development programmes. With the accelerated rate of the exploitation of its natural resources the Soviet Union could meet not only its own needs but also supply a significant part of the raw materials needed by the European socialist countries. At the same time, when forming its own production structure, the Soviet Union was able to reckon with the export potentials of these countries, too. Under these circumstances, the political decision of the communist parties of the CMEA countries were founded on a realistic economic basis.

It follows from the nature of things that in the relationships existing and intensifying among the CMEA countries the main principle is the ensurance of *planned development and mutual advantages, and international plan co-ordination is the method on the basis of which this principle can be asserted*. Not only the fact that the CMEA countries elaborate national plans and that they rely on these five-year plans in the management of their national economies is of utmost significance for the CMEA mechanism, but also the circumstance that these five-year periods are simultaneous. The latter facilitates the co-ordination of the plans to a high degree. Since the countries undertake international medium-term commitments simultaneously, the plans can be easily correlated with the exigencies of intensive co-operation within the CMEA. Economic co-operation in the CMEA is diversified, embracing the following fields:

1. *In technical and material relations*:

– the co-ordination of national economic policies,
– the co-ordination of the national plans,
– the organized supply of power and materials,
– specialization and co-operation in industrial production,
– the unification of standards,
– the co-ordinated development of agriculture and of the food industry,
– the co-ordination of transport,
– the co-ordination of technical and scientific research.

2. *In commodity and money relations*:

– the control of the exchange of commodities in a system of interstate agreements,
– the settlement of all kinds of financial operations on the basis of the CMEA's own collective currency,
– financing on the basis of its own banking and credit system,
– the introduction of regional contract prices.

The co-ordination of the national plans takes place under specific forms. The main objectives of economic development and the major investment projects are definitely co-ordinated in practice only if they are influenced by interstate trade agreements. There is no multilateral plan co-ordination, it is only the independently elaborated plan objectives of the CMEA countries that are summarized. This policy is particularly useful in that it provides information for the other members on the ideas the CMEA countries have about their own development. This means that there is no comprehensive CMEA economic plan, not even the co-ordination of the national plans extends to every element of economic development. *Plan co-ordination is developing in two domains:* the first is the *engineering industry* as an important branch of the manufacturing industry where, on the basis of a multilateral co-ordination, the CMEA countries sign *contracts for specialization* and *co-operation;* the second is the bilateral co-ordination of the material balances of the *more important raw materials, of semi-finished and finished products,* followed by bilateral foreign-trade agreements. A summary balance of the products which are most essential for the economic growth of the CMEA countries is also drawn up.

Thus plan co-ordination materializes in the system of *physical indicators.* It is on these indicators that the annual and five-year *interstate trade agreements* are based. Plan co-ordination plays an important part in the five-year interstate agreements. For countries dependent on raw-material imports, these agreements set rather strict limits to the rate of economic growth and to the structural transformation of their production. This feature is the more characteristic of the CMEA countries, the greater the number of commodity deliveries within the CMEA that tie up their export capacities, since in such a case their trade with countries outside of the CMEA can only be of a residual character.

As a consequence, at the consultative plan co-ordination conferences the national problems of economic development and their interrelations with the international division of labour emerge in their totality. It follows, furthermore, that *the national plans cannot be finalized and adopted before the five-year interstate agreements have been concluded.* Thus, in the system of foreign-trade agreements, the five-year interstate agreements become powerful regulators of the national plans in an indirect way. The forecasts for the growth and changes in the production structure of the national income must be harmonized with the five-year interstate agreements. These in turn exert an effect upon the entire system of plan indicators in a definite manner. Compared with the five-year interstate agreements, the annual operative interstate negotiations are of secondary importance only, provided naturally that the member countries consistently meet their obligations undertaken in the long-term contracts for reciprocal commodity deliveries. The annual trade protocols specify the deliveries falling due.

In this way, the CMEA mechanism is characterized by the features of a *self-sufficient economy.* Determinant in it are those criteria which motivate the negotiations co-ordinating the plan, because it is at these negotiations that the volume and commodity structure of trade are established. These in turn are determined by co-ordinating the considerations of the political strategy, the equilibrium of the balance of payments and of economic efficiency.

Political strategy is a criterion governing the relationship between the socialist and capitalist systems of the world economy. The contradictions and conflicts of the different socio-economic systems set special requirements to economic policy, which also manifest themselves in economic integration. In the productive spheres of key importance for the general development and for the military potential, it brings about certain elements of autarchy and enables the expansion of production on the CMEA's own basis.

The equilibrium of the balance of payments is a criterion underlying the internal relationships of the socialist system of the world economy. It is based on the principle that the CMEA countries should, as far as possible, sell their surpluses within the CMEA thereby ensuring balanced progress on the basis that investments to transform the production structure should be made with due consideration of proportionality on CMEA level.

Economic efficiency is a criterion which refers to the principle of the comparative advantage that can be asserted on a CMEA scale. What is involved here is a co-ordination of the development of the forces of production which enables the CMEA countries optimally to utilize of the productive forces available to them. This will be possible if achieving the optimum of the development of the forces of production, at least in the basic branches of production, is endeavoured on an international level and not exclusively within national boundaries.

The mere acceptance of these criteria, however, does not remove the possibility of conflicts in the co-operation within the CMEA. Strategy, equilibrium, economic efficiency can be interpreted in various ways. The scope of products of strategic importance (and with them the endeavour towards autarchy) may be limited or may be wide. Equilibrium within the CMEA may be bilateral or multilateral. The basis for mutual advantages may be

- comparative costs,
- the equality of labour-time inputs,
- the capital-intensity equality.

The CMEA integrates the economies of socialist countries with the same type of economic control, but widely different as regards foreign-trade sensitivity, production structure and the development of the forces of production. Therefore, for objective reasons, the generally formulated and generally accepted criteria show a divergence from the national aspects. This in itself may explain the choice of instruments in physical terms to resolve the problems of co-operation.

With co-operation controlled by way of physical terms *the function of currency and price is strongly restricted.* The categories of currency and price necessary only because the international division of labour takes place in the system of commodity trade and not in direct barter. The exchange rate and the price do not exert control over either the volume or the commodity structure of foreign trade. The only function performed by the *currency* is that of accounting, whereas *foreign-trade prices* control the terms of trade. With respect to currency, it seemed sufficient to indicate the kind of currency in which accounting takes place. As to foreign-trade price, it seemed sufficient to agree on the principle of pricing which regulates the terms of trade. The CMEA countries came to an agreement in 1950 to use the clearing rouble as a unit of accounting in their bilateral relations, in 1958 they agreed to accept the world-market price as the main criterion in determining the CMEA contract prices. The 1963 agreement introduced from January 1964 on the system of a multilateral settling of accounts, making the clearing rouble transferable (convertible within the CMEA).

The currency and price functions so interpreted in CMEA co-operation, particularly in the earlier years, seemed to be well adapted to the national economic mechanism of the member countries. Although each CMEA country determined the *gold content of its own national currency,* the currencies of the socialist countries are in fact non-convertible. In several socialist countries the officially determined gold content of the national currencies does not in fact reflect their actual value. In a foreign-trade mechanism controlled by obligatory plan indicators and operating under the system of a restrictive foreign-exchange policy, this is not absolutely necessary, since the exchange rate of the currency and the production costs are no regulators in foreign trade. The CMEA countries

– settle their accounts in capitalist currencies on the capitalist world market (mostly in US dollar or in pounds sterling),

– settle their accounts in transferable rouble when trading with on another,

– set the domestic producer and consumer prices of the export and import commodities administratively,

– level the difference between the domestic price of the export and import goods payable in the national currency and their foreign-trade rates in foreign exchange (dollar, clearing rouble, etc).

If the national currency is not convertible, if commodity trade is regulated outside the financial system, furthermore, if there is no organic relationship between the domestic and foreign-trade of the products, the exchange rate is not *relevant to commodity trade,* the only requirement being that the price in foreign exchange must be expressed in terms of the national currency, since otherwise foreign-trade equalization could not be effected technically.

The system of co-operation within the CMEA has permanent and variable elements. *A permanent* and increasingly powerful factor is planning and plan co-ordination safeguarding the former. This, among other things, is borne out by recent developments in which plan co-ordination in certain key sectors of the economy is shifting towards joint planning. *The variable elements can be perceived mainly in the way in which planning is being implemented.* The methods actually applied are periodically supervised by the CMEA Council which, on the basis of experience, looks for the alternatives best suited to the conditions.

From the second half of the 1950s onward, some peculiar problems began to crop up in the CMEA co-operation system. Whilst the economic system of the socialist world expanded faster quantitatively than the capitalist economy, it lagged behind in quality in many branches of production. Quantitative progress and qualitative decline gave rise, somewhat later, to quantitative problems. The rate of growth began to drop. In the 1960s it became evident that the potentialities of growth by extensive industrialization had been practically depleted, and that the *entire system of co-operation within the CMEA had to be adapted to the requirements of an intensive type of development.* This realization led to the resolution of the CMEA Council on *socialist economic integration.* Its Complex Programme adopted in 1971 lays down the main direction of perfecting the system of co-operation on the one hand, and specifies, on the other, the problems which need scientific study, as the analyses have revealed serious deficiencies. Therefore, it is not due to mere chance that since the adoption of the Complex Programme the debate on the CMEA mechanism has assumed international proportions.

The most debated issue is how best to improve planned co-operation: *by strengthenig the system of physical indicators or through monetization.* The discussions on the details can ultimately be reduced to this problem. In the present stage of the debate, however, no definite stand has taken shape yet from which unequivocal conclusions might be drawn for the future of the CMEA mechanism. So far only different views of economists can be registered. Before dicussing the different points of views, it would seem rational to elucidate the commodity and money relations in the CMEA mechanism in greater detail.

The Systems of Commodity Trade and Pricing

Commodity trade within the CMEA is regulated by *five-year* interstate agreements in a quota system, in which compulsory quantitative prescriptions are in force for raw materials exchanged in large volumes, for typical semi-finished goods and for the more important mass products. Trade is governed by combined (global) value quotas in groups of products which are characterized by a wide assortment and a fast product replacement. In this case, the interstate agreements stipulate the capacities needed and regulate the commodity composition (the technical parameters of individual products) within the framework of operative co-operation. Where there are agreements on specialization and production co-operation in force, the deliveries stipulated in them are also taken into consideration when setting the quotas. *The nomenclature of the products falling into the system of quantitative and value quotas is regulated bilaterally.*

The implementation of the five-year interstate agreements is supervised in the course of annual interstate negotiations. These have the task:

– to carry out *modifications,* if necessary, of the five-year agreements,

– to elaborate measures needed for the expansion of foreign-trade relations or for the *widening* of the scope of interstate agreements,

– to supervise the development of turnover and the orders on hand, and thereby to remove the obstacles hampering co-operation, which is based on an equilibrium position of the balance of payments.

The interstate agreements provide the framework for legally binding delivery contracts signed by foreign trading enterprises (or those vested with foreign-trading rights). Thus, interstate agreements involve compulsory contracting, and contracts involve compulsory commodity delivery. The undisturbed operation of this mechanism is safeguarded by *the state monopoly of foreign trade.* The enterprises producing the export commodity fund and those using (trading in) the import commodity fund participate in the preparation of both the interstate agreements and the delivery contracts, depending on the internal mechanism of the CMEA countries concerned.

As a general rule, up to 1971 the interstate agreements and delivery contracts had been signed without specifiying whether the then valid CMEA contract price was to be modified or not in the subsequent period. The *trade and price agreements were separated from one another.* The demand for an agreement in advance on the prices of some products emerged for the first time during the negotiations preparatory to the five-year interstate agreements covering the period 1971–1975. It is expected that for the period between 1975 and 1980 this demand will be met in a wider sphere. This fact, at the same time, expresses the new tendencies of the co-operation system, *viz.*

(1) that the obligation to supply commodities which are significant for the importing country, and

(2) that the obligation to take delivery of goods of primary importance for the exporting country

– should be determined as a function of price.

The CMEA countries set the contract prices applied to foreign trade in bilateral interstate agreements, taking as a basis the prices prevailing on the capitalist world market. In forming these prices, the CMEA countries follow the *guidelines (the so-called Bucharest Price Principle) determined by the CMEA Council in 1958.* The main directives for price formation are based on the fact that trade among the socialist countries is built upon the principles of mutual assistance and mutual advantages and is aimed at ensuring the participating countries' economic progress. Price formation within the CMEA – also taking into consideration the modifications introduced in the meantime – are as follows:

1. Capitalist world-market prices are taken to mean *prices prevailing on the principal world market.* This market should constitute an international trade centre whose share in the turnover of the commodity concerned is significant, a market where the deals are transacted under usual conditions.

If a product is traded in on several principal world markets, the selection of the market in question depends on the extent to which it is ready to carry on trade with the CMEA countries, and on how far it is geographically situated from the latter.

When selecting the principal world market, the seller's interests must also be taken into account, but basically the buyer's viewpoint matters, namely, on which main capitalist world market he would purchase the goods if he signed a contract not with his partner in the CMEA. In some cases, depending on the agreement, the contract price may also be based on two or more principal market prices.

The prices applied in the trade of CMEA-members with capitalist countries may also be taken as a starting price, particularly with products which the CMEA countries sell and buy in considerable quantities on the capitalist world market.

2. The capitalist world-market price must be *adequately documented.* For products that are dealt in at commodity exchanges, quotations are acceptable. In the case of minimum and maximum quotations, the minimum price should be taken as a starting price. If the items are not traded in at commodity exchanges, the prices quoted in the delivery contracts and verified by invoices, or quotations of respectable firms, price catalogues, price lists, etc. can be accepted.

If the subject of trade is a product on which no world-market price documentation is available, the price must be established in proportion to the world-market price of related products by comparing their technical parameters.

If the available price documentation is older than twelve months, the current world-market price should be established by a price-index method specifically adjusted to this purpose.

If the price documentation is available only in an agreement based on clearing dollars (etc.), the world-market price should be determined by taking into consideration the difference (discount) between the value of convertible and restricted foreign exchange.

3. When determining the CMEA contract price, the capitalist world-market price has to be cleared of all elements of irregularity which exist on the capitalist world-market as a result of state and regional protectionism, the operation of international monopoly organizations and cyclical market fluctuations. This clearing process takes place, as a general rule, with due consideration to the average prices of a longer period of time.

4. The difference (advantages, disadvantages) between the *transport costs* included in the capitalist world-market price and those incurred in the trade between CMEA countries must be divided half and half between the exporting and the importing CMEA country (the principle of "half-freight").

5. The CMEA contract prices formed on the basis of the capitalist world-market prices must, as a general rule, be fixed

for the duration of five-year interstate agreements. This must be achieved in such a way that the CMEA countries can organize their planned co-operation while preserving their state of equilibrium.

Therefore, in the five-year period of the interstate agreement the contract prices of new products should be established not on the basis of the current world-market prices, but according to the prices of the same period which serves as a basis for general price formation. If no such price can be identified, the price of the new product can be agreed upon on the basis of the prevailing world-market price, but account must also be taken of the price level of related articles already on the market.

Prior to a new five-year plan period, the CMEA countries jointly determine the period whose average prices will form the basis on which to check on the current contract prices, and which will be used as a basis for setting the contract prices for the subsequent five-year plan period.

Each CMEA country is entitled, by referring to the criteria of "price clearance", to raise objections to the world-market price documented in this way, or – on the basis of a new price documentation – to put forward concrete proposals for the modification of the prevailing contract price.

This system of price formation designed to determine CMEA contract prices was modified after 1971, mainly in the sphere of new (modernized) products. Some CMEA countries hold the view that in certain groups of products (particularly machinery) the contract prices were unjustifiably high. This gave rise to a tendency to reduce the contract prices in some product groups. However, owing to the prices fixed for five years, this endeavour can be effective in relation to new (modernized) products only.

Furthermore, the discussions conducted on how to implement the Complex Programme of socialist economic integration, may make us expect that *a more flexible price mechanism will take shape* during the period 1976–1980. There is a consensus of opinion that in concluding interstate agreements not only the prices must be agreed upon but also the conditions under which the prices can be modified during the plan period. The view has been generally accepted that the contract prices of products which are of a long-term significance for the economic development of the CMEA countries (basic raw materials, fuel, agricultural staples, specialized products and goods produced in co-operation) must be stable. At the same time, to promote technical progress in a number of industries, among others in engineering, emphasis should be placed on determining the criteria which will justify a change in the contract prices. With agricultural produce, whose production and storage is definitely seasonal in character, the contract prices must be differentiated according to the season or to the time of delivery.

The Three-Channel-System of the International Settling of Accounts

In the interrelations of the CMEA countries assets and liabilities may emerge for a variety of reasons. In conformity with the system of accounting now in force, they must be handled separately, depending on whether they belong to the sphere of

– "trade",
– "non-trade", or
– "other" operations.

The term "trade" operations means foreign-trade activities, respectively related ancillary (transport, insurance etc.) operations. "Non-trade" operations are those related to passenger traffic (for instance tourism) and assets and liabilities of the character of wages. This group also includes assets and liabilities arising in connection with the settlement of property claims of citizens, for example transfer of bequests, certain services (for instance the shooting or distribution of motion pictures, etc.). The "other" operations group comprises capital movements in connection with joint undertakings and, in general, the establishment and running of internationally organized institutions. Thus, every conceivable operation which is associated with the movement of money, falls into one of the three accounting methods, according to the main characteristics of the operation. From the point of view of accounting methods, the similar and dissimilar features of international operations may be summed up in the following:

1. The national currencies of the CMEA countries do not take part in the alimentation of foreign-trade operations. In this sphere, the transferable rouble is used as an accounting unit. However, *the national currencies of the CMEA countries do finance "non-trade" and "other" operations.* This is a necessity, since in the two latter fields both the expenses and the incomes appear in terms of national currencies, but as against "trade" operations in these two domains, the problem of the national currency cannot be evaded. Either the demand for the national currency must be satisfied (for instance in tourism), or it is necessary to contribute to expenses in the national currency (for instance to found an international organization), or else the earnings gained in national currency must be shared (as for in-

stance, in sharing profits gained by a joint undertaking). Therefore, for operations of this kind it is necessary to determine the relative values of the national currencies.

2. *In the national price systems of the CMEA countries the producer and consumer price levels differ to considerable, but varying, degrees.* This difference is substantial, for instance, in the Soviet Union, and is negligible in Hungary. This is due to differences in the two countries' tax systems. The difference between the price levels is substantial and, as a consequence, the producer price level is low where centralization by the budget of net incomes takes place through a turnover tax realized in consumer prices. And vice versa: the difference is negligible where the budget centralization of net incomes occurs through taxes realized in producer prices.

Owing to these dissimilarities in the price systems of the CMEA countries, *the relative values of their national currencies are different in respect of producer and in consumer prices.* This exactly was the main reason for a separate handling of "non-trade" and "other" operations in the international settling of accounts. For non-trade operations, which are mostly of a character of wages, that exchange rate seemed to be most appropriate which approaches the value relations of the national currencies on the basis of a definite commodity structure (consumption basket) by comparing the consumer prices. In the "other" operations, which are largely of a material character, the value of the currency can best be expressed in the system of producer prices.

3. In formulating the system of the international settling of accounts it had to be taken into consideration that, if in the relationship of two CMEA countries the assets and liabilities arising in "non-trade" and "other" operations are not equalized, then the problem can be solved only in the field of "trade" operations. The transferable rouble is a collective socialist currency which cannot be converted into any free foreign exchange; thus not into gold either. In other words: holdings arising within the CMEA must be made use of within the CMEA, and the best channel for this purpose is commodity trade. Therefore, the relationship among the three spheres of the settling of accounts had to be ensured. More precisely, the assets and liabilities created through "non-trade" and "other" operations had to be converted into transferable roubles.

The way in which the accounts of trade operations are settled was laid down in the agreement which established the International Bank for Economic Co-operation. It was put into force on the 1st January 1964 and amended in 1970. The settlement of "non-trade" operations is based on the Prague agreement adopted in 1963 and amended in 1971. It determines the scope (titles) of "non-trade" operations, the methods of settling them, the coefficients to be applied in converting the assets and liabilities arising in the non-trade field into transferable roubles. The guidelines for the accounting method of the "other" operations were elaborated by the 1963 Berlin methodology and the 1972 Varna model regulation respectively, which put the former into a more accurate working. The latter proposes methods for the conversion into transferable roubles of accounts (assets, costs, profits) held in national currencies. The parties concerned are free to choose from among the methods the one they want to apply.

Since 1964 the CMEA countries have settled their trading transactions with CMEA members in transferable roubles. According to the agreement, the gold content of the transferable rouble amounts to 0,987412 grs of pure gold. When concluding trade agreements, each CMEA country has to maintain a global equilibrium between its earnings and expenditures in transferable rouble over one calendar year, or over any other period of time mutually agreed upon. In doing so, the accumulation or utilization of transferable rouble reserves as well as credit operations have to be taken into consideration, too.

In accordance with the relevant agreements, *the non-trade rate of exchange is governed by the purchasing power parity* measured by the consumption basket internationally agreed upon. While retaining the system of accounting elaborated on the conditions of "non-trade" payments, the 1971 amendent to the 1963 Prague agreement, up-dated the structure of the "basket of goods" (the quantitative and qualitative parameters of commodities and services) and made allowance for changes that had taken place in retail prices and rates. Meanwhile, with increasing tourism, most CMEA countries have bilaterally modified the coefficient set down in Prague and used in the conversion into transferable roubles of the liabilities and claims in national currencies arising in "non-trade" operations. This induced the CMEA countries to introduce a new coefficient in 1971 for the conversion of "non-trade" payments into transferable roubles.

In line with the Varna model regulation concerning the settlement of *"other" operations,* the estimated value of jointly established projects is given in national currency and in accordance with the prices of the country on whose territory the project is to be erected. This value is agreed upon and accepted by the countries concerned. When the value is converted into transferable roubles, the countries may consider the following:

(a) The conversion of costs of a material character (materials, equipment, transport, depreciation, etc.) is carried out by comparing the domestic and foreign trade prices. The commodity-representation may not be less than 50 per cent of the inputs of a material character. The weighted average coefficient calculated in this way must be applied to the conversion of other material costs foreseen in the estimates. Depending on the agreement of the parties concerned, a separate coefficient may be calculated for building materials.

(b) Should the costs of the machinery and equipment represent more than 5 per cent of the value of materials, their transferable rouble value is determined on the basis of a calculation including the following factors: wages, material costs, depreciation, overhead costs. Material costs and depreciation are converted according to point (a); wages are converted according to the "non-trade" exchange rate and coefficient. The overhead costs are split into materials and wages costs and converted by the appropriate methods.

(c) If a country contributes a complete project (e.g. a plant) to a joint undertaking, the value in transferable roubles is calculated by means of the average coefficient formed in accordance with (a), but making allowance for depreciation. If components to a project jointly to be constructed are purchased on the capitalist market, the interested parties agree on financing it and on dividing the costs between them.

(d) When converting jointly earned enterprise profits, the interested parties may agree on applying a weighted average coefficient by which the conversion into transferable roubles of the capital invested by them is calculated. A conversion coefficient calculated on the basis of the ratio of the foreign-trade to the domestic price of the product of the joint undertaking is also acceptable.

The Varna model regulation serves the purposes of orientation. The interested parties may agree on the concrete system of the exchange rate depending on the character of the operation in question. It should be stressed, however, that owing to substantial differences between the systems of national producer and consumer prices in the CMEA countries, an extremely complicated system of coefficients concerning the method of settling accounts of "other" operations has evolved. Under this system, expenses given in national currency in the producer-price system of the country concerned, are converted into transferable roubles in the commodity structure broken down into its elements. Thus it is assumed that capital investment and profits are sets of use values to be handled in a differentiated way, depending on national price patterns. An example to elucidate this may be the case of a joint Polish-Hungarian enterprise (Haldex) established to utilize the pit heaps close to the Polish coal mines. Here, to express the parity rate of the Polish zloty and the Hungarian forint, some main coefficients differentiated according to the investments made and to the running costs and, within these main coefficients, no less than thirty-six secondary coefficients are used.

Therefore, the necessity of elaborating a simplified method of settling the accounts of "other" operations was justly raised. It applies a uniform coefficient agreed upon internationally and calculated by comparing national producer prices. To understand this it should be noted that in recent years the CMEA countries have quantified at producer prices the relative value of their own national currency to the transferable rouble separately within the CMEA export-commodity structure and within the national structure of production. This makes it possible to determine in an indirect way the value relations of the national currencies measured at producer prices. For the time being, however, the concrete method to be used and the conditions under which such a coefficient can be applied for settling the accounts of "other" operations, are still being discussed.

Multilateralism

The current system of multilateralism has developed step by step. Already in the mid 1950s, the CMEA countries realized that a bilaterally organized commodity trade would either stabilize the volume of foreign trade on the level of the country having a lesser export potential, or force the country with a greater export potential to take over goods which it does not need, or to buy commodities which are among the last items on the priority list of unsatisfied wants.

This situation resulted in the conclusion of a multilateral clearing agreement on the 20th June 1957. According to its basic principle, the payments made within a calendar year by one of the countries must tally with its receipts from the rest of the countries. This meant the *substitution of the principle of a global equilibrium for a bilateral equilibrium*. The agreement did not abandon bilateral accounting but laid down that if a country finds ways and means to use its claims arising in a given bilateral relation in another bilateral relationship, it is free do so. Since 1957, therefore the system of multilateral settlements has played only a complementary role alongside basically bilateral accounting. However, the 1957 agreement did not yield any appreciable results. Thus, in 1963 an agreement introducing the transferable rouble in multilateral settlements was concluded.

In the 1963 agreement the individual CMEA countries undertook the obligation to ensure by trade agreements the equilibrium within a calendar year of the earnings and expenditures in transferable roubles with the rest of the participating countries. This agreement lent *an institutional basis for the principle of global equilibrium*. The resulting features of the multilateralism may be summed up as follows:

1. Each CMEA country is entitled, even after the introduction of multilateral settlements, to *maintain the equilibrium in the system of bilateral relations*. The method of settling accounts at the International Bank for Economic Co-operation (IBEC) is adapted to this principle. IBEC keeps a combined record on accounts but it handles them analytically, according to bilateral relations. The debtor or creditor CMEA countries know exactly in what relation they have incurred debts or acquired claims. Since in trade agreements, even after 1964, the bilateral equilibrium of the balance of payments has continued to be the main criterion, a creditor-debtor position in bilateral relations can develop only because one country supplies more than originally planned, or another country supplies less then originally foreseen. The latter case occurs either because the country is incapable of making deliveries, or because there is no market for some products.

But under *such settlement arrangement there cannot be structural creditors, consequently there cannot be structural debtors, either*. Holdings in transferable roubles can be used only within the CMEA, and there is very little likelihood that claims arising in a given relation can be utilized in another. Moreover, a debtor position, owing to a lower rate of interest, can only be desirable if it serves to ease the balance of payments difficulties in capitalist relation, viz., if debts are incurred because a country sells on the capitalist world market products which it should have sent, by obligation, to a CMEA country. The situation is different if the product is non-convertible and the debt is incurred because a CMEA country which was obliged to take delivery of the goods in question refuses to do so. Irrespective of whether there is no demand for the product, which is shoddy, the indebted country will deem this extremely detrimental, as it will result in unsaleables and will put a brake on production. In such cases the debtor's position is regarded as a disturbance – caused by the creditor country – in planned co-operation based on equilibrium.

It should be stressed once more that the only system in which no structural creditor-debtor position can develop is that of *multilateral* settlements. There are numerous examples of CMEA countries granting short-, medium- or long-term credits under *bilateral interstate agreements* and ensuring thereby the equilibrium of the bilateral balance of payments. Should this not be the case, both parties may rightfully expect that the equilibrium be maintained year after year by regular deliveries as foreseen in the trade agreements. One of the objectives of operational annual trade agreements is exactly to correct the imbalances of the preceding period. The preparation of such agreements includes the endeavour to encourage the debtor countries to step up their exports and to make the creditor country increase its readiness to take delivery of the products. Debates in such events arise mostly with respect to the nomenclature of the goods.

2. Creditor-debtor positions may also arise in the relationships of the international financial bodies of the CMEA (IBEC and the International Investment Bank: IIB) and of the member countries. Their operations fall outside the scope and are independent of bilateral relations. Therefore, for instance at IBEC, the synthetic bills for each country consist of two parts: settlements (1) reflecting bilateral relations are supplemented by (2) movements on the *internal accounts* of banking operations.

The facts that goods can be obtained for transferable roubles in bilateral relations only, and that in payment for debts incurred in transferable roubles goods can be supplied in bilateral relations only, give rise to a peculiar situation. Should a country have a credit balance on an internal banking-operations account, this cannot be regarded to be liquid, because of the automatism of the co-operation system; it is in fact a frozen asset since it originates from outside the sphere of bilateral trade relations and has as such no commodity coverage. In the same way, the granting of credits outside bilateral relations does not in itself mean solvency in bilateral relations. A bank credit given on a multilateral basis has no independent commodity coverage unless the medium- (long-) term credit granted by the IIB is accepted by the CMEA countries in settlement of their exports within the framework of bilateral agreements.

This is one of the fields where *the contradictions of multilateral accounting and bilateral trade carried on simultaneously manifest themselves*. These contradictions, too, justify that the present system of co-operation within the CMEA should be regarded merely as a transitional stage in which the newer elements assert themselves by gradually ousting the old ones.

3. The CMEA countries set the contract prices in bilateral agreements. In this system the same product may have different

import prices in different relations, there might be differences in the price levels, too, ranging in certain relations between 7 and 12 per cent, and for certain products even between 25 and 35 per cent.

This peculiarity of the CMEA contract prices would, as a natural consequence, make the CMEA countries maximize their exports in the relation where the export-price level is the highest, and maximize their imports in the relation where the import-price level is the lowest. This policy would enable them to keep an equilibrium in their payments balances under the system of multilateralism in the easiest way. But this, again, points to the contradictions between multilateral accounting and bilateral price formation, because such endeavours would be doomed to failure in a bilaterally organized trade.

Prices can be differentiated bilaterally just because the balance of payments must be in a bilateral equilibrium. Under such conditions, a higher import price would be indifferent to the importing country if it could outbalance it by similarly high export prices. Anyway, bilateral relationships have the peculiarity that in such cases it is not the systems of commodity exports and commodity imports, but rather the export and import commodity structures that count. *What is compared is export and import price levels and not export and import prices proper*.

The principles multilaterally fixed for foreign-trade prices put constraints on bilateral agreements to a certain extent only. In the revision and change of prices fixed for five-year periods, the CMEA countries are interested to different degrees. It follows from the nature of things that the revision and change of prices are urged by those countries for which adaptation to current capitalist world-market prices means an improvement of their terms of trade. At the same time, the partner country is interested in averting or at least in alleviating a deterioration in the terms of trade. These problems vary from relation to relation, and it is exactly the endeavour to keep the terms of trade on a stable level that differentiates the prices formed in different relations.

4. Bilateral prices raise problems with regard to the *homogeneity of the transferable rouble*. This is characteristic of any clearing currency. In their bilateral relations established with most capitalist soft-currency countries, the socialist states do not use the currencies of these capitalist countries as accounting units. When, in bilateral clearing, the accounting unit is the US dollar or the pound sterling, in gold-parity quotations this must be regarded as US dollar or pound sterling. But since in capitalist soft-currency countries there is an organic relationship among domestic price, the rate or foreign exchange and

foreign-trade price, a drop in the value of the currency finds expression in the clearing-dollar or the clearing-pound-sterling prices as well, and these, too, will rise. What is the actual background of this problem? In gold-parity quotations the clearing currency cannot be regarded to be an independent currency, *indeed, when in a bilateral relationship the currency of a third country is used as an accounting unit, this currency will become a new foreign exchange which has a special feature*: its value is determined in bilateral trade, and any changes in its value will by and large adapt themselves to changes in the internal value of the capitalist soft currency concerned.

In the case of a correctly implemented price policy, the devaluation of a clearing currency accepted for trade has no detrimental influence on the equivalence of commodity trade in the bilateral relation of a socialist and a capitalist country. When the exporter in a capitalist country raises the price, the socialist country will also raise its export prices. This it can do all the more as the higher price will correspond to the internal price relations in the capitalist country. Higher import prices are thus compensated for by higher export prices. However, this holds true exclusively for this single bilateral relationship. This becomes obvious if a socialist country converts its claim in clearing currency into a convertible foreign exchange. The loss in rates incurred in such a transaction is the measure of the difference in value between clearing and convertible foreign currencies bearing the same name.

Relating all this to the transferable rouble, attention should be called to two main differences. (1) Deviations in the value of the transferable rouble in different relations are not due to differences between the domestic prices of the CMEA countries, or to the different movements of domestic prices, but to the bilaterally different commodity-structure of foreign trade, and to the conflicting interests in the terms of trade, respectively. (2) Deviations in the value of the transferable rouble in different relations remain latent because the claims arising in transferable roubles cannot be converted into free foreign exchange (gold).

The transferable rouble cannot be converted into capitalist currencies (gold), but convertible currencies have a role to play in the CMEA's co-operation system. As regards the institutional forms, this role manifests itself in the following: (1) Thirty per cent of the one thousand million transferable roubles' worth of capital stock of the IIB and a part of that of IBEC are available in convertible foreign exchange or in gold. (2) Under specified conditions, the IIB grants investment credits in convertible foreign exchange (gold) if a new technology can only be purchased on the capitalist world market (know-how, licences, capital machinery, etc.). (3) In the case of joint enterprises, sales receipts in convertible foreign exchange made on the capitalist world market are directly divided among the participating CMEA countries.

Greater attention is due to the phenomena caused by the fact that although the transferable rouble is not convertible, the CMEA countries need considerable amounts of convertible foreign exchange. This situation has led to the differentiation between *"soft" and "hard" products* in the commodity exchange within the CMEA. In the last analysis, owing to the non-convertibility of the transferable rouble, the CMEA countries find trade within the CMEA mutually advantageous only if, among other things, the "hard" commodities mutually compensate for one another in bilateral relationships. More precisely: a change in the given state of affairs in favour of convertible products only is regarded possible if the partner country introduces the same change in its export structure. As a consequence, the debates on the export and import quotas for convertible products have become keener. There are now several products – and their number is increasing – in which the export quotas lag far behind the supplying capacity of the country, viz. goods of which it can buy more than its quota, but only against convertible foreign exchange and at current world-market prices.

Commodity transactions settled in convertible foreign exchange may be explained by the exporting country in the following manner: if it supplies more than stipulated in the trade agreement, it uses up the commodity basis of its capitalist foreign-exchange earnings. It is therefore justified for that country to distinguish this export from planned trade transactions. Convertible foreign exchange does not necessarily figure in such deals, because the transaction may be of a barter type. In such a case, exports and imports mutually equate one another; products convertible on the world market appear on both sides, and the zero balance is formed at current capitalist world-market prices.

The same happens when *close-type agreements* on production co-operation are concluded. A typical example for such deals is the production of Zhiguli passenger cars in the Soviet Union under the Italian Fiat licence; the Soviet Union pays for the components supplied by co-operating CMEA countries by end-product deliveries, the equivalent being established on the basis of the price structure (component and end-product prices), adapted to the Fiat price catalogue. It is thus fully possible for the participating country to supply Zhiguli components at prices completely different from those of related articles in regular commodity exchange. Since, however, the value of these deliveries is determined by the value of imported cars, the price in itself is neutral for the countries concerned.

These phenomena, however, only further testify to the *difficulties caused by the currency problems not yet solved*. Thus deals in production co-operation in which the production of components in large, economical batches and the demand for the related end products coincide in the relation of the same country, are indeed very few. Therefore, the problem of the convertibility of the transferable rouble also had to emerge. According to the 1970 amendent of the statutes of the IBEC, the Council of the Bank has to study whether the Bank is able to carry out operations whose object is to change the transferable rouble into gold or freely convertible foreign exchange.

2. CMEA Contract Prices

World-Market Prices v. Socialist Price Basis

Foreign-trade price policy is an activity of the government profoundly different from price control in domestic relations. In the domestic field, the government appears as the owner of productive units or as the organ of state power. Quite different is the situation in foreign relations. On the world market, adaptation to prices at which sales are effected is necessary. World-market price relations can only be influenced by buyers and sellers. But to exert an impact on these relations, their position must be strong. If this is the case, the lowest price limit for selling and the highest for buying can be set. In principle, this possibility is given to any participant but only if he can do without a certain import product or if he can afford to renounce exporting a certain product.

The socialist state relies on a foreign-trade monopoly in organizing the international division of labour. It makes use of this in its foreign-trade policy. The establishment of the CMEA gave the European socialist countries a good opportunity of pursuing a novel foreign-trade price policy. In the first years following the Second World War, the European socialist countries considered the agreement on foreign-trade prices as an enterprise affair. Foreign-trade prices were formed in contractual relations between enterprises and in an adaptation to world-market prices. A change in this situation came in 1950 when, after the conflict in Korea, a process of speculative price rise started on the capitalist world market. The CMEA countries decided not to follow this tendency but to form an independent foreign-trade price policy, which was introduced *in 1950 by the price-stop agreement*. The "Bucharest Price Principle" is, at present, its form of manifestation. Thus the CMEA contract prices have become a specific category of world-market prices on the CMEA markets. While the European socialist countries pursue a virtually passive (adaptable) foreign-trade price policy in their relationships with capitalist countries, they follow an active (determinant) foreign-trade price policy among themselves.

When the 1950 price-freeze was introduced, the CMEA countries regarded it to be a temporary measure, and in the late

1950s, when the world market got normalized, they put on the agenda a revision of stop prices. This date also marked the beginning of the debates on CMEA contract prices. The following question was raised: do the stop prices have to be abandoned because of the adaptation to world-market prices, or in order to put price formation on the CMEA market's own value basis. *In these debates most economists took a stand for the adaptation to world-market prices*. This opinion is most consistently expressed by those economists who hold the view that international value can only be interpreted on a world-market scale.[129] Those who opted for the acceptance of world-market prices are still of the opinion that

– it is the relative prices of the world market that express internationally the technical standards of individual products, and that

– it is changes in the relative prices of the world market that express the tendencies in the development of the productive forces.

It was especially Bulgarian economists who expressed concern about the adaptation to capitalist world-market prices[130] saying that these prices had developed under capitalist production relations. Owing to the historically determined economic structure, to the difference between the levels of development and, last but not least, to the specific objectives of socialist economic policy, the production relations under capitalism are different from those prevailing in the socialist countries. The industrially advanced capitalist states exert their influence on the international division of labour as well as on price formation in their own political and economic interests. Most capitalist commodity markets are manipulated; there turnover and prices are formed under the capitalist monetary system, subordinated to the interests of monopolies, economic and financial associations, etc.

The 1958 CMEA agreement (the Bucharest Price Principle) tried to reconcile the conflicting opinions by a compromise. It

[129] Cherniyansky, V.: *Ekonomika sotsialisticheskoy vneshney torgovlyi* (The Economics of Socialist Foreign Trade). Moscow, 1963. Popov, K. I.: Über die Grundlage des Preissystems des Handels zwischen den sozialistischen Ländern. Sovietische Wissenschaft. *Gesellschaftswissenschaftliche Beiträge*, No. 3, 1966.

[130] Savov, N. V.: *O tovarnykh otnosheniyakh mezhdu sotsialisticheskimi stranami i tsenoobrazovanii na mirovom sotsialisticheskom rynke* (Commodity Relations among Socialist Countries and Price Formation on the Socialist World Market). Moscow, 1963. Gelev, G.: Sur la question du passage vers une propre base de la formation des prix du marché international socialiste (On the Switchover of the International Socialist Market to the Socialist Price Basis). *Planovo Stopanstvo i Statistica*, No. 5, 1964.

geared the adaptation to the world-market prices to the "clearing" of these prices of those elements of "irregularity" which were caused by the price policy of the monopolies, the cyclic nature of development, etc. This compromise, however, failed to reconcile the different views.

It was for this reason that those who advocated the principle of the world-market price suggested revoking the decision on the price stop in order to place commodity trade inside and outside the CMEA on a *uniform price basis*. In the period between 1950 and 1957 an awkward situation arose owing to the fact that the same products had two different prices because the socialist countries could buy or sell the same product variety on either of the two international markets. Under such conditions it seemed particularly advantageous to sell on the capitalist world market when the price was higher, and buy there when the price was lower. In this way, the two prices created conflicting interests in the relationships of the socialist countries. The buyer wanted to buy on the socialist world market when the seller preferred to sell his goods on the capitalist world market. For one socialist country it was more advantageous to sell on the socialist market, while the other socialist countries were interested in buying rather on the capitalist world market.

Although the economic relations of the socialist countries are planned relations with quotas fixed in bilateral contracts and, further, the advantages and disadvantages inherent in international trade can obviously be judged only in the context of total exports and imports, experience has proved that when the prices of the two world markets are completely separated from one another, then, in respect of material interests, the economic co-operation of the socialist countries becomes looser rather than closer. This is why it seemed logical to those who were in favour of the principle of the world-market price that the abrogation of the 1950 price stop should reinstate the pre-1950 state of affairs.

Those who argued for the principle of the "*socialist price basis*" reasoned in the following way. If it is not expedient mechanically to transplant the prices of the capitalist market into the socialist world market, is it practicable to separate the two world-market prices in such a manner as price "clearing" would mean? Is it not possible that, when the capitalist world-market price is applied in its "cleared" form, what actually happens is the substitution of the capitalist world-market price by its own distorted variety? Is there a criterion at all according to which it can be decided in practice what the world-market price would be like if it were free of its irregular elements?

As long as the socialist world-market price is the same as the capitalist world-market price, the question cannot of course be raised at all what the causes, in principle, of the relationship (or differences) of the prices prevailing on the two world markets are. But as soon as the socialist contract price diverges from the world-market price, it is inevitable to answer the questions relating to the essence of the CMEA contract price. Thus, among other things, an answer should be given to the question: if the world-market price changes in themselves do not give sufficient reason for causing price changes in the trade among the socialist countries, why should the price already in use be considered justified?

The debates have continued to be keener in the practical application of the Bucharest Price Principle. It is for the first time in history that the formation of foreign-trade prices has, as a general rule, become separated from the calculations of enterprises manufacturing export products, respectively of those using import products. In other words, *price formation takes place through the direct adaptation of the prices on the external market*. This means that a completely new problem, the *quantification and "clearing" of the world-market price should be solved*.

The coming into existence of the different national currencies, the commodity world becoming increasingly richer, the variety of the forms of intermediate trade, together with the ever-changing delivery terms, render *it extremely difficult to be well informed about the world-market price*. Analyses have evinced that world-market prices and free-market prices coincide only in the case of a very few products – mostly raw materials –, and only if commodity trade is entirely free, if there are no substantial export subsidies or import levies, quantitative controls etc. According to general opinion, the price used in international trade can only be regarded as a world-market price

– if it emerges in deals where the export and import operations are separated from one another,

– if payments are made in a free foreign-exchange and, finally,

– if the deal is transacted on an approved international export or import market.

However, it is much easier to set down these criteria in principle than to quantify – on their basis – the world-market price in concrete cases.[131] What is involved here is not whether a world

[131] Csikós-Nagy, B.: *Árpolitika a mai kapitalizmusban* (Price Policy in Up-To-Date Capitalism). Budapest, 1964. Kormnov, Yu. F.: *Sietsializatsiya i kooperatsiya proizvodstva stran SEVA* (Specialization and Co-operation in the Production of the CMEA Countries). Moscow, 1972.

market-price exists or not, but whether it can be recognized by an outside observer (not the business partner). Obviously, it is easier to get information on the world-market prices of goods traded in at the commodity exchanges (auctions) than on prices formed in direct inter-enterprise relations. It is true that nowadays international commodity exchanges transact only a marginal part of the trade, but their significance should not be judged by the share of their transactions in international turnover. In deals transacted outside of the commodity exchanges, buyer and seller usually accept the exchange quotation prices. And if in long established relations the price is fixed by contract for several years, a clause is often applied stipulating that should the price quoted on the exchanges deviate from the contracted price to a certain defined degree, or keep so over longer periods, the interested party reserves the right to change the rate.

The adaptation of the world-market price is much more complicated in the sphere of commodities not traded in at the exchanges since the enterprises' price documentations provide no reassuring basis for this adaptation. They indicate prices from which the actual transactions deviate to a varying extent. The complexity of the problem lies, however, mostly in the fact that the assortments of semi-manufactures and especially finished goods (machinery and consumer articles) in the intra-CMEA trade are not fully identical in size or quality (technical parameters) with the varieties whose prices are quoted by the documentations as world-market prices.

Particular difficulties arise if the semi-manufactures or finished articles are not convertible on the world market, that is, if they are produced according to such technical parameters that they represent use values within the CMEA only. If identical or nearly identical products can be sold on markets both inside and outside the CMEA, the price that they fetch on the world market may be of some help in forming the contract price. Of course, this is not always a reliable basis either. It frequently occurs that in their non-CMEA relations the socialist countries sell at prices below the world-market level because this is the only way to enter into the capitalist market, and to earn the convertible foreign currency they need.

With the development of the productive forces, the division of labour within the CMEA shifts increasingly towards specialization and production co-operation in the engineering industry. Along with this change in the commodity structure, the weight of articles traded in at the exchanges in the total volume of turnover is steadily diminishing, and thus the problems of adaptation to world-market prices is getting more and more difficult.

The ninth meeting of the CMEA Council revoked, on the one hand, the stop prices with a view to a better adaptation to the world-market prices and set up, on the other, a study group to find out under what conditions a switch-over could be effected to the "socialist basis" in forming the contract prices, and under what principles of calculation the value relations of the socialist world market could best be expressed. Within the CMEA the Standing Committee of Economics, which was operative until quite recently, a "Socialist Price Basis" Study Group was set up whose activities consisted in the first place of elaborating the principles of price formation concerning the value relations of the CMEA market. In the late 1950s and the early 1960s the "Socialist Price Basis" Study Group was engaged mainly in the *quantification of the regional international CMEA value*. Having given due consideration to the different points of view, the Study Group decided to prepare models for four types of price.[132]

1. In the Study Group it was primarily the Soviet economists who held the view that the contract prices should be determined *on the basis of the national producer prices in the CMEA Countries*. They argued by stressing that the internal producer prices of the individual countries were objectively founded, that not only the labour inputs were considered but also the totality of other factors of pricing (capital-intensity of the products, their use value, the relationship between demand and supply), which would greatly help in forming the contract prices. They also stated that it was important *to correct* the domestic producer prices because the principles of pricing varied from country to country.

2. It was mainly Bulgarian economists in the Study Group who advocated the concept of the *value-type (c+v+m) socialist price basis*. They based their opinion on the assumption that the magnitude of the socially necessary inputs needed for producing products were most correctly reflected by prices which correspond to the magnitude of value. Therefore, they suggested the construction of a contract price model based on wage plus net income where the latter is related to in wage input proportions.

3. Hungarian and Polish economists expounded the concept of a "socialist price basis" of the *production-price type*, since in their opinion the capital-intensity of production must also find expression in the contract price. They, therefore, proposed a contract price model based on wage plans net income where the latter is related to capital input proportions.

[132] *Socialist World-Market Prices*, Selected Conference Papers. Eds: FÖLDI, T., and KISS, T., Akadémiai Kiadó, Budapest – Sythoff, the Hague, 1970.

4. Romanian economists preferred *the concept of self-financing prices* to the production price. They proposed a contract-price model, where net income is partly related to capital inputs harmonized with planned investment activity.

The Principle of Mutual Advantages

When assessing the debate on CMEA contract prices – and it is advisable to stress this again – it should be borne in mind that the great majority of economists participating in the debate – at least at the very beginning – did not consider it as a possibility that the price should play a role in forming the volume and commodity structure of foreign trade. Under such conditions, foreign-trade prices could have a decisive role to play in the distribution and redistribution of the national incomes among countries only. In the price debate, therefore, the question came to the fore how mutual advantages could be ensured in the division of labour and how it would be possible to distribute among the CMEA countries part of the national income realized in foreign trade *without the redistribution of their national incomes.* This is feasible if the price conditions correctly reflect the socially necessary inputs measured internationally. Many attached great significance to the price modelling organized in the "Socialist Price Basis" Study Group as a means to quantify the situation which had evolved by applying the Bucharest Price Principle. Although the "Socialist Price Basis" Study Group was dissolved before the price models were elaborated, the methodology it had worked out and the exchange of price information provided a possibility for performing approximate calculations. Such a calculation was published by Zhukov and Olsevich.[133]

The effect of transition to the "Socialist-price basis" upon the terms of trade between 1966 and 1970

Country	Current contract prices = 100
Bulgaria	+ 15.3 per cent
Hungary	– 3.7 per cent
German Democratic Republic	– 17.3 per cent
Poland	– 8.1 per cent
Romania	+ 12.9 per cent
Soviet Union	+ 13.3 per cent
Czechoslovakia	– 7.3 per cent

Although these figures should be accepted with certain reservations, they reflect the trends and also reveal the roots of conflicting opinions. The two scientific conferences: the one held in 1967[134] on the subject of "Socialist World-Market Price", the other which took place in 1970[135] on "Nature and Problems of the CMEA Market" were organized for CMEA economists in Budapest. Most economists were unanimous in that *the CMEA should be regarded as a regional market,* into which the prices of the major capitalist market cannot be transplanted mechanically. Doubts emerged, however, as to either the "Socialist price basis" or the "cleared" world-market price provided a satisfactory solution to the regional-market problem.

Some Soviet economists suggest solving this dilemma *by a combined application of the world-market price of specialized products and of those produced in co-operative ventures of the engineering industry on the one hand, and the intra-CMEA costs, on the other.*[136] The idea was most pregnantly expounded by *Kormnov.* In his opinion both the ratio of specialized products in CMEA-trade and in the turnover in general ensured by co-operation and specialization agreements is increasing year by year. And since the most dynamic element, and economic efficiency, too, is the highest under such a system of co-operation, in the solution of price problems attention should be concentrated on how to ensure, by taking account of mutual advantages, maximum material interest in concluding co-operation and specialization agreements.

Kormnov argues as follows: the CMEA market is regional, consequently, a value-proportional exchange is, in fact, an exchange corresponding to regional value. The principle of regional value presupposes an upward or downward deviation

←

133 ZHUKOV, V. N. and OLSEVICH, Y. Y.: *Teoreticheskiye i metodologicheskiye problemy sovershenstvovaniya tsenoobrazovaniya na rynke SEVA* (Further Development of CMEA Pricing. Theoretical and Methodological Problems). Moscow, 1969.

134 See: Note 132.

135 *The Market of Socialist Economic Integration*. Selected Conference Papers. Ed: KISS, T. in coll. with FÖLDI, T. and SCHWEITZER, I., Akadémiai Kiadó, Budapest, 1973.

136 BOGOMOLOV, O. and TEREKOV, V.: Lenin i razvitiye mirovogo sotsialisticheskogo sodruzhestva (Lenin and the Development of the Socialist World Community). *Voprosy Ekonomiki*, No. 2, 1970, Moscow. KORMNOV, YU, F.: *op. cit.* SAMRAY, A.: Tseny na spetsializirovannuyu produktsiyu v torgovlye mezhdu stranami-chlenami Seva (Prices of Specialized Products in Trade among the CMEA Countries). *Voprosy Ekonomiki*, No. 5, 1970. TARNOVSKY, O.: Vzaimovygodny obmen na mezhdunarodnom rynke Seva (Mutually Advantageous Trade on the International CMEA Market). *Voprosy Ekonomiki*, No. 1, 1972.

from the national value. A deviation from the national value, however, does not mean that a commodity exchange under such price formation should necessarily be unfavourable for one of the partners. In an exchange based on regional value, every socialist country may obtain advantages by selecting such products for exportation and importation in which the ratio of national inputs to foreign-trade prices is the most favourable for the country concerned.

Hence, *Kormnov* gives a novel interpretation of the organization of the division of labour within the CMEA. According to this proposition, the agreements are concluded not independently of prices, but it is just the foreign-trade price which serves as a signalling system to be taken into consideration in making national decisions and thus in concluding international agreements. In his view, the foreign-trade price is the main incentive to specialization and co-operation through which the principle of mutual advantages materializes for every partner in the concrete variant of co-operation.

The best incentive for the consumer is a low price with a given quality of the product. For the producer the best incentive is provided by a price ensuring an adequate profitability of production. The dividing line of their interests is at the boundary of domestic efficiency derived from sales (from the point of view of the producer) and of domestic efficiency derived from purchases (from the point of view of the consumer), since specialization must enhance efficiency. *Kormnov* approaches the price ensuring these conditions on the basis of the national inputs of that CMEA country in which of all partner countries, the conditions are the most favourable. If the lowest national input is higher than the world-market price, this indicates that, with respect to the product concerned, the conditions for competitive production are not yet available and therefore it is more favourable to buy it on the capitalist market. This provides more advantages than the rational organization of the division of labour within the CMEA.

With *Kormnov the capitalist world-market price is a tool of measuring the level of efficiency achieved.* In other words, in the fields of specialization and co-operation, the CMEA contract price is always the lowest input price within the CMEA, but it is never higher than the world-market price. The world-market price is the upper limit. Should the lowest input price exceed it, the task of the reconstruction to be performed in the framework of specialization and co-operation is to create such production conditions which ensure the most favourable price for the exporting country. This should be promoted, if necessary, by joint assistance.

Kormnov hopes to promote specialization and co-operation in a negotiation mechanism which is based on the declaration of supply and demand prices (price limits), when the mutually favourable solutions are sought in the course of concrete negotiations. At such negotiations the importer will make efforts to attain that the foreign-trade price converted into national currency should not be higher than the domestic production input of the same commodity.

Several economists have commented critically on *Kormnov's* and on related concepts.[137] They have pointed out that this method will hardly ensure mutual advantages. These concepts will place the importers of primary products in an unequal position against the exporters at a time when their extraction costs are lower than the world-market prices. Raw materials have to be paid for in the world-market prices. Machinery exports, on the other hand, must be competitive with an engineering cost level based on raw-material prices below world-market prices. Thus, if otherwise all conditions are requal, the country importing raw materials will lose the difference between the national and international values of the raw material in machinery exports. Under the above-mentioned conditions, another consequence of this price concept is that the raw-material exporting country can achieve a higher profit in machinery exports than the country processing imported materials. Obviously, whoever exports raw materials must, even in machinery exports, compete with an engineering cost level in which the processed raw materials are considered at world-market prices.

The question was also raised whether, from the standpoint of prices, *foreign trade can be divided into trade in specialized and non-specialized products.* In such a price system, the enterprise (country) could achieve higher prices by selling non-specialized machines than if it exports them under specialization agreements. In this way, the interest of the enterprise (country) would conflict with the interest of integration, with the conclusion of co-operation and specialization agreements.

There were also doubts as to whether the differences in national costs express in fact differences between national production conditions, that is, whether they can be interpreted as differences in economic efficiency. It was exactly the incomparableness of national price systems because of differences in the systems of accounting, finances, etc. which, in the late 1950s, led to the creation of the CMEA Cost Study Group entrusted with the elaboration of the methodology of internationally

[137] This debate took place mainly in the CMEA Study Group on Prices set up to implement the Complex Programme and to stay operative until 1974.

comparable prime costs. The experience gained in this work led to a more profound study of the category of the "national producer price" and to the construction of the "ideal" foreign-trade price in the course of the examination of the "socialist-price basis".

Kormnov's price concept and the others related to it were inspired in fact by the intention to change the terms of trade which had evolved as a result of applying the Bucharest Price Principle. *Lyutov's* arguments run like this: The CMEA contract price shows the greatest upward deviation from the world-market price in the products of the processing and particularly of the engineering industry, which cannot be explained by the low productivity and high costs in the branches. At the same time, the CMEA contract prices of agricultural products are close to the world-market prices in spite of the fact that the latter are specifically characterized by elements of irregularity owing to budgetary subsidies, export supports, etc.[138] But in *Lyutov's* view, the solution of the price problem is part of a comprehensive reform of the economic mechanism. Those, however, who advocate the principle of prime cost combined with the world-price limit as a specific method of pricing for specialized products regard its application simply as a matter of decisions; they separate, as it were, the foreign-trade price from the system of co-operation in which it operates. *Kormnov's* concept differs from theirs in that he raises some problems of the reform and gives correct answers to them. At the same time, he disregards the existing and increasingly strengthening interrelationship between price and currency.

At the scientific conferences even such variants of the regional price were discussed which consider the world-market price in a uniform price system.[139] According to them, the foreign-trade price system of the CMEA integration will bring

[138] Lyutov, A.: Economic Integration and the Socialist International Market. In: *The Market of Socialist Economic Integration*. Budapest, 1973.

[139] Csikós-Nagy, B.: Mutual Advantages in Economic Co-operation. In: *The Market of Socialist Economic Integration*. Budapest, 1973. Of the different price concepts the *three-centric price system* deserves special mention. According to it, three commodity groups were formed on the world market depending on the degree to which their trade is linked to the capitalist or to the socialist world. If the major portion of the goods exchanged originate from capitalist relations, their international value is determined by the necessary input measured on an international scale. If the goods are in trade only *between the CMEA countries*, their value is determined by the necessary input measured on a regional scale. In the third group, there is a mixed market in which the international value is determined by the combination of the first two. Tarnowsky, O. and Mitrofanova, N. M.: *Stoimost i tsena sotsialisticheskogo mirovogo rynka* (Socialist World Market Value and Price). Moscow, 1968.

the mutual advantages to fruition only if the prices meet the following three criteria:

- the assertion of the principle of the world-market price,
- preferential treatment of intra-CMEA trade,
- the ensurance of material interest in co-operation.

The intensification of the economic relations among the CMEA member countries presupposes the co-ordination of the economic development concepts and of the national development plans. The policy of planned international development interpreted in this way is the main determinant of structural transformation. What is essential is that the national structural policy takes into consideration not only the conditions of a closed national economy, but also reckons with the structural transformations envisaged for the domains selected in agreement with the partner countries. This enables each socialist country to plan the optimum of its own development at a higher level than it would if planning took place only on a national scale. In this interpretation, structural transformation also implies the organization of the international division of labour. In this work, in selecting the most favourable solution from among the alternative possibilities, the price category is an important means of orientation. A harmonized structural policy provides definite production conditions. These are, in many cases, different from what is expressed by world-market prices. There are, for instance, natural endowments which are impossible, or very difficult to control by technical development. A rational transformation of the production structure must take into consideration numerous national peculiarities, such as the level of development, economic equilibrium, employment policy, etc.

The system of foreign-trade prices cannot disregard the productive-technical conditions brought about by a co-ordinated structural policy, nor can it countermand the common decisions taken for the development of the macrostructure. In the foreign-trade price system, therefore, possibilities must be provided for acknowledging, in an adequate way, the countries' own conditions of production. This can be achieved by granting preferences. If the principle of preferences is accepted, this will mean that the contract price is separated, in a specific sphere and manner, from the world-market price. Thus the contract price will be related to the world-market price in the same way as any regional-market price.

Mutual advantages are not ensured if the national inputs of the CMEA member countries are automatically acknowledged in the foreign-trade prices. This is the concept of the "socialist price basis", a concept in which the price performs no function of critical supervision, and therefore the autonomous structural policy of the individual countries takes no account of other countries' interests. The only requirement that the "socialist price basis" is designed to set is that the goods produced by a country's advanced export capacities should be bought by another country at a price which covers the costs of the country producing them. This will not serve mutual interests.

The common system of preferences can never be taken to mean the support of the development of the uneconomical branches of any country, neither can it means preferences granted to industrial branches in which there is an overproduction within the integration. Preferences cannot be an end in themselves, they cannot diminish the endeavour to achieve technical development. Nor can the preferential system become a general principle, lest the advantages of adapting to world-market prices may get lost. Preferences, however, are justified if it is advisable or necessary to become self-sufficient in regard to the products of an industry, or if the guaranteed preferences provide the economic conditions of creating, developing and raising the technical level of an industry.

The deviating economic and developmental levels of individual CMEA countries and their different standards of productivity may also cause significant disparities in the levels of their respective inputs. We cannot reasonably expect that price preferences will iron out the differences in the standards of development. But for this purpose the socialist countries have various other possibilities at their disposal. If, over and above the preferences ensuring mutual advantages, it should be justified – for a variety of reasons – to extend further support to a country, this should be given in some other form, by using direct instruments of assistance.

Two things must be reconciled: the internationally highest technical standard and the progressive development of the CMEA production structure. The price system must be subordinated to these two criteria. Therefore, the determination of the scope and degree of the preferences and of their deviation from the world-market price on this basis constitutes one of the central problems that has to be solved. What is essential in developing the common system of preferences, is the requirement that the best instruments suitable for every individual country and yet co-ordinated in an appropriate way should be found to determine those fields and product groups in which the partial acknowledgement of the national production conditions and inputs can ensure the expansion of mutually advantageous foreign-trade relations.

But the building up of a system of socialist preferences ensuring deviation from world-market price ratios may become necessary not only in respect of imports but of exports as well. To maintain and increase international competitiveness the countries support their exports, or part of them, in one form or another (export subsidies, compensation for differences between domestic price and export earnings, tax exemptions, etc.). Export subsidies should be used to promote the expansion of intra-CMEA trade, the aim being that the boost to be given by the socialist countries to their trade with outsiders by price and fiscal policy measures should be less than the aid by which to their intra-CMEA trade is to be fostered.

Nature of the CMEA Market

The adaptation to world-market prices may take place either in a *direct or an indirect* way. The "cleared world-market price" is the direct, and the "regional price" the indirect method of adaptation. The latter is the more favourable alternative. However, a switch-over from direct to indirect adaptation sets certain requirements to the system of internal economic control of the CMEA countries. The debates on this problem are similar in character to the internal price debates of the CMEA countries. In several socialist countries the price debate began as a debate on pricing only to continue later as a debate on the economic mechanism as a whole. The so-called *pure price debate* started from the hypothesis that the problems existing in socialist economies are due mainly to the deficiencies of the price system. This leads to the conclusion that the economic mechanism of socialism must and can be improved by the perfection of the price system. This criticism of the price system is based on the postulate of economic clear-sightedness. The requirement is that prices should reflect the socially necessary input. In such a case – it is assumed – every economic decision ensures a rational solution, and in the system of central planning, with due consideration of economic efficiency, the state can exercise control over expanded reproduction.

Later, however, the opinion came into prominence that the price problem could be raised and solved satisfactorily only within the framework of the economic control system. Consequently, attention was centred on the role and function of the price. If a parallel can be drawn between national and international price debates, it is justified to say that in the debate on the "socialist price basis" some economists took up a position showing characteristics similar to those which marked the first stage of the national price debates, while the standpoint of other economists was closer to the opinions which were voiced in the second stage of the price debates.

If the price performed the function of a regulator in the international division of labour, the CMEA would not be in a position to determine different price principles, and particularly to take decisions on them, because in such a case there should exist a price system which could only be modified in a manner adapted to the requirements of the commodity and money relations of the CMEA. If price participates in regulating commodity trade, all price problems can only be solved on the basis of the existing prices and with due consideration of the effects which a price change exerts upon the commodity structure. To revoke the whole price system and to replace it by a new one – only to express inputs better –, is only possible if there is no market, and if the role of price is restricted to accounting alone.

If price regulates the commodity structure – even if its function is severely limited by plan co-ordination agreements –, it must adapt itself to the conditions under which a division of labour among the CMEA countries can exist and develop. *A price which operates as an accounting device can be constructed on any basis or taken over from foreign markets. But a price which has a market function, cannot be directly taken over and adapted. Such a price must be the product of the market in which it operates.* In such circumstances, the dissimilarity of the price systems on the socialist and capitalist world markets can be economically derived from the regionally different characteristics of the commodity and monetary relations in the same way as an economically exact explanation can be given of the differences in the commodity relations prevailing on the various world markets. In other words, *the road to solving the problems does not lead through price formation but through the solution of the market problem.*

The system of the economic co-operation of the CMEA countries used to be characterized as one to which market relations were alien. More precisely, it was regarded as a market organized on the basis of co-ordinated national economic plans which, by this very fact, was no longer a market, but as far as its content was concerned, a system of international exchange relations developed in a planned way.[140]

The term "CMEA market" became established as a result of scientific debates. It was as early as the mid-1950s that *Kohlmey* characterized the socialist world-market relations as commodity relations, and pointed out that the commodity relations within and among the various countries were not the same.[141]

[140] RUDOLF, J.: Gemeinsame Preisbasis und Verrechnungsbeziehungen der sozialistischen Länder. *Wirtschaftswissenschaft*, No. 1, 1963, Berlin.

[141] KOHLMEY, G.: Der demokratische Weltmarkt. *Die Wirtschaft*, 1955, Berlin.

Later, at the conferences held in Budapest in 1967 and 1970, the view gained general acceptance that the attributes of the CMEA were determined by the regional market.[142]

Therefore, the question under discussion in our days is no longer whether market relations can or cannot exist in the CMEA system of co-operation, but rather what *the nature of the CMEA market really is.* The negation of the market still set planned development against the law of value.[143] Many economists were of the opinion that planned co-operation raised the optimization of the use value, as against that of profit, to the rank of a decision-making criterion.[144] It was only later that it become clear that this was nothing but the theoretical generalization of the practice of a given historical period. This view was already clearly formulated by *Senin* who set forth that the threatened state of the European socialist countries had introduced such elements into their system of the division of labour which contradicted the theory of labour value.[145]

The study of the nature of the CMEA market directed the attention to the theorem of *comparative costs.* At first it was generally held that this theory could not have any practical applicability to the international division of labour organized on a socialist basis, because – among other things – if the law of value operated in the international division of labour, then the economically more advanced countries would acquire one-sided advantages over the developing countries.[146] Indeed, an *observer* of the debates on the CMEA mechanism ought to bear in mind the peculiar conditions prevailing in the CMEA. The countries participating in this system of co-operation represent different levels of economic development. There are industrially advanced CMEA countries (for instance the Soviet Union, the German Democratic Republic, Czechoslovakia) and developing ones (for instance Mongolia, Romania). It should also be remembered that of the industrially advanced countries the Soviet Union plays a prominent role in the raw-material supply of the CMEA market.

In discussing the law of comparative advantage it is justified to refer to the commodity structure of exports. The unequal

[142] See the Proceedings of the said Conferences.

[143] Blessing, H.: Zu einigen Fragen der Theorie des kapitalistischen Weltmarktes. *Wirtschaftswissenschaft*, No. 5, 1954, Berlin.

[144] Cherniyansky, V.: *op cit.*

[145] Senin, M. V.: Sotsialisticheskaya integratsiya (Socialist Integration). *Mezhdunarodniye Otnosheniya*, 1969, Moscow.

[146] Anghel, I.: Critica teoriei costurilor comparative in legátura cu probleme tárilor slab dezvoltate (Criticism of the Theory of Comperative Costs in Relation to the Problem of the Less Developed Countries). *Probleme Economic*, No. 2, 1961, Bucharest.

position of countries in international trade is primarily a problem of the commodity structure. It is the export-commodity pattern determined by a monocultural production structure which puts the developing countries at a disadvantage against the industrially advanced ones.[147] And, from the point of view of comparative advantages, it is indifferent whether a country's export structure is monocultural because such is its production structure, or because this is the way it joins in the international division of labour. However, scientific studies have brought home the fact that for the assertion of an internationally measured economic efficiency, it is the theorem of comparative costs that provides the only acceptable basis. Economists, therefore, have set about finding out the rational core of this theory which may also be relevant to the system of co-operation within the CMEA.[148]

In their analysis many have come to realize that planned development cannot invalidate the theory of comparative costs, it only sets limits to spontaneity. Scientific research has proved, further, that the international division of labour based on mutual advantages can be approximated only through the theory of comparative costs. This explains the endeavours characteristic of the 1960s: to elaborate methods which make the international comparability of value indices possible.

However, the debate is still going on whether the consideration of the law of value should be interpreted exclusively as *a criterion of plan co-ordination, or whether it should be asserted by the activization of the market mechanism.* According to current opinion, price must play a role in forming the foreign-trade structure within the CMEA and, as a consequence, the price category must be made suitable to perform the function of a signalling system in decision-making. But while some regard this as a specific problem of planned administrative pricing, others interpret it as an all-embracing problem of the mechanism of co-operation.[149]

147 Kohlmey, G.: Karl Marx, Theorie von den internationalen Werten. *Jahrbuch des Instituts für Wirtschaftswissenschaften*. Bd. 5, 1962, Berlin.

148 Gusek, M.: *Prano kosztów komparatywnych i RWPG* (The Law of Comparative Costs and the CMEA). Warsaw, 1967. Mervart, J.: *Vyznam a vyvoj cen v mezinárodnum obchode* (The Significance and Trend of Prices in International Trade). Prague, 1960. Vajda, I.: A komparatív költségek elmélete és a szocialista világgazdaság (The Theory of Comparative Costs and the Socialist World Economy). *Közgazdasági Szemle*, No. 5, 1963, Budapest.

149 Ausch, S.: *A KGST együttműködés helyzete, mechanizmusa, távlatai* (The State, Mechanism and Perspectives of Co-operation in the CMEA). Budapest, 1969. Nyers, R.: *A szocialista gazdasági integráció elvi és gyakorlati kérdései* (The Principles and Some Practical Problems of Socialist Economic Integration). Budapest, 1969.

It is *Nyers*[150] who has most clearly expounded the market problem. Let us follow his train of thought. The national markets of the CMEA countries, which have as yet mutual contacts only in a relatively limited field, should gradually be developed into a common, integrated market. The aim set should be for the countries participating in the integration to *open their internal market for one another.* However, thinking realistically, account must be taken of the fact that within a foreseeable time this aim can be attained only to a limited and partial extent, and that its complete realization is possible only in the long run. The creation of an integrated market would by no means give free play to spontaneous market forces, since the principal processes of economic development would be controlled by a co-ordinated economic policy of the individual countries and by a jointly evolved CMEA regulation system. The integrated market would enhance competition among the enterprises in productivity, technology and quality, widen the horizon of economic and technical experts and speed up the pace of technological progress.

This calls for a system of foreign trade which combines planned development with flexibility. It would require changes in the system of foreign-trade agreements; the present barriers impeding the free flow of trade in certain commodities should be removed, and, in addition to fixed prices, a greater role should gradually be given to free prices. Mutual foreign trade within the CMEA would continue to be regulated primarily by long-term interstate agreements, and indeed, it is desirable that their significance should increase compared to that of the annual agreements. However, *in keeping with the nature and economic importance of the various commodity groups, the system of interstate agreements would have to become more differentiated.*

(a) The core of the trade agreements would continue to be materials and goods of basic importance for the national economies. For them, both the long-term and the annual trade agreements would provide itemized and quantified quotas and stipulate the conditions of delivery.

(b) In another group of commodities trade would be effected on the basis of global interstate quotas. In such cases, the inter-governmental agreements would set, by way of estimate, only limits in terms of value leaving it to the enterprises to fill them in with content.

(c) In a third group of commodities – mainly in the field of machinery and consumer goods – efforts should be made

[150] NYERS, R.: *op. cit.*

gradually to change over to liberalized trade within the economic community. Initially, this can take place in a rather narrow scope only, including, say, 10 to 15 per cent of the consumer goods and a smaller proportion of machinery, but later this trade channel could be expanded step by step. Thus, in this category, the turnover would be determined wholly by the demand of the national consumer market and the supplying capacity of the exporting country, without any restriction by quotas.

The suggested system makes it imperative that in the future productive units should obtain a greater autonomy in foreign trade and in shaping interstate agreements; international agreements between manufacturing and trading enterprises should be developed and the enterprises encouraged to conclude long-term contracts. All this requires, of course, more purposeful market activities on the part of the enterprises, a more thorough knowledge of the multilateral market of the CMEA countries, and a smoothly operating system of reciprocal market information.

The opening up of markets, interpreted in a definite manner, and the liberalization of foreign trade, will pave the way for a full assertion of the money function and will thus create the conditions for a more effective monetary regulation to be realized in the comprehensive system of a planned division of labour. This, however, must be ensured by suitable monetary measures.

Price and Currency

The gold content of a soft currency is fictious simply because it does not participate in the alimentation of international operations. Nevertheless, the international value of a soft currency can be determined. The CMEA countries quantify the relative value of their national currencies to the transferable rouble and to hard currencies in a way best suited to their purposes. For this they apply an internationally accepted method determined while they elaborated the methodology of internationally comparable prime costs. In these costs the input of imported materials is quantified by using the foreign-exchange "coefficient". It is by using this coefficient that the price of imported materials is converted into domestic currency. The relative values of national currencies to transferable rouble and to hard currencies are determined by calculating the amount in domestic currency needed to buy one transferable rouble in CMEA exports and one US dollar in the trade outside of the CMEA.

These calculations revealed that the transferable rouble was over-valued in relation to the hard currencies. According to calculations made in Hungary in 1967, 40 forints were needed to earn one transferable rouble, and 60 forints of domestic input were required to earn one US dollar. At gold parity, the equivalent of one transferable rouble was 66 forints and not 40. Calculations made in the other CMEA countries yielded more or less similar results.

What explains, then, this *disparity* when in adapting the world-market prices the CMEA countries convert the free foreign-exchange prices into transferable rouble at gold parity? A more detailed analysis has revealed that the devaluation of the CMEA national currencies in relation to free foreign exchanges would also take place if the complicated task of a direct adaptation of the world-market price could be satisfactorily solved. In this several factors are involved. The disparity is caused, first of all, by the *distorted export structure.* Owing to the peculiarities of the world-market price relations, a country contributing predominantly primary products to the international division of labour is in a less favourable position in utilizing of the advantages offered by this division of labour. As a consequence, if the exports of a country to two main markets are of fundamentally different commodity structures, the cost ratios of foreign exchange earnings must, by necessity, deviate from the gold parity.

When assessing this question it cannot be left out of account that the exports to the capitalist world market of most CMEA countries are not regulated primarily by considerations of economic efficiency but by the possibility to earn *the quantity of free foreign exchange needed to buy products and services for their economic development,* i. e. by export "compulsion" asserting itself simultaneously with the existing export constraints. The latter find their expression in the fact that the readiness of the world market to buy CMEA goods is confined to certain products and, further, that machinery and consumer goods can only be sold at a substantial discount. The unfolding of East-West trade, a few CMEA countries joining the GATT, etc. in the 1970s have increasingly contributed to easing what is broadly called "discrimination". According to calculations made for 1972, the disparity has diminished, owing, among other things, to the inflationary tendencies on the capitalist world market, or because the CMEA contract prices for the period 1971–1975 reflect the capitalist world-market price for the period 1968–1970.

The application of the Bucharest Price Principle causes disparity, too. The CMEA market operates as a duty-free zone.

The transacting of commodity trade is relatively less cost-intensive, and intermediate trade is practically excluded from most of the deals. The principle of "half freight" in certain commodity transactions leads to a price rise. Added to this all is the fact that in determining the CMEA contract prices of products that are not traded in at the commodity exchanges, the "fictitious" prices of the world market are taken into account, i.e. such quotation prices of the capitalist firms that are not applied to relations among capitalist countries.

If the collective socialist currency (the transferable rouble) is non-convertible, then the difference between its declared gold content and real value is of no consequence. In the case of a restricted foreign exchange policy it is not the price level but the relative prices, i. e. the terms of trade that are determinant in such relations in which this currency is used as an accounting unit. This might also be clear from the debates on the CMEA contract prices, and even more from the views voiced by *Kormnov* and others.

According to these suggestions the only aim of determining the currency value would be to find out the world-market price as an upper limit for forming the CMEA market prices. *But whilst the Bucharest Price Principle sets out from the hypothesis of the equality of the currency value and the price level, these views institutionalize their separation.* While the application of the Bucharest Price Principle caused the devaluation of the transferable rouble, the world-market price limit, i.e. a combined application of the lowest CMEA prime cost, causes the revaluation of the transferable rouble in relation to its own exchange rate. According to the followers of this view, this should find expression exactly in the fact that, owing to production specialization and co-operation, economic efficiency is higher within the CMEA than outside it, and the intensity of revaluation measures the improvement of efficiency, which is more dynamic than the international average. Although not explicitely formulated, these facts naturally follow from the logic of the concept.

But why solve a problem, which is in fact the task of the regulation of the exchange rate, by the revaluation of the socialist collective currency in relation to its own exchange rate (i. e. by a pricing giving rise to revaluation)? There is one possible explanation for this: world-market price relations unjustifiably prefer machinery trade. The profit realized in the world-market prices of machinery is disproportionately high compared to other commodity groups. To solve this problem, *Kormnov* and others use a *double price level.* Let the price level of raw materials, foodstuffs and consumer articles be regulated by the world market, and that of the engineering products by the lowest CMEA input. This takes us back to the problem of relative prices as the key question of the debates on CMEA contract prices.

On the non-CMEA markets, the problem of relative prices emerges in conjunction with the world-market price of agricultural products. The Common Market uses financial bridges to make the production costs, which are high in relation to world-market prices, regulate prices in the commodity trade within the Common Market. Within the CMEA, it is mostly Bulgarian and Hungarian economists who attach similar significance to the introduction of a common agrarian policy and of foreign-trade prices stimulating agricultural production. And yet it is not this principle but the capital-intensity of the exploitation of raw materials and the high prices of the engineering industry that have become the central issue of the price debates.

Thus, the theoretical debates on the CMEA co-operation mechanism are still characterized by their having got stuck in the stage of price debate. Monetary discussions in their proper sense have failed so far to materialize. The situation, however, would be basically different if we approached the relationship of currency and price on the basis of the requirements of a developed monetary system, that is, if we did not preclude the possibility of making the collective socialist currency convertible. Given this case, *the exchange rate already assumes the role of a regulator of the price level* because an organic relationship with the world monetary system – under the restrictions of regional markets and equilibrium exchange rates – reduces the foreign-trade price levels to a common denominator.

The Complex Programme of Socialist Economic Integration justifies the examination of such an alternative. Under this programme, a more active role should be assigned to the monetary relations in solving the problems of further developing and strengthening planned economic co-operation. To this end, the CMEA countries have agreed to study the ways and means to strengthen the role of the collective currency (the transferable rouble) and to take the necessary economic and organizational measures. This would enable the collective currency to perform all functions of money, which, to use *Marx's* formulation, are: measure of value, medium of exchange, medium of payment and medium of accumulation. *Marx* endowed with these properties only the money which in fact replaces gold. At the same time, the Complex Programme lays down that a collective currency so interpreted can develop only gradually. As a matter of fact, this is a process whose integral parts are the measures taken both in the monetary sphere and in the spheres of production and foreign trade.

From the point of view of a developed monetary system, it is primarily the *realistic rate of exchange* that constitutes a basic problem. This is why the Complex Programme declares that the CMEA countries establish the economically founded and mutually agreed exchange rates of their national currencies, and their conversion rates (coefficients) to the collective currency (transferable rouble) as well as to one another.

The CMEA countries will continue for a considerable time to organize the division of labour by using a double exchange rate. The introduction of a uniform rate is a complicated matter because it also involves problems of the price structure. To solve them, the thing likely to be done first would be the approximation of the system of national taxes (withdrawal of incomes). The complexity of this problem accounts for the dissolution of the CMEA Price Study Group in 1973. From 1974 on the CMEA Foreign Trade Standing Committee has been responsible for improving the system of CMEA contract prices, while the study of reconciling the national price systems will be delegated to the authority of the Conference of the Presidents of the Price Offices.

Thus, for the time being and for the subsequent years, attention will be focussed on the problems of settling accounts of the "trade" operations. As a result of the activity of the CMEA Socialist Price Basis Study Group, these problems were already discussed in the 1960s. In these debates, a prominent role was played by the endeavour of individual countries to set the value of their own national currencies as favourable as possible in relation to that of the transferable rouble and thus of the currencies of the rest of the member countries. The same can be observed in the debates in the Monetary and Financial Standing Committee of the CMEA. The question that inevitably arises is this: what is the explanation for the fact that while, under the capitalist monetary system, a country's interest is the devaluation of its national currency, it is, under the CMEA monetary system, the revaluation of its own currency. The reason for this must obviously be sought in the dissimilarities of the mechanism of international co-operation. The problem of the exchange rate emerges differently if the international division of labour is based on currency co-operation, and if it is based on a commodity exchange regulated by physical instruments.

In monetary co-operation, the smooth operation of the international division of labour can only be based on the *system of equilibrium exchange rates.* In such a case, the countries are interested in a policy of exchange rates which is able to ensure the equilibrium of the international balance of payments. And the devaluation of the national currency can be regarded as a measure of currency policy aimed at promoting exports and restricting imports. If, however, the international division of labour is organized in physical terms, it is only the accounting rates that are needed. As a result, the countries will be interested in an exchange rate policy which enables them to minimize their national input. And the revaluation of the national currency can be interpreted as the revaluation of the performance made by the country concerned as against that of other countries. The endeavour aimed at the revaluation of national currencies has a realistic background in the spheres of "non-trade" and "other" operations. At the same time, in the debates on the exchange rates, the CMEA countries also reckon with the fact that during the implementation of the Complex Programme a relationship can be established between national producer prices and CMEA contract prices.

The equilibrium exchange rate is a concomitant of currency convertibility and of foreign trade, while the accounting rate can only exist in a control system based on physical terms supported by a restrictive foreign exchange policy. Thus, the endeavour to revaluate the national currencies also expresses the prevailing opinion according to which the socialist collective currency, respectively the national currencies of the CMEA countries, will not become convertible into free foreign exchange (and ultimately into gold) within a foreseeable time. Moreover, many economists hold the view that this cannot be regarded as an essential problem of improving the system of co-operation. According to this view, the transferable rouble is already fulfilling in practice the basic functions of an international socialist currency and the barriers impeding its working objectively spring from its planned character.[151] Thus, the monetary debate also extends to the interpretation of the principles formulated in the Complex Programme.

Yet, the contradictions of a bilaterally organized trade and a multilaterally organized accounting system may justify the view that the present system of co-operation within the CMEA should be regarded as a *transitory state* in which new elements assert themselves by gradually ousting the old ones. It appears practicable to outline, first of all, such a *monetary* model as may

[151] VINCZE, I.: A pénz szerepe a KGST országok egymásközti gazdasági kapcsolatában (The Role of Money in the Economic Interrelations of the CMEA Countries). *Pénzügyi Szemle*, No. 5, 1973, Budapest.

emerge in the perspective, judged by the tendency of the current CMEA debates. Its principal elements may be the following:

1. Transition from the three to the two spheres of the *international settling of accounts*, the introduction of an accounting system based on the separation of "trade" and "non-trade" operations, the further development of multilateral settlements on this basis.

2. The increasing *role of national producer prices* in concluding agreements on trade, production co-operation and specialization based on plan co-ordination, in forming CMEA contract prices, until eventually the currency coefficients measured in national producer prices (foreign-trade price multipliers) perform the function of an exchange rate.

3. *National price reforms,* which can create the conditions for abolishing the two spheres of the international settling of accounts, and for introducing a uniform exchange rate of the national currencies, this should also further develop multilateral settlements on this basis.

4. The convertibility of the transferable rouble.

Already in the debate preceding the 1963 agreement, *the question had been raised whether it was possible to switch over from bilateral to multilateral accounting without simultaneously ensuring the convertibility of the clearing rouble to free foreign exchange.* The debate was decided simply by the fact that nobody held external convertibility to be realistically feasible, while the multilateralization of settlements seemed quite natural, merely because within the CMEA the same currency was used for settling accounts in bilateral relations. Of course, already then multilateralism was meant to imply more than just a reform of the accounting technique. All the more so as the substitution of the principle of global equilibrium for the principle of bilateral equilibrium, and the gradual transition to multilateral trade as an endeavour was already formulated as early as in the second half of the 1950s, and it was generally assumed that the 1963 agreement would directly put this into effect. As a result, development would have taken a turn in which the requirement to give more weight to the function of the socialist collective currency as a medium of payment would have been more pronounced.

The socialist collective currency cannot become a real medium of payment unless it is accepted as such on a worldwide scale. Multilateralism within the CMEA cannot unfold either until it is related to the other monetary systems of the world economy. This would enable the CMEA to become an organized regional market, in which the member countries prefer one another to the outside world, and in which, at the same time, they can organize their economic relations with due regard to economic efficiency.

Currency convertibility is a *relative* concept. The gold currency has ceased to exist exactly as a result of the restrictive measures taken by the foreign exchange policy of countries. Each country, whose currency participates in transacting international operations and is thus engaged in a world-wide circulation, derives from the requirement of maintaining the equilibrium of the international balance of payments those restrictions on the capital and money market and on commodity trade which ensure the convertibility of its national currency. Nevertheless, it is justified to differentiate between restrictive and trading currencies, or, in other words, between soft and hard currencies.

A trading currency aliments international operations, a characteristic which is due to the fact that the central bank issuing it can guarantee its officially declared value (gold content). To this end, it transacts open-market operations. A soft currency, on the other hand, functions within a country's boundaries. Its exportation is prohibited. This currency, too, circulates in international trade, but its circulation is declared illegal by the issuing bank, which does not guarantee its value. The bank of issue is also indifferent to discrepancies between the currency's officially declared value and its "black-market" rate.

The characterization given of trading and soft currencies applies to *national* currencies only; *the transferable rouble occupies an exceptional position.* It has no black-market rate, since it operates exclusively as banking money. The IBEC does not perform issuing activities, the transferable rouble does not circulate in the form of banknotes, traveller's cheques, etc. It is an instrument of the multilateral settling of accounts within the CMEA, and is as such convertible within the CMEA at the level of the banks of issue. It has no external convertibility and in this sense it is a soft currency. Yet, in examining the monetary system of the CMEA, it is justified also to consider the position of the national currencies of the CMEA countries, primarily because, according to a fairly typical opinion, the national currencies of the CMEA countries may, step by step, develop into trading currencies even if the external convertibility of the transferable rouble cannot be achieved.[152]

In the case of a foreign-trade sensitive economy, the country can only have a trading currency *if it fits into world economy on*

[152] This opinion was expressed in interviews, documents of financial research institutes, etc. In Hungary Pécsi, K. deals with problems of currency convertibility in greater detail.

a monetary basis. The larger proportion of the exports of most European socialist countries are sold on the CMEA market where the system of co-operation is at present not of a monetary character. The economic structure (export potential) of these countries is adapted first and foremost to the requirements of the CMEA market, and it is on this market that they can pursue a foreign-trade policy which enables them to build up money reserves. In their relations outside the CMEA they find it difficult to keep their international balance of payments in equilibrium even with import restrictions and currency restrictions imposed on their own nationals.

This is the point at which a country insensitive to foreign trade (for instance the Soviet Union) and one with a high foreign-trade sensitivity (for instance Hungary) may come to different conclusions. It would be an awkward situation if the national currencies of the CMEA countries operated as trading currencies, while the transferable rouble were convertible within the CMEA only. This, among other things, would mean that the function of these currencies as means of payment would come into force in a more perfect form than that of the collective currency, and their value, too, would be higher outside the CMEA than inside it. They could not function as trading currencies in relation to one another unless the assets and liabilities arising in national currencies from the "non-trade" and "other" operations were kept apart from multilateral settlements made in transferable roubles. This, however, would undermine the role of the socialist collective currency. However, these national currencies circulate not only on bank accounts, but also in the form of actual banknotes. They can be converted into any currencies in proportion to their value (gold content) officially declared on the international monetary market. Extremely rigorous restrictive measures, which would be very difficult to control at that, should be taken if non-residents of the CMEA were to be prevented from taking advantage of this possibility.

It is, therefore, easy to understand that some economists, particularly in foreign-trade-sensitive CMEA countries, hold the monetization of the mechanism of co-operation, that is, the external convertibility of the transferable rouble desirable. In such a case their own national currencies, too, would more easily become trading currencies. Of course, the national and international prerequisites of the convertibility should be correctly interpreted. The advanced monetary system of the international division of labour provides merely the conditions for turning a country's currency into a trading one. In the last analysis, however, the position of a country's currency is determined by its national economic resources and its economic policy.

A problem is caused, from the point of view of the *external convertibility of the transferable rouble*, by the fact that the readiness to buy some products within the CMEA would surely diminish if the buyer country had to settle its debts within the CMEA in gold. This might become the greatest dilemma of a switch-over of economic co-operation based on a highly developed monetary system. This is the reason why the realization of external convertibility is an intricate problem. A better co-ordinated development on a multilateral basis, the raising of the technical level of production and, as a result, the expansion of the export potential seems to be the only realistic way in which the currency problem can eventually be solved. For several socialist countries, the convertibility of the transferable rouble can logically lead to introducing trading currencies.

The *interpretation of "gradual" introduction* gave rise to controversies between Polish and Hungarian economists.[153] They agreed on the point that co-operation within the CMEA should be perfected toward a highly developed monetary system and also that this presupposes the convertibility of the currency used as a CMEA accounting unit, which can be achieved step by step. Thus, their basic view was identical in this respect, too. But as to the method proposed for its implementation, their opinions differed. The *concept elaborated by the Polish economists can be* summarized as follows:

1. Liberalized trade should be kept apart from multilateral accounting.
2. In the framework of multilateral clearing, accounting takes place in transferable rouble and parts of the debt must be settled in free foreign exchange (finally in gold).
3. For the purposes of liberalized trade, a new international socialist currency should be introduced. As a security for debts payable in this currency commodity reserves should be provided whose nomenclature has previously been agreed upon by the CMEA countries. Since there can only be such goods on the list which are convertible on the world market at any time, the socialist international currency operating in the sphere of liberalized trade is, by necessity, a convertible currency.

[153] Some of the papers submitted to the Symposium organized by the Polish Economic Association between 9th and 11th January, 1969: PAJESTKA, P.: Currency Rates and Economic Co-operation; RACHKOWSZKI, S.: Principles of the Operation of the National Socialist Currency; CSIKÓS-NAGY, B.: Problems in the Further Development of Co-operation among the CMEA Countries.

4. Liberalized trade develops at first in a rather narrow field, usually in the sphere of consumer goods. Later, this sphere will expand until finally it ousts the transferable rouble entirely.

Hungarian economists participating in the debate took a stand for the convertibility of the transferable rouble to be introduced gradually, saying that the relative values of the national currencies to the transferable rouble would have to be regulated differently in the "trade" and the "non-trade" spheres. And graduality should be manifested in the fact that an annually increasing proportion of the credit and debit balances held in transferable roubles would have to be settled in free foreign exchange. By way of summing up, the essential difference between the Polish and Hungarian views on the currency mechanism is this:

Temporarily, both views call for a double currency valuation. But unlike the Hungarian view, which qualifies double valuation according to foreign-trade and non-foreign-trade relations, the Polish proposal differentiates according to liberalized and non-liberalized turnover within international trade as a whole. Foreign-trade and non-foreign-trade relations can be separated unequivocally. At first sight, it would seem that separation is also unambiguous in international trade, since the products in the liberalized sphere are excluded from multilateral settlement. Nonetheless, this relationship does come about through the commodities serving as security for the new international socialist currency, since it is exactly these commodities which are the most significant factors of multilateral trade.

Thus, the two currency spheres are, in an indirect way, in the closest relationship with one another. This is brought about, in addition, in a most peculiar manner, setting, as it does, the most easily convertible products (e.g. raw materials) against those which are the least convertible (consumer articles) on the world market. In this way, the two currencies exert different influence on economic processes which are in fact identical, that is, they put into force the so-called Gresham law. True, this law would work in a singular manner: it would either prevent liberalized trade from unfolding, or would lead to more negative effects in the main sphere of trade (in multilateral settlements) than the positive effects that the initial results of liberalized trade would represent. This was the reason why Hungarian economists held the view that multilateral trade and a convertible currency should be developed gradually in a uniform monetary system.

The external convertibility of the transferable rouble also raises problems with regard to *international monetary co-operation*. The monetary co-operation of the industrially advanced capitalist countries came about on the basis of the Bretton

Woods agreement signed in 1944. As a result of this agreement, the US dollar was linked to gold and became a key currency. Since then, the role of the US dollar in the monetary system of the capitalist world has diminished. It was laid down as a general principle that no national currency should be regarded as a standard in relation to any other currency, and development should proceed in the direction of a reserve currency which is subject to collective responsibility. In 1968, a document establishing the so-called SDR (Special Drawing Rights) was adopted as a first practical step towards creating a neutral international currency. This gave rise to a situation in which there are better possibilities of establishing a closer relationship between the different international monetary systems.

3. The Relationship between Foreign Trade and Domestic Prices

Comparative Analysis of the CMEA National Price Systems

The monetization of the CMEA co-operation system requires, among other things, that the national price system of the CMEA countries should be brought closer to each other. This issue came into the fore in the 1970s. The *national features* of price (prime cost) are interrelated with

1. the productivity of labour,
2. the standard of living of the population and
3. the self-accounting mechanism of the enterprises.

If two countries with the same natural endowments and technical conditions produce a product with the same efficiency of labour, this means that they turn out the same quantity of products per unit of time. Although the *productivity of labour* in relation to the product in question is identical in these two countries, their prime costs are different since prime cost expresses money cost and not labour time. Accordingly, it is in this category that the processes of the production, distribution and redistribution of the national income or those peculiarities which are involved in the national money relations also find expression.

As far as the other circumstance connected with the national peculiarities of price (cost) i.e. the *living standard* is concerned, its factors are these: private consumption of the members of society, and public consumption, which can be distributed among the various social strata. The standard of living consists of two factors, because the distribution of goods produced for consumption takes place in different forms. Working people purchase from their incomes most of the products and services they need. However, commodity exchange is the main but not the only form of distribution. Consumption which is not, or not wholly, transmitted by trade, is ensured, partly or entirely, by incomes accruing to society as a whole. This means that the members of society are paid wages on the one hand, and receive social benefits, on the other.

Price (cost) relations are connected not primarily with the living standard in general, but rather with definite distribution forms of consumption, i.e. with wage incomes that appear as the wage cost component of the prime cost. If two countries with the same natural endowments and technical conditions produce their goods with the same efficiency of labour, the cost will be higher in the one in which

(a) the living standard of the population is higher and,

(b) given the same living standard, the average wage income of the population is higher.

A higher living standard (assuming a higher wage-income level) will result in higher costs because the price (cost) categories reflect wage incomes. In the same way, if in two countries the same labour productivity is achieved in the entire sphere of production and the wage levels are also identical, but the relative wages are different in various productive branches, the national characteristics of the wages policy will also manifest themselves in the price (cost) relations. If the standards of living of the working population are identical in two countries, but in one of them a larger proportion of the products consumed by the population is paid for out of wages (and thus the role of social benefits is less significant), this deviation will have the same effect on price (cost) relations as the difference between living standards.

Finally, the *characteristics of prices and costs are closely interrelated with the enterprises' self-accounting.* With the help of the documents of the CMEA Cost Study Group, the Price Study Group analysed the similarities and dissimilarities of the national price systems of the CMEA countries.[154] They have found that the social production relations and the economic laws working under such conditions place the national price systems of the CMEA member countries on a common basis. This finds its expression in the planned character of pricing and the central control of its processes, in price stability and in the endeavour to approximate prices to the socially necessary input of labour. Every socialist country sets out from the requirement that the price system should ensure undisturbed self-accounting of the enterprises operating in the spheres of production and distribution: that the producer prices should realize not only current costs but should also express, to a certain extent, the capital intensity of production.

At the same time, owing to dissimilarities in natural endowments, economic and historical conditions determining the developmental levels, in the systems of economic management and organization, in the methods of planning and financing, the *individual countries are using different methods when applying the common principles of pricing.* In this way, despite the com-

[154] KOBZAR, E. and STROMOTSOV, A.: Sblizhenie metodov vnutrennego tsenoobrazovaniya (Approaching the Methods of Domestic Pricing). *Economicheskaya Gazeta*, 3, I, 1974, Moscow.

mon principles, the methods applied by the CMEA member countries in forming their domestic prices show fundamental differences. These may be summed up as follows:

1. *Differences in the price mechanism.* In some CMEA countries price plays an active role in forming inter-sectoral proportions, while in other countries these proportions are based on central directives. In the former case price (profitability) has a role to play in structure-forming processes, while in the latter it has not. Although this is not a difference directly influencing the price system, its effect on it is significant. This holds true particularly for those CMEA countries where the active role of the price is more or less linked up with the enterprises' freedom of decision-making with regard to their product mix, material supply and pricing. Under such circumstances, the self-accounting price assumes the form of a self-financing price, and the role of demand and supply in price formation is more decisive.

With regard to those CMEA countries where the administrative fixing of prices is the general method of planned price formation, the following differences can be found in the price mechanism: (a) The alteration of fixed prices is effected, as a general rule, by periodic price rearrangements. In setting prices some CMEA countries take the costs of the accounting period as a basis, while others leave certain costs out of the actual costs (they adjust e.g. the overhead costs if the capacities in the period surveyed were insufficiently utilized). Other CMEA countries again take planned costs as a basis instead of those of the accounting period. This means that in the price revision they take into account of the (estimated) changes in the conditions of production over the years ahead. (b) In different CMEA countries price rearrangements do not take place at the same time. As a result, the "degree of obsolescence" of their prevailing prices differs at any given time. The longer the time which has elapsed since the last price revision, the less faithfully current prices reflect the real conditions of production. (c) Some CMEA countries adhere to the practice of carrying out comprehensive producer price rearrangements every six to ten years, while others prefer "continuous" revisions to keep their producer prices up to date.

All these differences are ultimately expressed in considerable deviations as regards the profit differentiation from country to country. These deviations, however, cannot be considered as differences in economic efficiency, but as consequences in different practice of planned price formation.

2. *Differences in the methods of forming the domestic prices of export and import products.* In some CMEA countries the

domestic prices of export and import goods are adapted to the national conditions of production. Planned pricing is ensured by the methods of equalization and proportionality. In such a system, the enterprise is paid the same price for the product it manufactures regardless of the fact whether it is sold at home or abroad. The difference between foreign-trade and domestic prices is settled by the budget with the foreign trading enterprise. In the same way, the enterprise pays the same price for the goods it buys regardless of the circumstance whether they are produced at home or are imported. If they are imported, the difference between the foreign-trade and domestic prices is settled by the budget with the foreign trading enterprise. If the product imported is not produced at home, the domestic price is set in proportion to the price of a home product which is closest to the imported article in question.

Other CMEA countries are trying to establish a relationship between the receipts of the enterprise producing export goods and the price attainable in foreign trade, or to integrate the import product in question into the production costs in proportion to the import cost. But this system works differently in the different CMEA countries. The differences are attributable to two factors: the one is that some CMEA countries consistently adhere to the principle of uniform prices, and thus they consider foreign-trade prices merely as a criterion of price arrangements. Others regard it possible to apply differentiated prices. The other factor is that it seems to be more practicable to establish and maintain an organic relationship between foreign-trade and domestic prices in the CMEA countries where the spheres of authority are decentralized, that is, where the state does not guarantee the domestic input necessary for the manufacture of export articles and enables the enterprises' to form their sales prices with due regard to the actual purchase price of the imported goods.

3. *Structural differences in the price (prime cost).* (a) In the category of the *industrial producer* price there are differences as regards the degree and the way of evaluation of the individual cost factors. The system of self-accounting lends itself to different interpretations. Formally, the requirement the producer price has to meet is that in the case of rational management it should cover prime cost, when the profit realized in the price is a yardstick of effectiveness measured on the micro-economic level. In this respect, it is only a difference in judgement that one country forms its preference-ranking of efficiency according to the recovery period of capital, and another to the rate of profit related to production cost. As far as its content is concerned, self-accounting is determined by what is considered to

be the production costs. In a socialist economy this depends on the system of financing. From this aspect, the national price system of the CMEA countries show the following differences:

– Differences in *material costs* arising from the fact that the materials and semi-finished goods used (bought) are often passed on not in conformity to their inputs (to the money paid for them in the case of imports); the state budget imposes taxes on certain materials and semi-finished goods and increases thereby their cost price, while in other cases it makes them cheaper by subsidizing them. Deviations from the cost of the prices of goods subject to further processing can be observed in all CMEA countries, but the sphere of application, the degree and direction of these deviations vary from country to country.

– The enterprises of all CMEA countries are obliged *to pay taxes on wages at a rate ranging from 7 to 36 per cent in different countries.* The taxes levied upon wages in most CMEA member countries cover by and large the budgetary expenditures for social insurance, but there are also CMEA countries where the social charges on wages (to be paid by the enterprises) are designed to provide a fund for social benefits in their wider sense. This difference in policy alone causes a 2.5 per cent difference in the industrial production cost-level differentiated according to the labour-intensity of the product.

– CMEA countries regulate in a different way the costs that can be written off as an allowance for the *depreciation of fixed capital.* Examinations have shown that differences in the less capital-intensive productive branches and in depreciation norms exert no appreciable influence on costs; but in some industries, where the depreciation allowance amounts to 12 to 20, sometimes even to 30 per cent of the production cost, there are very considerable differences in the production cost, owing to different rates of depreciation. Further differences arise from the different methods applied in evaluating and re-valuating fixed assets.

– In certain CMEA countries, most of the costs incurred in *geological research* and prospecting, the costs of scientific-research-designing and construction activities connected with technical development are largely financed by the budget, while in others these costs are fully or partly realized in the prime cost.

– In the national price systems, the *transport costs* are also expressed in different ways. As a general rule, uniform administrative prices are fixed with due regard to an average amount of transport cost, and thus they become regionally uniform prices. But in the case of transport-cost-sensitive products (for instance building materials) the price refers to the place of destination in one country and the uniform price applies to the place of production in another; in this case the price is differentiated according to the place of utilization. There are again countries, in which part of these costs are covered from central sources.

– In the prime costs of some CMEA countries there are also items which in other countries are considered either as constituent elements of the profit or are not applied at all. Such are: charge on capital engaged in production, rent for land use, fees for the use of water of artifical reservoirs and for the exploitation of ground water, property insurance fees, road tolls, taxes on enterprise vehicles, interest on bank credits used as circulating capital, socio-cultural costs, etc.

(b) As regards the category *of the agricultural procurement price* there are differences both in purchase prices and in forming the industrial delivery prices of farm produce intended for further processing. The incomes of agricultural co-operatives are jointly determined by the procurement price, budgetary subsidies of a non-price character, and agricultural taxes. Some CMEA countries combine the relatively low procurement prices with a broadly interpreted budgetary non-price subsidy, while others intend to use these subsidies to support exactly defined development objectives and grant budget subsidies only to co-operatives which, owing to unfavourable natural factors, are in adverse circumstances. The latter use the procurement price for solving such financing problems for which special budgetary funds are available in the former countries.

Further deviations arise from the fact that in most CMEA countries part of the foodstuffs are sold at a deficit consumer price. The CMEA countries solve the budgetary subsidizing of agricultural consumer prices which are lower than their procurement prices in a variety of ways. In some countries the price at which foodstuff is sold to industry is determined on the basis of the procurement price supplemented by trading costs with the budget reimbursing the food industry for the difference. In other countries the budget grants subsidies to the procurement and distribution network.

(c) With respect to the *consumer-price* the differences are substantial in three fields;

– In some CMEA countries the budget centralizes the financial fund needed to satisfy social demand primarily through consumer prices, while in others this is realized rather through taxes levied on producer prices. In accordance with this practice, the difference between the level of producer and consumer prices varies in the different CMEA countries.

– Some CMEA countries have a highly differentiated *turnover-tax system* based on the so-called selective tax system. This is motivated by the endeavour to make cost-proportionality of producer prices in the field of related articles and proportionality based on use value in the case of consumer prices the main criterion of pricing. In such case it is considered that the consumers' and producers' points of view cannot be reduced to a common denominator, and this must be also expressed in keeping the producer- and consumer-price systems apart. In other CMEA countries the problem of planned price formation is approached from the standpoint of a uniform market value judgement. They apply the deflection of the relative consumer prices from the relative producer prices as an exception rather than a rule.

– The CMEA countries use the consumer price to a different extent for the purpose of income redistribution. There are countries where hardly any deficit prices or none at all, in others the prices of necessities (foodstuffs, public services) are subsidized by the budget in a wider sphere. Their financing absorbs more or less the turnover tax realized in the prices of other products.

The Approximation of National Price Systems in the CMEA

After the characterization of the national price (cost) patterns, the question arises what exactly should be understood by the approximation of the national price systems. To comprehend this we should first clarify what differences must be eliminated to make the national prime costs homogeneous.

The category of prime costs is suitable for an international comparison only if the calculations are performed for an *identical cost type.* For comparative cost analysis it is also objectively necessary to eliminate the differences that exist in respect of the enterprises' self-accounting systems. The elimination of the national features of enterprise self-accounting and the application – for the purposes of comparative analyses – of uniform cost-calculation principles are objectively necessary because these are national characteristics inherent exclusively in the accounting conditions, and it is exactly they that hinder a comparison of the conditions of production. When eliminating the national differences of the accounting relations from the prime costs constructed for the purposes of an international comparison, a uniform cost type is obtained. In other words: the price structure in which the cost is calculated becomes uniform.

The cost category streamlined specifically for the purposes of international comparison *removes the differences in the accounting relations, but it does not eliminate the differences in labour productivity and in income relations*. It eliminates the national traits of enterprise self-accounting, but reflects the natural endowments, technical and economic characteristics of production in the CMEA countries, and also the differences in their standards of living. With such a cost type it is only the price structure and not the price which is uniform. Thus, for example, the price of coal calculated in the cost of electric power is determined in every country by national endowments and technical conditions as well as by national wage relations. In this way, all preconditions for the comparability of costs are given:

1. The price structure being uniform, the costs (for instance the costs of electric power) can be directly compared.

2. It is the actual cost relations which are compared, since in the calculation of costs all previous stages of production are taken account of in the calculations at cost prices (e.g. the price of coal in the cost calculation of electric power).

3. In comparative products analyses, this category may be used as a yardstick of economic efficiency.

4. And if the conditions of production are to be compared in a closed circle, in a well-defined phase of production (for instance in the electric power industry), it is not the costs but the value added (for example the prime cost of electric power without material inputs) which are examined.

In connection with this category of prime cost constructed for international comparison, it is necessary to make some supplementary statements. The requirement may arise that the national features should be eliminated not only from the accounting but also from the *income relations. This is a category for which the relevant calculations performed have revealed the existing differences in the productivity of labour*. Such a requirement may arise primarily on behalf of those who wish the cost category to be used in the international comparison of the different variants of investments made for the expanded reproduction of identical or mutually substitutable goods. When prime cost also reflects income relations and when this category is used, for example, to decide in which country it would be more economical to develop a certain industry, it is not sure that the optimum variant is obtained. A country may have the most favourable natural endowments and technical conditions, yet, compared to another country, the investment may appear to be less economical merely because the wage incomes of the workers are higher.

It may also appear to be necessary to eliminate *not only the national features inherent in the accounting and income relations, but also the national differences in labour productivity*. Such request may come from those who attach importance to this category from the point of view of the switchover to the "socialist-price basis" in intra-CMEA trade. This standpoint may be based on the assumption that for the creation of the "socialist price basis" the uniformity of the price structure is not sufficient, the prices themselves must be uniform. The "socialist price basis" demands a unified foreign-trade price system which is detached from the world-market price system and is built upon the averaged value relations of the socialist world market. Such a price system can really be established if the prime costs cleared of the national characteristics inherent in the conditions of accounting in each phase of production are expressed in a common currency, that the price is determined in conformity to the (average) costs necessary from the point of view of the socialist countries, and finally that the material costs are realized at the so obtained prices in the prime cost of the products gained through further processing.

What exactly is the difference between the cost category as it appears in the unified price structure and in the unified price system? In the former, prices are constructed in order to make national cost relations comparable, in the latter costs are constructed in order to form uniform prices. In the former, cost calculation is based on national, in the latter on international prices. By cost calculation made in the unified price system the same is achieved on an international scale as is attained by the CMEA countries when rearranging their producer prices separately on a national scale. The only difference is that the enterprise is replaced by the country and the country by the CMEA.

We have come to the point where it is reasonable to point out *the conflicting opinions with respect to the approximation of the price systems.* We may disregard the "socialist price basis" concept since its followers do not demand the approximation of the national price systems, they stand for CMEA contract price detached from the national price systems. The debate about the approximation of the national price systems was going on primarily between Polish and Hungarian economists.

They agreed on the necessity of establishing an organic relationship between foreign-trade and domestic prices, but while Polish economists took a stand for approximating the national price structures, Hungarian economists emphasized the importance of introducing flexible price mechanisms.[155] Hungarian economists argued in the following way:

155 The Symposium organized by the Polish Economic Association on "*Timely Problems of Co-operation in the CMEA*" between 9th and 11th January, 1969. Knyziak, Z.: Home Prices and Prices in the International Commodity Trade. Glinkowski, B.: Changes in the Mechanism of Socialist Co-operation and their Effect on the System of the Home Economy.

1. The national price systems are not expressed in a uniform price structure. Owing to objective reasons, the structure of industrial producer prices differs from the structure of agricultural procurement prices. Moreover, planned pricing both in industry and agriculture calls for specific solutions to set proportionate prices for products in substitution relationship. In this respect, the task of proportionality based on use value must be solved. Each country solves the task of product substitution according to its greater interest in utilizing the product variety to which it has the easiest access. Thus, by asserting price proportionality, peculiar national market conditions are incorporated in the price system. These cannot be eliminated from the price systems, because the economic control systems of the different CMEA countries develop in the direction of activizing commodity and money relations, of increasing the role of price in a planned control of the economic processes. All that may seem to be the "technique" of the national accounting systems is in fact a significant element of autonomous national economic policies.

2. The most essential elements of the differences between the national systems of calculation are primarily reflected in the *price level.* If, therefore, an economically determined rate of foreign currency is available, the differences in the price structure become largely neutralized. If a country applies self-financing prices and not self-accounting ones, if it accounts inputs among costs which another country excludes from the sphere of prices by budgetary financing, the resulting difference in the price structure is largely neutralized by the currency of the latter country being revalued in relation to that of the former. Therefore, what the concept based on the unification of price structures intends to solve as a price problem, should essentially be treated as a currency problem.

3. If the price structures of the different countries were unified, but administrative price formation (the policy of freezing prices) were maintained, the requirement in whose interest the concept was formulated would be met only formally. Thus, the problem which each CMEA country has to face separately, would appear on an international scale. When, in keeping with the guiding lines of price formation, new prices are fixed by the central authorities – even if all calculation were faultless – the desired price structure will have validity for the selected basic period only. Subsequently, prices will become "outdated" as a function of changes in value relations. If the producer price is interpreted in this sense, as the basis of the CMEA contract price, there is no way decisions to be taken with due regard to the prevailing value relations in the rational organization of the international division of labour.

These are the deliberations which account for the fact that according to Hungarian economists participating in the debate, the international comparability of the conditions of production is not a matter of the unification of the price structure but, primarily, of creating an organic relationship between domestic and foreign-trade prices, and of whether the socialist countries are capable or not in their internal control systems of regulating price in a flexible mechanism which renders a better adaptation of changes in value relations possible.

The Domestic Price of Import and Export Products

The most intricate questions relating to the national price systems of the CMEA countries are undoubtedly encountered in the organic relationship between foreign-trade and domestic prices. One of the forms in which planned price formation is manifested in the socialist countries is that *of general and partial price rearrangement.* Most socialist countries solve this task in the administrative price system, where fixed price is the prevailing price form. This led to the introduction of the category of the "initial" price. This is, in fact, a reference to those principles of price formation which have to be considered when a new price is set. It is namely possible to conceive the initial price as the quantification of these guidelines with the difference that it is confined only to the initial period serving as a base for price rearrangement. With the passing of time a frozen price loses its relationship with the guidelines.

Owing to the dual character of the guidelines of price rearrangement and price changes, the relationship between foreign-trade prices and domestic prices cannot be revealed in the system of general principles. This intricate problem must be broken down into its elements, and it is expedient to approach the question first of all in relation to the "initial" price.

In socialist countries whose national economies are sensitive to foreign trade, *the formation of initial domestic prices of import products* is one of the most controversial questions in the debates on the guidelines of price rearrangement.[156] In these

[156] BRADA, J.: Vliv cen dovázenych surovin na efektivnost vyroby (The Effect of the Prices of Imported Prime Products on the Efficiency of Production). *Finance a uver*, Nos. 8–9, 1970, Prague. BRUDER, H. and NICK, H.: Nationale und internationale Werte und Preisrelationen. *Wirtschaftswissenschaft*, No. 11, 1966, Berlin. DREISCH, W. and SILTER, R.: Zur Preisbildung für Importerzeugnisse. *Wirtschaftsrecht*, No. 1, 1971, Berlin. LUCA, N. and SPOTHAIM, S.: Cum sa stabilim preturile la produsele din import

debates the answer is usually sought to the question how production inputs and the inputs of foreign-exchange earning could be applied simultaneously and in such a way that the initial price should give correct orientation in economic decisions. In the debates in Hungary – apart from the policy of a national price system consistently based on the world-market price – three possible policies were formulated:[157]

Formula I: is a uniform and proportionate price system based on the principle of domestic inputs (where the foreign-exchange price of imports can play a role only in a very limited scope). According to this formula, in domestic price formation the price of import products has also to adjust itself to domestic inputs except for the prices of exclusively or mostly imported raw materials. The effect of the different inputs of the various sources of supply cannot be brought to bear on price formation as it disturbs the normal course of the economy. Therefore, the source of supply which is of crucial importance for the whole of a group of products (for example sources of energy, rolled goods) is regarded decisive for pricing. In the sphere of semi-finished and finished goods import price can be applied only to such product groups where there is no domestic production (for example passenger-car production), or where this production is of a complementary nature (for example passenger-car components). Therefore, the role of the foreign-exchange multiplier as a price regulator is of a very limited scope.

Formula II: is a price system based, according to the origin of products, on two price centres. In this price system, there is no price proportionality and only such "fully identical" products command a uniform price the origin of which cannot be identified in the process of their utilization. This makes a more consistent assertion of the principle of a double cover, i.e. of the two price centres possible. Under such a price system, the price

←

(How to Set the Price of Import Products). *Viata Economica*, No. 29, 1970, Bucharest. STOURACOVÁ, J.: Vyvoj vztahu ceskoslovenskych vnitrich a zahranicne-obchodnich cen (Perfectioning the Relationship between Domestic and Foreign Trade Prices). *Politická ekonomie*, No. 6, 1969, Prague. TUDORAN, C.: Interactiunea dintre preturile mondiale si preturile interne (Interrelationship between World Market and Domestic Prices). *Probleme de Preturi*, No. 6, 1970, Bucharest.

157 BAKONYI, B.: A külkereskedelmi devizaárfolyamról (On Foreign-Trade Exchange Rates). *Pénzügyi Szemle*, No. 1, 1965, Budapest. BALÁZSY, S.: Termelői árak–devizaárak–árkiegyenlítés (Producers' Prices–Foreign-Exchange Prices – Price Equalization) *Közgazdasági Szemle*, No. 9, 1964, Budapest, – A devizaárfolyam vitához (Contribution to the Debate on the Foreign Exchange Rate). *Pénzügyi Szemle*, Nos. 8–9, 1965, Budapest. BRÓDY, A.: Az importszorzóról és alkalmazásáról (The Import Multiplier and its Application). *Közgazdasági Szemle*, Nos. 7–8, 1964, Budapest.

of domestically produced goods adapts itself to the conditions of production, and the price of imported goods to the import price. In the former case the price expresses the cost of the product, and in the latter it provides information about what price corresponds to the cost of export production. For so-called "fully identical" products either the cost of domestic production, or the import price must generally be asserted depending on whether the bulk of the demand is satisfied by goods of domestic origin or by imports. If neither case prevails, an average must be formed from the different prices.

In the case of the free assertion of the two price centres, actual input prices tend to approach certain average values in the prices of industrial semi-finished goods and products produced with the utilization of import materials. One of the essential requirements of the two price centres is that the joint effect of different input prices should be allowed to work freely up to that phase of utilization where the difference of prices leads to rational economic decisions. In case prices are fixed administratively, this fixing must be performed in the phase where enterprises can exercise the greatest influence on rational decisions.

Formula III: According to this formula, the costs of that source must be chosen as a basis of price formation from which *the satisfaction of additional domestic needs are foreseen by the plan.* Decisive for its choice is the consideration that the costs of the source should be the most unfavourable. (Marginal-cost formula.) Prices adjust themselves to domestic production conditions only if imports are insignificant relative to production. According to the marginal-cost formula, stimulation to rational economic decisions (import substitution, etc.) is provided only by a price which takes into account that rising demands can only be satisfied by the more expensive sources of supply. (Such a price indicates that in the case of decreasing demands the most expensive source of supply must be omitted; an import substitution, however, which is cheaper than that source, can automatically be applied only at a price consistent with marginal costs.) According to the marginal-cost fomula, the uniformity and proportionality of prices must always be ensured by considering the most expensive but still necessary inputs in the relation required by that formula.

Some imports are necessary because what is produced domestically of the given products is not sufficient (quantitative imports). Other products are imported because, for various reasons, they cannot be manufactured domestically at all, or not in an adequate quality (qualitative imports). According to this variant of the formula, a realistic possibility appears to be quantitative import substitution. This must, then, be reflected in the price policy. In other words: according to a certain variant of this formula, the prices of the most expensive source of supply must be taken as a basis only in the case of the so-called "quantitative imports" and not of "qualitative imports".

Each of the three formulae reckons, of course, with the fact that it may be, in certain cases, in the interest of a socialist country to set domestic prices which deviate from relative foreign-trade prices. The furthest goes in this respect the marginal-cost formula, which establishes a whole system of price deflection by taking into account as a basis the most expensive, but still necessary source of supply. But the rational assistance of socialist international co-operation, the support of individual sectors of domestic industrial production, if needed for a shorter or longer period of time, as well as other factors may justify the application of price deflections in any formula.

The Hungarian price reform of 1968 approached this problem in a differentiated way in the case of raw materials, intermediate and finished products, and even within each of these categories. *In setting* the "initial" prices of raw materials the following *factors were considered*: (1) Is the supply based on products manufactured domestically, or is it based exclusively in imports? (2) If it is based on imports, is its source within or outside the CMEA? (3) If the supply of certain products is effected in different relations, what are the shares of these relations in supplying these products, and which is the source that can best be depended upon in the case of additional demands? The mere enumeration of the factors to be considered will suffice to show that in determining the "initial" domestic prices of imported raw materials it is possible and expedient to apply differentiated approaches.

From the point of view of a socialist country with a high foreign-trade sensitivity, the essence of the problem may be summed up like this: the production cost concerning nearly all materials deviates from CMEA contract prices, and the latter from world-market input prices (in case the supply is effected from markets outside the CMEA). Since the initial price can be made uniform for any of these prices and, indeed, a mixed (averaged) price can also be applied for this purpose, the relationship between the foreign-exchange and domestic initial prices of imported products has emerged in the context of *four possible price centres*. The Hungarian price reform has applied all the four price centres according to the following considerations.

1. There are branches of production in which *domestic production* constitutes the main basis of material supply. If production is the primary determinant of consumption, and if the requirement that the planning of economic development is ex-

pected to fulfil is the expansion of raw-material extraction to meet increasing needs, it may appear to be justified to determine the initial price according to the conditions of production. In this case, the domestic price of imported raw materials will also be set accordingly. Thus, for example, the price level of the sources of energy has been fixed under the consideration of national production conditions. From this point of view, the sources of energy can be regarded as a "single" product, as they are utilized in a substitution relationship, and thus their relative prices must be regulated by making them proportionate on the basis of use value. Therefore, though the production conditions of coal mining – in view of their being unfavourable – are not reflected in prices, the inputs are realized in the price level of the various sources of energy; lower coal prices are financed by the rent incomes of carbohydrates.

2. There are production branches in which the main basis of material supply is *intra-CMEA imports*. If CMEA imports predominantly determine domestic production, and if the requirement expected to be met by the planning of economic development is to take into account the possibilities of expanding raw-material imports from CMEA countries, it may appear to be justified that the initial price is determined by the CMEA contract price. In the case of several raw materials, this price was lower than the domestic cost price, or the input price of imports from non-CMEA countries. Therefore, this is the alternative in which price is determined according to the *lowest* price. Thus, for example, the price level of the materials of metallurgy has been determined by CMEA contract prices. From this, however, it does not follow that the price level of the *products of metallurgy* adjusts itself to CMEA contract prices. In the producer-price level of the products of this industry it is already the national production conditions of metallurgy that find expression.

3. There are production branches in which the supply of materials equally relies on imports both from CMEA and non-CMEA countries, and in planning the process of structural transformation it appears desirable *not to confine their development to import quotas laid down in inter-state agreements within the CMEA*. The development, faster than planned, of these branches of production is possible only if it is based on additional capitalist raw-material imports. Additional (above quota) material imports from the CMEA had also be considered as capitalist imports, since these commodity transactions usually do not apply contract prices, but current capitalist world-market prices. Therefore, it appeared to be expedient to set the initial prices of materials in these production branches *in confor-*

mity with capitalist world-market prices. This was typical, for example, of the textile industry – and of the light industries in general – which develop largely in reliance on capitalist material imports.

4. There are production branches in which material supply depends on these three markets to a varying degree. The final product is processed through several phases of production, and intermediate (semi-finished) products are exported and imported practically at every phase. In these branches of production it appeared to be appropriate to determine the *initial prices* of raw materials (semi-finished products) by the method of *averaging* (mixed prices). This was the case in most branches of the chemical industry.

As we have seen, in the relationship of the foreign-exchange prices and domestic initial prices of imported raw materials there are four alternatives: prime-cost prices, CMEA contract prices, import prices outside the CMEA, and mixed prices. Whichever solution is chosen, the foreign-exchange price of imports will be reflected in the domestic price system in a peculiar way. The problem lies rather in the fact that the interdependences of the production branches also have to be reckoned with. The substitutability of base metal and non-ferrous metal, of traditional materials and synthetic material etc. sets specific requirements with regard to *relative prices*. The principle of price proportionality inserts new elements of deflection from import prices in foreign-exchange into the national price system. These problems become even more intricate in the sphere of *semi-finished and finished products*. Here the possibility of carrying out a price rearrangement based on foreign-exchange import prices depends on whether the principle of "one product – one price" is or is not insisted upon. The consistent application of this principle leads us of necessity to Formula I, because even in a moderately developed industry there can nearly always be found a domestically manufactured product from the price of which, by means of technical parameters, the domestic price of the imported product can be deduced by the method of price proportionality. *Non-standard investment machinery* may be regarded as exception. But it is not advisable to give up the principle of making domestic prices uniform and proportionate (of switching over from Formula I to Formula II) unless the rigidities of the administrative price system are relaxed; unless price is really a device of economic decisions; unless, as a result, the contradictions between the guidelines of price rearrangement and price changes are resolved. It is precisely in this respect that the Hungarian price reform of 1968 differs from any earlier price rearrangements.

In applying Formula I, the coincidence of the *initial and foreign-exchange prices of export products* can only be due to chance. If the national price system is consistently to reflect national production conditions, and the producer price of products is set accordingly, then it is natural that the initial price of export products differs from their foreign-exchange price. Here account must also be taken, of course, of the fact that price appears in a medium in which it regulates the export-commodity pattern not directly by its international competitiveness. The interrelationship of the two prices in the sphere of export products presupposes the application of Formula II.

Financial Bridges

The administrative price system comes to fore together with very definite principles of price changes. When administrative prices are fixed, domestic prices are usually not changed simply because foreign-trade prices change. Similarly, domestic prices can also be changed when foreign-trade prices remain unchanged. In other words: the price movements are different in the domestic and foreign-trade spheres. The mechanism of foreign trade price levelling is used to surmount this problem.

The systems of foreign-trade price levelling can be *distinguished* according to

(a) how far they are active instruments of domestic price formation itself. In this sense, we can speak of the systems of mobile price-levelling independent of foreign-exchange price, mobile price-levelling proportionate to foreign-exchange price, and constant price-levelling proportionate to foreign-exchange price,

(b) how they serve, within the framework of the already existing price system, the practical levelling of domestic and foreign-trade prices. In this sense, we can speak of differential mobile and differential constant price-levelling systems.

In the former case, we shall analyse the price-levelling systems as methodological tools of socialist price formation, and in the latter, as operative devices of the domestic accounting of national commodity transactions.

It is under the system of the mobile price levelling independent of foreign-exchange price that the "complete" independence of domestic prices of foreign-trade prices can be realized. The amount of price-equalization is not determined in advance for any product. This is invariably formed in commodity turnover and according to the actual difference between prices. In this system, price levelling is not a factor of price formation, prices are formed independently of it, it is only a system of transacting commodity exchange which connects prices already formed and equalized price differentials. It is precisely due to this fact that relative domestic prices can freely deviate from relative foreign-trade prices, that is to say that one price may be set independently of the other. If such is the levelling system of foreign-trade prices, the state budget also performs its accounting with foreign-trading enterprises usually on the basis of price differentials as in the case of any commodity transaction.

The system of mobile price-levelling independent of foreign-exchange prices is justified to apply when the domestic sales price of export products is determined on the basis of prime cost, and the domestic purchase price of import products is set in proportion to the price of related products produced domestically. Therefore, its rate is different even for a given range of products. And the proportionate prices of imported means of production are determined by calculating them in retrospect, from the prices of semi-finished (finished) products gained by their utilization.

The system of mobile price-levelling independent of foreign-exchange price is not the only possible form. This system suggests the possibility of completely separating the two prices. Even under the mechanism of obligatory plan indicators, the state may have an interest in forming domestic price relations in the sphere of related products in line with foreign-exchange import prices. Taking into account foreign-trade prices implies that in certain cases of domestic price formation, foreign-trade prices must be regarded as a price centre. When the domestic price is based exclusively on the foreign-trade price, the price levelling is no longer a transacting system but an active factor of price formation.

In the system of mobile price-levelling proportionate to foreign exchange, the domestic price is formed from the foreign-exchange price of the product by means of a definite rate of conversion resulting in a foreign-exchange-proportionate domestic price. This price-levelling system is characterized primarily by the fact that domestic prices adjust themselves to the foreign-trade price relations of a selected period, (period of price rearrangement), and the prices of newly imported products to the prices of the first business transaction. But after that domestic prices of import goods are fixed. This system, looked upon in movement, is related to the constant system independent of the foreign-exchange price. Difference exists only in the method of asserting the principle of *price proportionality*.

In the system of a mobile price levelling independent of foreign-exchange prices, there is a possibility of equalizing the varieties of a given raw material available at different foreign-trade prices from the point of view of the domestic price. But if the industry can buy at an identical price varieties which have different foreign-trade prices, the demand of the industry may shift towards more expensive varieties requiring more foreign exchange.

It may also harm the foreign-exchange interest of the national economy if the relative domestic prices of varieties substantially deviate from relative foreign-trade prices. Industry assesses, of course, its material consumption from the point of view of prime cost. It will choose such sort of materials (formula, mixture, construction, etc.) which decrease its cost. For industry it is only domestic prices that count, as it is only these prices that affect product cost. When the relative prices of assortments substantially differ from the price proportions of foreign trade, it may also occur that the cost reduction of industry is combined with additional foreign exchange inputs. This arises as a problem in such industries where several varieties of a given sort of material can be used to turn out products of the same or nearly the same use value. This is, for example, the case in the cotton, wool and leather industries.

When a transition takes place from the system of moving price levelling dependent on foreign-exchange price to *a moving system proportionate to foreign exchange*, the relative prices of varieties are formed from below, in an upward direction. It is a common feature of both systems that they receive the domestic price level of a given raw material in a form already established in the domestic producer-price system. A difference exists therefore only in making the prices proportionate to varieties. What is another a common feature in the two systems is that domestic prices do not automatically change with foreign-trade prices. That is why the latter is called a foreign-exchange-proportionate mobile system. In other words: in setting producer prices, the foreign-trade price proportions of a given period are taken to be the basis, and these prices are fixed. Thus, price-levelling changes depending on changes taking place in foreign-trade prices (price proportions).

Taking into account foreign-trade prices in the case of predominantly imported means of production provides the solution to two problems. The price may be, on the one hand, informative for decisions in domestic production of a marginal nature. On the other hand, it may shape an evaluation among the users which takes into account in their economic management the foreign-exchange interests of the national economy. Therefore, this system is applied where it is expected to yield such advantages. Here, however, the interest of the national economy generally requires *a constant harmony between relative domestic and foreign-trade prices*. It is obvious that this harmony ceases to exist when foreign-trade prices change with domestic prices left unchanged. The advantage that the moving price-levelling system proportionate to foreign exchange ensures by the provision that it carries out the proportionality of assortments according to the foreign-trade price, may, sooner or later, be offset by the fact that in this system the interrelationship of the two prices can only be realized by fixing the domestic price. From this it follows that this system is applicable mainly to such products of which the constant character of foreign-trade price proportions is typical. But a characteristic of the world-market price formation of intermediate materials of the light industries is the possibility of price proportions changing substantially according to varieties.

Thus the interrelation of the two prices can only be maintained under *the system of constant price levelling proportionate to foreign exchange*. The essence of that system lies in the fact that, in the interest of taking advantage of current price changes in the world market, fixed prices are modified by changing surcharge resp. allowance coefficients. The domestic price level at which raw materials are made available to industry cannot change, consequently, only price proportions according varieties can be modified. If, at a given point of time the fixed price of a variety is increased by a surcharge, then the fixed price of another variety has to be made cheaper by an allowance. The levelling of changing prices by surcharges resp. allowances takes place within a limited scope. It is regulated by the marginal rate of substitution in industry. Therefore, when the restricted mobile-price system is implemented, the scope of imported raw materials that are in a mutual substitution relationship is, at the same time, determined separately.

A closer relationship between foreign-trade and domestic prices can be ensured by the transition from Formula I to Formula II, namely, by switching over from the price levelling system to the system of *financial bridges*. This transition is effected by changing the planning, regulation and organization of the national economy. Here it is already assumed that the exchange rate of currencies (foreign-trade currency coefficient) has a price-regulating function, consequently, domestic prices are formed by a flexible price mechanism, making it possible, among other things, for domestic prices to change as a function of foreign-trade prices. Under such circumstances the two types of prices cannot be separated from one another even institutionally. Under the system of foreign-trade price levelling it is possible for foreign-trading enterprises to handle foreign-exchange prices as an internal affair if the enterprise manufacturing the export product is not aware of the price the foreign importer pays for it, and if the enterprise using the imported product is not informed about the actual burden on the national economy. Foreign-exchange prices cannot be indifferent to the manufacturer, or to the user either, if the foreign-exchange price of exports is regarded as an enterprise price receipt, and the foreign-exchange price of imports as a production (investment) cost. Therefore, it is necessary even in the institutional system to find an adequate solution by Formula II.

But the organic relationship of the two prices needs correct interpretation. The abolition of the autarchic system of economic policy does not mean the surrender of an independent economic policy. The qualitative difference between *autarchy and an independent economic policy* on the one hand, and *an independent and world-market oriented economic policy on the other*, must equally be emphasized.

The economic policy of autarchy gives rise to the view according to which economic efficiency and thus price categories, too, may not have an important role to play in forming the production structure; the producer price must always adjust itself to the national conditions of production, the domestic price cannot be changed merely because the foreign-exchange price changes. Looked at from the viewpoint of the policy of autarchy, all development (production) decisions can be justified that have their foundation in the system of the physical balances of raw materials, semi-finished and finished products. All this sufficiently proves that these decisions cannot be made questionable in relation to prices. On the other hand, a *world-market-oriented economic policy* assesses everything on the basis of international competitiveness, it resolves national prices in the system of world-market prices.

A country pursuing *an independent economic policy* wishes to develop the national economy by keeping an eye on international competitiveness, and uses therefore consciously the price category in the system of economic control and management. For the successful application of such an economic policy efficiency measured by international standards is to be directly evaluated in the interrelationships of national price-cost-profit. The price is, in such a case, not merely a tool of physically founded planning, but an active signalling system of decisions. But such a role can only be played by price in a foreign-trade-sensitive national economy if the deviation of foreign-trade prices from domestic ones is economically determined. The deviation cannot be regulated in the system of foreign-trade price levellings as this system is based exactly on a conceptual differentiation between the two prices. *The objectives of an independent economic policy must be formulated in specific financial bridges*. Their main forms of manifestation are customs duty in the case of import products, and budgetary support in the case of export products.

In the course of socialist economic transformation, several countries have maintained their *systems of customs duties* in unchanged or modified forms. In these countries, customs duty has been incorporated into the system of foreign-trade price levelling. It appears not as a price-forming factor but as a factor of financial accounting within price levelling. If the import price increased by customs duty exceeds the fixed domestic price, the difference is offset by an import subsidy, otherwise, the difference is skimmed off. Here subsidy and skimming are not financially determined. Both are determined by the fixed domestic price. Under such circumstances, of course, a differentiation of the customs duty, according to magnitude, relations and products is different from the point of view of foreign-trade relations and price proportions. The case is different if the exchange rate (foreign-trade coefficient) is a price regulator, and customs duty is a price factor.[158] It was for this reason that Hungary connected the price reform of 1968 with the *creation of a new tariff system*. This is designed to operate as a system of customs which can orientate with sufficient safety

– in a structure-transforming development policy aimed, among other things, at achieving economic efficiency,

– in the policy of foreign-trade relations, in relations inside and outside economic integration, in relations outside the CMEA, in establishing relations with socialist and non-socialist countries, or advanced and developing countries.

In the case of exports, subsidies from the budget (tax refund system) are designed to ensure that material interest in exports is created at the level of import needs determined by planned development. The foreign-trade coefficient stimulates exports in branches with higher than average foreign-exchange earning capacity. In branches, however, with a lower than average capacity, it exercises a curbing effect. The foreign-trade coefficient may make exports realized below its *average level* unfavourable for a large number of enterprises or even for whole branches, and may cause them to decrease or even discontinue their exports. Though one of the basic ideas of the economic reform has been that the organizational power of the market

[158] NYERGES, J.: *Vámpolitika* (Import-Duty Policy). Budapest, 1973. VENERA, Z.: Ceny a cla (Prices and Import Duties). *Svetové finance*, No. 1, 1969, Prague.

mechanism should also work under a planned economy, the market forces cannot be allowed to have an unrestricted play. Thus the regulation of the exchange rates must be supplemented by the mechanism of export subsidies.

The system of export subsidies is one of the factors of controlling foreign trade by economic instruments. What is at the core of the question is the supplement of the uniform coefficient in order to make possible, if necessary by government subsidies, exports that are indispensable from considerations of the balance of payments position in a given period of time. Under certain conditions, the money receipts of the enterprise can be raised by subsidies to a level which ensures that its exports are not less favourable from the point of material interest than its other activities.

A general requirement that the system of subsidies is justly expected to meet is that it should *promote* – in compliance with a co-ordinated weighing up of the considerations of economic policy and other regulating devices of the mechanism – *exports in a* volume needed by the national economy, but also to restrict uneconomical and therefore undesirable export activities to an extent in which this restriction can be tolerated by balance of payments considerations. The system of subsidies should be for the enterprises an objective regulation ensuring their safe and economical operation on the one hand, and the full assertion of their responsibility and risk-bearing capacity, on the other. *Export subsidies must be distinguished from the system of price levelling*. The difference may be summarized in the following:

– *State subsidies* are a supporting system at the *sectoral level*. This support is not aimed at levelling the two types of prices in respect of individual products. The state does not skim off favourable export prices and does not refund losses sustained by the export of individual products, and primarily not on the basis of price differentials.

– Export subsidies are granted to enterprises manufacturing the exported products, while price levelling is a matter of foreign-trading enterprises and of the state budget. The administratively fixed domestic prices of export products and the acknowledgement of high prime costs leave the enterprises unaware of their real economic efficiency.

– Price levelling adjusts itself to changes in the foreign-trade price. Export subsidies, however, are stable for several years. Changes in the foreign-trade price cannot, as a rule, exercise any effect on the amount of subsidies.

The relationship of the two prices established by inserting between them financial bridges asserts itself *within definite limitations* in a *mixed* price mechanism using simultaneously fixed, maximum and free-market prices. This restricts, in the first place, the organic relationship of the two sorts of prices in the case of imports, since when a product has a fixed (maximum) price, this generally applies to imported products as well. The situation is different in the case of exports. Here the price receipts of the enterprise are regulated by the foreign-exchange price of exports even if it is compelled to sell part on them on the home market at a fixed price. The only exception to this is, in the case of exports, agricultural products. It follows from the price system of state procurement of agricultural products that their prices, apart from some prominently market-type goods, are fixed, consequently the price receipts of agricultural producers are in no direct relationship with the price paid by foreign importers.

In shaping the relationship between domestic and foreign-trade prices, specific problems also arise from the *fact that the cyclical movement of world-market prices and, in the 1970s, inflation make even such socialist countries adopt a defensive attitude which otherwise attach great importance, in the interest of efficiency interpreted in the sense of international competitiveness, to an organic interconnection between domestic and foreign-trade prices*. In order to eliminate cyclical price movements, Hungary, for instance, has introduced a self-financing price fund for all strategically important products. Where such "funds" are in operation, the "accounting" price used in domestic calculation has been fixed according to the "initial" world-market price, and world-market price movements are accounted for in the import price fund. If the world-market price level is stable, cyclical price movements are offset in the system of self-financing by the import price fund, and price losses resulting from price rises are financed by price gains in the periods of price decreases. In the case of inflation, import price funds develop a deficit. How social interest in a relative price stability is to be reconciled with the interest of the national economy in establishing an organic relationship between the two prices is perhaps one of the greatest dilemmas of today's socialist price policy.